FOURTH EDITION

Helping Children Learn to Read

Creating a Classroom Literacy Environment

Lyndon W. Searfoss
Arizona State University

John E. Readence
University of Nevada, Las Vegas

Marla H. Mallette
Southern Illinois University at Carbondale

Allyn and Bacon

Boston ▪ London ▪ Toronto ▪ Sydney ▪ Tokyo ▪ Singapore

Series Editor: *Arnis E. Burvikovs*
Vice President: *Paul A. Smith*
Editorial Assistant: *Patrice Mailloux*
Executive Marketing Manager: *Lisa Kimball*
Editorial Production Service: *Lifland et al., Bookmakers*
Manufacturing Buyer: *Julie McNeill*
Cartoonist: *Gayle Levee*
Cover Administrator: *Jennifer Hart*
Electronic Composition: *Omegatype Typography, Inc.*

Copyright © 2001, 1994, 1989, 1985 by Allyn & Bacon
A Pearson Education Company
160 Gould Street
Needham Heights, MA 02494

Internet: www.abacon.com

Library of Congress Cataloging-in-Publication Data

Searfoss, Lyndon W.
    Helping children learn to read : creating a classroom literacy environment / Lyndon W. Searfoss, John E. Readence, Marla H. Mallette.—4th ed.
        p.   cm.
    Includes bibliographical references and index.
    ISBN 0-205-27019-0
    1. Reading (Elementary)   I. Readence, John E., 1947–   II. Mallette, Marla H.   III. Title.

LB1573 .S39   2001
372.4—dc21   00-038622

Printed in the United States of America

Photo credits: Photo credits can be found on page 394, which should be considered an extension of the copyright page.

CONTENTS

6 Decoding   142

7 Vocabulary   174

10 Writing and Reading   277

11 Assessing Reading Abilities   310

PREFACE

This fourth edition of *Helping Children Learn to Read: Creating a Classroom Literacy Environment* is an elementary methods text for use in teacher-preparation programs at the undergraduate and introductory graduate levels. The text provides students with a detailed understanding of how to implement a developmental reading program. Throughout the text, instruction is set in a child-centered, print-rich classroom environment.

To assist readers of this text, study aids appear before, during, and after the core material in each chapter. *Before* reading, students are presented with a **Graphic Organizer** and **Objectives**. The Graphic Organizer provides advance structure for each chapter; the Objectives outline the major concepts to be discussed. *During* the reading of a chapter, students encounter **Process Guides,** which assess understanding of key concepts through questions, simulations, and self-checking exercises. *After* reading a chapter, students find three final study aids that reinforce key concepts and offer a variety of activities to extend understanding of ideas presented in the chapter. **Follow-Through Activities** provide two levels of independent activities: Level 1 Activities require little or no access to children, whereas Level 2 Activities usually assume such access. **Working with Parents** summarizes the chapter's key concepts in a form that can be used in communication with parents. Finally, a **Resources** section lists additional readings and practical teaching references related to the topics of the chapter.

Our thanks go to Doreen Bardsley of Arizona State University for her suggestions during the revision process. In addition, we thank the education editors at Allyn and Bacon, Virginia Lanigan and Arnie Burvikovs, for supporting us in our work on this edition of the book. We extend our thanks also to our reviewers: Mary E. Blake, College of Charleston; Solveig A. Bartz, Moorhead State University; Joan Knickerbocker, Ashland University; and Dolly S. Baldwin, Bluefield State College.

It is our hope that this text provides the support and encouragement teachers need to create a literacy environment that will help children learn to read.

LWS
JER
MHM

CHAPTER

1

Setting the Stage for Literacy Instruction

INTRODUCTION

The title of this book, *Helping Children Learn to Read,* was carefully chosen to emphasize the importance of making children the focal point for planning, organizing, and implementing reading programs. In this chapter, we discuss literacy and provide a definition of reading. The major portion of this chapter presents language principles related to helping children learn to read. Teachers must continually make decisions about how to incorporate commercial materials, school district curriculum guides, and advice from college and university professors into a classroom reading program that makes sense for their children year after year. Sound decisions require informed teachers who grow each year in their understanding of children's language and especially of how children learn to read and develop into literate adults.

GRAPHIC ORGANIZER

This graphic organizer summarizes the structure of Chapter 1:

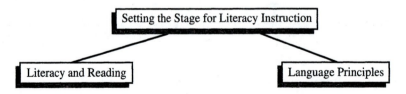

OBJECTIVES

When you finish reading this chapter, you should be able to understand and discuss each of these statements:

1. Literacy and reading have multiple definitions, functions, and uses.
2. Helping children learn to read becomes communication-centered through instruction and practice using methods and materials that treat language as a whole process.
3. Children bring to school a vast amount of language knowledge which can be used as the basis for reading instruction.
4. Instruction in reading is enhanced when it is integrated with opportunities for children to interact and to use speaking, listening, and writing as part of that instruction.

Literacy and Reading

As we discuss reading in the context of literacy in this chapter, we ask you to consider the importance of defining literacy and reading, as well as to examine your beliefs about each. You might ask, Isn't this just another academic exercise in a reading methods text? What do definitions and beliefs about either literacy or reading have to do with how I teach my class on Monday morning? Definitions and beliefs are important in life. For example, let's assume that while you were growing up, your family defined education as being important for your moral and intellectual development and believed it should have a high priority. Your actions, both as an individual and as part of a family unit, were shaped by these beliefs. Your parents expected you to attend school each day, do your homework, and participate in school activities. They, in turn, took an active interest in school functions and in your academic progress. They may have opened a special bank account before you entered elementary school, to begin saving money in case you decided to attend college. When you entered college, you may have begun to work part-time or full-time to help finance your education. All of these actions reflected the beliefs you and your family had about the importance of getting an education.

Similarly, your individual beliefs about literacy and reading will influence decisions you make about the teaching methods and strategies you select, the materials you use, and the ways in which you organize reading instruction. Thus, defining literacy and reading and developing some beliefs about how to help children learn to read are important parts of becoming a teacher. To help you begin thinking about literacy and reading, we will first discuss definitions of literacy and then present a definition of reading based on that discussion.

Defining Literacy

We can begin to help you define literacy by asking you to consider some definitions from a variety of sources:

> *Literacy* (n.) the ability to read and write. (*Oxford Encyclopedic English Dictionary,* 1995)

> The term literacy means an individual's ability to read, write, and speak in English, and compute and solve problems at levels of proficiency necessary to function on the job and in society, to achieve one's goals, and develop one's knowledge and potential. (*Public Law 102-73*, 102d Congress, National Literacy Act of 1991, Sec. 3)

> Until quite recently, literacy was generally defined, in a very limited way, as the ability to read or write one's own name. A much more ambitious definition of literacy today includes the capacity to accomplish a wide range of reading, writing, speaking, and other language tasks associated with everyday life. (*Standards for English Language Arts,* 1996, p. 73)

> To understand what literacy is and how students learn to be literate in a particular classroom, we must examine how members of a particular social group (a culture) construct and reconstruct literacy as part of everyday life. Literacy, therefore, involves more than reading and writing processes; it also involves the communication processes through which it is constructed. (Santa Barbara Classroom Discourse Group, 1994, p. 125)

These definitions represent different views of literacy. The first one, taken from a dictionary, is simple and clearly limits literacy to the reading and writing of printed matter. It could probably be more accurately labeled a definition of *print literacy,* since it focuses on how people use print to communicate through reading and writing. The second definition, from an act of Congress, is much more complex. After initially defining print literacy, it then goes beyond reading and writing. Although the definition of a literate individual is limited to one who reads and writes well in English, the act implies that being literate can help one be a successful citizen, realize personal goals, and develop one's potential. It is no coincidence that the second definition, no doubt written after some political compromises, combines a number of views of literacy. The third definition contrasts a traditional view of print literacy with a definition that broadens reading to include the other language arts.

The fourth definition views reading and writing as two of the many symbol or sign systems people use to communicate (Harste, 1994). Both reading and writing are influenced by the particular culture and everyday life of the people communicating.

However you interpret the above definitions, they reflect issues often raised in discussions of literacy and reading. Kaestle (1990), in his review of the many definitions of literacy that have emerged, concludes that literacy can be defined in multiple ways, ranging from narrow definitions of literacy as *a set of skills used to meet the literacy demands of the workplace* to much broader and loftier definitions of literacy as *the means by which people can enhance their lives and be prepared for life in an increasingly complex society.* Definitions of literacy have changed over time. The terms *literate* and *illiterate* are Latin in origin. In the Middle Ages, *literacy* came to mean a minimal ability to read, but the word did not appear in the English language until near the end of the nineteenth century, according to Venezky (1991). The literate person of 1750, 1850, or even 1950 would be astonished by the literacy demands of today—especially the uses of reading and writing.

In the 1930s the Civilian Conservation Corps (CCC), formed as a much needed make-work federal project, used the term *functional literacy.* A third-grade education was all that was believed necessary to meet the basic literacy demands of society. By the early 1940s, the United States Army had changed the level of functional literacy to a fourth-grade education. Subsequent changes have included slowly raising the grade-level designation of functional literacy until it was defined in the 1970s as graduation from high school. Recently, though, definitions of literacy have been broadened to include reading and writing ability in all of the social and cultural contexts in which people need to communicate. *To us, literacy means being able to communicate through reading and writing. It requires the acquisition of reading and writing skills and the ability to apply those skills in interactions with others in a variety of contexts.*

Will definitions of literacy continue to change in the 21st century? The popular press and professional sources offer many intriguing definitions of literacy that will only continue to grow in number in the coming years. We compiled a list of the types of literacy found in the literature (see Figure 1.1). We began our list with print literacy, the topic of this book, and the two other most frequently mentioned literacies, functional literacy and cultural literacy. Each time we thought we had found the last type of literacy, another article landed on our desks with still another term to describe another type of literacy. This is as it should be. Literacy evolves as society changes. We hope you will find other types to add to our list. Think about the many literacies in your life; can you imagine what new ones lie ahead as we move through a whole new century?

Defining Reading

As our discussion of literacy indicated, reading, like writing, is a basic form of print literacy. Reading is used as a language tool for communication, purposefully and intentionally. As a process, it involves the reader in constructing literacy in classrooms through interactions with others and interactions with and through

FIGURE 1.1   **The Multiple Literacies**

Place each term listed in front of the word *literacy* to create one of the
multiple literacies. Add any others you might find.

literacy

print	emancipatory	mechanical
functional	environmental	scribal
cultural	essay-text	spatial
aesthetic	general	graphic
alphabetic	global	symbolic
cash-cultural	lay	technological
community	measurement	visual
computer	motivated	artistic
content area	school	ideal
economic	mathematical	hieroglyphic
school-constructed	ideological	critical

texts (Santa Barbara Classroom Discourse Group, 1994). It goes beyond simply understanding what is read. As Glazer and Searfoss (1988) explain:

> Reading is receiving ideas, experiences, feelings, emotions, and concepts. It is an ac-
> tivity that permits one to gain vast knowledge. When reading, we can live and travel
> vicariously and become acquainted with people and events of the past that have
> shaped our worlds. Reading creates for us mental maps of events so that ideas can be
> transmitted from the mind of one, the author, to the mind of another—the receiver/
> reader. (p. 2)

Language Principles

We believe that a classroom reading program should be grounded in the following
language principles:

- The function of language is to communicate.
- Reading is a constructive and meaning-making process.
- The vast amount of language children bring to school should be recognized
  and used in helping them learn to read and write.
- The whole of language is not the sum of its parts.
- The interaction of thought and language is essential for both cognitive devel-
  opment and language development.
- The language of classroom instruction differs from other language found
  outside of school.
- Reading is *one* of the communication tools.
- Assessment guides and directs language instruction.

In this section, we will look at each of these principles and its implications for helping children learn to read.

Principle 1: The Function of Language Is to Communicate

Language use always occurs in some context and for some reason. To children before they come to school, language *is* communication. Their world is full of language, especially oral language, which is meaningful, relevant, and natural. Children use oral language efficiently, fluently, and frequently. They discuss, explain, report, negotiate, create, describe, and retell for physical, social, and emotional survival, as well as for creative purposes.

Reading, like oral language, is a social activity, always occurring for someone or to someone, even if that someone is yourself and the reason personal and private. Edelsky (1991) writes that when language is used more goes on than just language events. Speakers, readers, and writers are engaging in a complex activity that includes more than just talking, comprehending, or producing a composition. Edelsky observes:

> Whenever language is used, it is used in events—events that capture and create relationships among people and between people and objects (materials and otherwise) in the culture. What is learned when people learn language includes all those relationships that were part of the events carried out through language use. The language used within those events is usually used for some purpose other than instruction or in evaluation of the language use itself—for informing, persuading, joking, warning, teasing, explaining, cajoling, and so forth. (pp. 80–81)

Bloome (1985) explains that children must understand and interpret stories or other texts they read according to what is acceptable culturally. He relates an example about a character who worked hard and was more successful than his peers (sounds like *The Little Red Hen* plot to us). In school, the character was interpreted by the teacher as a positive model of what happens when you work hard. Out of school, the same ambitious behavior may be interpreted in some cultures as individualistic, noncooperative, and competitive and present a negative role model. Part of understanding language, then, is understanding the culture of language users, their values and ways of thinking, and potential points of difference with the values expressed in commercial reading materials and school reading instruction. Cultural differences in the way children think about what they read should be understood, accepted, and discussed by teachers, not ignored or viewed negatively.

Principle 1, applied to helping children learn to read, means that classroom instructional activities, strategies, and methods must involve children in authentic reading, for real purposes, and not in exercises that are simply instruction for instruction's sake. By becoming immersed in activities that incorporate choice and interaction with others, such as producing classroom books and newsletters, projects for science fairs, or a booklet of holiday poetry for senior citizens, children will learn much more about how to use reading than they will by completing exercises in workbooks assigned solely to provide practice in isolated skills.

Principle 2: Reading Is a Constructive and Meaning-Making Process

As you read the definition of reading presented earlier in this chapter, we hope you noted that reading is a dynamic process. It asks the reader to use the words on the page, or surface structure, to construct the author's message, or deep structure. *Surface structure* refers to the choice of words actually used in a language message, whether that message is expressed in speaking or in writing. In reading, surface structure is communicated by means of what readers see on the printed page, usually little black squiggles called letters, words, and sentences. Surface structure reflects an attempt by an author to express a message. *Deep structure* refers to the meaning of the message at the time it was created by the author.

A simple example or two will demonstrate the distinction between these two levels of language. Consider these statements:

> She dives into the spray and waves.
> The butler serves tea and rolls downstairs.

Think a moment about how these two rather ambiguous statements illustrate the obvious differences between surface structure and deep structure. The deep structure is the intended meaning of the statement in its original context in the author's mind. In the absence of the original author, however, readers must use the surface structure they see in order to create meaning.

Readers dig away at the surface structure, searching for meaning.

Another example closer to real life is a sign found in a college cafeteria:

SHOES ARE REQUIRED TO EAT IN THE CAFETERIA!

Underneath the sign, a creative undergraduate had printed "Socks can eat wherever they want!" Obviously, the author of this message did not clearly represent it in print so that readers could accurately create the meaning—much to the dismay, no doubt, of the cafeteria manager.

The basic task of readers is similar to the task of a prospector. Just as the prospector picks away at the surface to discover the gold hidden underneath, readers dig away at the surface structure, searching for and demanding meaning. Hard work? Yes, at times; but for both readers and prospectors, the rewards can be great.

Constructing meaning is often complex, for a number of reasons. First, the prior knowledge and language skills the author uses to represent ideas in print are different from the prior knowledge and language skills of each reader. How different? Every one of us has a unique set of prior experiences and a unique facility with language. These differences are a factor in every reading situation. Second, authors vary in their ability to use language to convey a message in print for readers to comprehend. Some authors simply do not have much success in making their meaning clear through print. That can be a real problem for readers who must try to figure out what was meant by an author who is not present to clarify vocabulary, syntax, or meaning. Third, what readers construct depends on factors outside of the cue systems found in print. As we mentioned in our discussion of Principle 1, reading is a social process. The reason for reading, where it is being done, and for whom it is being done are all important. Reading for pleasure, reading directions to construct something, and reading a social studies chapter are different in the kind of meaning they demand.

Principle 2, applied to helping children learn to read, means that teaching strategies should show children how to become actively involved in the search for meaning, provide them with strategies for independent, strategic reading, and lead to self-monitoring and self-questioning. Helping children learn how to take control of the reading process and what to do to keep meaning flowing as they read is a major goal of the classroom reading program.

Principle 3: The Vast Amount of Language Children Bring to School Should Be Recognized and Used in Helping Them Learn to Read and Write

Children bring a vast amount of language to school, practiced and polished during preschool years. The exact nature and extent of this language knowledge is often underestimated or misunderstood, instead of being recognized and used to help children learn to read. Certainly the formal language instruction found in school settings is not the first encounter children have with learning about language. Although the setting (using a common text to teach whole classes or small groups of children) may be new, learning about language is not. There is much evidence to support the view that preschool children have sophisticated language abilities in three areas: (1) knowledge of the sound/symbol relationship, (2) vocabulary levels, and (3) functional uses of language.

Before they enter school, children possess considerable knowledge of the relationship of the symbols (graphemes) to the sounds (phonemes) of English. Examination of children's self-created, or invented, spellings reveals that both preschool and primary-grade children use this knowledge to make guesses and predict how words are spelled. This can be seen in what might appear, to the untrained eye, to be a simple message scrawled carelessly on a page. Figure 1.2 shows Marissa's attempt in September of grade 1 to write a recipe for making a peanut butter and jelly sandwich.

Process Guide 1.1

Break into pairs or small groups. Read Marissa's recipe (in Figure 1.2) for making a peanut butter and jelly sandwich. Is the message clear to you? What language strengths can you find? In what areas will Marissa continue to develop? Share your pair or group responses with the whole class.

Additional evidence of the amount of language that children bring to school can be found in the word knowledge or vocabulary level of young children. A quick survey of language-acquisition research disclosed that estimates for the size of the vocabulary of 6-year-olds range from 4,000 to 8,000 words. The exact number is probably not all that important, and it is hard to fix accurately. What can be concluded, however, is that the vocabulary level of young children is quite impressive and should provide teachers with a solid foundation upon which to build formal language instruction.

Evidence obtained from simple observations of children using language in everyday, functional ways further documents the complex language abilities of preschool and primary-grade children. Children 4, 5, and 6 years old are literally language machines, using listening and speaking and even writing and reading to manipulate and control an environment dominated by adults. One such use of language can be observed in grocery stores all over the country, every day, when children decide they must have a particular kind of cereal, candy, or toy. A listener can only observe, "Wow! Can they use language efficiently and effectively to change a parent's mind!"

Older children, too, through the oral and written language they bring to school, can tell us what they know. This prior knowledge can be used as a springboard for new learning. Whether children are beginning or older readers, it is clear that they come to classrooms each day with considerable prior knowledge about language and the world.

Principle 3, applied to helping children learn to read, suggests that teachers look at children's language production, especially their writing, for signs of what

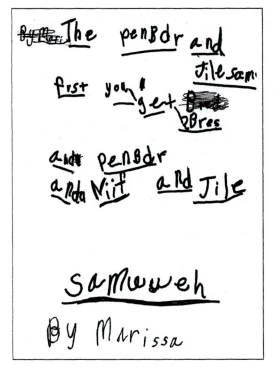
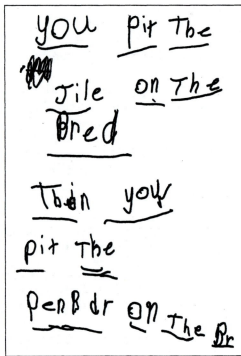

FIGURE 1.2   Marissa's Recipe for Peanut Butter and Jelly Sandwich

Permission to use Marissa's recipe has been granted. We thank Marissa for allowing us to use it.

children can do and what strengths they bring to school to support reading instruction. Children's early attempts to write are serious efforts and reveal much more than a quick glance would indicate—if teachers will look past the form to the message. Chapter 3 will present more ideas on how to use the vast amount of language children bring to school.

Principle 4: The Whole of Language Is Not the Sum of Its Parts

Language is very complex at times. Four essential systems interact during the reading process: the graphophonic cue system, the syntactic cue system, the semantic cue system, and the pragmatic cue system.

The *graphophonic cue system* is the system of relating sounds, or phonemes, to the symbols, or graphemes, of print. Learning the names of the letters and the various sounds they stand for is often part of beginning reading instruction. Such instruction relies heavily on the fact that English is an alphabetic language, in which a large number of sounds have a one-to-one correspondence with their symbols. Chapter 6 discusses this instructional issue in greater detail.

The *syntactic cue system* is the set of underlying natural rules by which the language operates. Language is arranged and rearranged according to these rules. For example, the order of words is a part of the syntactic cue system. "The green car is mine" is syntactically arranged according to the rules of the English language, whereas "Car the mine is green" is not so arranged. How are we able to distinguish between the two? Many linguists agree that syntactic knowledge is a natural part of the language, which all native speakers possess. This knowledge is acquired rapidly in a somewhat predictable sequence and without direct instruction, beginning at birth. In general, the acquisition of syntactic knowledge is accomplished without our being able to state formally the rules of syntax that we use.

The *semantic cue system* gives meaning to words, sentences, and longer units of print. It is the knowledge, gained through prior experiences, that all readers carry around in their heads and bring to each reading situation. Words must mean something—individually and in a variety of contexts. Semantic development includes not only how much vocabulary is acquired, but also how words are used and understood at various stages of cognitive development and in different contexts. It is a complex process about which much more needs to be learned.

The *pragmatic cue system* incorporates the cultural and social aspects of using language. Tompkins (1997) explains the pragmatic cue system in this way:

> People use language for many different functions, and how they talk or write varies according to purpose and audience. Language use also varies among social classes, cultural and ethnic groups, and geographic regions. (p. 19)

The way you speak and write varies with your purpose (whether you are speaking to a friend or to your boss), the geographic area in which you live (whether you speak of *submarine sandwiches* and *pop* or *hoagies* and *soda*), and the environment in which you are reading (whether you are scanning a magazine at home or studying a chapter in a science book at school). All of these forms of language reflect your attempts to communicate. None is correct or incorrect. It is the effectiveness with which you communicate that is important. In reading, sensing the author's intent is an important part of constructing a message from what you read.

Thus far we have considered, briefly, the systems that interact in the reading process. There is, however, some danger in separating these systems, even for purposes of explanation. When separated, they do not retain the properties of the total process, just as flour, water, yeast, and salt do not possess the unique properties of bread.

When all cue systems are present in a reading situation, we can reasonably predict that the reader will be able to construct meaning from print. If one or more of the cue systems are missing, however, constructing meaning may be more difficult or no longer the task. For example, in test settings where one reads isolated lists of words as part of an informal reading inventory, neither the syntactic nor the semantic cue system is present. When one answers test questions after reading a standardized test paragraph, the pragmatics are distorted; real reading doesn't end with multiple choice questions.

*When separated, flour, salt, yeast, and water
do not possess the unique properties of bread.*

Principle 4, when applied to helping children learn to read, gives us the message that reading instruction should occur with whole, intact samples of language. Whole stories, poems, and other forms of print with real messages give children opportunities to use all cue systems in constructing meaning and provide the language support they need to be successful in making meaning.

Process Guide 1.2

Read the words below, and try to write a short definition of each one. Then use those definitions to try to understand the meaning of the whole sentence constructed from the list of words. How easy or difficult was this activity for you? Compare your responses with those of others in your class, and discuss which cue systems you used.

mobile	nonmetallic	mineral
matter	thwarts	the
congregation	of	bryophyta

Sentence: Mobile nonmetallic mineral matter thwarts the congregation of bryophyta.

Principle 5: The Interaction of Thought and Language Is Essential for Both Cognitive Development and Language Development

Reading begins with communication between author and reader. As a reader constructs meaning from what the author has written, language and cognition interact. The more you know about a topic, therefore, the easier it is to understand an author's message if it is presented clearly. Suppose that you were familiar with nuclear physics at a very superficial level, but did not have sufficient prior knowledge or a rich enough background of experiences to make reading a college text on the subject very rewarding. How would you learn about nuclear physics? By reading about it, of course, and thinking about and discussing what you had read with a teacher, fellow students, or an expert in nuclear physics. As you struggled to increase your knowledge of nuclear physics, you would find reading easier and easier if you had many opportunities to manipulate concepts relating to nuclear physics.

Young children, too, increase their store of prior knowledge and background of experiences by *reading* about what they hear and talk about; *writing* about what they read, hear, and talk about; and *talking* about what they read, hear, and write about. By nailing down their thoughts, clarifying meaning, and cementing understanding, language becomes a tool for helping children learn. Principle 5, applied to helping children learn to read, suggests that the focus be shifted from teaching reading and writing as ends unto themselves to defining them as the means by which children gain access to knowledge in the classroom.

Process Guide 1.3

Divide into pairs or small groups, and discuss the following question about language arts instruction: Should reading and writing be abolished as separate parts of the curriculum and instead be taught through science, social studies, math, and other curricular areas? Make a list of the pros and cons of your point of view. Pool your lists for a whole-class discussion.

Principle 6: The Language of Classroom Instruction Differs from Other Language Found Outside of School

As discussed earlier in this chapter, children bring considerable learning about language and about the world with them to school. However, out-of-school settings are very different from in-school learning. Juliebo (1985) studied the learning interactions of kindergarten children at home and at school, especially those related to literacy development. Learning interactions differed significantly in these ways:

1. Children initiated literacy learning at home; teachers initiated learning in school.
2. At home, when children did not understand, they were given explanations that were linked to the past and the future. In school, they did not appear to understand the rationale behind the goals for many literacy activities.
3. Readiness for school literacy tasks often was not grounded in the children's own experiences.

4. Parents tended to modify their language to ensure understanding; in school, at least some of the time, children did not understand explanations or directions.
5. School learning experiences were selected by the teacher to meet the needs of all children. At-home learning experiences were likely to be tailored to the age of the child and paced accordingly.
6. Predetermined, generic kindergarten curriculum appeared to hinder literacy development more than foster it.

In addition to the contrasts between the settings, there are other crucial differences between out-of-school learning and in-school learning, especially in the nature of classroom language. As Pinnell and Jaggar (1991) conclude in their review of the research about one type of language—conversations—classroom language has much to do with control and power relationships between teacher and students. Students learn, for example, that

> Lessons are different from ordinary conversation. In everyday conversation, speakers share responsibility and they negotiate turns. In situations where it is very difficult to get a turn, speakers often reform into smaller groups. In classrooms, however, the number of speakers are contained in one space for a long period of time. The teacher is pressed to keep order so that information can be transmitted; so, teachers control turns (Edwards, 1979). There is one speaker at a time, to which everyone is supposed to listen, few gaps in conversation, and little overlap of speakers. Teachers usually speak between turns. (p. 707)

Stubbs (1979), in observations of classroom language, pointed to crucial ways in which classroom language differs from non-classroom language.

1. Teachers talk most of the time, and children talk a small part of the time.
2. Teachers ask a large number of questions, generally knowing the answer to each one *before* they ask it (pseudoquestion).
3. Control of conversations is clearly in the hands of one person, the teacher.
4. Question-and-answer dialogues between teachers and pupils, which dominate much instructional time, can lead children to believe that knowledge is largely factual and acquired in little bits, presented sequentially. Also, such ping-pong, teacher-to-pupil-to-teacher dialogues reinforce the false notion that *all* questions have a single, short, correct answer.

Two of Stubbs's observations deserve closer examination: first, the notion of pseudoquestions and, second, the ping-pong nature of many classroom dialogues. Pseudoquestions are confusing to young children when they enter school. Outside of school, most questions are genuine; that is, when someone asks a question, it is to seek an answer to a problem or clarify some confusion. The person asked a question expects that the questioner truly does not know the answer. Inside school, though, the questions that teachers use for reading instruction often do not fit these constraints. The questions teachers ask may not be their own but may have been taken from a teacher's manual. Also, the answers may be obvious or may have been supplied for the teacher. So, the social rules, structure, and roles children have become accustomed to concerning questions are violated, and the purpose of school questions becomes more testing than information-seeking.

Second, the ping-pong exchanges between teacher and students are not the natural kind of conversation found outside of school. This type of conversation can lead to passivity on the part of students, who simply learn to wait! A short sample of a dialogue between a teacher and students in a small-group reading lesson serves as an example of ping-pong:

> TEACHER: Now, read the next page of our story to find out where the boys are going.
>
> *(Students read silently.)*
>
> TEACHER: Let's talk about our story. Susan, where were the boys going?
>
> SUSAN: To the store.
>
> TEACHER: What for? Glen.
>
> GLEN: Because they wanted to.
>
> TEACHER: Is that the only reason, Alicia?
>
> ALICIA: Uh-uh, no. They were going to buy a new toy.

The pattern illustrated above of "now read, now answer, now go away" can lead to reading instruction that is active for the teacher and passive for the students, who simply wait to be activated. Waiting for the next question and a turn to talk, rather than initiating conversation, becomes the habitual pattern for success. Turn-taking rules are different in ping-pong exchanges, because students are expected to talk *in between* the teacher's questions, a pattern that is not normally a feature of out-of-school conversations. As simple observation of children's conversations will confirm, rules for turn-taking are much more flexible outside of school. Whether among 4-year-olds or 14-year-olds, out-of-school talk rarely contains statements such as "I'm sorry to interrupt" or "Let's be polite and take turns."

Principle 6, applied to helping children learn to read, asks teachers to recognize that there are significant differences between the language of instruction and the language children use in settings outside of school. If classroom and individual discussions are expanded to help children talk through what they are reading, learning in school can become easier for them. These discussions should allow for maximum interaction among students and be conversational in nature, not a ping-pong type of teacher-dominated exchange.

Principle 7: Reading Is *One* of the Communication Tools

Basic to understanding the reading process is comprehending its relationship to the other tools of communication. First, we will discuss the relationship of oral language (speaking and listening) to reading, especially from the viewpoint of language development and use before children enter school. Next, we will consider some common characteristics that oral language, reading, and writing share. Finally, we will look at the ways in which reading and writing are related.

Oral Language and Reading.   When children come to school for their first formal instruction in reading, their oral language is full of extra-meaning clues, such as facial expressions, body gestures, and voice inflections. These extra-meaning clues, however, do not exist as obviously in print, where the richness of oral language is not available. To expect that they will supply these missing clues while reading for themselves is a poor assumption. The following story was dictated to a third-grade teacher, who faithfully recorded it. As you read it, think about how you would react if the young author were standing in front of you, hands and arms flying, voice excited, and eyes bright and sparkling with a secret adventure to share.

The Wine Bottle

Me and Matt, well our mother made me and Matt go to our room. I don't know why now. Well—

There were two windows in our room that had screens and one didn't, so we opened the window with no screen and climbed out. We had some tall bushes on the side of our house that we always called our secret fort. The reason we called it that was because it was all hollowed out inside and we went down that and found a full wine bottle so we shook it up a lot and neither one of us wanted the job of opening it and so sooner or later I volunteered to open it and then it squirted wine all over me because Matt was far enough away that it wouldn't squirt wine on him. And we knew Mom wouldn't want us to get wet, so we went over our friends' house and they had a swimming pool in their backyard and a slide attached to it and so for about a half hour after that we were playing in the water to get rid of the smell and jogged around the block about three times and sooner or later that dried us out and so we went home.

by C. S.

Of course, the young author dictated a wonderful story, but all the accompanying oral language clues are not there in print for the reader. Punctuation in this story was an aid, but certainly a poor substitute for the author's being there telling the story.

When they enter school, children are accustomed to using oral language—speaking and listening—as their primary communication tools. Even as adults, we still depend heavily on facial, body, and voice clues when someone is talking to us. What does a mother really mean when she says "Come over here" to a 7-year-old? These three little words on paper do not communicate the mother's real meaning. Missing are the clues that help the 7-year-old create a context for the message. Is the mother angry? Is she merely interested in sharing an interesting picture in the comics section? Is she indicating a desire to help the child with a task? Or does she just want to give a hug or kiss for being helpful with a household task?

The extra help that enables you to detect the real or hidden meaning of an oral message may not always be readily found in print. You have to put forth effort to make print mean something. Context for oral language is easy to find. In print, though, the context must be carefully pieced together over time. Readers must be guided to learn self-monitoring strategies for creating context. They need strategies to replace the oral language clues in order to know when to slow down and read carefully, speed up and skip information, stop and reread, question, or seek help. Readers, while creating context, must also sustain their attention; the print is not going to do this for them.

Oral Language, Reading, and Writing.   Reading, writing, and oral language (speaking and listening) share some very important characteristics:

1. All four tools enable you to communicate with yourself, another person, and your environment for a variety of reasons.
2. All four tools share underlying linguistic elements, such as a common lexicon and grammar. The English *lexicon* can be thought of as the giant bank of words we all are able to draw from as we read, write, speak, or listen. Of course, we all do not use the same quantity or variety of words, but they are still there for us to use, just like the words in a dictionary. Of equal importance is the grammar shared by the tools of communication. This *grammar*, or form and structure, is the customary arrangement of words in phrases and sentences. The rules of grammar apply across all four tools, even though we do take liberties with them at times.
3. All four tools are essential for the total communication system a literate society requires. They include both *primary literacy tools* (listening and speaking) and *secondary literacy tools* (reading and writing). The primary tools of literacy are developed first and largely prior to any formal education. The secondary tools of literacy develop later and rapidly during formal education. These tools of literacy can be thought of as means of dealing with information. Each tool can be categorized either as a *receptive process* (listening and reading) to gain or receive information or as an *expressive process* (speaking and writing) to send or produce information.
4. All four tools are developmental in nature; that is, fluency and proficiency improve with practice over time. The exact developmental stages of each individual tool are still the subject of debate, especially in any sequence associated with reading and writing. But, stated simply, children begin by using each tool in a rather primitive, tentative way and gradually become increasingly sophisticated as they see the necessity for gaining control over its use.

Reading and Writing Processes.   Research on the relationship of reading and writing has brought to light new ways in which reading and writing are parallel processes. Tompkins (1997) explains:

> Reading and writing have been thought of as the flip sides of a coin—as opposites; readers decoded or deciphered written language, and writers encoded or produced

written language. Then researchers began to note similarities between reading and writing and talked of both of them as processes. Now reading and writing are viewed as parallel processes of meaning construction, and readers and writers use similar strategies for making meaning with text. (p. 249)

Tompkins also outlines key features or stages of each process:

Reading	*Writing*
Preparing to read	Prewriting
Reading	Drafting
Responding	Revising
Exploring	Editing
Extending	Publishing

Principle 7, applied to helping children learn to read, illustrates how instruction and practice in one process enhances growth in the other processes. As children talk, read, and write, they improve their fluency in using oral language, reading, and writing as communication tools. The structure of the school day should encourage integration of language processes in classroom activities. Separating reading, writing, and oral language into distinct subjects taught at different times in the day discourages integration of language and learning. Every attempt should be made to integrate the curriculum goals and objectives of these communication tools. Using different curricular goals and different instructional materials for each process seems inefficient and unnecessary when their interrelatedness is understood.

Principle 8: Assessment Guides and Directs Language Instruction

In each chapter of this text, we have included assessment strategies along with instructional strategies, because we firmly believe that assessment guides and directs language instruction rather than existing apart from it. The purpose of assessment is to document change over time for teachers and students, to encourage growth, and to direct instruction (Searfoss, 1994). In the present era, assessment of states, school districts, students, and teachers is expected. The public wants to know whether children are making progress in learning, and where they are not, change is expected.

As you read this text, we want you to view assessment as one way of guiding daily instruction. Language assessment should be broad, covering traditional areas such as decoding, comprehension, and vocabulary, as well as oral fluency, writing, and the classroom learning environment. Assessment tools should go beyond paper-and-pencil tests to include observation, interviews, individual conferences, student self-assessment, and portfolios. Figure 1.3 shows a broad view of language assessment tools.

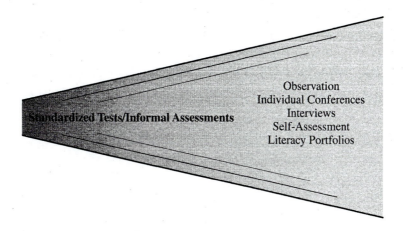

Observation
Individual Conferences
Interviews
Self-Assessment
Literacy Portfolios

Standardized Tests/Informal Assessments

FIGURE 1.3   Broadening Language Assessment Tools

Principle 8, applied to helping children learn to read, stresses the important role assessment plays in daily instruction. Broadening language assessment by extending it beyond traditional areas and by adding new assessment tools allows it to become a major factor in guiding and directing daily instruction.

Summary

In this chapter, literacy and reading were defined and discussed. Eight principles of language were presented as guidelines for planning an effective, child-centered reading program. In Chapter 2, these principles will be put into action, to help you make the classroom a print-rich environment.

FOLLOW-THROUGH ACTIVITIES

Note: Level 1 activities require no access to children or classrooms. Level 2 activities should be completed using children and classrooms.

Level 1 Activities

1. Keep a log of your language activities for at least one day. Include only those that involve interactions with others. Note whether you are reading, writing, or using oral language, as well as the following factors about each communication:

   a. Place (home, school, work)
   b. Nature of communication (classroom discussion, giving directions, asking for something)
   c. Party or parties involved (friend, parent, bank clerk)

Refer to the list of types of literacy in Figure 1.1. Which of these are reflected in your log of language activities? Cite specific examples from your log to support your responses.

2. What is *ideal* literacy in our society? Re-read the list of literacies in Figure 1.1. How many of these types of literacy can be included in the elementary school curriculum? Should one type of literacy be valued or prized more than another? Develop a two- or three-page paper that addresses these questions.

3. Consider this question: Are recent immigrants from Asia or Eastern Europe illiterate because they cannot read and write fluently in English? Form a discussion panel with people in your class who have differing views on this question, and stage a debate for the whole class.

Level 2 Activities

1. Collect and present to this class samples of preschool-age children's writing that illustrate their early attempts to use writing as a communication tool.

2. Observe one classroom for a full day or several classrooms for part of a day, to find examples of teachers' efforts to include multiple literacies in the school day. Look for examples of functional literacy, environmental literacy, and other types of literacy listed in Figure 1.1. Keep a record of the literacies you observe, and collect samples where possible.

3. Interview people about their views of literacy and how important it is to learn to read and to write. Get a cross section of the population by asking a variety of people, such as school personnel, peers, parents, business people, and others. Look for similarities and differences among responses. Refer to the list of purposes of being literate, discussed in the section on Defining Literacy. Which of those purposes came up in the interviews you did? Compile the results of your interviews in a two- or three-page paper or a short oral presentation.

RESOURCES

Browne, R. B., & Neal, A. G. (1991). The many tongues of literacy. *Journal of Popular Culture, 25,* 157–186.

After examining the controversy surrounding cultural literacy, these authors argue that literacy "comes in more colors than a laser show" (p. 185).

Edelsky, C. (1991). *With literacy and justice for all: Rethinking the social in language and education.* New York: Falmer Press.

Chapter 5 of this text deals with distinctions between "exercises" and authentic reading.

Gallego, M., & Hollingsworth, S. (1992). Research directions—Multiple literacies: Teachers' evolving perceptions. *Language Arts, 69,* 206–213.

The authors discuss how teachers can extend their understanding of literacies from an academic, school-bound definition to the literacies of students' communities and personal lives.

Hall, N. (1997). Real literacy in a school setting: Five-year-olds take on the world. *The Reading Teacher, 52*, 8–17.

In an article full of examples of children's reading and writing, the author describes the differences between school literacy and literacy outside of school.

Wormser, R. (1996). *American childhoods: Three centuries of youth at risk.* New York: Walker.

In one particularly readable chapter, the author relates the struggle children have had learning in America's schools, beginning with the Puritan era. The whole book is a fascinating and disturbing view of the "good old days."

Wray, D., & Lewis, M. (1997). *Extending literacy: Children reading and writing non-fiction.* New York: Routledge.

The authors tie basic insights about learning to a current view of teaching literacy.

REFERENCES

Bloome, D. (1985). Reading as a social process. *Language Arts, 62,* 134–142.

Edelsky, C. (1991). *With literacy and justice for all: Rethinking the social in language and education.* New York: Falmer Press.

Edwards, A. D. (1979). Patterns of power and authority in classroom talk. In P. Woods (Ed.), *Teacher strategies: Explorations in the sociology of the school* (pp. 237–253). London: Croom Helm.

Glazer, S. M., & Searfoss, L. W. (1988). *Reading diagnosis and instruction: A C-A-L-M approach.* Englewood Cliffs, NJ: Prentice-Hall.

Harste, J. C. (1994). Literacy as curricular conversations about knowledge, inquiry, and morality. In R. B. Ruddell, M. R. Ruddell, & H. Singer (Eds.), *Theoretical models and processes of reading* (pp. 1220–1242). Newark, DE: International Reading Association.

Juliebo, M. F. (1985). To mediate or not to mediate? That is the question. *Language Arts, 62,* 848–856.

Kaestle, C. F. (1990). Policy implications of literacy definitions. In R. L. Venezky, D. A. Wagner, & B. S. Ciliberti (Eds.), *Toward defining literacy* (pp. 63–68). Newark, DE: International Reading Association.

The Oxford encyclopedic English dictionary (2nd ed.). (1995). New York: Oxford University Press.

Pinnell, G. S., & Jaggar, A. M. (1991). Oral language: Speaking and listening in the classroom. In J. Flood, J. Jensen, D. Lapp, & J. Squire (Eds.), *Handbook of research on teaching the English language arts* (pp. 24–29). New York: Macmillan.

Public Law 102-73. *National literacy act of 1991.* Washington, DC: Congress of the United States.

Santa Barbara Classroom Discourse Group. (1994). Constructing literacy in classrooms: Literate action as social accomplishment. In R. B. Ruddell, M. R. Ruddell, & H. Singer (Eds.), *Theoretical models and processes of reading* (pp. 124–154). Newark, DE: International Reading Association.

Searfoss, L. W. (1994). A holistic/wellness model of reading assessment: An alternative to the medical model. *Reading & Writing Quarterly, 10,* 105–117.

Standards for the English language arts. (1996). Newark, DE: International Reading Association.

Stubbs, M. S. (1979). Language, schools, and classroom (an interview by D. A. Dillon). *Language Arts, 56,* 941–949, 1016.

Tompkins, G. E. (1997). *Literacy for the 21st century: A balanced approach.* Upper Saddle River, NJ: Merrill/Prentice Hall.

Venezky, R. L. (1991). The development of literacy in the industrialized nations of the West. In R. Barr, M. L. Kamil, P. B. Mosenthal, & P. D. Pearson (Eds.), *Handbook of reading research: Volume II* (pp. 46–67). New York: Longman.

CHAPTER

2

Creating a Community of Literacy Learners

INTRODUCTION

Now we move on to the job of helping children learn to read by putting into action the definitions of literacy and reading and the language principles from Chapter 1. The classroom needs to be a print-rich environment, organized in a way that contributes to the development of a community of literacy learners. Classroom design can help to establish physical, social, and emotional settings in which children and teachers can read and write for real purposes, interacting and sharing language. This chapter will help you create a classroom environment that, as Searfoss (1993) states,

1. Encourages children to take risks while producing language so that they learn not only to read and write, but also to use reading and writing as communication and learning tools.

2. Shares control and decision making in language learning so that children can make decisions, solve problems, and become responsible for their own language learning.

3. Merges instruction and assessment so that the process of how children produce language can be observed and used to guide instruction.

GRAPHIC ORGANIZER

This graphic organizer summarizes the structure of Chapter 2:

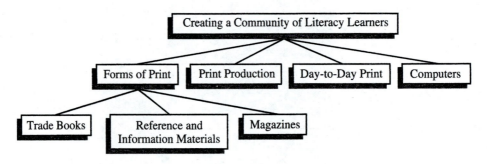

OBJECTIVES

When you finish reading this chapter, you should be able to understand and discuss each of these statements:

1. Schools have the responsibility of showing children that learning to read is a personal, worthwhile goal.

2. Children, parents, and teachers must cooperate in creating a classroom reading environment for helping children learn to read.

3. Practice in reading a wide variety of relevant print establishes sound purposes for children to read.

4. Independent reading, in school *and* out of school, is both a necessity and a responsibility for children if they are to learn to read.

5. Having opportunities to produce print (that is, to write) facilitates learning to read.

Creating a Print-Rich Classroom Environment

We believe that regardless of the materials or methods you choose to use to help children learn to read, the nature of the classroom environment is critical. It is often the most neglected element in a classroom reading program, since much time is spent in selecting materials and choosing approaches and strategies for teaching reading. The place where all this activity takes place, the classroom, must be a rich and fertile ground for language growth. A sterile, illiterate environment, devoid of print, will doom any method of teaching reading to failure. We envision literate classrooms full of "literacy droppings," completed and in-process language products shared and displayed everywhere one can look—floors, walls, corners, and even ceilings. Literate classroom environments provide a place where children's language growth and your teaching can come together.

"Children enter school having learned different things in different ways in different cultures and communities" (Clay, 1998, p. 1). School, therefore, has the job of showing children, through concrete and relevant experiences, that learning to read is a personal, worthwhile goal for each of them. A child will learn to read and will practice reading in a classroom where reading a wide variety of print is actively encouraged. Experimenting with reading print, just like mastering a musical instrument or athletic activity, requires regular, sustained practice. Such practice, however, must eventually become intrinsically motivated—that is, come from within the child—if reading is to become fluent. Extrinsic motivation, provided in school by teachers, can only serve to whet a child's appetite for learning to read. The initial taste provided by the teacher must be rich and exciting enough for children to want more on their own. No one has ever learned to play a piano or any other musical instrument simply by taking lessons or practicing only under parental or teacher pressure. Those of you who continued to play an instrument for pleasure in adulthood developed a genuine love of playing and practiced without being forced to do so. In order to foster a love of reading, classrooms should provide an environment that says to children, "It is safe to practice here; there is exciting reading here, so dive in and read!"

The first step in creating a print-rich classroom that promotes a literacy learning community is to consider the organization of the room. We suggest beginning with the following four areas:

1. A text area that contains various types of print such as trade books, reference materials, and magazines
2. A print production area
3. A computer area
4. A day-to-day print area

To create the text area, begin with one type of print, such as trade books, and collect a small number of them, say 20 to 30. Discuss their organization and their use with the children, and introduce the children to a few books at a time. Encourage them to add to the collection or to make suggestions about specific titles or interests they may have. Then move to a second type of print, such as magazines or reference materials.

If they slowly build the area over the first few months of school, children will feel involved and have a sense of ownership in the literacy learning community. Try to avoid constructing a picture-perfect text area, which you have decorated, for children to enter on the first day of school. Almost every first-year teacher has had the experience of preparing beautiful bulletin boards, games, or classroom displays that, while eye-pleasing, are only briefly noticed by children and quickly abandoned. One of the authors observed a teacher who had prepared an elaborate corner consisting of a bulletin board, table display, and collection of books, all on a single topic—the seashore. The teacher had spent many happy hours by the sea-shore during summer vacation and had collected all kinds of items related to the sea. By creating this attractive interest area, the teacher hoped to motivate children to read books on the topic of the seas. Well, the center generated some initial, first-school-day interest from a few students who had also been near the sea during the summer, but not much from the other children. After a month or so, the teacher re-moved the entire corner one day after school. On the next school day, when the children had arrived and were settled, the teacher asked them to put their heads down on the desks, close their eyes, and think about what was missing from the room. The response was deafening silence, except for one child who said, "Tommy is absent!" In spite of considerable prodding, only two students were able to recall that something related to the sea was missing from the corner.

That teacher learned a valuable lesson. Constructing displays—including text areas—must not be viewed as a creative, aesthetic experience for the teacher. If text areas are to be functional, children must be involved in their planning and use. The teacher and the children must work together to create the area, right from the beginning of the school year.

Trade Books

Trade books are those books generally written and published for children to read for pleasure and information. They are often called library books, and they can be distinguished from books published specifically for reading instruction, such as basal readers. Trade books also can be used for major aspects of reading instruc-tion (see Chapter 5). In the present chapter, their role as part of a text area is ex-plained. Trade books come in all sizes, large and small, and in all kinds, paperback and hardbound, and they cover the widest range of topics imaginable. In a recent year, more than 3,000 children's books were published in English alone. If you can think of a topic, someone has probably written a book about it for children. This rich, diverse reservoir should be tapped as an integral component of creating a community of literacy learners.

Here are a few guidelines for choosing trade books:*

1. Choose trade books for the quality of the writing. Who judges the quality? You, the teacher, using your professional and personal criteria, are the best

---

*Portions of guidelines 1–4 were developed on the basis of a discussion by Moffett and Wagner (1992, p. 167) and applied to selecting trade books.

judge of quality for your classroom. Children need to be surrounded by examples of good writing.

2. See that trade books represent a wide range of topics of interest to children in your classroom. You are the expert at judging what the children you teach are interested in reading. Talking with the children, observing their library choices, and asking the school librarian for suggestions are good ways to develop an initial list of children's reading interests.

3. Be sure that the range of difficulty is *very* broad, fitting the reality of the classroom, not some fancied typical third or fourth grader. A rough rule for getting started is to aim for trade books with reading levels 3 years above and 3 years below the grade level of your students. Of course, in the lower primary grades, this rule will need bending. As the classroom text area grows, books with even a wider range of difficulty may be added, especially for the upper elementary levels, when scientific and reference texts become useful to children.

4. Include trade books with a wide variety of formats and types—books with many illustrations and those with only a few, large and small books, thick and thin books, soft-cover and hard-cover books, and plain black-and-white books. The greater the variety, the more the text area will model the real world. The diversity of a text area is also enhanced by books of poetry, riddles, fables, myths, plays, jokes, limericks, tongue twisters, proverbs, and other similar types of literature. Variety is the key.

5. Have multiple copies of some trade books. Small groups of children can then read the same book at the same time, engage in literature study, conduct impromptu plays or panel discussions, and develop art or musical projects based on the book.

6. Plan to use a variety of lists and sources recommending trade books for children. (See the Resources section at the end of this chapter.)

7. Include multicultural literature for children.

Multicultural Literature for Children

During the past few decades, there has been an increasingly important movement to expand the types of literature made available in classrooms to include multicultural literature. Multicultural literature is described as literature that focuses on people of color, religious minorities, regional cultures, the disabled, the aged, and, often, women and girls in roles that do not perpetuate common stereotypes (Harris, 1992). The importance of including multicultural literature was expressed by Bishop (1992):

> If literature is a mirror that reflects human life, then all children who read or are read to need to see themselves reflected as part of humanity. If they are not, or if their reflections are distorted and ridiculous, there is the danger that they will absorb negative messages about themselves and people like them. Those who see only themselves or who [are] exposed to errors and misrepresentations are miseducated into a false sense of superiority, and the harm is doubly done. (p. 43)

Although teachers realize the importance of including multicultural literature, they may have little knowledge about how to select this type of literature. Bishop suggests these principles as guidelines:

1. Strive for cultural authenticity in the multicultural literature you choose for the classroom. Accuracy is important if we are to avoid presenting stereotypical or distorted themes, characters, and actions of a particular culture.
2. Become aware of the various types of multicultural literature by reading literature written by *insiders*. Literature reflecting the social behaviors and mores, values, attitudes, and themes of a particular cultural group is probably more easily accepted as authentic when the person writing about the culture can claim it as his or her own. There is some debate, however, on this issue, as Bishop notes.
3. Judge books by their literary quality, too, not just by their multicultural nature. Multicultural books should offer a good read and have something to say to children—criteria that should be applied to all books in the text area. Balance your collection across cultures, and present cross-cultural viewpoints on the issues. For example, along with the standard military history of World War II, present the role of the United States from the perspective of Japanese-Americans who were interred in camps in this country.

Equally important to consider is the use of multicultural literature. Discussions of multicultural literature serve as a basis for considering one's own ethnicity (Bean, Readence, & Mallette, 1996) as well as a starting point for a social-action curriculum (Enciso et al., 1999). As students have opportunities to place themselves in the roles of others, they begin to see the societal forces that perpetuate racism. Teachers can build on these events through in-depth discussions of literature. Multicultural literature can play an important role in helping all students learn about racism. It "opens the door for literature to be used as a springboard toward critical literacy—reading the word in order to read the world" (Enciso et al., 1999, p. 191).

Sources of Trade Books

Selecting which trade books to include is a big job for both the teacher and the children. Once the books have been selected, a practical consideration arises: Where do you *find* these wonderful books? There never seems to be enough money to purchase all the books needed, but the following resources have been used by the authors in helping teachers create text areas on small budgets.

1. *School librarian.* The school librarian will often allow a teacher to check out, on a rotating basis, a core of trade books, perhaps 25 or 30 every few weeks.
2. *Public library.* If each child has a library card and is encouraged to visit the public library and check out books regularly, these books can then be shared in the classroom.
3. *School book budget.* Classroom teachers need to know how books are purchased for the school, who does the purchasing, and if any money is allocated for individual classroom purchases.

4. *Basal reading program lists.* Most basal reader companies provide lists of supplementary trade books that can be purchased to accompany the regular reading series.

5. *Parent and community organizations.* Sometimes you just have to ask. Teachers will be surprised how many parent and other community organizations are willing to donate books or money for classroom text areas.

6. *Children's book clubs.* A number of national children's book clubs offer inexpensive paperback books for sale to children in a system similar to that of adult book clubs. The largest club is

> Scholastic Book Clubs
> 2931 East McCarty Street
> P.O. Box 7503
> Jefferson City, MO 65102

7. *Parents.* Parents can be a rich source of books for the classroom. They can be asked to donate books no longer in use. A library pocket can be prepared with the notation "This book was donated by _____. Thanks!"

8. *Book fairs.* Local paperback book distributors (listed in the *Yellow Pages*) can be contacted to support school book fairs. Parent organizations can conduct book fairs, with the dual purpose of helping children to acquire books and at the same time raising funds for the treasuries of the organizations.

9. *Discount stores, supermarkets, and drug stores.* With large sections devoted to the sale of books, these stores have provided places for people to purchase children's books at greatly reduced prices.

To summarize, the first task in making trade books an integral part of the classroom is collecting them. The sources are many, and teachers will need to use all the inventiveness they and their students can muster to build a large and varied collection of trade books. But the more effort teachers, parents, and children put into the collecting, the greater the feeling of pride and ownership by all.

Process Guide 2.1

Locating and becoming familiar with sources of trade books outside school is an important part of creating a text area. What are the resources available to local schools in your community? In small groups, prepare a short list of specific places and sources a teacher might easily find and use. Review the pages on trade books in this chapter before you begin.

Organizing and Arranging Trade Books

After a number of trade books have been collected, organizing them for easy use is the next step. Browsing among a collection of trade books is a worthwhile activity for children, but, unfortunately, many of them are unsuccessful at finding books and are reluctant to ask for help. To create an independent browser, some organized arrangement of trade books is necessary. There is no best way to physically arrange books, shelves, tables, or centers. The space available in each classroom will vary, so it is difficult to design an all-purpose scheme. Two major points should be kept in mind as the books are arranged: The arrangement should (1) allow for quick, easy access to books and (2) be attractive and inviting to the children. Some teachers combine a recreational reading area with the collection. This has the advantage of providing a comfortable area in which children can read, right next to the raw materials—books. But if the collection is widely used during the day, the constant coming and going of children selecting books can be distracting to a child who is trying to find a quiet corner in which to read. It also may be necessary for the teacher to set up other forms of print (such as the magazines, the reference collection, or the day-to-day print center) near the trade books. For these reasons, we suggest that the quiet corner, with its pillows or bean bag chairs, pieces of carpet, and other creature comforts, not be placed near the collection of trade books.

Here are some other suggestions for creating a reading corner or area:

1. Start the corner, and then let the children help create it. The corner should evolve, not be born full-grown.
2. Follow the guidelines discussed earlier in this chapter for selecting trade books.
3. Include a variety of print, such as trade books, magazines, and reference materials.
4. Update the corner with the help of children and parents.
5. Encourage children to use the corner every day. Make it a source of pleasure and information for you and the children.
6. Organize the corner so that you and the children can find things. Be willing to change the organization as the corner grows.

For the primary grades, one effective scheme is to arrange books by subjects and pictures. For beginning readers, pictures are used to identify categories of books (e.g., a picture of a clown for books on wit and humor). For the intermediate and upper grades, the scheme can include a small card catalog arranged alphabetically by subject and placed in a file box.

Children should take over the maintenance of the text area as much as possible. A rotating library committee might be elected or appointed every week to share the work. The committee can add new subjects and subtopics and can replace pictures as needed. In the intermediate grades, the card catalog can be developed and maintained by the children. Recent additions to the area might be displayed on a separate shelf or in a special spot. These additions can then be introduced to the children by the teacher or by a child, especially for books on personal loan. Children can be given time to *sell* a book to other children who might be interested in the same subject. If time is set aside for it, this sales activity can generate much interest in new additions to the collection. Through the involvement of all the members of the classroom, a community can flourish.

Using Trade Books

The role of trade books in helping children learn to read will be discussed in detail in Chapter 5. In the present chapter, we simply want to introduce some general categories of activities involving trade books, together with a few examples of tried-and-true activities every teacher can use. (See the Resources section of this chapter for a list of the many activity books published for teachers.) There are four categories of activities that can be used with any reading program:

- Reading by the teacher
- Reading to the teacher
- Reading by children to other children
- Independent reading in school and at home

Reading by the Teacher.   In reading prose to children, the teacher may want to adopt the read-and-tell strategy, which allows the story to be tailored to the audience. For poetry, the read-a-poem approach ties the poem to the classroom environment.

Read-and-Tell.   In read-and-tell, the teacher selects a book and then, over the course of a week, reads or tells a portion of the book each day. The portions selected for oral reading to children should be crucial ones, relating directly to the plot, actions of characters, or special parts of the setting. This approach allows the teacher to read longer books to children in a short period of time, while preserving the story line and maintaining the children's interest. Storytelling an entire story from the trade book collection can be a highly effective means of generating children's interest in shorter stories. Ross (1996) explains in great detail the art of storytelling. We offer the modified steps he describes, with a brief summary of each one.

1. Find the story you want to tell. The right story to tell must be one *you* like and want to share with children. Reading widely, asking for suggestions from librarians and other teachers, and trying out a number of stories until you feel comfortable with one are all part of finding a story to tell. We suggest you develop one story at a time, gradually building your repertoire.
2. Prepare the story. To prepare a story, first read it aloud to yourself several times, trying to think of major actions or incidents that could each be told as a unit. Next, develop a sense of the characters in the story by forming mental pictures of how they look and act. Imagine the setting of the story, and draw a rough sketch or map of it. Look for key phrases that are especially scary, funny, or vivid and good for telling. Plan a few gestures that will add to the story, but keep these to a small number. Finally, practice the entire story, and time yourself to see if you need to cut it down or to schedule several story sessions. A tape recorder is useful at this stage, as is a mirror for practicing gestures.
3. Share the story. When it is time to tell the story, pick a quiet time of the school day, with no deadlines pressing. Make yourself and the children comfortable—and tell your story.

Read-a-Poem. In read-a-poem, the teacher keeps a "poem in the pocket" ready for instant reading when there is time. Rather than schedule a regular time, Larrick (1987, p. 25) suggests that the teacher fit poetry reading to occasions. She offers these suggestions for teachers:

1. Select a short poem to read aloud each day, sometimes about the weather, sometimes funny, sometimes sad. Print the poem on a sheet of construction paper, and post it in a prominent place where children can reread it easily.
2. Invite children to help you choose a poem for the day and present it for class participation. This is a good time to repeat favorites heard earlier.
3. Give the children frequent opportunities to become involved in impromptu choral reading, not to teach a lesson or analyze the poem, but to revel in the melody.
4. From time to time, focus your selections on a theme—sports, people, weather, the moon and stars, or just plain fun. A week of funny poems may be the pick-me-up everybody needs.
5. Have a week devoted to the work of one poet, such as Jack Prelutsky, Myra Cohn Livingston, or Shel Silverstein.
6. Focus on poems related to an upcoming holiday.
7. Help children select appropriate music to play as background while a poem is being read or a song to sing softly as the setting for a poem. Show the children how to improve background music with rhythm instruments, water glasses, bells, or wooden sticks and blocks.

In addition to engaging in Larrick's spontaneous poetry moments, Perfect (1999) suggests using poetry as a link between narratives and life experiences, as well as a bridge to common experiences.

Reading to the Teacher. Children can be taught the same basic read-and-tell strategy that was just described for teachers. They can share exciting, interesting parts of a book as they read it. The purpose for sharing should be *fun*; the teacher should sit back and enjoy the moment with each child. This is not the time for reading instruction or an individual conference. Nemeth (no date) offers the following guidelines for listening to children read. They are also useful for helping parents who ask what to do when their child reads aloud.

1. Sit down…and give your undivided attention and listen with obvious interest and enjoyment. Listen to *what*, not *how*, the child reads.
2. Always let the child practice silently before reading aloud, especially if brothers and sisters are to be part of the audience. Such silent reading practice will help the child read more fluently and quickly and can reduce possible embarrassment.
3. When the child reads silently or orally and doesn't know a word, provide the word for the child. Insisting that the child sound or spell out the unknown word interrupts the flow of the story, causes comprehension loss, and forces the child to lose self-confidence.

Reading by Children to Other Children.   The idea is a simple one. Children share favorite books with one another. In the experiences of the authors, though, a bit of structure is necessary for this sharing to be worthwhile. Paired reading, buddy reading, and reading to a group are simple activities that are easy for children to follow.

Paired Reading.   The strategy of paired reading, adapted from one originally created by Greene (1970b), is reminiscent of a parent's reading a story to a child. The technique requires the pairing of two children of *different* reading abilities. Children take turns reading to each other from their favorite books at their own levels of reading competence. The children should sit side by side so that one can follow while the other reads. It is important that the more competent reader not become an overbearing prompter, thus discouraging the less competent one. If either reader encounters a difficult word that causes the reading to stop, the other reader can be asked for help in pronouncing the word. Each child should read about 10 to 15 minutes, for a total activity time of 20 to 30 minutes. Of course, teachers can adjust these time limits for younger and older children. Some teachers, as a comprehension check, will want to add a few minutes of oral retelling or discussion time by each child. If this is done, it should not add time to the activity; the oral reading time limits may be shortened to allow time for discussions. Paired reading is an excellent method of increasing oral reading, having children share books, and freeing the teacher to work with small groups of children while the remainder of the class reads in pairs.

Buddy Reading.   The strategy of buddy reading differs from paired reading in that the children choose a buddy with whom they want to read and the reading ability of each child is unimportant. Veatch (1978) presented the directions for a similar activity as follows:

> Have the buddies sit together, choose the story they want to read—either the same one or two different ones—and begin reading silently and then to each other. Help them organize their activity something like this: "Before you start to read to yourselves, decide how much you will read, and plan it so that you both will be through at the same time. Then when you are done, read together or to each other, or in some way swap the ideas of what you have read. If you want to, you can begin to plan a project about what you have read—if it is that kind of material." (p. 61)

Buddy reading requires the children to make more decisions, and teachers will want to demonstrate it to the entire class several times before having children participate. Also, children may need plenty of planning time and may want to spend several sessions together.

Reading to a Group.   Paired reading and buddy reading do much to build children's confidence in sharing books. As they gain confidence, individual children could volunteer to read to a small group of children, following the read-and-tell directions (presented earlier for teachers). A child might want to initially practice with a buddy and then enlarge the audience to four to six children.

Children need many opportunities to practice reading on their own.

Independent Reading in School and at Home. Children will need many opportunities to practice reading silently on their own, both in and out of school. The trade books in the text area can be checked out to individual children for their use in school and at home. Developing an independent reading habit requires two ingredients: a large collection of good books and a means for children to select books. The Goldilocks strategy, described by Ohlhausen and Jepsen (1992), is a decision-making process children can use when self-selecting books. Children are encouraged to ask themselves the following questions:

Too Easy Books
Ask yourself these questions. If you are answering YES, this book is probably a *Too Easy* book for you. Have fun reading it!

1. Have you read it lots of times before?
2. Do you understand the story (text) very well?
3. Do you know (can you understand) almost every word?
4. Can you read it smoothly?

Just Right Books
Ask yourself these questions. If you are answering YES, this book is probably a *Just Right* book for you. Go ahead and learn from it!

1. Is this book new to you?

2. Do you understand some of the book?
3. Are there just a few words per page you don't know?
4. When you read, are some places smooth and some choppy?
5. Can someone help you with this book? Who?

Too Hard Books

Ask yourself these questions. If you are answering YES, this book is probably a *Too Hard* book for you. Spend some time with it now. Give it another try later (perhaps in a couple of months).

1. Are there more than a few words on a page you don't know?
2. Are you confused about what is happening in most of this book?
3. When you read, does it sound pretty choppy?
4. Is everyone else busy and unable to help you?

Children will select books at different levels on different occasions. As Ohlhausen and Jepsen make clear, the key here is that the books be their choice.

Teachers cannot provide all the practice children will need to become fluent readers. Independent reading in school *and* at home is a necessity. Children have to assume some of the responsibility for practicing on their own. Structure and direction are necessary for this practice to be productive for some children, however. Two successful approaches to independent practice are SSR (sustained silent reading) for use in school and alarm clock reading for use at home.

SSR, or Sustained Silent Reading. Once called USSR (uninterrupted sustained silent reading), SSR has been around for a number of years. It was originally intended to provide everyone, including the teacher, with a quiet time to read. With everyone in the classroom reading at the same time, both peer pressure and the modeling effect serve to help children increase and sustain their independent reading for increasingly longer periods of time. Over the years, many variations of the SSR rules have been suggested:

1. Don't try to sell SSR to the whole school. First graders and sixth graders require different amounts of SSR time, and even a different time of day for scheduling SSR. Also, individual teachers will want to schedule SSR to fit individual classroom schedules and programs. We strongly urge that children be involved in planning and scheduling SSR times and in determining the amount of time given to SSR.
2. Discuss SSR with the children, and post your interpretation of the rules. Tierney and Readence (2000) present three cardinal rules of SSR:

   Everybody reads.

   There are no interruptions during SSR.

   No one will be asked to report what he or she has read.

Use a kitchen timer instead of the classroom clock to signal the beginning and end of the SSR period. Remember: *you*, the teacher, are a model fluent reader for your children. If you spend the SSR time glancing back and forth from the clock to what you are reading, this is hardly good modeling.

3. Read with your class. SSR is not "shut up and read" time, so take some time to relax with a favorite piece of writing and enjoy it. Try a novel, a professional book, a new children's book, poetry, the newspaper—but be sure to select something for *your* pleasure reading.

4. Start SSR with the phrase "Does everyone have something to read?" Avoid saying "a book to read," since that implies that only books are good enough for SSR.

5. Adjust the SSR time to fit your children, gradually increasing it. Beginning with 5 minutes and moving slowly to 20 or 25 minutes is the general pattern.

6. Be consistent and follow the rules. Handle fidgeters and disruptive children quickly and without lectures on proper behavior. Simply inviting yourself to sit next to a potentially disruptive child often has a calming influence in a hurry. If only a few children are fidgeters, see that they place themselves out of the line of sight of the others. Make them comfortable near you or in their own little corner.

SSR can provide an excellent opportunity for children to silently practice reading. It is simple, cheap, and easy to implement and keep going. A last word on SSR: Keep the students involved in planning the SSR daily time period and the length of the period and also in finding ways to be certain that everyone has a chance to read, quietly and without interruptions.

Alarm Clock Reading. The purpose of alarm clock reading is to give some direction and structure to children's at-home reading. The exact steps in the technique, suggested originally by Greene (1970a), are certainly adaptable. The important element of alarm clock reading is the regular recording children do as they read each day at home. This recording is crucial to starting a habit of reading independently at home. The basic steps are these:

1. Select an easy book to read for alarm clock reading.
2. Set a stove timer or alarm clock so that it will ring 15 minutes after you begin to read.
3. Read your book as rapidly as you can until the alarm rings.
4. After the alarm rings, count the number of pages (to the nearest half page) and record it somewhere. Keep your daily log in a place where you can find it.
5. Close your book, and tell yourself out loud what you just read.
6. Do alarm clock reading each day, and keep your record up to date.

Log format will vary with the grade level of the children. Whatever the form, space should be provided for recording daily progress, as shown on the next page.

> Book Title:
>
> Number of Pages: Mon. _____   Tues. _____   Wed. _____   Thurs. _____
>
> Fri. _____   Sat. _____   Sun. _____

Some parents keep the log sheet on the refrigerator door. If children have a special place to study, a log can be tacked to a small bulletin board. Weekly logs can be transferred to a reading folder in school, so that the teacher can review the log with each child. Some teachers might wish to develop a log format with simple drawings, duplicate it, and provide it for children to get alarm clock reading started. Later, children might design their own logs. Some children will already be reading regularly at home and may find alarm clock reading unnecessary. Teachers can suggest they continue with their independent reading and not use an alarm clock reading log. The authors have found, though, that these children adjust to almost any system of recording their at-home reading, since it is already a habit for them.

Process Guide 2.2

Locate several popular children's trade books. Use them to try SSR and alarm clock reading as part of this class for a week or so. Share your reactions with the class.

Reference and Information Materials

The reference and information materials section of a text area should contain the kinds of materials children will use to gain information, such as dictionaries, encyclopedias, and maps. If children are to envision reading as a learning tool, though, the range of information materials must be expanded beyond these traditional ones. Including historical fiction (Johnson & Ebert, 1992), information books (Pappas, 1991), and nonfiction trade books in the text area gives children many sources to explore and helps them use reading as a learning tool. (See the Resources section of this chapter for some suggested readings on how to use nonfiction trade books, information books, and historical fiction in the text area.)

Children's nonfiction trade books have emerged as a type of literature that can be used in addition to content area textbooks (Moss, 1991). Moss believes that dated, unappealing content area textbooks provide limited opportunities for indepth exploration of a topic and may be too difficult for children to read. Children's nonfiction trade books have these advantages, as listed by Moss:

1. Teachers can more readily individualize content area instruction through the use of nonfiction trade books. Books closer to the reading levels of children can be selected.

2. Nonfiction trade books have both content and visual appeal and also provide in-depth information on a particular topic.
3. Nonfiction trade books are often more current than content area textbooks, which are usually revised every five to ten years.

Variety is the key to building a reference section that is continually used by children. Following are some suggestions for the contents of this part of the text area:

Encyclopedias. A set of encyclopedias is useful, especially in the intermediate grades. A set should also be included in the primary grades for the teacher to use in finding answers to children's many questions, thus providing a model for them.

Dictionaries. If the text area is the only source of dictionaries in a classroom, then it is crucial that a variety of types be provided, ranging in difficulty from picture dictionaries through those published primarily for adults.

Atlases, maps. A generous selection of world, national, regional, and local maps and atlases is an indispensable part of a text area.

Directories. Telephone books, especially the pages that are devoted to services, should be a part of the text area. Other kinds of business and restaurant directories, along with community calendars, may be collected and added to this section.

"How-to" references. References that explain how to do something should be a part of the text area reference section—cookbooks, songbooks, catalogs of all types, arts and crafts books, plant and animal information books, first-aid manuals, Boy Scout and Girl Scout handbooks, travel guides, and so on. Many of the materials for this section are available at no cost in multiple copies. One of the authors gathered nearly 50 brochures and manuals at no cost on a Saturday morning by visiting local supermarkets and collecting them from store displays. A few titles from a day's hunting were *Traveling with Your Cat, Breaking Cats' Bad Habits,* and *To Market with Metric.*

Government publications. The United States Government has a catalog of free and inexpensive government publications on hundreds of topics. For this list, write to

Government Printing Office Bookstore
720 North Main Street
Pueblo, CO 81003

State, county, and local government offices also publish many helpful references that are free or inexpensive and that cover topics ranging from safety and energy conservation to agriculture and home economics.

Magazines

Magazines should be part of every text area. Two kinds may be included: magazines specially written for children and general-circulation magazines, such as *Time* and

Many "how-to" reference materials are available at no cost.

Consumer Reports. More than 30 national magazines for children are published in the United States. The following list has been selected to start your collection. There are others that probably should be included, and these can be added after observing the interests of the children and consulting with school and public librarians.

> *Cricket: The Magazine for Children.* Age range 9–14. This general-interest magazine includes a variety of stories, poems, and articles. 315 Fifth Street, Peru, IL 61354.
>
> *Highlights for Children.* Age range 2–12. In keeping with its motto "fun with a purpose," this magazine has articles, stories, puzzles, and activities that prepare children for reading and encourage creative thinking. P.O. Box 269, Columbus, OH 43216-0269.
>
> *Jack and Jill.* Age range 6–12. Published by the Children's Better Health Institute, this magazine focuses on stories that promote healthy living. 1100 Waterway Blvd., P.O. Box 567, Indianapolis, IN 46206.
>
> *Kids Discover.* Age range 8–12. Each issue of this science magazine for children is devoted to a single topic, with short articles, photos, diagrams, drawings, and bibliographies related to the theme. P.O. Box 54205, Boulder, CO 80322-4205.
>
> *New Moon: The Magazine for Girls and Their Dreams.* Age range 8–14. Devoted to encouraging girls to become strong, positive women, this magazine has articles on girls and women from many diverse backgrounds and countries. P.O. Box 3620, Duluth, MN 55803-3620.

Odyssey: Science That's Out of This World. Age range 8–14. Each issue of this magazine focuses on a single science theme, raising issues to which students may respond via the Internet. 7 School Street, Peterborough, NH 03458.

Ranger Rick. Age range 6–12. Published by the National Wildlife Federation, this magazine is geared toward teaching elementary students about animals and the environment. 8925 Leesburg Pike, Vienna, VA 22184.

Skipping Stone: A Multicultural Children's Quarterly. Age range 8–14. This magazine's stories, articles, and pictures provide information about students from diverse backgrounds. P.O. Box 3939, Eugene, OR 97403-0939.

Sports Illustrated for Kids. Age range 8–13. This colorful magazine, focused on sports and athletes, makes for wonderful recreational reading for students interested in sports. Time and Life Building, Rockefeller Center, New York, NY 10020-1393.

The school librarian can be approached about creating a mobile magazine cart that can be circulated around the school building on a schedule. Teachers, with the help of the school librarian, can design the cart with a good selection of magazines from the school library and see that the cart is shared throughout the school. The goal of placing the magazines on a cart and moving them around the school is to make them accessible to children. Without convenient access, many children might not make the initial effort to begin reading magazines.

Process Guide 2.3

The next time you visit a school, public, college, or university library, locate the children's magazine section. Browse through the collection, and compare it with the list in this chapter. Keep a record of children's magazines that you find. Share your list with others in your class.

Print Production Area

A classroom dedicated to creating a community of literacy learners should offer children not only opportunities to read a variety of print, but also a place to produce print for others to read. A print production area is such a place, and it will need to contain resources to produce a variety of writing. The production area can also be the place where children's writing is displayed and stored for others to read and share. Major components of a writing/publishing area include the following:

Paper in a variety of qualities, sizes, and colors. Newsprint or other inexpensive paper serves for first or rough drafts, with finer grades for final drafts.

Markers, pencils, and felt-tip pens of many sizes and colors.

Writing models that show capital and lowercase letters, for use as editing aids.

Spelling aids, such as dictionaries and lists of high-frequency words, color and movement words, and words from units under study in the classroom.

Models of different kinds of writing, such as riddles, jokes, poetry, and newspaper headlines.

Supplies such as a paper cutter, paper punch, glue, tape, sewing equipment, and arts-and-crafts items for creating book covers, binding stories, and illustrating writing.

If the classroom does not have a computer area, there should also be a typewriter for children to use.

Computer Area

The computer has become an extremely important tool in our society. The enormous amount of information rapidly available through this technology has launched us into the information age. Through the use of computers, children now have the opportunity to communicate with children throughout the world. While there are many applications for computers in classrooms, this section highlights the three that we deem most beneficial in creating a classroom of literacy learners: (1) using educational software, (2) word processing, and (3) logging onto the Internet.

Software

There is an abundance of educational computer software designed for literacy instruction. This software ranges from drill-and-practice programs to electronic books. When selecting reading software you must take care not to get distracted by the graphics and other bells and whistles. It is crucial to evaluate the software's educational importance: How will this software be used by children? Often, drill-and-practice software is nothing more than *electronic worksheets*. The children push buttons or keys to indicate answers to drill exercises, are told whether they are right or wrong, and move on. There is little or no interaction between child and program. Such a use of the computer seems like a waste of money—worksheets are cheaper! To achieve its potential, the computer, along with its software, should enable children to interact with ideas and concepts.

This is not to suggest that there isn't any valuable software for use with literacy learners; on the contrary, there is plenty. When selecting software, however, look for programs that will engage children and encourage creative thinking. For example, electronic books such as *Just Grandma and Me* (Broderbund, 1994) provide opportunities for students to interact with text and play within stories. These books cover a broad range of difficulty levels and so can be used with children of all ages.

Word Processing

In their role as word processors, computers make a great supplement to the materials in the print production area. Computers give students a way to rewrite their pieces without much labor. Additionally, they provide graphics and templates for constructing a variety of items ranging from newsletters to resumes. For example, the teacher and children together can publish a monthly newsletter to send home to parents, informing them of classroom events and special activities and sharing news of the day-to-day happenings in the classroom. This type of project constitutes a real-life application of literacy in the classroom, promotes the classroom community, and, in addition, involves the parents as part of that community. All this can be accomplished with great ease with the use of computers and word-processing software. Numerous word-processing programs are available, designed for use with children of all ages.

Internet

An increasingly common way to use the computer to enhance literacy is to take advantage of the vast network of computers known as the Internet (Moore, 1999). The Internet has many applications in an environment designed to create a community of literacy learners. First, the Internet provides access to a plethora of data, both graphic and text. Students can use the Internet to locate information on just about any topic they choose. Second, the Internet provides opportunities for communication through electronic mail (e-mail) and chat rooms, allowing students to become participants in global conversations. Third, the Internet—through the World Wide Web—gives students the ability to locate and create web sites, a new forum for publishing.

Leu, Karchmer, and Leu (1999) suggest that literacy learning can be achieved through new *envisionments*. They describe these envisionments as taking place "when teachers and children imagine new possibilities for literacy and learning, transform existing technologies to construct this vision, and then share their work with others" (p. 636). Such Internet projects, or envisionments, range from sharing ideas with other classrooms to collecting stories from multiple classrooms to dialoguing across countries on particular topics. The information one can access on the Internet is continually expanding and evolving. We encourage you to use newly published resources, such as the periodicals listed below, to keep current on sites that will provide the best resources for you and your students:

Computers in the Schools
The Haworth Press, Inc.
Sample Copy Department
10 Alice Street
Binghamton, NY 13904-9981

T.H.E. Journal
150 El Camino Real
Suite 112
Tustin, CA 92680-3670

*Information Technology
  in Childhood Education*
Association for the Advancement
  of Computing in Education
P.O. Box 2966
Charlottesville, VA 22902

Technology Teacher
1914 Association Drive
Reston, VA 22091

*Learning and Leading
  with Technology*
International Society for
  Technology in Education
1787 Agate Street
Eugene, OR 97403-1923

The Reading Teacher and *Language Arts* both publish monthly columns on using the computer in language education.

Day-to-Day Print Area

Creating a day-to-day print area is the last step in making the classroom resemble the real world of print. Materials in this center introduce children to the kinds of print containing information that changes frequently.

Newspapers

An important part of the day-to-day area is the daily newspaper. There is no substitute for having a newspaper available for both the teacher and the children to use in a classroom. It contains news stories and features that give children a window on the world outside the classroom. Of course, classroom activities using newspapers will vary across grade levels, but the importance of their being an integral part of classroom instruction cannot be overstated. The successful integration of the newspaper into classroom instruction depends heavily on two factors—the availability of the newspaper on a regular basis *and* a teacher who reads the paper and relates it to classroom instruction.

    Where do teachers get a newspaper, which obviously costs money, to appear each day or periodically during a school week? From experience, the authors have found three sources. First, just as for trade books, teachers may ask the school administration to provide regular funding from the following year's school budget. Second, weekly or monthly donations or sponsorships can be solicited from parents, parent organizations, and community groups. Third, children can bring newspapers from home after they have been read by the family. The third source will provide multiple copies of the same paper or copies of several different papers for classroom use. Whatever the source or combination of sources, regular availability of newspapers is crucial.

Newspapers can provide children with a window on the world outside the classroom.

We suggest incorporating three categories of activities that demonstrate how informative and entertaining the newspaper can be:

- Current events
- Classroom projects using the newspaper as a resource
- Humorous and recreational activities

Current Events.   Helping children to develop a regular habit of reading the newspaper and to be informed should be the goals of current events activities. The key to making current events a part of classroom life lies in making them part of the daily schedule and not an extra set of activities that occasionally take place when time allows. A few suggestions for regular classroom current events activities follow.

1. In the primary grades where reading skills may be a problem, select a *few* stories of local interest and read and discuss them with the students. A read-and-tell format will save time. Topics at the state and national levels can gradually be added. Don't try to read too many stories; a small number will allow more discussion time.
2. Keep a variety of maps on the classroom wall. Include international, national, regional, state, and local maps. Use large pins, with flags made from colored tape at the top of each one, to indicate the places where events under discussion are taking place. Make this a regular feature, and follow through on stories over a week or longer.
3. Keep a classroom sports log of various school teams' records over a season, adding to the logs after each sports event.
4. Use the major headline stories to prepare a short daily broadcast for the classroom or entire school. Using the public address system, a committee of newscasters can make this a regular activity.
5. Encourage children to become familiar with other features of the newspaper by following one of particular interest. They could choose to read their horo-

scope for a few weeks and note any patterns, follow a particular company's stock market reports, develop a favorite cartoon series, or keep a personal scrapbook of a favorite sports figure or team.

Classroom Projects.   Crucial to helping children read the newspaper and develop a sense of its value as a resource is its use in classroom projects or units of study. The following activities illustrate how the newspaper may be integrated into daily classroom instruction. Note that we have included some examples at the primary grades.

Primary Grades

1. The details of a news event can be predicted from a picture of the story. Children may work in groups of three to five to develop a short oral or written story to accompany a picture. The stories should be presented to the entire class by each group, with the teacher finally reading the actual stories from the newspaper for comparison with the children's versions.
2. Children can construct "wish menus" of a breakfast, lunch, and dinner that they *wish* they would be served at home. Grocery and restaurant ads can furnish pictures and simple vocabulary for each child to use. This project might be assigned early in the week, so that on Friday each child can present a final menu, using pictures, words, or both.
3. Advertisements for furniture and feature stories on home decorating provide words and pictures to reinforce general vocabulary. Children, either individually or in small groups, can design a home and furnish it with items from the newspaper. They can cut out pictures and words from the newspaper and paste them onto floor diagrams of the house.

Grades 4 and Above

1. Editorial cartoons, news stories from several papers, and letters to the editor on the same topic may be collected and critically compared and contrasted. Points of agreement and disagreement should be discussed.
2. Computation skills may be practiced by having children chart the weekly fluctuation in costs of single grocery items or the weekly cost of a supply of groceries for their families.
3. Weather maps and temperature summaries from around the country and the world furnish material for functional practice in computation. For example: How much colder is one place than another? What is the range in degrees of Celsius and Fahrenheit temperatures in today's paper?

The activities suggested above are just a few examples of how the newspaper can be a useful resource for classroom projects. For additional ideas contact

Newspaper Association of America
1921 Gallows Road
Suite 600
Vienna, VA 22182

Humorous and Recreational Activities.   Perhaps the best way to promote enthusiasm for newspapers is to introduce children to those features of the newspaper intended to be read for fun and pleasure.

1. In the primary grades, the teacher can begin the habit of reading selected cartoons or comics to children daily. At higher grades, children can be encouraged to find a favorite cartoon strip and read it regularly.
2. Once a week, a small group of children can be responsible for presenting to the entire class a short newscast titled "Good News This Week" or "Funny Things from the Paper."
3. Reading "Dear Abby," medical advice, or a similar column and preparing alternative answers for presentation, either orally or in the classroom newspaper, can combine fun with reading, writing, speaking, and listening.
4. Children can pretend that they have been given $1,000 to purchase anything they wish from an issue of the newspaper. They might compare purchases orally in small groups.
5. Activities from children's sections of Sunday editions and crossword or other word puzzles can make for quick, lively, and fun small-group or paired vocabulary activities.

Other Day-to-Day Materials

In addition to the newspaper, the day-to-day area might include materials such as restaurant menus and a coupon-exchange box.

Restaurant Menus.   A collection of current menus from a variety of restaurants may be used for problem-solving activities in math, nutrition, and consumer education. The teacher might pose questions that require children to use menus as a resource for answers. For example: "Could a family of four eat dinner for under $_____?" "If I had $_____ and wanted to eat breakfast, lunch, and dinner, where could I eat?" Small-group, paired, and individual solutions can be shared with the entire class. Children might select meals from a menu and then evaluate each of them using a nutrition chart of the basic food groups and calorie or carbohydrate counters.

Coupon-Exchange Box.   Consumer education skills may be functionally demonstrated by having the children develop a coupon-exchange box and trade their grocery coupons. The day after grocery ads appear in the newspaper, practical shopping tips (bargains of the week, stores with sales) could be posted on a chart by a rotating committee in charge of the coupon-exchange box.

Miscellaneous Materials.   Teachers and children will tailor the day-to-day print area to individual grade levels and classrooms by contributing relevant materials. Materials the authors found in one fourth-grade classroom indicated how teachers and children had personalized the center and kept it growing. The center included multiple copies of inserts from monthly utility bills with power-saving hints, the monthly school newspaper, sample ballots for an upcoming city election, a recent list of new acquisitions by the city library, and a free weekly guide that listed secondhand items for sale.

Summary

Throughout this chapter, children have been involved in planning, organizing, and implementing a print-rich classroom that contributes to the development of a community of literacy learners. It is time-consuming to help children learn to read by pushing, encouraging, and helping them to become part of their own learning, but the eventual rewards are certainly worth the time and energy for both children *and* teachers. In this chapter, we have presented two useful measures of the relevance of teaching—the first is active child involvement in learning, and the second is the act of bringing the world of print from outside the classroom into the classroom.

FOLLOW-THROUGH ACTIVITIES

Note: Level 1 activities require limited access to children or classrooms. Level 2 activities should be completed using children and classrooms.

Level 1 Activities

1. Visit a supermarket, convenience store, department store, or discount center, and collect printed materials that might be part of a print-rich classroom.

2. Visit a bookstore and a library (school, public, or college) to determine the most popular recent trade books that children are reading. Select one or two of them, read them, and try to figure out why they are popular. Share your ideas with others in the class.

3. Visit a school library and a public library, and select two or three magazines that librarians tell you are popular with children. Read several issues of each, and make a list of the features that you think make each magazine popular.

Level 2 Activities

1. Interview three to five children of the same age level about their favorite kind of reading (e.g., ask "What do you like to read?"). Be careful not to use the word *book* in your question. Repeat the same interview with older or younger children, and compare and contrast the children's responses.

2. Observe and analyze the literate environment of a school. In classrooms, the library, halls, and other school areas, what specific examples of literacy droppings can you find that demonstrate a literate school environment?

3. Review the guidelines for storytelling in this chapter. Pick a story, prepare yourself, and then tell the story to a group of children. Tape-record your telling, along with any reactions the children have to the story. Share these reactions with other members of your class and the instructor.

WORKING WITH PARENTS

Involving parents right from the beginning of the school year in the development of a print-rich classroom ensures their support and understanding of your reading program. At the beginning of the year, schedule an open house or special hours for parents to visit the classroom *before* the literacy areas are created. Tell them what you and the children would like to do, show them some rough floor plans that you and the children have sketched, and then ask for help. Parents can contribute books and other print, sponsor magazine and newspaper subscriptions, and plan ways to raise money to buy materials for the classroom.

Ask parents to provide additional input into the design of the classroom by sharing the literacy activities they engage in at home. Then incorporate these types of activities into the classroom. This will give you the opportunity to weave children's home literacy practices into their school literacy practices and will have the further benefit of helping to develop a community where all children and their families feel a sense of belonging.

RESOURCES

Carter, B., & Abrahamson, R. F. (1991). Nonfiction in a reading program. *Journal of Reading, 34,* 638–642.

> Nonfiction offers readers books that teach, entertain, and provoke thought—the "stuff of life," as the authors of this article say.

Cullinan, B. (Ed.). (1987). *Children's literature in the reading program.* Newark, DE: International Reading Association.

> This book is an excellent source of ideas on using literature. Chapter 3 on using poetry by Nancy Larrick and Chapter 10 on resources for identifying children's books by Arlene M. Pillar are especially useful.

Cullinan, B. E. (1992). *Invitation to read: More children's literature in the reading program.* Newark, DE: International Reading Association.

> A sequel to Cullinan's 1987 book, this wonderful resource has chapters on many topics, including how to use information books and author study, and list after list of resources for using literature in the print lab.

Cullinan, B. E., Scala, M. C., & Schroder, V. C. (1995). *Three voices: An invitation to poetry across the curriculum.* York, ME: Stenhouse.

> This book provides a wonderful collection of strategies for using poetry with children of all ages and for integrating poetry throughout the curriculum.

Englehardt, T. (June, 1991). Reading may be harmful to your kids. *Harper's, 282*(1693), 55–62.

> This critical essay on the children's book publishing industry describes how it has become big business and discusses how quality may suffer when profits come first.

Fielding, L., & Roller, C. (1992). Making difficult books accessible and easy books acceptable. *The Reading Teacher, 45,* 678–685.

> As the title suggests, the authors present ways to encourage children to interact with and learn from books that may be too difficult or too easy for them to read.

Harms, J. M., & Lettow, L. J. (1991). Recent poetry for children. *The Reading Teacher, 45,* 274–279.

> As new poets emerge and join well-established ones, their work should be added to the collections in classroom print labs.

Harris, V. J. (Ed.). (1992). *Teaching multicultural literature in grades K–8.* Norwood, MA: Christopher-Gordon.

> In an excellent collection of easy-to-read chapters, recognized authorities explain how to use multicultural literature in the classroom.

International Reading Association publishes yearly lists of new children's literature. Three collections are offered: *Children's Choices, Young Adults' Choices,* and *Teacher's Choices.*

> Send a self-addressed, stamped envelope for *each* one, stamped with two ounces of first-class postage (six ounces for all three) to International Reading Association, P.O. Box 8139, Newark, DE 19714-8139. Bulk copies are also available.

Johnson, N. M., & Ebert, M. J. (1992). Time travel is possible: Historical fiction and biography—passport to the past. *The Reading Teacher, 45,* 488–495.

> Using literature to teach history is exciting for both teachers and children when historical fiction is added to the text area.

Language Arts. Published by the National Council of Teachers of English, 1111 Kenyon Road, Urbana, IL 61801.

> Make it a habit to skim each of the nine issues per year of this journal for teaching suggestions and discussions of current issues in language instruction.

Moss, B. (1991). Children's nonfiction trade books: A complement to content area texts. *The Reading Teacher, 45,* 26–32.

> Nonfiction trade books can be used to overcome some of the weaknesses of content area texts.

Putnam, L. (1991). Dramatizing nonfiction with emerging readers. *Language Arts, 68,* 463–469.

> Dramatizing and nonfiction books go hand-in-hand for beginning readers.

REFERENCES

Bean, T. W., Readence, J. E., & Mallette, M. H. (1996). Selecting multicultural young adult novels: Identifying criteria for use with Banks' typology. In D. J. Leu, C. K. Kinzer, & K. A. Hinchman (Eds.), *Literacies for the 21st century: Research and practice.* 45th yearbook of the National Reading Conference (pp. 296–305). Chicago: National Reading Conference.

Bishop, R. S. (1992). Multicultural literature for children: Making informed choices. In V. J. Harris (Ed.), *Teaching multicultural literature in grades K–8* (pp. 37–53). Norwood, MA: Christopher-Gordon.

Clay, M. M. (1998). *By different paths to common outcomes.* York, ME: Stenhouse.

Enciso, P., Rogers, T., Marshall, E., Jenkins, C., Brown, J., Core, E., Cordova, C., Young-steadt-Parish, D., Robinson, D., & Tyson, C. (1999). Social justice and social action in everyday worlds: Literature bridging history, hope, and action. *The New Advocate, 12,* 191–207.

Greene, F. P. (1970a). *Alarm clock reading.* Unpublished manuscript, Syracuse University.

Greene, F. P. (1970b). *Paired reading.* Unpublished manuscript, Syracuse University.

Harris, V. J. (1992). *Teaching multicultural literature in grades K–8.* Norwood, MA: Christopher-Gordon.

Johnson, N. M., & Ebert, M. J. (1992). Time travel is possible: Historical fiction and biography—Passport to the past. *The Reading Teacher, 45,* 488–495.

Just grandma and me [Computer software]. (1993). Novato, CA: Broderbund.

Larrick, N. (1987). Keep a poem in your pocket. In B. Cullinan (Ed.), *Children's literature in the reading program* (pp. 20–27). Newark, DE: International Reading Association.

Leu, D. J., Karchmer, R. A., & Leu, D. D. (1999). The Miss Rumphius effect: Envisionments for literacy and learning that transform the Internet. *The Reading Teacher, 52,* 636–642.

Moffett, J., & Wagner, B. J. (1992). *Student-centered language arts and reading, K–12* (4th ed.). Portsmouth, NH: Heinemann.

Moore, P. (1999). Reading and writing on the Internet. In J. Hancock (Ed.), *Teaching literacy using information technology: A collection of articles from the Australian Literacy Educators' Association* (pp. 48–65). Newark, DE: International Reading Association.

Moss, B. (1991). Children's nonfiction trade books: A complement to content area texts. *The Reading Teacher, 45,* 26–32.

Nemeth, J. (n.d.). *Some helpful hints for parents.* Unpublished handout.

Ohlhausen, M. M., & Jepsen, M. (1992). Lessons from Goldilocks: "Somebody's been choosing my books but I can make my own choices now!" *The New Advocate, 5,* 31–46.

Pappas, C. C. (1991). Fostering full access to literacy by including information books. *Language Arts, 68,* 449–462.

Perfect, K. A. (1999). Rhyme and reason: Poetry for the heart and head. *The Reading Teacher, 52,* 728–737.

Ross, R. R. (1996). *Storyteller* (3rd ed.). Little Rock, AK: August House.

Searfoss, L. W. (1993). Assessing classroom environments. In S. Glazer & C. Brown (Eds.), *Portfolios and beyond: Collaborative assessment in reading and writing* (pp. 11–26). Norwood, MA: Christopher-Gordon.

Tierney, R. J., & Readence, J. E. (2000). *Reading strategies and practices: A compendium* (5th ed.). Boston: Allyn and Bacon.

Veatch, J. (1978). *Reading in the elementary school* (2nd ed.). New York: John Wiley.

3   Early Literacy

INTRODUCTION

I can remember my feeling of amazement and power when I began to recognize words in the magazines my mother and father had around the house. I had always liked looking at the pictures in those magazines, but the print had never been anything but a dense jumble of letters. And then one day I found that some of that jumble was beginning to form itself into words that I knew, words I'd learned in school. It was a little like bringing a blurry television picture into focus—suddenly things made sense. And I was hooked. (Babbitt, 1986, p. 42)

Natalie Babbitt's adult recollections of her early reading experiences illustrate the almost magical feeling of learning to read. Some of us may have different memories of how we began to read or little memory at all; but we now know our early encounters with print began long before we came to school. We might ask these questions about how young children begin to learn to read:

> When do children begin to read?
>
> What do children need to know or be able to do in order to learn to read?

These questions will be explored in this chapter as we discuss the beginnings of learning to read—a journey for children that seems magical, even when they recall it as adults.

GRAPHIC ORGANIZER

This graphic organizer summarizes the structure of Chapter 3:

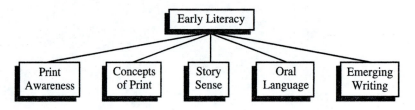

OBJECTIVES

When you finish this chapter, you should be able to understand and discuss each of these statements:

1. Learning to read has undergone a reexamination and redefinition.
2. Print awareness, concepts of print, story sense, oral language, and emerging writing are areas of early literacy.
3. Children's early encounters with print before coming to school serve as a foundation for and a bridge to reading and writing instruction.
4. Activities for encouraging early literacy occur as part of a print-rich classroom.
5. Assessment of early literacy must be merged with instruction.

Young Children and Reading— An Historical View

During much of the 20th century, until the 1980s, children were viewed as non-readers before they entered school and began formal reading instruction. Little attention was paid to the reading behaviors of young children before they entered school. *Real* reading was thought to begin when children entered school. It was believed that getting ready to read, or *reading readiness*, was rooted in the experiences of children before they came to school. Some children had more experiences at home and needed less reading readiness instruction than other children. For a number of children, though, reading readiness instruction continued for a protracted amount of time in kindergarten and first grade.

Usually the reading readiness of young children was tested using a standardized test with an established cut-off score. If a child scored above the cut-off score, he or she went on to formal reading instruction; however, if a child scored below the cut-off score, more reading readiness was in order. Unfortunately, in many cases the readiness factors tested either (1) were not important to success in reading, (2) were important but were out of the control of the school, or (3) could best be developed by beginning reading instruction, not delaying it.

A simple list of factors taken from methods texts of the 1960s and 1970s will be useful for our discussion of the changing role of reading readiness in beginning reading programs:

Intelligence	Listening ability
Physical condition and health	Preschool, kindergarten
Auditory discrimination	Background of experiences
Interest in books	Language development
Hearing	Visual discrimination
Speech articulation	Sex
Motor coordination	Attitude toward reading
Physical development	Age
Social and emotional adjustment	Cognitive ability
Vision	Language facility
Directionality (left to right)	

These factors came under reexamination in recent years for several reasons. First, as a beginning teacher trying to use such lists to plan instruction, what do you do on Monday morning with intelligence, age, vision, and emotional adjustment? Only a few of these factors—such as directionality, auditory discrimination, visual discrimination, and interest in books—may be of real value to teachers in planning lessons.

Second, some of the factors listed are directly related to maturation of physical and cognitive abilities, and individual children will naturally vary in levels of functioning. These are the individual differences among children that challenge teachers at all levels. Quite simply, no two children ever seem to be alike in social, emotional, physical, and language development. Some educators question the validity of providing activities that are designed to increase the pace of children's maturation. Although some studies do report success in this area, it is doubtful that entire school districts and classrooms can adopt and implement programs with the same success found in carefully controlled research studies. To create large-scale programs with the goal of accelerating children's physical, emotional, social, intellectual, or language maturation requires defined, commonly accepted sequences of development, hierarchical in nature. Such step-by-step sequences have been established with considerable agreement in some areas (physical), but in other areas of maturation (social, emotional, intellectual) less agreement among experts is evident.

Finally, this historical view of reading and reading readiness kept many children from exactly what they needed—reading instruction and practice. Readiness tests became gates through which some children would pass only with great difficulty, causing their first encounters with reading in school to be marked by feelings of failure, certainly not a positive way to begin their many years of schooling.

Do teachers, then, simply ignore readiness factors that cannot be used as the basis for specific skills lessons? Of course not. A child's physical health, vision, emotional adjustment, and other factors *are* related to success in school, to the development of positive attitudes toward school and reading, and to the building of a positive self-concept. However, these factors should be considered as developing in a classroom environment that builds on children's abilities and is founded on the basic principles of language discussed in Chapter 1.

Young Children and Reading—A Current View

As we discussed in Chapter 1, definitions of reading and the nature of reading instruction have undergone profound changes in recent years. These changes have mandated a critical look at the reading of young children before they enter school. Since the 1980s, the exploration of literacy among children from birth through the end of kindergarten has become a topic of intense study and investigation. The term *early literacy* has been used to describe the reading, writing, and encounters with print that young children have before entering school (Clay, 1991; Sulzby, 1991; Sulzby & Teale, 1991). The explosion of research studies in early literacy led us to new understandings about the early stages of learning to read, which begin at birth. As Sulzby and Teale (1991) explained, early literacy

> is concerned with the earliest phases of literacy development, the period between birth and the time when children read and write conventionally. [It] signals a belief that, in a literate society, young children—even 1- and 2-year-olds—are in the process of becoming literate. This literacy is seen in not-yet-conventional behaviors; underlying the behaviors are understandings or hypotheses about literacy. Literacy learning is seen as taking place in home and community settings, in out-of-home care settings, and in school settings such as Head Start, prekindergarten, and kindergarten. (p. 728)

The concept of early literacy makes legitimate the reading and writing children attempt before they are of school age. Young children will often pick up a book and model adults by turning pages and reading aloud, even though the book may be upside down and the oral rendition of the story only loosely related to the print version. This pretend reading is real reading in the mind of a young child. Similarly, when young children write messages, such as birthday cards to grandmothers, using scribbled writing and drawing, they are creating a real message in print. These reading and writing activities by young children are carried out for genuine purposes. They are legitimate explorations in learning about and using language. Are they the conventional type of reading and writing we expect of older children and adults? No, but they are the foundation for conventional reading and writing and should be celebrated and encouraged at home, in preschools, and in the early years of formal schooling.

Early literacy is a time of exploration and discovery for children. The extensive research conducted in this area has led to the conclusion that it is at this period in children's literacy development that teachers need to intervene. Instead of waiting until children fail at learning to read, teachers need to accelerate their learning early on. Many early-intervention projects have therefore been developed and implemented all over the world. These projects are all based on helping children acquire literacy on time with their peers.

Our view of the early reading and writing of young children is based on Principle 3 in Chapter 1: *The vast amount of language children bring to school should be recognized and used in helping them learn to read and write.* Understanding young children's early literacy before they enter school is a necessary step in translating Principle 3 into classroom instruction. In this chapter, we will discuss the reading and writing of young children and their early encounters with print. Our discussion will focus on the following areas of early literacy:

- Print awareness
- Concepts of print
- Story sense
- Oral language
- Emerging writing

First, however, we would like to acknowledge the ever-changing knowledge base within the field of early literacy. McGee and Purcell-Gates (1997) suggest that the explosion of research in the 1980s successfully changed our views about the beginnings of reading, leading to many changes in curricular decisions. They point out that this research is still progressing today, contributing to the adoption of an even broader view of early literacy. Early literacy research today is carried out within a sociocultural perspective; that is, it is grounded in the assumption that learning to read is a social process. Vygotsky (1978) introduced the concept of *zone of proximal development.* This concept suggests that learning occurs in social settings through the process of scaffolding. As children begin to make discoveries about print, knowledgeable others (e.g., parents, teachers, and other children) mediate this learning. Our discussion of the five areas of early literacy is framed within the construct that early literacy learning occurs in a print-rich environment through social interactions.

Before moving on to a discussion of each of the five areas of early literacy, we will address the important role of assessment. We believe that assessment needs to be the driving force of instruction. Thus, throughout this chapter we have included descriptions of various types of assessment tools, which teachers can use to obtain a more socioculturally based perspective on children's early literacy development.

Assessing Early Literacy

How and why do we assess early literacy? We assess to document change and growth and to guide our instruction. By observing (or *kidwatching*, as Yetta Goodman would say), listening, collecting samples, and interacting with children, we learn about them and try to interpret how they are using language (Y. Goodman, 1985; 1991). As Strickland (1990) pointed out, fundamental to an early literacy perspective is the integration of assessment and instruction. She stated:

> Increased reliance on systematic observation, record keeping, and analysis of children's classroom participation and work products and less reliance on standardized tests are the hallmarks of student evaluation and teacher planning. (p. 23)

Assessing early literacy requires looking at the variety of research and writing on the topic for some focus and direction. Two underlying principles emerge to guide us:

1. Assessment of print awareness, concepts of print, story sense, oral language, and emerging writing must be functional, relying on the observation and recording of children's behaviors during reading and language-related tasks. Careful observation of children's interactions with print will yield much more information than standardized, objective tests administered to young children who lack test-taking skills.
2. Assessment and instruction must be merged, because good teaching requires that both processes work together in a constant interplay (Salinger, 1998). If assessment measures require children to complete tasks that are not related to classroom instruction, then assessment contributes little to helping children learn to read.

These two principles suggest that three major elements should be incorporated into the assessment of early literacy. These are unstructured teacher observation, structured teacher observation and interviews, and observational records combined with samples of children's language production.

Unstructured Teacher Observation.   Unstructured observation by teachers of children engaged in natural reading and reading-related tasks is the first element of assessment. Over the years in education, there has been a reluctance to rely on teachers' judgments gained from classroom observation because of their unreliable nature. Teachers' intuitions or feelings about what children are and are not able to do have usually been relegated to the status of supplementary information ("nice to know, but do not need to know!"). Formal, standardized tests with published reliability figures often carry more weight. However, teachers can be reliable observers, particularly when they conduct multiple observations and situate observations of individual children within the context of other children (Salinger, 1998). If teachers can be guided in how to observe something—say, print awareness—in the same children under similar conditions over time, the reliability of their judgments will naturally be increased. For each of the basic prerequisites for reading, we will present situations conducive to unstructured observation, along with behaviors for teachers to note.

Structured Teacher Observation and Interviews.   The use of informal instruments will provide teachers with the opportunity to observe reading under more controlled conditions. In assessments of print awareness, for example, if some children appear confused during unstructured teacher observations or if the teacher is unable to gather enough information to make a judgment about their proficiency, these children may be administered an individual inventory of environmental print. Items can be presented individually, and the child's responses recorded. Adding this controlled observation and interview to the less structured multiple observations will increase the reliability of teacher judgment.

Observational Records Combined with Samples of Children's Language Production.   Written records of both unstructured and structured teacher observations should be combined with samples of children's language productions and kept in individual, cumulative folders. The child's folder becomes a living portfolio, with samples of stories, books, projects, and other language activities completed and collected periodically throughout the school year. Tape recordings of oral language activities that are repeated every so often might also be included as firsthand, real illustrations of a child's attempts to gain control over and use language. The samples will make reporting to parents and children much easier and further increase the reliability of teacher judgment.

In the following sections, we discuss the five areas within early literacy. Each discussion begins with an overview, followed by a presentation of assessment techniques and then suggested teaching strategies.

Print Awareness

Y. M. Goodman (1980) was among the first to suggest that in examining children's awareness of print we are exploring the roots of literacy. She states:

> I believe that the beginnings of reading development often go unnoticed in the young child. Neither children nor their parents are aware that reading has begun. This lack of sensitivity occurs because the reading process is misunderstood; because learning to read and being taught to read have been conceived as one-to-one correspondence; and because we have been led to believe that the most common sense notion about learning to read suggests that it begins in a formalized school environment. (pp. 10–11)

Print awareness begins long before formalized schooling. Children explore the vast world of print that surrounds them and begin to make many discoveries about it. These initial discoveries serve as a foundation for literacy development.

For example, when 3½-year-old Kasey wanted her mother to jump on the trampoline with her, she pointed to the warning label on the trampoline and said, "It says mommies have to jump with their children!" Kasey had made an important discovery about print—she had discovered that print carries meaning—and she assigned the meaning she wanted to the print.

Clearly children respond to print in their environment, such as signs and logos for favorite foods or places. In an interview with Betsy, a lively 3-year-old, Hudelson (1981) asked her to identify various items involving print, such as her favorite cereal boxes, soup cans, and candy wrappers. When presented with a carton of Jello pudding, Betsy thought and thought and finally said, pointing to the word *Jello*, "Pudding in a cloud, it says pudding in a cloud, right there" (p. 67). While Betsy was using the context to figure out meaning, an important discovery— similar to Kasey's—was occurring. Betsy recognized that the carton *said* something, thus realizing that print represents meaning. She made the almost magical connection between print and meaning and took a giant step on the road to reading more complicated messages and texts.

What do children learn about print during the print-awareness stage of reading development? Following are some major concepts that children seem to acquire, presented from the child's viewpoint:

1. Print always means something, whether we can understand it or not.
2. Print tells something, because it shows us how to find things we like, such as favorite foods or television programs.
3. Print helps us gain control over our world because it's dependable. A sign or a label goes the same way and says the same thing day after day.
4. Print and talk seem to go together. Adults seem to spend lots of time talking about print.
5. Print, adults, talk, and us go together, too. We have plenty of talks every day about print, with adults and with each other.

In summary, awareness of the functions and uses of print develops early among preschool children. This awareness occurs because children share the same print environment we all do.

Assessing Print Awareness

Unstructured Observation. Teachers can make unstructured observations of print awareness while children are engaged in print-related activities. Behaviors to observe are discussing uses or purposes of print, using verbal labels correctly, and pointing to print.

Structured Observation and Interviews. On an individual basis, the structured observation of children can be accomplished by constructing a simple print-awareness inventory (see Figure 3.1). Items should be selected carefully from the children's environment and presented one at a time for identification. A tape re-

FIGURE 3.1   Print Awareness Inventory

	Identified (Yes/No)	Notes:
1. Milk carton	_____	
2. Picture of STOP sign	_____	
3. Toothpaste carton	_____	
4. Cereal box	_____	
5. Fast-food restaurant items	_____	
6. Soap carton	_____	
7. Soup can	_____	
8. Soda bottle or can	_____	
9. Public phone sign	_____	
10. Picture of highway signs of local interest	_____	
11. Other?	_____	

Note: Specific brand names were not used in this sample inventory; teachers should use brands available in their locale. For example, fast-food restaurant items will vary, depending on which leading restaurants are accessible. Also, additional items may be added, such as school signs and other places of interest locally. Where possible, the actual item should be used; pictures should be substituted only when it is not practical to obtain the real item.

corder may be used to create a more relaxed atmosphere, since it will free the teacher from attending too much to the mechanics of administering the inventory. To personalize the list, the teacher should include food and other household items used by children, as well as local street and business signs. Empty cartons may be used for perishable items. Following is a list of potential interview questions:

What is this?
What does it say?
Where does it say that?
What do you do with this?
Have you ever seen this before?

Activities for Developing Print Awareness

Print awareness can be fostered in the classroom through activities such as the following:

1. *Include an environmental print area.* Displays and bulletin boards with various nutrition and consumer education themes can serve as the focus of environmental print. The four basic food groups can be portrayed with actual objects, pictures, or empty containers used to illustrate each group. These ingredients may be used to plan nutritious meals, which can then be depicted

on a display table. Magazine and newspaper ads are readily available, inexpensive sources of pictures to be clipped and turned into collages, with central themes such as safety signs, words related to specific occupations, and directional indicators.

2. *Take environmental print walks.* Walks around the school and neighborhood, with children searching for examples of environmental print, reinforce print in its natural context. Each trip can center around searching for words related to a particular topic under study in the previous activity.

3. *Incorporate play stations.* Organize stations in your classroom where children have opportunities to approximate literacy in authentic settings (Neuman & Roskos, 1997). These stations could include a post office, restaurant, bank, or store. In each station, provide tools for literacy use that would naturally be in that setting. For example, in the restaurant include menus, supplies for writing orders and bills, and recipe cards. The children will then have opportunities to use literacy in integrated play. As Hall (1998) suggests, children can *use* literacy as opposed to studying literacy.

Process Guide 3.1

Create a list of all the centers typically found in preschool and primary-grade classrooms. Then think of how each of those centers could be literacy enriched. What types of materials are already included in the centers? What new materials need to be added?

Play stations offer children a place to use literacy as a tool.

Concepts of Print

Print, especially in the form of books, dominates beginning reading instruction. It seems logical that if children develop an awareness of the functions and uses of print in their environment, this awareness will carry over into concepts about print arranged in book form. You may be puzzled by the preceding statements and wonder what exactly concepts of print are. Print is print, just as roses are roses. Simple enough, isn't it? For fluent readers who are familiar and comfortable with the mechanics, conventions, and uses of many kinds of print, concepts of print are subconscious; we rarely think about them. But for beginning readers, the concepts of print listed below cannot be assumed. Beginning readers may possess them in varying degrees. This compilation incorporates the work of several writers and researchers on the topic (Downing & Oliver, 1973–1974; Hiebert, 1981; Lomax & McGee, 1987; Mason and McCormick, 1981; Roberts, 1992; Worden & Boettcher, 1990; Yopp, 1992).

1. *Building blocks of reading and writing print.* Included in this category is *phonemic awareness* (awareness that speech is composed of sounds; see Chapter 6), alphabet or letter-name knowledge, use of punctuation, and concepts of word, sentence, and paragraph. As fluent adult readers, we may find it difficult to understand how anyone could not know what a word or sentence is. But assigning the label *word* to the concept is important, since teachers use this label frequently (e.g., "What is the first word in the title of the story?" "Point to the word you do not understand," and "Find the word that shows how the dog in the story behaved"). The language of reading and writing instruction is full of terms children need to know. Many children come to school not knowing what a word is (Roberts, 1992). Similarly, concepts such as letter, sentence, and paragraph may also be unfamiliar.

2. *Form and direction, or "how print goes."* Included in this category are concepts related to direction and how print, books, and stories are arranged. Books have a beginning, middle, and end. Pages go from top to bottom, lines move left to right, and illustrations and text work together. Also included in this category are the order or sequential nature of words, sentences, and paragraphs (first word, second sentence, last paragraph). Questions teachers ask that relate to these concepts include "What does the picture on the second page tell us about what might happen next?" and "Who can find and read the first sentence and tell us the name of the dog?"

3. *Use of print.* Included in this category are all the uses of reading and writing that young children discover and explore. Print gives us directions, information, and pleasure (when our favorite stories are read over and over) and has many other uses. Similarly, writing allows us to send messages, get responses, and communicate with others in a new way.

Assessing Concepts of Print

Unstructured Observation. Teachers can make unstructured observations of children's concepts of print while children are involved in SSR and while they are browsing through the classroom and school libraries. Behaviors to observe are willingness to participate in SSR and adhere to the rules, independent browsing and selecting of library books, talking about books, and simulating fluent reading by pretending to read.

Structured Observation and Interviews.   An assessment strategy for determining a child's knowledge of concepts of print is based on the work pioneered by Marie Clay (1972). Clay developed two books, *Sand* and *Stone,* to use in this assessment. We have modified the assessment tool for easier use (see Figure 3.2). This assessment will provide you with information on children's knowledge of book orientation, print awareness, directionality (i.e., left to right and top to bottom), and terminology (i.e., *letter, word,* and *sentence*). Begin this assessment by presenting the child with a familiar book. Ask the child to point to the front of the book. Then ask the child to point to the back of the book. Open the book and ask the child where to begin reading (note whether the child points to the print or the illustration). Ask the child to move his or her finger along to show you how to read the text. Note whether the child makes the sweep to the left at the end of the first line. Ask the child to point to a word, a sentence, and a letter. This quick inventory will supply you with the basic information you need to determine a child's knowledge of concepts of print. Remember to follow up by conducting unstructured observations with children.

One aspect of concepts of print that is essential to assess in early readers is concept of word. Concept of word is most often defined simply as speech-to-print match (Morris, 1981, 1993), and it serves as a good indication of the transition from early reader to beginning reader. To assess concept of word, begin by teaching the child the first two lines of a nursery rhyme—for example, "Humpty Dumpty sat on the wall. Humpty Dumpty had a great fall." After the child has memorized these lines, write the words down in front of the child, saying each word as you write. Then, point to the words while you read the two lines. Next, hold the child's

FIGURE 3.2   Concepts of Print Checklist

Name: _____   Date: _____

Concepts of Print

_____   Points to the front of the book

_____   Points to the back of the book

_____   Knows that print, rather than the illustrations, tells the story

_____   Knows left to right directionality

_____   Knows top to bottom directionality

_____   Can identify a word

_____   Can identify a sentence

_____   Can identify a letter

Notice how the child, when presented with a familiar book, holds it.

finger and point to the words together. Then, ask the child to read the two lines and point to the words. Finally, ask the child to point to individual words (e.g., *great* and *Dumpty*). Morris suggested that three levels of concept of word could be determined from this assessment:

1. *No concept of word.* The child does not have speech-to-print match and thus cannot track print.
2. *Rudimentary concept of word.* The child is developing speech-to-print match; however, the match is usually based on syllables instead of words. A child at this level has difficulty with words of more than one syllable. Additionally, a child at this level often starts at the beginning of each line to locate specific words.
3. *Full concept of word.* The child has speech-to-print match. The child can locate specific words in the text.

Activities for Developing Concepts of Print

Mechanical and form concepts may be developed and reinforced through activities such as the following, which relate to letters and words in context.

1. Label classroom objects and areas (e.g., sink, books, play, gerbil, seeds).
2. Place children's names on their desks, cubbyholes and lockers, and classroom-duty rosters.

3. Set aside time for shared reading. Holdaway (1979) describes shared reading as a simulation of parent-and-child lap reading. Shared reading is done with big books, to give all the children a chance to see the printed page as the book is being read. In addition, directionality and book orientation can easily be modeled with big books. After reading the book several times, you can conduct follow-up activities that focus children's attention on book-related terminology (e.g., *word, sentence,* and *letter*). When using big books, always remember to read the story straight through the first time, to allow the children to hear the uninterrupted flow of the story (just as a parent might read to a child).

4. Introduce nursery rhymes, pattern books, and predictable books. Nursery rhymes can be easily used to help children become aware of the speech-to-print match. Print the rhymes on chart paper and reread them, using a finger to point to each word in a smooth movement that preserves the sense of rhythm. Then, you and the children read together, perhaps alternating lines in choral-reading fashion. Finally, individual children can take turns at reading the rhymes or can lead the group by taking the teacher's role. Pattern books and predictable books (Bridge, 1984; Heald-Taylor, 1987a, 1987b) feature repeated patterns of language, natural-sounding language, familiar concepts, and dependable or traditional stories with familiar sequences. All of these features help beginning readers experience early success in reading by gaining and predicting meaning easily; they also offer beginning writers models or patterns of writing to emulate.

Orientation and directionality concepts may be further developed and reinforced through writing activities found in this chapter's section on emerging writing.

Story Sense

Much of beginning reading instruction relies on the story as a major vehicle for teaching reading skills, whether those stories are written for children or by children. The story is the heart of many beginning reading programs. Understanding stories as a whole and the characteristics or elements that form a story is called *sense of story.* The structure of stories has been extensively explored by Applebee (1979) and others. As with concepts of print discussed earlier, it is often difficult for fluent adult readers to understand the importance of a well-developed sense of story in beginning-level reading instruction, because their own story sense is taken for granted.

Various researchers have concluded that frequent storybook reading between parent and child is a social event and should be full of interaction between participants. Simply reading to young children may not be an effective way to help internalize story sense. As Sulzby and Teale (1991) note, "it appears that a key factor in the effect of storybook reading across home and school is how the adult mediates the reading in response to the child's reactions and initiations" (p. 737). In other words, adults who read to children need to do more than simply present the story. Stopping the reading to acknowledge children's reactions, using an illustration to help understanding of the story, and calling attention to some personal experience in the children's lives related to the story are important parts of story reading. Finally, for young children, reading and talking about a favorite story while seated on a friendly lap in a comfortable chair, with an occasional hug and a smile, creates not only the environment for storybook reading, but healthy social interaction as well.

Issues surrounding the development of story sense have been much discussed in recent years. Research has shown that children have different experiences with stories at home (Heath, 1996; Taylor & Dorsey-Gaines, 1988) and thus enter school with varying knowledge about stories. Thus, story sense should provide only one index of a child's early literacy development—we cannot discount the many types of literacy experiences children bring from their homes in favor of accepting story sense as the only valid one. As you read through the following assessment and teaching techniques, bear in mind that sense of story development needs to be nurtured throughout a child's early schooling experiences. Equally important is connecting the story knowledge children have with the formal sense of story you want them to develop.

Assessing Story Sense

Unstructured Observation.   Teachers can make unstructured observations of children's story sense by examining their responses to wordless picture books, the drawings they make to illustrate a story read to them, and the stories they dictate or compose.

Structured Observation and Interviews.   Sulzby (1994) has identified five stages in children's development of story sense:

1. *Attending to pictures, not forming a story.* A child in this stage will focus solely on the pictures. The child will not weave a story together and often will simply label the pictures.
2. *Attending to pictures, forming an oral story.* At this stage, the child is still attending to the pictures, yet now the child is connecting these ideas to form a story. The story at this level sounds more like one related by a storyteller.
3. *Attending to pictures, mixing reading and storytelling.* The child at this stage will fluctuate, at times sounding like a storyteller and at times sounding like a reader.
4. *Attending to pictures, forming a written story.* The child will sound as if he or she is reading a story.
5. *Attending to print.* At this stage, the child is attending to print. Sulzby identified four strategies that a child may adopt: (a) refusal—the child refuses to read because she or he has print awareness and does not know the printed

words; (b) aspectual—the child chooses to read only some words on the page; (c) imbalance of strategies—the child often omits or substitutes for unknown words or exhibits a lack of control over reading processes; and (d) independent reading.

Children's story sense can be charted by observing their reading throughout the year and determining in which of these stages they fall.

Activities for Developing Story Sense

Developing story sense is an integral part of many of the previous activities in this chapter. Each of those activities had a purpose or function, and each attempted to provide beginning readers with genuine reading and writing situations. A few additional guidelines that are useful in developing story sense follow:

1. *Read regularly to children.* Reading regularly to children is a not-so-new recommendation. For the beginning reader, though, a few special suggestions are in order if concepts about story sense are to be developed. First, using big books, read to small groups of children who are situated so they can follow along as you read aloud. Young children need to see the print and illustrations while you read the story to them. So, get on the floor, or gather the children around you so that their line of sight is the same as yours. Second, read a variety of stories to children. In addition to stories, read items of interest from the newspaper or reference books such as the *Guinness Book of World Records* or *Book of Lists.* Discuss briefly the purpose for reading each kind of print. Third, have other people read to the children. Older children from the upper grades can be invited to read to beginning readers. Parents, grandparents, senior citizens, the school secretary, the school nurse, the principal, and any others who can be enlisted to volunteer their time become models of fluent readers for children.

2. *Involve media and print.* Use read-along story records and tapes. One note of caution is in order regarding these materials: Children still need some teacher, adult, or peer time to share their stories. The teacher's occasional interest in the activity will assure that read-along story time is not simply a time during which children are to be seen and not heard. Videos and films based on children's stories are often available through the school library, district office, church groups, public libraries, and college and university libraries. These are always a special treat and generate a high level of interest in stories.

3. *Try wordless picture books.* Wordless picture books get children off to an early feeling of successful reading (Degler, 1979; Hoskisson & Tompkins, 1991). Children's storytelling, using wordless picture books, can be fostered in these ways:

    Ask prompting questions as children tell the story, in order to help them expand on their ideas.

Use probe questions to help children express an idea more precisely ("What kind of birds are in the story?" or "What is on the table?").

Discuss elements of story structure, such as setting, time, and character feelings, with the children.

Have multiple copies available so that stories may be shared or developed in small-group settings.

Introduce or clarify new concepts not familiar to children through discussions about these concepts.

4. *Use predictable books.* Predictable books, discussed earlier in this chapter under Activities for Developing Concepts of Print, are also useful for helping children acquire a sense of story.
5. *Share stories through repeated readings.* Reading the same stories again to children offers them a second chance to enjoy a wonderful story and the teaching opportunity to focus their attention on an aspect of the story that was not considered during the first reading.

Oral Language

Oral language plays two roles in learning to read. First, oral language serves as a foundation on which learning to read can be based. Second, it serves as a bridge between the language and experiences children bring to school and those they encounter in formal reading instruction in school. Remember, we are defining oral language as using speaking and listening to communicate, just as we did in Chapter 1.

In its first role as a foundation for reading instruction, oral language shares with reading the significant feature expressed in Principle 1: *The function of language is to communicate* (see Chapter 1). Language use always occurs for some reason and in some context. Communication, then, is the common goal of oral language *and* reading. We suggest you take a few moments to review this principle before reading on. Other common features shared by speaking, listening, and reading are found in Chapter 1 under Principle 7: *Reading is* one *of the communication tools.*

The second role of oral language, as a bridge for children between the language and experiences they bring to school and those they encounter in formal reading instruction, is reflected in Principle 3: *The vast amount of language children bring to school should be recognized and used in helping them learn to read and write.* In Chapter 1, we delineated areas of language in which there is clear evidence of the sophisticated language abilities of preschool children: (1) knowledge of the sound/symbol relationship, (2) vocabulary levels, and (3) functional uses of language.

These roles of oral language lead to three basic guidelines for oral language instruction:

1. Oral language instruction should utilize real experiences children have both in and out of school. The experiences and the language that children bring to

school should be valued, accepted, and used to further develop their language. Real experiences provided in school should have *sense power,* which enables children to create a vivid, sharp, and personal identification with each experience.

2. Oral language development should be viewed as an integral part of the whole school day, planned but arising from naturally occurring events in the classroom. Social studies, science, art, and other school subjects become the real stuff used to practice language. There is so much going on in classrooms that is part of daily learning and that intimately involves (or could involve) the use of oral language, it seems natural to use these opportunities to foster growth in oral language.

3. Oral language (speaking and listening) activities should lead naturally into using the tools of reading and writing. Activities designed to develop oral language should be integrated with reading and writing. Written language becomes a natural extension of oral language activities as children, on the road to literacy, write their own stories, read stories they have dictated to the teacher, and learn all the advantages that reading can bring them.

Designing and implementing classroom oral language instruction requires making some practical decisions and choices. What will be taught? How will it be taught? These questions are at the heart of curriculum planning. For the design and implementation stage of oral language programs, strategies that attempt to put into practice the guidelines established earlier include using activities designed to elicit language functionally and structuring the oral language program into language-based units.

Assessing Oral Language

Procedures designed to assess children's oral language should elicit samples that are representative of their typical oral language performance. Assessment must be based on information gathered in a variety of ways, including multiple observations, interviews, and informal tests. Each of these ways of assessing oral language should *encourage* children to communicate, rather than discourage oral language production. Further, the interactive nature of speaking and listening must be taken into consideration. Performance in each cannot be assessed separately.

A number of formal, or standardized, tests have been developed to measure oral language. Oral language tests should be viewed with much skepticism, because children's performance on unfamiliar test tasks is often used to classify children as proficient or nonproficient language users. It is questionable whether such tests can accurately estimate oral language ability when they do not resemble real school language situations. We believe that objective tests given in short testing sessions under timed conditions, and often using paper and pencil, generally will not yield valid or reliable data on the effectiveness with which children use language.

We would argue that *determining children's effectiveness in using oral language to communicate with other children and adults ought to be the goal of assessment.* The crux of this approach is an insistence that features of children's language such as syntax or vocabulary cannot be separated from the social context in which they occur. To do so denies the tremendous influence that purpose for using language has on the way children choose to use it, as well as the many different reasons children have for needing to use language. Teachers should assess children's oral language by observing children *during activities designed to elicit oral language as naturally as possible*. The variety of functions that the children use then becomes the basis for making judgments about their ability to communicate.

Unstructured Observation.   Most teachers carry out unstructured observations of children's oral language every day and all day. As children engage in a variety of learning activities and informal contacts with one another, oral language is evident everywhere. A specific list of behaviors to observe during unstructured observation is difficult to construct. However, teachers should note how effective children seem to be in completing language activities, getting their physical and emotional needs met, and interacting with the variety of children and adults found in a school. It is possible to gain a general impression of those children who appear to use oral language confidently and easily. Children who seem to be struggling with language can be observed under more structured conditions.

Structured Observation and Interviews.   For structured observation, three or four children can be selected each week for closer study as they engage in oral language activities. The activities that are part of a language-based unit offer teachers excellent opportunities to observe oral language in use. We suggest that the children selected each week for observation be followed all week and that the functions they exhibit be recorded on a simple checklist with explanatory comments where relevant. The rotation of structured observation throughout the school year allows teachers to conduct multiple observations over time, thus improving reliability. The checklist should be a guide and a place to store information, and it should be modified as necessary. Multiple copies can be made, with one checklist summarizing each week's observations.

Dramatic role-playing situations offer assessment settings in which to observe oral language functioning and to interview children. Glazer and Searfoss (1988) suggest using group settings and having students plan the role-playing situation, beginning with a brainstorming session to identify the topic of the role playing.

> Selecting topics for role playing should be collaborative ventures. Brainstorming provides the vehicle for joint decision making in small and moderate sized groups. The generation of ideas by "storming one's brain" encourages students to observe possibilities without making judgment about those ideas. A scribe writes these ideas in front of the group on a chart or chalkboard, without comments or censorship, so that all "storms" are accepted. This activity provides information about student interests. Brainstorming supplies ideas for oral as well as written drama. (p. 76)

Once a topic has been selected, the children plan the specifics of the role-playing situation. The teacher interviews the group as they plan, probing, guiding, and observing language functions being used. The Oral Language Checklist in Figure 3.3 can be used to record responses for group interactions or those of one individual

FIGURE 3.3   **Oral Language Checklist**

Child: _____

Date: _____

Activity: _____

Functions to Be Elicited: _____

                              ✓ = Observed
                              0 = Not observed
                              ? = Can't tell

                                              Notes and Comments:

1. Self-Maintaining   _____
2. Directing   _____
3. Reporting   _____
4. Logical-Reasoning   _____
5. Predicting   _____
6. Projecting   _____
7. Imagining   _____

Note: See pages 72–74 for definitions of the seven functions of language.

child under study. As an example of how teachers can use role playing to elicit and assess oral language, Glazer and Searfoss (1988) provide a list of questions used with a group of children who had decided to role play a restaurant scene as part of a unit on foods (see Figure 3.4). Of course, the teacher did not use all the questions in Figure 3.4, but Glazer and Searfoss listed as many as the teacher who worked with the children was able to generate. These questions can be adapted to stimulate oral language drama in other content areas.

Activities for Developing Oral Language

Activities designed to elicit many kinds of functional language are the core of oral language instruction. In essence, functions replace the skills usually found in programs. There is no skills sequence implicit in a program that uses functional language activities. The focus is on the *use* of language in an activity; that is, the activity is the vehicle that allows children to use language in specific ways for definite purposes. The outcome of an activity, whether it is a making a cake or a drawing or something that goes home to parents, is not the concern. What is important is the language and the learning that take place while the activity is being completed and the satisfaction children get from using language as part of learning.

Functions and Eliciting Activities.   Joan Tough (1979) cites seven functions of language: self-maintaining, directing, reporting, logical reasoning, predicting,

FIGURE 3.4   Focusing Oral Language Drama: Questions about Food

Questions that seek student interests	What should we do a play about? What do we need for the play? How will we get the materials? What will we do with the materials when we get them? How many people should be eating? Who should be the focus (the cook, eaters, visitors, etc.)? Where do we want the restaurant to be located? What will be the problem? What will be the "mistaken ingredient" that causes the people to leave the restaurant? How would you plan to get the people back to the restaurant? Who should be the character to do this? What happens to the person who eats the bad food?
Questions that define the moment	What is the time of day? What is the time of year? What will you be wearing to dinner? What will you be carrying? What do you think the atmosphere is like? At what point do you want to suggest that the food is bad?
Questions that require research or interviews with informed persons	What does a Spanish restaurant look like? What special ingredient would give a rancid taste even if it were not bad? How do Spanish cooks dress? What kind of special utensils would be needed to eat that special food?
Questions that help to control the group for organization into drama activities	*Course of Action Questions:* Should this play happen now, in the past, or in the future? How many girls and boys should be in the play? Should the play be about helping the people who are sick from the food or helping the chef who ruined the food? (point of view) Who should help the people (owner, customer, public health officer)? *Branching Action Questions:* How can we keep the cook from hearing the bad comments about the food? How can we look like very upset customers? How can we set the action so that we get mad at the owner for purchasing the wrong spices for the food? When do you want to stop the action?

projecting, and imagining. The overview presented below includes a definition of each of the seven functions (taken from Tough's work), examples of each function, the key element necessary for the function to be elicited from children, and a few sample activities (Maddox & Searfoss, 1982).

Self-Maintaining Language.   Language used primarily by children in an attempt to satisfy their physical and psychological needs is self-maintaining language. Examples of self-maintaining language are "I want my milk now," "That's my game, so go away!" and "It's my turn." The element that is necessary is the presence of a desired object or task that is not available to all children at once.

Suggested Activities
1. When conducting an activity using magnets, give the child who needs to develop self-maintaining language a strong magnet and others weak ones.
2. When making a pudding or some other food, assign one child to lick the spoon and others such jobs as beating, measuring, and counting.
3. Make a class *What I Can Do Book.* Have children illustrate and write or dictate a sentence for each page. Begin each sentence with "I can...."

Directing Language.   Language that is used by children to direct and monitor either their own actions or those of others is directing language. Examples of directing language are "Put the ruler here," "You cut the paper and I'll stick it," and "Play the record with me." The element that is necessary is a project—making or doing something—in which children work in pairs or small groups.

Suggested Activities
1. Provide a model of a colorful flower, simple pattern pieces, and other materials needed to assemble a flower. Children may work in pairs to make one flower. After it is finished, they can make another one so that each child has a flower.
2. Have children construct clay or papier-mâché models of large sea and land creatures as part of a classroom display. Children may work in groups of three or four, agree on which creature they want to build, and construct it from either clay or papier-mâché. They should be provided with pictures or models to work from and should make their own clay or papier-mâché. The recipe for each can be discussed with the whole class, and then each group can divide tasks and proceed.

Reporting Language.   Language that is used by children to report present and past experiences (giving a commentary on what is or was seen, observed, and recalled) is reporting language. Examples of reporting language are "That little bus has a door in the back that opens," "The nurse said we should go at 2:30," and "We went to the zoo on Saturday and saw the new baby elephant." The element that is necessary is reporting and recalling an experience to others who may or may not have participated in it.

Suggested Activities
1. Have show-and-tell. Like discussions of current events, show-and-tell can become the focus of reporting language.
2. Ask someone such as the school bus driver to discuss the bus rules with the children. Later, have the children in small groups summarize the rules, and have each group present its version of the rules. Expand this activity to other school personnel, such as the nurse or custodian, and to community helpers, including the police, fire-fighters, and others.

Logical-Reasoning Language.   Language that expresses relationships within an experience, such as explaining cause and effect, drawing conclusions, making judgments, and discussing comparison and contrast, is logical-reasoning language. Examples of logical-reasoning language are "I don't think we better take the clock apart, because we couldn't put it back together," "This one is larger and will hold more water," and "You shouldn't do that, it'll break." The element that is necessary is a problem or situation that needs to be explained or resolved.

Suggested Activities
1. Collect materials of various kinds for a floating experiment. Have the children determine which materials will float by trying them out. If they discover some that will not float, ask them to try to find a way to make them float using the materials they have at hand.
2. Read and discuss two short stories with the children, such as *The Three Bears* and *Three Billy Goats Gruff.* Have the children either in small groups or as a class tell ways in which the stories are alike (three animals, all talk) and ways in which the stories are different (setting, ending).

Predicting Language.   When children attempt to anticipate or predict an outcome on the basis of past experience, they use predicting language. Examples of predicting language are "I'll put this flag on and it'll come crashing down," "I'm going to paint a picture when I finish my milk," and "Last time we used blue and you couldn't see it; use red this time." The element that is necessary is a situation in which children need to anticipate or predict an outcome.

Suggested Activities
1. Have a container big enough for children to reach into, and fill it about two-thirds full with small objects, such as erasers or beads. Children then predict how many each one can pick up in one hand. Have each child pick up a handful and count the objects. Make a chart of both the predictions and the actual numbers picked up by each child.
2. Read the children some weather forecasts for various parts of the country. Assign one forecast to each small group of three or four children. Their task is to determine what kinds of clothing would be appropriate for each weather condition. Then, using either pictures the children cut out from catalogues and magazines or their own drawings, have them develop a display illustrating each forecast in clothing.

Projecting Language. Language children use to place themselves into other people's experiences or into situations they have not actually experienced is projecting language. Examples of projecting language are "He spilled all the red paint and doesn't like to clean it up" and "If I were in the story, I'd get on the horse and get away fast!" The element that is necessary is projecting into the experiences of others or into situations that are unfamiliar.

Suggested Activities
1. Make a 12-inch by 18-inch book using construction paper, stapled or tied with yarn. Before putting it together, mark off each page in squares. Label each square with a feeling word (*happy, sad, lonely, puzzled*), and then place the book in the activity center. Have the children find magazine pictures that illustrate each word, cut them out, and glue them in the book. Children may work in pairs.
2. Give situations, and have children discuss how they might feel in each one. For example: (a) Your brother just borrowed your best toy and broke it; (b) You just made a wish, and it came true; (c) You wake up and discover you are in a new school. Children can role-play the situations, too.

Imagining Language. Language children use to develop an imaginary situation or story is imagining language. Examples of imagining language are "You be Snow White, and I'll be a dwarf," "The car is going to crash through the gate with the monkey driving!" and "Once upon a time there were three big dinosaurs...." The element that is necessary is any situation that allows children to produce an imaginary response or to fantasize.

Suggested Activities
1. Allow children to lose themselves in imaginary situations in dramatic play centers, such as a classroom restaurant, store, or beauty shop. Include a prop box of old clothes, hats, objects, and puppets for dressing as characters.
2. Ask children to draw, or find and then cut out, pictures to illustrate three wishes they have. They can then share their wishes with one another. Have available magazines, catalogues, and newspapers full of pictures.

Oral Language–Based Units. If functional activities are the core of oral language instruction, then the organization and structuring of those activities become important. Structure for oral language instruction is provided by organizing activities into language-based units. Without structure, an activity-centered program can appear to lack direction and goals. A unit approach can provide organization for both the teacher and the children. Each unit in an oral language program is dominated by a central theme, utilizes as wide a variety of resources as is available, and involves children as active learners.

We outline below a language-based unit that includes functional oral language activities, reading, and writing. The outline is a brief one, with only a few activities presented. Its central theme is the rainbow, and the title is "The Rainbow Connection."

Each unit should contain at least one activity under each heading.

Introduction. Each unit begins with the teacher's reading or telling a story or poem to the children for motivation. Children talk about the unit topic, relate any previous experiences with the topic, and predict what is likely to happen in the story or poem. For further motivation, children can make a bulletin board related to the unit topic. In the rainbow unit, a story about goblins who steal the rainbow is read to the children (Rico, 1978).

Arts, crafts, and cooking activities. When children work together in pairs or small groups to complete "hands-on" tasks, they must use purposeful language. In the rainbow unit, children make rainbow Jello. They also use the following precut semicircular pattern, which they glue to a sheet of paper and transform into a new shape. Each transformation is titled "First I was a rainbow, then I was a...." A class book is then assembled from these transformations.

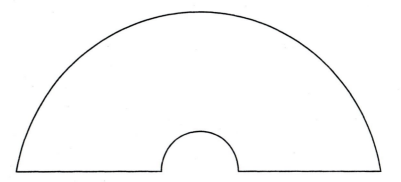

Creative play and drama activities. Games, puppet plays, and informal skits can be part of a unit. In the rainbow unit, the children dramatize the goblin story that introduces the unit, and they play color games.

Music and movement activities. Records, tapes, and other rhythm activities may be appropriate for language use. A song can be learned and sung for fun, or sing-along records related to the unit topic can be included. In the rainbow unit, the song "The Rainbow Connection" (Williams & Ascher, 1979) is learned and practiced.

Related reading and writing. Reading and writing activities grow out of the other unit activities. Experience stories, poems, and other kinds of writing complete the unit. In the rainbow unit, children construct individual color-alphabet books and read from a collection of picture books related to color. The picture books may be taken from the school library and arranged in a display in the classroom.

A few final notes on designing and implementing an oral language program are necessary. The variety of resources and activities used in a language-based unit is limited only by those available to the teacher in the school and community.

Librarians are the best friends a teacher can have in developing a unit. Music, art, and physical education teachers are also invaluable resources in many schools. Arts-and-crafts books, language-activity books, and stores specializing in teaching supplies are additional sources of ideas and materials.

Finally, we must mention *teacher patience* as the last important ingredient in developing and implementing a language-based unit—patience that

Allows children to figure things out for themselves.

Permits them to make mistakes on the way to completing an activity.

Leaves the unit time line and schedule open as it grows and expands and takes new directions along the way.

Contributes to the view that children's language development always looks forward, not backward, on the not-so-straight road to gaining control over language.

Process Guide 3.2

Read the following summaries of two classroom observations. Each teacher had the stated objective of "providing oral language practice." Discuss each situation with others in your class in small groups or pairs, and note the functions of language you think might have been elicited in each classroom. How are the lessons alike? Different? Which one better fits the rationale discussed in this chapter for an oral language program?

Class A.   The teacher holds up small plastic pieces of fruits and vegetables. Individual children are asked to volunteer the name of each piece and tell something about its color, smell, or taste. Finally, the teacher writes the name of each piece on the chalkboard.

Class B.   The class is planning to make popcorn. The children develop a recipe chart story, with the teacher recording the steps and ingredients that children wish to use in making the popcorn. Next, the children decide who will be responsible for collecting each ingredient and when during the next few days would be the best time to make the popcorn. It is finally decided that the best time would be Friday afternoon just before story time.

Emerging Writing

Interest in the writing of young children before they enter school is relatively new, compared to concern with other areas of early literacy. That young children attempt to communicate through writing is evident from observations of their spontaneous writing (Sulzby, 1991). Their attempts to spell conventionally are called *invented spelling* (see Principle 3 in Chapter 1). Because the early writings of young children often appear to be nothing more than scribble accompanied by drawings, for many years they were ignored or mislabeled by researchers and educators as simply drawings. But Sulzby (1989) suggests that "nonletter forms such as early scribbling or drawing frequently function as writing for the young child" (p. 278).

In fact, there is a rough series of developmental stages that young children pass through as they move from scribbling and drawing to invented spelling and finally to conventional spelling. These stages are not separate stages; for example, some children will mix invented with conventional spelling in kindergarten and first grade. Return to Chapter 1, Figure 1.2, and notice how Marissa mixed invented spelling with conventional spelling.

Marissa's Invented Spelling	*Conventional Spelling*
jile	jelly
bred	bread

Process Guide 3.3

Working in pairs or small groups, examine Marissa's recipe for making a peanut butter and jelly sandwich. This time, notice the invented spellings and the conventional ones. Note each invented spelling and write its conventional spelling.

Sulzby (1989) and Sulzby and Teale (1985) offer the following sequence, which traces the development of writing from its beginnings to the appearance of conventional spelling. They caution that their sequence is not rigid, and overlapping of stages occurs frequently when young children's writing is studied over time.

1. *Scribble writing.* When asked to read the message, young children typically construct it from the scribble.
2. *Drawing.* A picture is worth a thousand words, and young children will often recall and retell stories or events from drawings they have made, sometimes adding scribbles.
3. *Nonphonetic letter strings.* Strings of letters are written that stand for a word or words, usually with an unconventional combination or order of vowels and consonants. For example, Jeremy wrote this note to this mother, reminding her that his birthday was coming soon and listing his choices for presents:

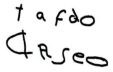

The strings of letters helped Jeremy construct and read his message to anyone willing to listen.
4. *Invented spelling.* Messages consisting mainly of invented spellings can usually be read by readers other than the young author. Marissa showed her in-

vented spelling ability when she wrote her recipe for a peanut butter and jelly sandwich. This stage appears in most children in kindergarten and first grade, occurring earlier or later in some children.

5. *Conventional spelling.* Often called dictionary spelling, or the way we should (or wish we could) spell, conventional spelling arises toward the end of early literacy.

Assessing Emerging Writing

Unstructured Observation.   Teachers can make unstructured observations of emerging writing while children are engaged in writing activities. Behaviors to observe include using writing for specific purposes, talking about writing, and moving toward conventional print from invented spelling.

Structured Observation and Interviews.   Individually, or when a small-group activity involves writing, children can be encouraged to talk about their writing. The teacher can keep a record of these conversations by taking notes or by recording responses and reactions on a simple checklist (see Figure 3.5), which includes questions related to the purposes of writing, use of invented and conventional spellings, and type of writing (e.g., story, recipe, or letter).

FIGURE 3.5   Checklist for Assessing Emerging Writing

Child: _____

Date: _____

1. What was the purpose or use of the writing sample, as expressed by the child?

2. Did the writer use invented and conventional spellings? (List samples of each, or circle them on the child's work.)

3. What type of writing was the sample you selected to discuss with the child?

    _____ Story   _____ Letter   _____ Other (please note type below)

    _____ Description   _____ Note   _____

4. After adding this sample to the portfolio or cumulative writing folder of the child, take a moment to compare this sample with earlier ones. Note below any changes and growth in the purposes for writing, type of writing, and writing mechanics (handwriting, spelling, use of lines, spacing between words).

Activities for Developing Emerging Writing

Emerging writing can be fostered and encouraged through classroom activities such as the following:

1. *Use journals with beginning readers.* Elliott, Nowosad, and Samuels (1981) explain how journals can be a powerful learning tool, starting with preschoolers. A journal is defined in their program as "a collection of children's statements, ideas, and thoughts, transcribed by adults, and possibly including illustrations" (p. 688). The children's journals travel to and from home. Results of the program include: (a) better communication between home and school, (b) improved understanding by parents of their own value in their child's learning, and (c) increased interest by children in reading and writing. The journals in the program developed by Elliott and her colleagues open with a "me" page, which is followed by topics designed to familiarize the children with school. The pages are reproduced in advance, with a separate topic printed at the top of each page to serve as the title. Plenty of room should be left for a drawing, the child's dictation, or even a photograph or picture cut from a magazine or newspaper. Here are some of the topics for the first few months:

School	*Home*
Toys at school	Toys at home
Friends at school	Friends at home
Cooking at school	Cooking at home

Journals may be sent home every few weeks on a Friday, to be returned on Monday. Of course, parent orientation through conferences, special workshops, or regularly scheduled parent meetings at school is necessary for the journals to be most effective. In school, the journals are shared and reviewed by teachers and children, placed in the classroom text area, read to other children, and displayed for all to see. Laura's recipe for chocolate cake, illustrated in Figure 3.6, was taken from her journal entry called "Cooking at Home" and was accompanied by her drawing of a chocolate cake.

2. *Make books.* Every classroom should contain a print production area (see Chapter 2 for a list of materials). An excellent way to help children learn about books is to have them make books, lots of them. Clavio (1980) has used two types of books that are good to begin with: *The Shape Book* and *The Me Book*.

The Shape Book is an exercise in creative thinking. It allows each student to make at least two pages quickly, and it can usually be completed in one period. Each student is given an abstract shape cut from tagboard. Be sure they are all the same. The students are to make as many drawings of real things as possible, using the outlined shape as part of the drawing. The shape must be visible in the drawing and should be traced from the tagboard cutout for uniformity. It can be turned in any direction. The words are simple and repetitive, with only the name of the object changing. For example, given a simple circle, some first graders made a

A chocolate cake

you put candles. You put a dozen chocolates, I dose of flour, I secret amount of butter, 2 scoops of sugar. Mix it up. You don't have to bake it. You have a bunch of pieces.

FIGURE 3.6   Laura's Recipe for Chocolate Cake

circle book: "At first it was a sun, and then it was a clock, and then it was a wheel, and then it was a ball." In virtually no time, this large-group project can show a whole class all the steps in the bookmaking process.

The Me Book is a longer project which gives students a chance to learn more about the process by writing about themselves. Since the students know about their own lives, there is no lack of material. Even the youngest students can make this kind of book with the help of dictation. By the time the students have written about and illustrated the many facets of their lives, they will have learned the bookmaking process page by page. These books are self-concept builders, written about the students' lives. A good activity at the start of the school year, making this type of book lets the students open up, shows that the teacher accepts them and their work, and gives the teacher a chance to learn about the students. These books can include general biographical data: family, friends, hobbies, loves, and hates. Possible titles include *The Book About Me, My Book,* and *There Is Nobody Just Like Me.*

3. *Write without a pencil.* As creative alternatives to having children use pencils, Tompkins (1981) describes some activities that involve a wide variety of materials through which children can be stimulated to communicate. Some of Tompkins's alternatives include

Flannelboard	Letter cookies
Letters cut from newspapers	Letter blocks

Magic slates	Foam letters
Pudding fingerpaint	Shaving cream
Glue with beans and popcorn	Blocks
Typewriter	Magnetic letters

4. *Use oral language and writing.* Oral language and writing activities can be integrated through thematic units such as the rainbow unit presented earlier in this chapter. Unit topics can be taken from science and social studies in order to provide a variety of opportunities for children to write.

Summary

This chapter discussed five areas of early literacy: print awareness, concepts of print, story sense, oral language, and emerging writing. Activities to encourage literacy and procedures for functionally assessing these activities were also presented.

FOLLOW-THROUGH ACTIVITIES

Note: Level 1 activities may require limited access to children or classrooms. Level 2 activities should be completed using children and classrooms.

Level 1 Activities

1. Brainstorm and list as many types of play stations as you can think of that incorporate authentic literacy. Then list all the materials you think would need to be included within each station. Share your results with your classmates.

2. Develop a wordless-picture-book activity by following the procedures in this chapter. Try it out on a small group of your classmates.

Level 2 Activities

1. "Preschool Use Soars" reads the headline of a newspaper story reporting that 37 percent of children ages 3 to 4 are attending some kind of preschool program. Make arrangements to visit a preschool class, and note any activities you observe that appear to be developing areas of early literacy discussed in this chapter.

2. Interview two or three kindergarten teachers about their views on beginning reading and what constitutes a sound beginning reading program.

3. Select one of the structured observation instruments for assessing early literacy and administer it to at least one child.

WORKING WITH PARENTS

Parents are genuinely interested in helping their children be successful in learning to read. Yet, schools often try to impose views on how parents should help their children.

As Y. Goodman (1997) pointed out, we can't expect all families to follow one prescription (reading to their children) as the only means of helping their children learn to read:

> Such a belief places heavy responsibility on families who do not read aloud regularly in the home; they often accept the notion that since they do not read books to their children, they are irresponsible and the cause for their children's lack of literacy. I want to dispel that notion: not to diminish the importance of reading aloud as one road to literacy development, but to document that there are many ways, equally important but different, in which children are immersed in literacy events that positively influence their development. (p. 56)

Teachers and parents can work together to validate the many ways children use literacy in their lives. Children make discoveries about print throughout their development as early readers. All of these discoveries need to be viewed as important.

RESOURCES

Buckley, R. (1987). A funny thing happened on the way to "reading readiness": A teacher learns from the learners. *Language Arts, 64,* 74–77.

> One teacher testifies to how her beliefs about reading readiness changed dramatically.

Clay, M. M. (1991). *By different paths to common outcomes.* York, ME: Stenhouse.

> This text, by one of the leading experts in the field of early literacy, contains excellent chapters on literacy before schooling, oral language, and introducing children to print in school.

International Reading Association & National Association for the Education of Young Children. (1998). *Learning to read and write: Developmentally appropriate practices for young children.* Newark, DE: International Reading Association.

> This comprehensive position statement was compiled by the two leading organizations concerned with literacy and young children. A must read!

McGee, L. M., & Purcell-Gates, V. (1997). "So what's going on in research in emergent literacy?" *Reading Research Quarterly, 32,* 310–318.

> These authors dialogue about the past, present, and future of research in early literacy.

Neuman, S. B., & Roskos, K. (Eds.). (1998). *Children achieving: Best practices in early literacy.* Newark, DE: International Reading Association.

> This edited volume synthesizes the research in early literacy and makes recommendations for sound instructional practices.

Smolkin, L. B., & Yaden, D. B., Jr. (1992). O is for mouse: First encounters with the alphabet book. *Language Arts, 69,* 432–441.

> Alphabet-book readings can orient children to the ways all book learning will be accomplished in school. This article presents teaching suggestions for making the most of alphabet books.

Strickland, D. S. (1990). Emergent literacy: How young children learn to read. *Educational Leadership, 47*(6), 19–23.

> New insights into how children learn to read and write are summarized in a readable, easy-to-follow article.

REFERENCES

Applebee, A. N. (1979). Children and stories: Learning the rules of the game. *Language Arts, 56,* 641–646.

Babbitt, N. (1986). My love affair with the alphabet. In *Once upon a time: Celebrating the magic of children's books in honor of the twentieth anniversary of Reading Is Fundamental* (pp. 42–45). New York: G. P. Putnam's Sons.

Bridge, C. (1984). Predictable books for beginning readers and writers. In M. Sampson (Ed.), *Literacy learning and instruction* (pp. 55–95). Dubuque, IA: Kendall/Hunt.

Clavio, D. (1980). A student author project: Integrating language arts. *Proceedings of the Annual Reading Conference of Arizona State University, 3,* 11–18.

Clay, M. M. (1972). *Concepts about print test, sand and stones.* Exeter, NH: Heinemann.

Clay, M. (1991). *Becoming literate: The construction of inner control.* Portsmouth, NH: Heinemann.

Degler, L. S. (1979). Putting words into wordless books. *The Reading Teacher, 32,* 399–402.

Downing, J., & Oliver, P. (1973–1974). The child's conception of "a word." *Reading Research Quarterly, 9,* 568–582.

Elliott, S., Nowosad, J., & Samuels, P. (1981). "Me at school, me at home": Using journals with preschoolers. *Language Arts, 58,* 688–691.

Glazer, S. M., & Searfoss, L. W. (1988). *Reading diagnosis and instruction: A C-A-L-M approach.* Englewood Cliffs, NJ: Prentice-Hall.

Goodman, Y. M. (1980, January). *The roots of literacy.* Paper presented at the Annual Claremont Reading Conference, Claremont, CA.

Goodman, Y. (1985). Kidwatching: Observing children in the classroom. In A. Jaggar & M. T. Smith-Burke (Eds.), *Observing the language learner* (pp. 9–18). Newark, DE: International Reading Association.

Goodman, Y. (1991). Informal methods of evaluation. In J. Flood, J. Jensen, D. Lapp, & J. Squire (Eds.), *Handbook of research on teaching the English language arts* (pp. 502–509). New York: Macmillan.

Goodman, Y. (1997). Multiple roads to literacy. In D. Taylor (Ed.), *Many families, many literacies: An international declaration of principles* (pp. 56–62). Portsmouth, NH: Heinemann.

Hall, N. (1998). Real literacy in school settings: Five-year-olds take on the world. *The Reading Teacher, 52,* 8–17.

Heald-Taylor, G. (1987a). How to use predictable books for K–2 language arts instruction. *The Reading Teacher, 40,* 656–661.

Heald-Taylor, G. (1987b). Predictable literature selections and activities for language arts instruction. *The Reading Teacher, 41,* 6–12.

Heath, S. B. (1996). *Ways with words: Language, life, and work in communities and classrooms.* Cambridge, UK: Cambridge University Press.

Hiebert, F. H. (1981). Developmental patterns and interrelationships of preschool children's print awareness. *Reading Research Quarterly, 16,* 236–260.

Holdaway, D. (1979). *The foundations of literacy.* Sydney: Ashton-Scholastic.

Hoskisson, K., & Tompkins, G. E. (1991). *Language arts: Content and teaching strategies* (2nd ed.). Columbus, OH: Merrill.

Hudelson, S. M. (1981). *Print awareness in three-year-olds.* Unpublished manuscript. Arizona State University.

Lomax, R. G., & McGee, L. M. (1987). Young children's concepts about print and reading. *Reading Research Quarterly, 22,* 237–256.

Maddox, E. J., & Searfoss, L. W. (1982). *A structure for oral language development programs* (Oral Language Project Paper #1). Phoenix: Phoenix Elementary School District #1.

Mason, J. M., & McCormick, C. (1981). *An investigation of prereading instruction from a developmental perspective: Foundations for literacy.* (Tech. Rep. No. 224). Urbana, IL: University of Illinois.

McGee, L. M., & Purcell-Gates, V. (1997). "So what's going on in research in emergent literacy?" *Reading Research Quarterly, 32,* 310–318.

Morris, D. (1981). Concept of word: A developmental phenomenon in the beginning reading and writing processes. *Language Arts, 58,* 659–668.

Morris, D. (1993). The relationship between children's concept of word in text and phoneme awareness in learning to read. *Research in the Teaching of English, 27,* 133–154.

Neuman, S. B., & Roskos, K. (1997). Literacy knowledge in practice: Contexts of participation for young readers and writers. *Reading Research Quarterly, 32,* 10–32.

Rico, U. (1978). *The rainbow goblins.* New York: Warner Books.

Roberts, B. (1992). The evolution of the young child's concept of *word* as a unit of spoken and written language. *Reading Research Quarterly, 27,* 125–138.

Salinger, T. (1998). How do we assess young children's literacy learning? In S. B. Neuman & K. Roskos (Eds.), *Children achieving: Best practices in early literacy* (pp. 223–249). Newark, DE: International Reading Association.

Strickland, D. (1990). Emergent literacy: How young children learn to read. *Educational Leadership, 47*(6), 18–23.

Sulzby, E. (1989). Assessment of writing and children's language while writing. In L. Morrow & J. Smith (Eds.), *The role of assessment and measurement in early literacy instruction* (pp. 83–109). Englewood Cliffs, NJ: Prentice-Hall.

Sulzby, E. (1991). The learner develops: The development of the young child and the emergence of literacy. In J. Flood, J. Jensen, D. Lapp, & J. Squire (Eds.), *Handbook of research on teaching the language arts* (pp. 273–285). New York: Macmillan.

Sulzby, E. (1994). Children's emerging reading of storybooks: A developmental study. In R. B. Ruddell, M. R. Ruddell, & H. Singer (Eds.), *Theoretical models and processes of reading* (4th ed., pp. 244–280). Newark, DE: International Reading Association.

Sulzby, E., & Teale, W. (1985). Writing development in early childhood. *Educational Horizons, 64,* 8–12.

Sulzby, E., & Teale, W. (1991). Emergent literacy. In R. Barr, M. L. Kamil, P. B. Mosenthal, & P. D. Pearson (Eds.), *Handbook of reading research: Volume II* (pp. 727–757). New York: Longman.

Taylor, D., & Dorsey-Gaines, C. (1988). *Growing up literate: Learning from inner city families.* Portsmouth, NH: Heinemann.

Tompkins, G. E. (1981). Writing without a pencil. *Language Arts, 58,* 823–833.

Tough, J. (1979). *Talk for teaching and learning.* London: Ward Lock Educational.

Vygotsky, L. S. (1978). *Mind in society: The development of higher psychological processes.* Cambridge, MA: Cambridge University Press.

Williams, P., & Ascher, K. (1979). *The rainbow connection* (song). Los Angeles: Welbeck Music.

Worden, P. E., & Boettcher, W. (1990). Young children's acquisition of alphabet knowledge. *Journal of Reading Behavior, 22,* 277–294.

Yopp, H. K. (1992). Developing phonemic awareness in young children. *The Reading Teacher, 45,* 696–703.

CHAPTER

4 Instruction Using Commercial Materials

INTRODUCTION

There has been a decline over the past few years in the number of schools using basal readers. In many schools, though, commercial materials—especially the basal reader in updated new editions—are commonplace because they are still very attractive to teachers. School districts have pressured publishers into incorporating many features of holistic reading instruction into the basal readers that they publish. Fears that teachers would use basal readers automatically and without thought have proved largely to be false (Baumann & Heubach, 1996). Good teachers appear to be adept at picking and choosing what they find useful in helping children learn to read; they ignore or modify other features of basals. The basal today is seen as a resource for teachers that empowers through suggestions for teaching. The teacher's editions of basals are often the primary source on a day-to-day basis of new techniques for teaching reading.

We believe that no commercial, published material, by itself, can teach children to read. Effective use of the basal reader means stressing the root word, *base,* in basal. The basal can be the core of a reading program, but not the total program. Successful use of the basal reader in the classroom year after year will depend on how you adapt it to your teaching style and knowledge and to the needs of each class you teach. The purpose of this chapter is to provide you with the information you need to make sound decisions about using the basal reader in your classroom.

The definition of reading as a communication tool, explained in Chapter 1, is the foundation upon which we believe reading programs should be built. Chapter 2 presented the print-rich classroom environment in which the basal reader should be used. Quickly review both of these chapters before reading Chapter 4.

GRAPHIC ORGANIZER

This graphic organizer summarizes the structure of Chapter 4:

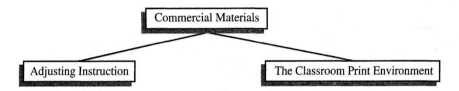

```
            ┌──────────────────────┐
            │ Commercial Materials │
            └──────────────────────┘
              ╱                  ╲
┌──────────────────────┐   ┌──────────────────────────────┐
│ Adjusting Instruction │   │ The Classroom Print Environment │
└──────────────────────┘   └──────────────────────────────┘
```

OBJECTIVES

When you finish this chapter, you should be able to understand and discuss each of these statements:

1. By taking control of the teacher's manual, the teacher can adapt basal reader lessons to make them more meaning-centered and child-centered.
2. Teachers should play a major role in selecting the basal reader series they are expected to use.
3. Integrating writing and oral language activities into basal reader lessons increases growth in reading, writing, and oral language.
4. Providing opportunities for children to read and write whole stories is an effective way of integrating the basal story into the classroom environment.
5. A strong decoding approach is needed in the early grades.

Basal Reader Approach

In this chapter, we will attempt to give you enough information to understand the essential structure of the basal approach and some ways to vary its use. Basal readers generally reflect a skills view of reading, in which a set of skills serves as the framework for the approach. These skills are roughly sequenced, and lessons and tests are developed to teach them. The entire *scope and sequence of skills,* as it is usually called, is then blended into the reading and discussion of stories and other selections. Add some supplementary parts, and a basal reader has been constructed.

Basal readers are composed of selections in which the difficulty of the vocabulary is carefully controlled. The selections begin at lower reading levels for beginning readers and gradually increase in difficulty as children move from level to level. A standard series of teaching steps or lesson plans is used consistently within each individual basal reader series. At one time, these steps were fairly common across leading series and were called the *directed reading activity,* or DRA for short. Recent editions of basal series vary in teaching procedures, although the teaching steps are generally arranged in a three-stage sequence: (1) preparation for reading, (2) guided reading, and (3) postreading skill or strategy development and enrichment activities.

Adjusting Basal Reader Instruction

Basal readers are written for average readers—those children who progress normally, grade level by grade level, through the series. In other words, a second-grade basal reader is intended for children in grade 2 who are *reading on grade level.* When children are either above or below grade level in reading, some adjustments may be necessary in the basal reader teaching steps. In fact, all leading basal reader series acknowledge this need and make efforts to meet it.

For above-average readers, we offer these suggestions:

1. Accelerate the pace of instruction by moving children through higher grade levels of readers. Above-average readers can be placed first at their instructional level and then allowed to proceed under teacher direction through the series at the fastest rate they can handle. If children can benefit from a certain text, then that text should be used, regardless of grade-level designation.
2. Enrich the basal reader lessons by supplementing them through a wide variety of print and nonprint activities. If a basal reader unit has a theme, such as "danger and daring," children could investigate special feats of daring that appeal to them. Children will need to identify a specific event, ask questions about it as they investigate, gather information from reference sources, and determine a way to share their results with others. A variety of ways to share should be encouraged, such as oral and written reports, plays, puppetry, pantomime, posters, models, and maps.
3. Supplement the basal reader with plenty of self-selected reading.

For below-average readers, we have these suggestions:

1. Use flexible grouping, as described later in this chapter, so below-average readers are not isolated or always placed together.

2. Allow additional time for below-average reading groups when making the daily classroom schedule.
3. Monitor comprehension carefully during the guided reading of a selection. Clear up confusion during the guided reading stage.
4. Spend extra time introducing new vocabulary before a selection is read. Build background for reading, motivation, and purpose setting carefully, and ask children to tell you why they are reading the story and to make some predictions about its content.
5. Reteach skills that are causing confusion *before* assessing children's mastery of them. Increase practice time if necessary.
6. Ask children to tell you or show you how they get an answer or complete a task. Probe their understanding of why they are completing a task and what they are learning. This helps them to relate one lesson to another.
7. Provide plenty of oral discussion of the selection after it has been read. Begin postreading discussion of a story with questions from the teacher's manual that focus on elements of the story, such as plot, main characters, setting, and time. Then ask other questions. In some cases, longer discussions of fewer questions may be more beneficial for comprehension.
8. Take special care to relate the postreading discussion to the original purposes set for reading and to review vocabulary that was introduced before reading.

Process Guide 4.1

At this point, we could continue to describe the basic structure of a typical basal and its uses. But one element is missing—the basal. We suggest that if you really want to understand the basal reader, a hands-on activity is essential before we go any further. The checklist in Figure 4.1 is designed to acquaint you with any basal. It is intended not as an evaluation checklist, but as an informational one. You can work alone, in pairs, or in small groups. Your instructor may want you to do some of the sections as part of an in-class project or may assign some of them as an independent activity. However the assignment is arranged, dig in and get to know the basal reader.

The Basal Reader in the Classroom Print Environment

This section will present ways to adapt the basal reader so that it can be used in a print-rich classroom. Our goal is to help you learn to make decisions about how and where to modify the teacher's manuals of basal readers to make them more effective. The following list summarizes the modifications that we believe will shift the focus of instruction from the basal reader to the children in your classroom.

- Know the basal reader you are going to be using.
- Organize your classroom as a print-rich environment.

- Take control of the teacher's manual.
- Teach only high-utility decoding skills.
- Integrate reading instruction with oral language and writing.
- Use workbook and workbook-type materials for meaningful reinforcement.
- Use flexible grouping.

Know the Basal Reader You Are Going to Be Using

Getting to know the basal reader before you begin to use it is essential. You can do so by completing the checklist in Figure 4.1.

Organize Your Classroom as a Print-Rich Environment

The availability of places to produce and display print, reference materials, current magazines, trade books of all kinds, bulletin boards full of notices, and other forms of print suggested in Chapter 2 promotes literacy and places the basal reader in the context of meaningful, functional print.

Take Control of the Teacher's Manual

Vary the structure of the lessons by providing more involvement by the children and by increasing the number of comprehension-centered activities. The activities

When the teacher takes control of the teacher's manual, students become more actively involved in learning.

FIGURE 4.1   Checklist for Getting to Know the Basal Reader

Directions: Complete the checklist, using as many as possible of these sources:

1. One teacher's manual or resource guide for a grade level between 1 and 4. The first part of each manual or guide usually contains a common core of information about the series.
2. Materials supplied by the publisher that explain the series, such as brochures on scope and sequence of skills and strategies or lists of what is taught.

Name of Series and Publisher: _____

Copyright Date:_____

	Yes	No	Notes
Evaluating Organization and Content			
1. Locate information about the approach to reading instruction taken by the series. Is it skills-based? literature-based? integrated language arts? a combination? other?			
2. Are grade equivalents given?			
3. Does the series appear to contain a balance and variety of literary forms and types of writing? Check (✓) the ones you find _____ Information, fact selection _____ Suspense _____ Fantasy _____ Plays _____ Fiction _____ Biography/autobiography _____ Legends, myths _____ Historical fiction _____ Poems _____ Content-area selections _____ Humor from social studies, science, and health			
4. Are award-winning children's stories, as well as contemporary stories, presented?			
5. At each level, does the series appear to be organized in thematic units?			

(continued)

FIGURE 4.1   Continued

	Yes	No	Notes
Examining the Teacher's Manual Locate a section in the teacher's manual at the beginning of a unit or story. Now answer these questions: 6. Are you able to follow the lesson plan or routine to teach a selection?			
7. Do you think an inexperienced teacher could teach from the manual without much additional guidance?			
8. Are pages from the children's texts reproduced in the manual?			
9. Are there suggestions at the end of each lesson for follow-up activities that involve *transfer* of skills (for example, transfer to a variety of print, including trade books, newspapers, and magazines, as well as transfer to content areas, such as social studies, science, drama, art, and music)?			
10. What are the *major* steps involved in teaching each story (for example, Introduction and Motivation, Guided Reading, and Follow-up Discussion)?	List steps here:		
Determining Scope and Sequence of Skills Use information you find in the teacher's manual to complete this activity.			Other areas included:
11. Does the series include instruction and practice in comprehension? decoding (word attack)? vocabulary? studying? listening? writing? oral language?			Other areas not included:
12. As you read through the teacher's manual, does it appear that each lesson integrates instruction in comprehension, decoding, *and* vocabulary?			
13. Are students taught specific *strategies* for decoding, comprehending, and studying, in addition to *skills* in these areas?			
14. Does the manual provide activities to integrate reading with writing, oral language, music, drama, and the arts?			

Judging the Format and Features			
15. Are the books appealing, inviting, and attractive?			
16. Do pictures and illustrations contribute to understanding or appreciating the stories?			
17. Are the bindings durable on children's text? teacher's manual? workbook or activity books?			
Examining the Components of the Series			
18. Is a testing or assessment program included?			
19. Is there a management system for keeping track of indicators of children's progress? Does it include individual checklists, folders, or portfolios? class-summary data sheets? test-summary data sheets?			
20. Have modifications been made for children with special needs, ESL/BLE students, and advanced learners?			

and suggestions presented below are designed to take the place of part of the basal reader lesson plan.

Directed Reading-Thinking Activity (DRTA).   The DRTA was developed by Stauffer (1969) as an alternative to the DRA lesson format. See Chapter 8 for a discussion of using the DRTA to encourage children to develop their own purposes for reading.

ReQuest.   An acronym for *reciprocal questioning*, ReQuest (Manzo, 1969) involves the children and the teacher in taking turns asking and answering questions while reading a basal reader story. See Chapter 8 for directions on how to use ReQuest as an alternative to the DRA.

Expectation Outline.   An adaptation of a technique suggested by Spiegel (1981), the expectation outline is appropriate for use with a factual selection from a basal reader. It could also be used with selections from science, social studies, or health texts. The steps to follow are simple:

1. Ask children to tell what they *expect* to learn from reading a selection—for example: "What do you expect to learn from this story on cave dwellers?"

Picture clues can be the source of children's questions if the children are reluctant to ask questions or are beginning readers.

2. As the children ask questions about the topic of the story, you can jot them down in rough categories. To encourage questions, we recommend placing some adjectives on the board and writing the questions generated by the children under the appropriate column. *What, where, who, why, how,* and *when* generally cover most children's questions. Of course, other category labels can be added as children ask questions that do not fit your choice of labels. As the children become familiar with expectation outlines, they will ask more and more questions, and the category labels may no longer be necessary to get them started. You can group the questions after the children have exhausted their questioning. This way you are not trying to group questions when they begin to come fast and furious from the children.

3. Have the children read the selection. Focus the discussion on the questions they expected to get answers for while reading the story. Unanswered questions can simply be dropped or can serve as motivation for additional reading or some library searching.

4. Use the follow-up activities suggested in the teacher's manual.

As with our other suggestions for taking control of the teacher's manual, the expectation outline in its adapted form should be used to vary the lesson format of the basal reader, not to replace that format entirely.

Radio Reading.   Radio reading (Greene, 1970, 1979) provides children with practice in communicating a message orally. It may replace the guided reading and discussion step of a directed reading activity. In radio reading, the focus of oral reading is comprehension and communicating, rather than articulation or word-by-word perfection. Searfoss (1975) suggested some revisions of Greene's original procedures. He developed four steps for teachers and children to follow:

1. *Getting started.* A small-group setting works well for radio reading, although it may also be used in a one-to-one setting. The teacher leads the activity by explaining the four steps to the readers, emphasizing the responsibility of the reader to communicate a message as a radio announcer does. The story selected for radio reading should be challenging—near the readers' instructional level, but not their frustration level. No silent reading is necessary prior to the oral reading. Each child reads orally a portion of a story of reasonable length, perhaps a paragraph or two in the lower grades and as much as a page in the upper elementary grades. The listeners are instructed to attend closely to the announcer (reader), since they will not have a copy of the story.

2. *Communicating the message.* The reader is responsible for deciding when he or she needs help with a word. If a difficulty arises, the reader simply puts a finger on the unknown word and asks one of the listeners for help. Since the teacher and other listeners have no copy of the story in front of them, their job is to listen for a message, not to correct or prompt. Some teachers initially

have difficulty in refraining from prompting or from beginning a phonics lesson when the reader requests help. Such tactics are clearly inappropriate. Phrases such as "Sound it out," "It rhymes with...," or "Begins with a b... b...b sound" are to be avoided. The place for a word-attack lesson is not during radio reading.

3. *Checking for understanding.* If the reader has read an accurate message, then a short discussion of what was heard moves quickly. The teacher may lead the discussion by simply asking someone to volunteer a brief summary of what he or she heard. Others in the group are asked to confirm the message. After the discussion, the reader, as a reward for sending a clear message, may be asked to continue. In a group setting, a new reader (announcer) may be selected and the activity continued.

4. *Clarifying an unclear message.* If the reader has not communicated a clear message and the listeners give conflicting statements of what they heard, then the reader is responsible for returning to the story and rereading the portion in question. It is the reader's job to do this clarifying; again, the teacher must avoid prompting.

Readers' Theatre. Readers' theatre (Bardsley & Foley, 1997) can be adapted for use with basal readers. It is similar to radio reading in that it provides practice in oral reading while creating high student interest and involvement. The first step is to select basal reader stories or plays that involve a number of characters and dialogue. In the case of basal stories, the script should be an adaptation, written by the teacher and students in dialogue form.

Working in groups of four to six, students select or are assigned parts to read. Each group uses a different basal reader story or play so that the groups can perform for one another. Although facial expressions, gestures, and some simple props may be used, emphasis is on the message being carried through the reading. Because students have an opportunity to rehearse before they perform, they are motivated to focus on the message and have a positive reading experience.

Readers' theatre may be done as a follow-up to a basal reader selection or as an alternative to an independent or guided reading activity in the teacher's manual. Audience members may be asked to discuss plot development or character portrayal as shown by the readers' voices. Audience participation improves story interpretation and comprehension by both the students performing and those listening and watching.

Selecting and Adding Questions. As you prepare to teach a basal reader selection, skim the questions suggested in the manual to guide comprehension and match them with the story or selection structure. For example, if a story is titled "Mystery of the Dark Swamp," it is reasonable to expect that the setting of the story and events occurring in a dark swamp are the focus of the story. It therefore seems only logical that if you are to guide children through a discussion to comprehend this story, most of the comprehension questions included in the teacher's manual should relate to the setting and events taking place there. If your goal is to involve the children in a good discussion of the story, then you will want to build the discussion around the setting, rather than asking a smorgasbord of questions that do not relate to one another. Asking one question about a character, a second about the time of day, and a third about the color of the horse's eyes will probably not lead to a coherent discussion that focuses children's thinking and increases their comprehension of the story.

The same direction applies to the patterns of organization used to develop comprehension of a factual selection. If a selection is on the life cycle of bees, then it is reasonable to expect that the focus of the discussion guiding children's comprehension of the selection will be the sequence of steps in the bees' life cycle. Questions on topics such as the commercial uses for bees, while interesting, will not guide children's comprehension of the life cycle that bees follow.

In selecting questions to be used to guide children's discussion of a story or factual selection in a basal reader, it is useful to analyze the story elements and patterns of organization employed by the author. Those questions directly related to either the major story elements or the pattern of organization used to develop the topic of a factual selection will probably be the most effective in encouraging children's comprehension.

Teach Only High-Utility Decoding Skills

Skills that are useful to children outside of the setting of the basal reader group should receive highest priority. Teachers can make decisions about which high-utility decoding skills to teach. They can also design lessons that take skills often taught in isolation and combine them into strategies for helping children unlock the meaning of unfamiliar words. Chapter 6 covers both these areas in detail.

Integrate Reading Instruction with Oral Language and Writing

Integrating instruction and practice in reading with the use of other communication tools is another modification of the standard lesson format of the basal reader. The activities that follow were designed with that purpose in mind. (See Chapters 5 and 10 for additional integrated language strategies that go beyond the basal reader.)

Listening-Thinking Activity.   Combining listening and thinking with reading instruction emphasizes the relationship between listening and reading. As part of teaching a basal reader story, the teacher could read some of the assigned story aloud to children before they try to read it on their own. For instance, the teacher might read the opening paragraphs and have students follow this oral reading with their own silent reading of the remainder of the story. This focusing of attention could get readers over the initial reluctance to read, and it could establish both motivation and purpose for continuing to read and for demanding meaning. When part of a class is devoted to helping children get started, they can relax and develop a sense of where they are going from the beginning—rather than waiting until a postreading discussion is conducted. If a story is long, children could finish reading it outside of the scheduled lesson for the basal reader group, thus freeing the teacher to give additional attention to other groups. Follow-up or enrichment activities from the teacher's manual may be used.

Retelling and Writing Activity. The follow-up discussion part of teaching a basal reader story can be replaced with retelling and writing. After children have read a story, they can try retelling it in this sequence:

1. Teacher and children retell the story into a tape recorder, in story sequence, with each child telling a part of the story.
2. Next the entire tape is played back, and as each child's part comes up, that child writes his or her part of the story, slowing down or replaying the tape as needed.
3. While each child is writing down his or her part, the other children make pictures on paper to illustrate their parts of the story.
4. After all the children have transcribed their parts of the story and drawn pictures, they play a sequencing game. The teacher shuffles the pictures and asks the children to put them in the order of the story plot. Later, the same can be done with the written parts of the story.
5. The pictures can be displayed on a bulletin board or easel, and the display can be used in telling the story to other members of the class or to children in a lower grade, or even as part of a presentation to school staff and parents.

Use Workbook-Type Materials for Meaningful Reinforcement

Workbooks are designed to provide children with individual, independent practice. Unfortunately, workbooks can have some unintended effects if they are poorly designed. Osborn and Decker (1990) report inherent flaws in some workbooks, such as ambiguous language, poorly designed directions, confusing tasks, and tasks inappropriate for a paper-and-pencil format. Of course, even well-designed workbooks, if not used properly, can lead to busy work. For all of these reasons, they are becoming less popular, especially with teachers who view them as providing skill-and-drill exercises not related to reading. Osborn (1981) suggests some guidelines for evaluating and using workbooks:

> Workbook tasks should be relevant to the instruction that is going on in the rest of the lesson.
>
> Workbooks should reflect the most important (and workbook-appropriate) aspects of what is being taught in the reading program.
>
> The language used in workbook tasks must be consistent with that used in the rest of the lesson and in the rest of the workbook.
>
> Instructions should be clear, unambiguous, and easy to follow; brevity is a virtue.
>
> Some workbook tasks should be fun and have an obvious payoff to them.

Use Flexible Grouping

Much of the instruction using basal readers is conducted in small, stable groups arranged by clustering children with similar reading ability. This arrangement allows the teacher to have more contact with children and to tailor instruction to their reading levels. Such formal, small-group settings, however, may not be familiar to all children; many children rarely encounter this type of grouping prior to coming to school. It cannot be assumed that children, because they play together in groups or score similarly on formal and informal tests, will automatically function together effectively in small-group instruction. Of special concern when children are grouped by ability for reading instruction in high, average, and low groups is the effect of being placed in the various groups, especially the low groups.

Some suggestions for improving reading instruction across *all* groups (especially low groups) are listed below:

1. Try not to allow low reading groups to become the dumping ground for children with behavioral problems. Reading ability should be treated separately, as a language tool to be acquired; children cannot benefit from instruction when grouped together for being discipline problems.
2. Resist parental pressure to move children too quickly from lower groups to higher ones. Explain why children are placed in particular groups, keep parents regularly informed of their children's progress, make certain that children understand their strengths and areas needing improvement, and make decisions to move children to another group based on their reading performance.
3. Monitor your own attitude toward low groups. Although they may require instruction that is adjusted to their learning rate and needs, they deserve the same sound teaching techniques as higher groups—delivered by the same smiling, motivating, empathetic teacher.
4. Try some self-assessment of the instruction you are providing poor readers. Tape record several instructional sessions with low reading groups, review the tapes, and note any behaviors that might need to be changed.
5. Remember that group labels are relative. A child may be in the low reading group in a school where average is really above average, such as in high socioeconomic communities. That same child, if moved to another school in another community or different part of town, might be in a high reading group. One of the serious consequences of grouping is that some children may, incorrectly, believe that being in the low reading group means they are inadequate, stupid, or dumb and begin to transfer those feelings of low self-esteem in reading to other academic and nonacademic areas.

Cleland (no date) offers some suggestions for using flexible grouping in reading instruction:

1. In the *whole group*, children can

    read chorally, rap, or echo read.

    brainstorm and share prior knowledge about the topic.

set common purposes for reading.

plan investigations and response activities.

perform puppet shows, plays, readers' theatre, charades, or TV/radio simulations.

debate.

construct class books.

share findings and products of reading.

carry out service projects.

2. In *teacher-directed small groups,* children can

work on vocabulary, concepts, or comprehension strategies they need to develop.

serve as models, talking aloud about how they figured out the meaning of a new word.

participate in teacher-directed discussion or other response activities.

prepare for whole-group sharings.

3. In *student-directed small groups and with partners,* children can

read and reread with peer or cross-grade support.

practice retelling.

write shared compositions.

interview each other about a story or selection.

work on projects or contribute to a group project.

use peer coaching for revising or editing.

prepare for whole-group sharings.

4. *Individually,* children can

listen to tapes of selections.

practice reading as "experts" or in character roles.

write in journals or literature logs.

confer with the teacher one-to-one.

read silently for pleasure.

prepare reports, create poems, or write newspaper articles.

work on individual contributions to a group project.

Summary

This chapter discussed effective ways to teach reading using the basal reader. The use of the basal was presented, along with ways to modify it so teachers can take control of the teacher's manual and integrate basal reading instruction into the classroom environment.

FOLLOW-THROUGH ACTIVITIES

Note: Level 1 activities may require some access to children and classrooms. Level 2 activities should be completed with children in classrooms. The Process Guide in this chapter may be substituted for one of the Follow-Through Activities listed below.

Level 1 Activities

1. Interview a teacher who uses the basal reader approach. Ask questions about the teaching steps recommended in the manual, children's reactions to the stories, and how the workbook is used.

2. Develop a list of advantages and disadvantages, *as you see them,* of the basal reader approach.

3. In small groups, role-play or microteach a basal reader selection, following the teacher's manual carefully. You may need to prepare some activities ahead of time. Be sure to discuss the lesson steps with the group after you complete them.

Level 2 Activities

1. Arrange to teach one basal reader selection to a group of children. Tape record the lesson so that you can replay it to determine how closely you followed the lesson plan in the teacher's manual. Teach another selection, if at all possible.

2. During a week or two in a classroom, observe how the teacher uses the basal reader for instruction. Take notes on how closely the teacher follows the teacher's manual. Prepare a list of similarities and differences between what you observed and the instructions in the manual.

3. After each of the above activities, reread the checklist on getting to know the basal reader (Figure 4.1), which you completed earlier. Revise or add information on the basis of each experience with the basal.

WORKING WITH PARENTS

Parents usually welcome suggestions for working with their children at home, as long as the suggestions are reasonable in terms of time required. We would like to suggest that parents can help with the sharing and celebrating that children do when they complete books. The following list can be sent home, several suggestions at a time, or can be used as part of parent conferences throughout the school year.

Eight Ways to Celebrate a Book with Your Child

1. Sit down, just you and your child, for even a few minutes and listen to your child tell about his or her book. Avoid questions—just listen!

2. Provide materials such as paper, crayons, finger paint, glue, scissors, scraps of material, yarn, colored paper, and clay, so that your child can celebrate by drawing, painting, or making something to illustrate a special part of the book. Display the work for all to see, perhaps on the refrigerator door.

3. Read the book yourself, and talk with your child about it. Did you like it? Read your favorite part or a section you found exciting, and ask your child to do the same.

4. Talk with your child about how this book compares with others he or she has read recently.

5. Help your child write a short summary of the book as a book-jacket blurb or advertisement. Write it for him or her, if necessary. A few sentences are all that are required. The summary can be illustrated, too, with drawings by *both* of you or with pictures that you cut out together from a magazine or newspaper to go along with the story.

6. Talk with your child about how the book made him or her feel. You might play a word-association game while you are busy in the kitchen, yard, or garage. Vary the list for the age level of the child. Tell your child:

   "I'm going to say a word and then you tell me if any part of the book you read made you feel that way."

Happy	Excited	Frustrated
Sad	Surprised	Sympathetic
Mad	Afraid	Confused

7. For books that involve building or making something, help your child assemble the necessary materials and then follow directions for completing the task.

8. Reward your child with a special treat (such as a favorite food or doing something together) for completing a book.

RESOURCES

Allington, R. (1991). The legacy of "slow it down and make it more concrete." In J. Zutell & S. McCormick (Eds.), *Learner factors/teacher factors; Issues in literacy research and instruction*. Fortieth Yearbook of the National Reading Conference (pp. 19–29). Chicago: National Reading Conference.

This article reviews the literature on how a single view of individual difference has dominated our school practices, especially in providing instruction for children who do not succeed in reading.

Baumann, J. F., & Heubach, K. M. (1996). Do basal readers deskill teachers? A national survey of educators' use and opinions of basals. *The Elementary School Journal, 96,* 511–526.

The authors' argument, based on an extensive survey, is that, basal readers rather than being a negative force, offer ways to empower teachers. Good review of this whole issue, from many points of view.

Flood, J., Lapp, D., Flood, S., & Nagel, G. (1992). Am I allowed to group? Using flexible patterns for effective instruction. *The Reading Teacher, 45,* 608–616.

Many classroom-based suggestions for using flexible grouping patterns are presented in this article.

Wepner, S. B., & Feeley, J. T. (1993). *Moving forward with literature: Basals, books, and beyond.* New York: Macmillan.

Chapter 2 presents a thorough analysis of leading basals and some concerns and considerations about using basals.

REFERENCES

Bardsley, D., & Foley, D. (1997). Readers' theatre. In *Guidebook for America Reads tutors* (available from the Office of Professional Field Experiences, College of Education, Arizona State University, Tempe, AZ 85207-1111).

Baumann, J. F., & Heubach, K. M. (1996). Do basal readers deskill teachers? A national survey of educators' use and opinions of basals. *The Elementary School Journal, 96,* 511–526.

Cleland, J. (n.d.). *Flexible grouping.* Lexington, MA: D.C. Heath.

Greene, F. P. (1970). *Radio reading.* Unpublished manuscript, Syracuse University.

Greene, F. P. (1979). Radio reading. In C. Pennock (Ed.), *Reading comprehension at four linguistic levels* (pp. 104–107). Newark, DE: International Reading Association.

Manzo, A. V. (1969). The ReQuest procedure. *Journal of Reading, 13,* 123–126.

Osborn, J. (1981). *The purposes, uses, and contents of workbooks and some guidelines for teachers and publishers* (Reading Education Report No. 27). Urbana, IL: University of Illinois, Center for the Study of Reading.

Osborn, J., & Decker, K. (1990). *Ancillary materials: What's out there?* (Tech. Rep. No. 507). Urbana, IL: University of Illinois, Center for the Study of Reading.

Searfoss, L. W. (1975). Radio reading. *The Reading Teacher, 29,* 295–296.

Spiegel, D. L. (1981). Six alternatives to the directed reading activity. *The Reading Teacher, 34,* 914–920.

Stauffer, R. (1969). *Direct reading maturity as a cognitive process.* New York: Harper & Row.

CHAPTER

5 Balanced Literacy Instruction

INTRODUCTION

Throughout most of the 20th century, a debate has raged regarding the best way to teach reading. From the 1920s, with the progressive education movement, through the 1990s, with the whole language movement, one thing has remained constant: Reading educators cannot agree on how to teach reading. The plethora of research conducted in the 20th century has led to some important conclusions about reading instruction:

1. There is no one best method for teaching reading.
2. Research supports conflicting views.

As we begin the 21st century, the buzz phrase for reading instruction is *well-balanced literacy,* a term about which we can anticipate controversy: How do you define balance? Who defines balance? How do we create a balanced, multifaceted, and sound reading program? To begin with, it is of utmost importance, that we be clear on our conception of balance. While for some, balance may conjure up a picture of a scale with equal weights on both sides, we think that a metaphor provided by P. David Pearson is more appropriate (personal communication, September 9, 1999). He suggested that balance in reading instruction is similar to the ecological balance in nature. It reflects not merely an evening of the score, but rather an ensemble of skills, strategies, processes, and practices that work synergistically to provide a full and rich curriculum for all students. This conception moves beyond the assumption that well-balanced literacy can be achieved through a random eclectic combination of instructional approaches. Balance requires thoughtful eclecticism (Duffy & Hoffman, 1999), encompassing consideration of the learner and the learning environment.

GRAPHIC ORGANIZER

This graphic organizer summarizes the structure of Chapter 5:

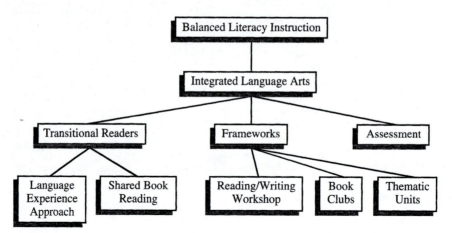

OBJECTIVES

When you finish this chapter, you should be able to understand and discuss each of these statements:

1. Reading instruction must be based on children's ability to use their language, interests, and backgrounds of experience.
2. Children expect reading instruction to give them the power to communicate.
3. Integrating reading instruction with instruction in other language arts is a natural and desirable way to create balance.
4. Trade books and other forms of print should drive reading and writing instruction.
5. Writing plays a major role in reading instruction.

Defining Balanced Literacy Instruction

The following principles of balanced literacy instruction were compiled from the work of many researchers and scholars who have written in this area:

1. Student ownership is critical to the learning process (Au & Carroll, 1997). Students need to feel that literacy learning is not something being done to them, but a reflection of their needs and interests that empowers them as learners.
2. Authenticity is key to literacy learning (Pearson, 1996). Students need opportunities to read and write for real purposes. They learn to become literate through the real literacy events in which they participate.
3. Literacy learning is best accomplished through a thoughtfully planned program (Strickland, 1998) in which teachers are viewed as informed decision makers (Freppon & Dahl, 1998; Spiegel, 1998). Teachers need to plan balanced instruction by implementing the curriculum in ways meaningful to their students. Because each group of students one teaches is different, no single model for literacy instruction will suffice. Teachers must make instructional decisions based on their knowledge of best practice and the dynamics of the group they are teaching.
4. Literacy instruction should take place in the context of a community (Pearson, 1996)—that is, with teachers and students working together to create a community where literacy can develop.

As you will recall, Chapter 2 suggested ways to create a community of literacy learners. This chapter will illustrate how to make that community flourish through a well-balanced literacy program.

Process Guide 5.1

To help you shape and state your own beliefs about balanced literacy instruction, reread the four principles of balanced literacy instruction and generate a list of words or phrases that you feel describe balanced literacy. Share your list with others in the class.

Rationale for an Integrated Language Arts Curriculum

Having defined well-balanced literacy instruction and listed our beliefs, we can now move to presenting a curriculum for making balanced literacy come alive in classrooms. A curriculum is not simply a paper-and-pencil exercise or a list of classroom activities with accompanying objectives. It is an expression of beliefs.

Integrated language arts is a term that respects the attempts of numerous pioneers (such as Dorris May Lee, Roach Van Allen, and Jeannette Veatch) to view language learning and teaching holistically. Much of what we know today builds on their efforts. *An integrated language arts curriculum translates beliefs about well-balanced literacy instruction into practice.* It is a curriculum based on creating a community of literacy learners who read and write for authentic purposes. As an integrated curriculum, it uses organizing themes. Generating these themes from students' interests is central to developing their sense of ownership in learning. Through the integration of language and content, this curriculum accelerates children's language growth, and their knowledge of content expands simultaneously. An integrated language arts curriculum places the teacher in the position of an informed decision maker who plans the instruction.

Starting a Journey of Change

If you are a beginning teacher, you may remember being taught to read and write by means of skills-based approaches and commercial materials. If you are an experienced teacher, you probably began your teaching career using the same skills-based approaches. Although the commercial materials have been updated, the basics of instruction remained constant for you as a learner and as a teacher. Changing to an integrated language arts curriculum means moving from a curriculum dominated by textbooks to one based on the choices and interests of you and your students. This shift to a student-centered curriculum is not always easy. Although you may be concerned about planning day-to-day activities and getting from Monday to Friday each week with new ideas and new teaching strategies flying through your head, we want you to take a few moments to gain some perspective. Remember the old saying "You can't see the forest for the trees"? Step back, and let's discuss change and how to begin your journey. Here are some suggestions for changing your existing views and practices about helping children learn to read.

Consider Yourself in Good Company

Many new and experienced teachers in schools all over this country are trying to implement an integrated language arts approach. They begin their journey with all sorts of beliefs about reading instruction. We find teachers at every point on a continuum from traditional, textbook-bound teachers to those who have already made giant strides toward an integrated curriculum.

Be Prepared for the Tension That Comes with Change

Knowing the sources of tension can sometimes make change easier. Pace (1992) identifies three sources of tension:

> Old beliefs clash with new ones, requiring us to rethink how children learn and language is acquired.
>
> New curriculum being implemented clashes with old curriculum.

Teachers engaged in change may find some teachers supportive and other teachers in the same school hostile.

Learn to Find Your Own Literate Voice

Routman (1991, p. 27) lists the stages she went through in changing her instructional approach:

> I can't do this. It's too hard, and I don't know enough.
> Maybe if I find out about it, it's possible.
> I'll do exactly what the experts say.
> I'll adapt the experts' work to my own contexts.
> I trust myself as an observer-teacher-learner-evaluator.

Routman also adds some wise words of advice: Allow time for change, trust yourself, be willing to give up some control of the classroom, and finally, don't view the basal reader as the enemy. In the hands of some teachers, even wonderful trade books can become unproductive if used without purpose or choice and if reading is followed by workbook-type exercises that do not relate to what has been read. Conversely, some teachers have made good use of basal readers in well-balanced literacy instruction.

As teachers begin to integrate language instruction, they will need to move away from dependence on commercial materials, including basal readers. Some advocates of a holistic or integrated language arts approach reject the use of any commercial materials, while others—ourselves included—suggest that teachers place them in perspective by lessening dependence on them. We favor allowing teachers to determine the nature and extent of what they will use to teach reading—that is, empowering them with the right to choose what materials they believe are right for their children each school year. Although this view may not satisfy those who wish to completely reject commercial materials, we believe it offers teachers self-selection in how to teach reading. Self-selection recognizes and considers the teachers' rights, individual personalities, and varied levels of understanding about the reading process and the teaching of reading.

Look for Allies

Find another teacher or, preferably, a small group of teachers who are also on a journey of change. Meet, talk, discuss, share, go to workshops and conferences together, and read, read, read all you can about balanced literacy and integrated language arts. In many areas of the country, teacher support groups meet regularly to offer the kind of support and interaction you will need. Isolation is the enemy of change; find a friend or two, and work together.

Write, Write, Write about Change

Sit quietly and reflect on what worked, what did not, and how you would do it next time. Record these thoughts in a personal log, journal, or diary of your journey. Do this at the end of each school day at first and weekly later on when your journey is underway. Share these written thoughts with others, and you will all learn from each other. There is something helpful and calming in reflecting, writing, and planning before going on to the next stage of your journey.

Find a Focus

It can seem as though you will never read enough to know all that you think you need to know. Someone will always find a book or article you have not read. We suggest that you begin by studying one textbook or article and focus on implementing the ideas in it in your classroom over time. A first-grade teacher selected Routman's book entitled *Transitions* (1988) and literally made the book come alive from the beginning of school until the children returned from vacation after New Year's. She had four months to try out Routman's ideas, reflect on them, share them, and revise them until they were either accepted as part of her classroom curriculum or rejected as not appropriate. If you are a bit nervous about committing that much time to one source, select a shorter journal article and follow the same process.

This single focus suggestion has been mentioned to us by a number of teachers who have found it successful. It does require some risks (including the willingness to trust yourself), as well as the support of administrators, who must not worry about whether everything in the old, printed district curriculum is being covered while the new one unfolds in your room. Listed in the Resources section of this chapter are some sources teachers have found useful; the list is a sampling to get you started.

Get Out of the Building and Out of Town Whenever Possible

There is something very exciting about attending a conference or workshop and hearing new voices talk about integrated language arts. New voices stimulate new thinking and help recast old ideas into new formats. When possible, attend, enjoy, and share your reactions with other teachers.

Implementing an Integrated Language Arts Curriculum

You may want to review Chapter 2 on creating a print-rich classroom environment before you read the rest of this chapter, which will be devoted to our suggestions for organizing, implementing, and evaluating an integrated language arts curriculum. Integrated language arts instruction and a literate classroom environment evolve together. There are many ways to organize the elements of an integrated language arts curriculum. We suggest that you keep it simple at first, gradually refining your organization as you become more informed and confident. Some overall scheme is necessary—one that you can keep in mind as you make decisions to add activities from your text and journal reading. We recommend that you incorporate the following elements as you translate beliefs into curriculum:

- A variety of settings for language learning and practice, including individual, paired, small group, and whole group
- All types of print found in and out of school, from literature to content materials to newspapers—any form of print available for the audience
- Oral language (speaking and listening), integrated with the reading and writing activities. (Children should talk about what they read and write, together and with other audiences.)
- Organizing themes for individual and group thematic units from literature and across the curriculum (social studies, science, arts, and music)
- Direct instruction through teacher modeling and demonstrations of reading and writing
- Sharing of language within the classroom and with a wider audience outside of the classroom. (For example, if a child writes a letter, it should be mailed.)
- Opportunities for you, the teacher, to read and write and grow

Now that we have explored the foundations of an integrated approach to literacy instruction and the aspects of change to consider, we are ready to look at ways to implement this type of instruction in the classroom. First we will discuss strategies for transitional readers. Then we will consider three frameworks for

New voices stimulate new thinking and help recast old ideas into new formats.

organizing balanced literacy. Finally, we will discuss various assessment techniques that can be used within each of these frameworks, to make assessment a regular part of day-to-day instruction.

Strategies for Transitional Readers

Chapter 3 focused on early literacy and the many discoveries children make about print. Teachers can build on this foundation by planning instruction that helps children transition into conventional reading. The following two strategies—the language experience approach and shared book reading—are ideal for children at this level. Later in this chapter you will see how these strategies can be integrated into each of the three frameworks for reading instruction.

Language Experience Approach

Hall (1981) calls the association of meaning with print through children's personally dictated stories and messages the key to helping children view reading as a communication tool. She outlined the characteristics of the language experience approach (LEA) in this manner:

Use of whole language. Children's talk presents their whole ideas, expressed naturally and meaningfully. In this approach, there is no attempt to simplify the vocabulary level or sentence length for children.

Pupil-composed materials. The basis for reading materials used in LEA is the talk that children generate and have written down for them (or later write for themselves).

Interrelationship of language processes. LEA makes use of oral language and writing an integral part of learning to read.

Language experience stories and charts provide children with the opportunity to utilize their own experiences and vocabulary as the basis for learning to read. Children dictate stories or messages that are recorded for them in print and then used for reading. It is through language experience that children begin an intensive use of printed language. Not only do they expand their listening, speaking, reading, and writing vocabularies, but they also begin to develop an awareness of common vocabulary and of the high-frequency function words, such as *the, said,* and *does,* that are the glue words of our language. Additionally, language experience provides children with models of pronunciation and spelling and the variety of meanings a word may take in different contexts.

The basic steps in completing a language experience story or chart are listed in sequence below.

1. *Getting started.* Motivate the child to talk by asking about a recent experience you are aware of or have provided. It is of the utmost importance that the experience be real, not vicarious. Unless the experience has sense power—that is, involves nearly all of the child's senses—the experience is not real to the child. The child's words serve as an excellent source of motivating experiences, since these words represent experiences that are real to the child. Field trips, classroom visitations, and experiences at home can be rich sources of dictation.

2. *Writing the story or message.* Record the child's story or message exactly the way it is said to you. You are not an editor at this point, only a secretary. With you as secretary, ownership of the story or chart rests with the child; if you are an editor, ownership begins to shift away from the child and onto you as teacher (recorder).

3. *Reading the story or chart.* After it is written, read the story or chart with the child. First read it back to the child to make sure that what was recorded is exactly what the child wanted to say. Once that has been confirmed, read the story or chart with the child several times, so that the child can become familiar with the newly dictated words. Teacher and child may alternate sentences, or each may take a turn reading the entire story or chart.

4. *Independent activity.* Provide immediate reinforcement after the rereading so that the words gradually become part of the child's reading vocabulary. There are numerous activities that children can do independently:

> Read the story or chart to a friend.
> Illustrate it.
> Think of a good title or two.
> Prepare to read it to the class.
> Tape record the story or message.

Children can dictate stories, which then can be recorded for them in print.

5. *Reviewing.* Provide opportunities for reinforcement later in the day or the next day. You, an aide, an older student, or a volunteer should review the story or chart with the child. A *few* words the *child* wants to learn and is having difficulty with can be placed on index cards to form a word bank. Only two or three really special words should be selected for writing on cards. Both the unknown word and the whole phrase or sentence from the story or chart should be included on the card, to avoid isolating words and to keep the reading situation as natural as possible. These word cards can then be used as the core of several vocabulary development exercises. The following are examples of such exercises:

> Look for these words in other forms of print, such as newspapers and magazines; circle or cut out the words and paste them onto a large piece of paper.
>
> Classify words that have something in common, such as names, actions, objects, animals, things to eat or wear, or words that begin or end alike.
>
> Study the words in a paired review situation. Two children could pair up together to review their words.

As a culminating activity, the child may draw a picture to accompany the story or chart. The illustrated story then becomes a part of an individual collection of stories.

A cautionary note is in order about the expectations you may have about how many words children dictate. For many children, a "story" may be one line or two at first. Later, as you read to them and they encounter models in the form of picture books with increasingly more print, their stories will become longer. Some children, however, will always be noted for brief stories or messages, as fits their communication style. Some children's stories will vary in length, depending on the intensity of the experience they are relating. Finally, the experiences children dictate may vary in type or style and may include stories, messages, directions, poems, jokes, and other literary forms. From the first dictation opportunities, such diversity should be encouraged by using opening statements that avoid biasing the children's dictation style. You might try "Can you tell me about...?" rather than "Tell me a *story* about...." The authors have observed that children model their dictation style after a book that has recently been read to them and that relates to some experience they have had. For example, Carlos, a first grader, dictated a story (see Figure 5.1) about an experience he had that was similar to those encountered in a children's book about a day that does not go well at all: *Alexander and the Terrible, Horrible, No Good, Very Bad Day*, by Judith Viorst (1972).

You will discover many variations of the basic steps in the language experience approach as you read the sources we suggest. One common variation that also allows teachers to expand the amount of time devoted to LEA is to use group-experience charts or stories. Small groups of children or the entire class can dictate a message, set of directions, or story to the teacher, based on a common experience or need. The teacher will need to be more of an editor in a group-dictation setting, since many children will be contributing to the dictation.

Me and the Terrible, No Good,
Dirty Rotten Day
by Carlos

I went to bed with bubble gum in my mouth and when
I woke up it was in my hair. My sweater fell in the sink with
running water and Kevin got a toy in his cereal box and I didn't
get anything. So, I knew it was going to be a terrible, no-good,
dirty rotten day!

FIGURE 5.1 Carlos's Language Experience Story

The steps to completing a group-experience dictation are as follows:

1. Children have a common experience or need. Holidays, field trips, the daily calendar, community events, class or school regulations, and directions for an experiment or art project are only a few of many subjects that can be the focal point of a group dictation.
2. Children discuss the experience with the teacher and clarify their ideas.
3. The teacher makes rough notes on a chalkboard or chart paper during the discussion.
4. A second draft of the dictation is made, with children *and* teacher molding the final form and word choice.
5. The children and teacher reread the chart as a whole.
6. The chart is displayed for rereading later and may be filed with other charts for future reference and review. For example, charts for holiday stories can be grouped into a class booklet, or the exploits of classroom pets can be recorded and kept together.

After reading about the language experience method, you must be thinking how nice it would be to have another set of helping hands in the classroom. You're absolutely right! Now where do you get this extra set of hands? Children in the upper grades can volunteer to work with you for short periods of time, and parent volunteers can be regularly scheduled to work with your class. Some schools are now realizing the wealth of talent in our seniors, especially grandparents, and are getting them involved in school volunteer work. They are a rich resource, and you should actively pursue using them.

Shared Book Reading

In addition to LEA, shared book reading is another approach that can be used with beginning readers. Shared book reading, as you might recall from Chapter 2, is based on the parent-child lap reading experience. This approach is thought to simulate, with the learning-to-read process, the natural way that children learn spoken language. Through shared book reading, children experience reading in a positive and relaxed atmosphere. Big books are used to allow a large group of children to reap the benefits of one-on-one reading.

1. Begin by reading the big book to the group. Remember to allow interaction during this reading. When children ask questions or make comments as you read, they build their comprehension abilities so as to better understand the test; this is an important aspect of scaffolding the reading experience.
2. Read the book a second time, and ask the children to join in on the reading. During this reading, you will want to model directionality by pointing to the words as you read. This is also a good time to discuss the author, illustrator, and parts of the book.
3. Provide the children with copies (little books) of the same story. Children may read these independently or buddy read.
4. Carry out a brief learning activity based on the needs of the children. There are a variety of activities you can do; for example, you may want to focus children's attention on particular words or letter/sound relationships.
5. Plan an extension activity for the story. There are many ways to extend the reading experience. Have children make their own big books, engage them in dramatic play based on the story, or have them respond artistically.

Shared book reading creates a comfortable atmosphere in which reading instruction can take place. Through the use of big books, children have opportunities to see the text as it is being read. For this reason, there are some important considerations in selecting big books:

1. *Choose books that are predictable.* This will enable children to build comprehension strategies.
2. *Choose books that are repetitive.* This will enable children to develop sight vocabulary as they continue to see similar words in the text.
3. *Choose books that have only a limited amount of text on each page.* This will enable the children to stay focused on the text. If a big book has too much

text on each page, it becomes nothing more than a sea of words to an emergent reader.

Both shared book reading and LEA provide sound integrated instruction for beginning readers. Through either approach, children are encouraged to make a successful transition into conventional reading.

Frameworks for Organizing Balanced Literacy

Three frameworks that we believe can be used effectively as comprehensive approaches to integrated literacy instruction are the reading/writing workshop, the Book Club, and the thematic unit. We have highlighted these particular frameworks for two reasons. First, they are in line with our conception of well-balanced literacy. That is, within each framework, literacy is not viewed as the sum of its parts; instead, it is viewed as holistic and complex. Second, they are comprehensive and integrated approaches to literacy instruction.

Reading/Writing Workshop

The reading/writing workshop, based on the work of Nancy Atwell (1987, 1998), is a way of organizing reading instruction that truly promotes balanced literacy. First, the workshop affords children both time to read and time to write and allows them to choose their materials. Second, through the use of mini-lessons, teachers can focus on selected skills and strategies based on the needs of their students. Third, small and large group discussions nurture a thriving community of literacy learners. Generally, a workshop contains the following elements:

1. Opening share time (5–10 minutes)
2. Mini-lesson (10–15 minutes)
3. Self-selected reading/writing and response (30–60 minutes)
4. Closing share time (10–15 minutes)

Opening Share Time.   Opening share time provides an opportunity for the teacher to set the mood for the workshop, by reading to the students or giving a book talk. When the teacher comes across a new book she or he wants the children to read, a book talk is a good way to promote it. The teacher might read a passage from the book or show illustrations. It is important to make sure the book is then left available for those students whose interest was piqued.

Mini-Lesson.   The mini-lesson is the second part of the workshop. This lesson is done with the whole group. At the beginning of the year, mini-lessons often center on workshop procedures (e.g., selecting books, responding to literature). As the year progresses, mini-lessons become a time to teach skills and strategies. It is important, however, that the ideas for the mini-lessons be based on the needs of the students.

Self-Selected Reading/Writing and Response.   The next part, self-selected reading/writing and response, is the heart of the workshop. Atwell has suggested many rules for students to follow during this time period. We have condensed that list into two:

1. You must be reading or writing.
2. You may not be working on homework or assignments for another class/subject.

What is most important is that the children read or write something of their choice. Listed below are some suggestions that can help children decide how to respond to what they have read.

1. Write in your response journal.
2. Prepare to read part or all of your selection aloud.
3. Plan for and rehearse telling an exciting, interesting, or funny part of a reading.
4. Find and read another book by the same author or about the same topic.
5. After reading two or more books about the same topic or by the same author, write a short paragraph telling why you liked them or what you learned from all of them.

Drawing, painting, or making a clay model gives children a chance to use what they read.

6. Tape record an exciting or interesting part of the book.
7. Prepare a demonstration for the class of something you learned to make or do.
8. Develop a short skit for others, working with someone else who has read the same book.
9. Plan a way to *sell* this book to someone else in your class who you think might enjoy it.
10. Form a panel of classmates who have read similar books or who have read information about the same topic. Write some questions for the panel to discuss.
11. Find a review of the book by a critic in the library, read it, and then write your own reaction to the review.
12. Make a list of things from what you read that you still do not believe happened or are true. Support your doubts!
13. Pretend that you are the author of the book and your fans ask you to write a sequel. Tell, briefly, what your book would contain.
14. Use reference books from the library to find out more about the author or illustrator.

While the class is engaged in self-selected reading/writing and response, the teacher can hold reading and writing conferences with individual children.

Individual Reading Conferences. To be certain that individual reading conferences are worthwhile for both child and teacher, some simple management steps are necessary. First, children should volunteer for conferences when *they* are ready. Second, a sign-up procedure for daily appointments is useful. The teacher can list times available each day on the chalkboard or a piece of chart paper and instruct children to sign their names or initials next to an available time. Third, children need guidance in how to prepare for a conference. A checklist can be posted with some questions the children should ask themselves before signing up for a conference. The difficulty of the questions can be adjusted to various grade levels; for beginning readers, the list can be regularly reviewed orally. Here are some questions that might be included:

What did I read? (Title, author)

Why did I read it? (Pleasure, report, or current events)

Can I tell the teacher about what I read in a few sentences? (Younger children might draw a picture or use an illustration from the selection to help in the telling; older children might jot down a few notes to help themselves.)

Are there some parts I still do not understand? (Note which pages.)

Are there some words I'm not sure of? (Write them down.)

What am I going to do now? (Share, select another book, or ask for help in getting another selection.)

We suggest using the *teacher's observation record form* to summarize the results of individual reading conferences. These records are an invaluable, cumulative source of information for evaluating children's reading skills, interests, and progress. Since the number of conferences that can be conducted with each child is somewhat limited during a grading period, careful records are important. You may have time for only one conference per child over several weeks. A simple form, similar to the one in Figure 5.2, can be developed to meet your needs, duplicated, and completed as part of each individual reading conference.

FIGURE 5.2   Teacher's Observational Record Form for Individualized Reading Conference

Child's Name: _____   Date: _____

Title and Author:_____

_____ Fiction   _____ Nonfiction

1. Reason child gave for choosing reading material_____

	Good	OK	Poor	Can't Tell
2. Comprehension of				
Central thought or theme	_____	_____	_____	_____
Plot (if story)	_____	_____	_____	_____
Details	_____	_____	_____	_____
Sequence	_____	_____	_____	_____
3. Critical thinking-through:				
Relates to other reading	_____	_____	_____	_____
Makes inferences, predictions	_____	_____	_____	_____
Evaluates accuracy	_____	_____	_____	_____
Has personal opinions	_____	_____	_____	_____

4. Did child seek help with words or ideas that were confusing?   _____ Yes   _____ No

(List words, ideas)

5. What will the child do with what has been read? (report, sharing activity) _____

_____

6. What will the child read next? _____

7. Estimate the child's overall reaction.

5	4	3	2	1
GREAT!		OK		UNINTERESTED

Estimated time for conference: _____ min.

Other notes:

Closing Share Time.   The final part of the workshop, closing share time, provides an opportunity for children to share their work. They may choose to read aloud a passage from the text they are reading or share the product from their reading response time. Because children will be working on different things and be at different places in their work, it is important to allow them to sign up to share when they are ready. Allowing multiple ways of sharing ensures that children have some ownership in how and what they choose to share.

Individual Writing Conferences.   Individual writing conferences can be scheduled or can occur informally for a specific reason. Tompkins (1990) advocates conferences in which the teacher serves as a listener and as a guide, demonstrating the writing strategies and skills needed by the child. She lists these types of writing conferences:

1. *On-the-spot conferences.* Often lasting less than a minute, these conferences occur when the teacher stops by a child's desk while he or she is writing to see how the writing is going.
2. *Prewriting conferences.* Teacher and child discuss plans for writing, including the nature of the topic, how to present ideas, and what resources the child may need.
3. *Drafting conferences.* Teacher and child work together on the trouble spots and discuss problems and solutions.
4. *Revising conferences.* Teacher and child meet with a small group of the child's peers, who give feedback on how the writing is progressing.
5. *Editing conferences.* Mechanics, spelling, grammar, and other conventions of language are the focus of these conferences.
6. *Instructional mini-lesson conferences.* A specific skill or two with which the child is having difficulty become the subject of a short lesson by the teacher (e.g., when to use exclamation points).
7. *Assessment conferences.* After the writing has been completed, teacher and child meet to reflect on it and to talk about future writing plans and goals.

Tompkins indicates that each of these conferences can also be conducted in a small-group setting. For some children, though, individual conferences will be more effective, especially for solving specific problems quickly. The Resources section of this chapter lists Tompkins's work on writing instruction, which is well worth reading.

Book Club

The Book Club, based on the work of McMahon and Raphael (1997), is like the reading/writing workshop in that it promotes the principles of balanced literacy instruction. In the Book Club approach, however, students read a common text in small literature groups. Through Book Club, children interact within communities and are afforded a level of choice in their reading; this puts the teacher in a key decision-making role. Book Club is grounded in the assumptions that (1) literacy learning is a social endeavor and (2) written and oral activities must be as authentic as the reading materials to which they are connected.

At first, Raphael and McMahon (1994) conceived of instruction as a separate component of Book Club. However, as they implemented and refined the approach, they found that instruction actually was embedded in all of its aspects.

Following are the four components of Book Club:

1. Community share
2. Book Club discussion
3. Reading
4. Writing

Community Share.   The community share time provides an opportunity for the teacher to meet with children in a whole-group setting. Community share can take place either before or after Book Club meetings. Before reading, this time is used to prepare the children for the upcoming text. After Book Club, the time is used to share ideas from different Book Clubs and to debate issues from the readings. During this time, teachers may model appropriate ways of responding to text and dialoguing about text.

Book Club Discussion.   During the Book Club discussion component, children meet in small groups to discuss the book or books they are reading. McMahon and Raphael (1997) conceived of this time as an opportunity for children to engage in discussions of issues important to them. They did not want this discussion to follow the norms of classroom discourse, with teacher-initiated questions followed by student response. However, open discussions do not always occur automatically. For example, Seely-Flint (in press) observed that fourth graders engaged in a group discussion positioned themselves and were positioned by others within the discussion, giving more power to some children's voices and silencing others. Thus, some facilitating and monitoring of these group discussions may be necessary. McMahon and Raphael (1997) also suggest that caution and consideration be exercised in selecting books. Books chosen for Book Club should be ones that are of interest to children and useful in instruction; additionally, they should represent diverse populations.

Reading.   During the reading component, children have the opportunity to read the text as well as be instructed in it. Teachers, again, must be thoughtful decision makers as they determine on how best to spend this time. We suggest that children be given the opportunity to read each day. The time allotted for reading can vary depending on the other instructional activities planned. Also, the method for reading—for example, silent reading, buddy reading, or reading aloud by the teacher—can vary. Instruction during this time often focuses on reading strategies and skills to improve independent reading abilities.

Writing.   Writing is the last component of the Book Club approach. McMahon and Raphael (1997) suggest that students keep response logs. At first, these logs can be based on ideas generated by the teacher—for example, wonderful words and character maps. As students become more proficient responders to text, though, they should begin to generate their own ideas for reading logs.

Book Club is a comprehensive yet flexible framework that affords children the experience of learning literacy through authentic engagement in texts and discussions. Instruction is embedded within all areas of Book Club. Although four components can be identified, they are not discrete elements—they build on one another.

Thematic Units

While reading/writing workshop and Book Club provide authentic means for integrating language arts, thematic units provide a means for integrating other subjects within the curriculum. The thematic unit approach to instruction is not new in education. However, it is being dusted off, revised, and given a language arts emphasis in current literature related to integrated language arts instruction. We recommend two types of units: (1) small-group or whole-group units and (2) individual inquiry or process units.

Small-Group and Whole-Group Units.   Small-group and whole-group thematic units were described in Chapter 3 as part of beginning reading instruction. They do have a wider use, though. Planned integration is much facilitated by use of thematic units built around science, social studies, and literature themes. We suggest you review the language unit on rainbows presented in Chapter 3. It is a good model for use in the primary grades. For older students, the sophistication of the unit topic increases and the types of activities broaden as well. For example, older students could use instant cameras to record images related to a topic. Videotapes can be made quite easily by students as part of a unit. Computers and desktop publishing further enhance and enrich units for older students. The key to using whole- and small-group units is to be certain that you include all kinds of books and other forms of print as part of the unit. Also, units do not have to be massive undertakings—they can last for a few days or for weeks.

Where do themes for units come from? How do you organize and manage a thematic unit? These sources of themes are suggested by Thompson (1991):

1. Let the children help you pick a theme. Use a suggestion box in your classroom on a regular basis.
2. Take a class survey of children's interests, role models, favorite foods, and out-of-school activities.
3. Review curriculum guides in language arts and content areas.
4. Observe what children talk about; consider favorite movies, news events, or holidays coming up.
5. Pick a subject you are interested in, too.

Thompson also suggests a simple four-phase plan for organizing thematic teaching, similar to plans suggested by other writers:

Phase I. Introduce the theme, and have children brainstorm ideas about it. Share a song, poem, or story related to the theme. Expand on the theme with a group activity based on the song, poem, or story.

Phase II. Read about the theme together and individually in all types of print. Share, and then respond to what has been read.

Phase III. Plan independent activities based on the theme.

Phase IV. Complete a whole-group project related to the theme.

Individual Inquiry and Process Units.   In individual inquiry or process units, children select a topic and explore it on their own, with guidance and encouragement as needed.

Inquiry units (D. W. Moore, 1985) allow students to independently study a topic of their choice. This is not a structured approach; rather, a cluster of informal procedures help students conduct independent investigations. Inquiry units are essentially the same as independent study or research reading. There are four basic steps:

1. *Identify topics.* Children begin an inquiry unit by identifying specific topics that they are interested in studying. Final topic choices are based mostly on the interest they have in learning more about a subject. In fact, exploring interests is the foundation of an inquiry unit, and elementary school children are interested in a great variety of topics. Following is a list of topics they frequently pursue through inquiry units:

Animals	Indians	Precious stones and metals
Bodies of water	Land formations	Prehistoric times
Body systems	Machines and tools	Seasons
Clothing	Middle Ages	Space
Diseases	Myths	Sports
Foods	Natural disasters	Superstitions
Foreign countries	Occupations	Transportation
Genealogy	Optical illusions	Weapons
Holidays	Plants	Weather

2. *Formulate research questions.* After identifying a topic or area of inquiry, children formulate questions. This task is often difficult, because they tend to ask questions that are either too general or too specific to be answered satisfactorily. Some children ask "What do we know about air?" while others ask "What molecules make up air?" The first question can never be answered, and the second can be answered with a quick look at an encyclopedia. The rule of thumb is to help children ask questions that will sustain about four weeks of inquiry and that can be answered convincingly. "What causes the wind to blow?" and "What were the worst storms in the United States?" are possible questions that would guide students through worthwhile inquiry projects.

3. *Locate references.* The next step is to locate materials and people to provide answers to questions. Typical reference books are encyclopedias, periodicals, library trade books, almanacs, and textbooks. Along with these traditional references, children can direct their inquiries to firsthand sources of information. For instance, they can write directly to a state's Chamber of Commerce for informational brochures as part of a report on an individual state; children who are studying transportation can contact bus, train, and airplane agencies for information. Not only can they rely on written information, but they also can conduct personal interviews with authorities in their field of inquiry. This activity lends a touch of reality to investigations. Children will need to identify whom they will interview, set up a meeting time, prepare interview questions, conduct the interview, and then summarize what they have learned. The authorities can be parents, relatives, teachers, and professionals in the community. It is important to note that children require help in locating the sources described here and in extracting and organizing the relevant information. Ensuring that the original research questions are clearcut and manageable does much to help them conduct these research activities.

4. *Share results.* As children identify inquiry topics, ask questions, and begin gathering explanatory information, they also are determining how they will share the results of their inquiry. Among ways to share are written compositions, oral reports, demonstrations, performances, and artistic or functional constructions. For instance, if children focused their inquiry on how air disturbances caused rainstorms, then they could share what they learn by submitting a report, performing an experiment before a group, or designing a poster. Of course, children also can combine these formats in a multitude of ways.

After an appropriate length of time, children share the results of their inquiry. The sharing is best done before groups, rather than only with the teacher, because children then learn what their classmates have taken the time to discover. The sharing sessions work best when they are staggered throughout class meetings. Sitting through an entire week of presentations becomes as tedious as sitting through a whole week of any other single activity.

In process units, children investigate their world by learning to perform a particular process. A process is a way of doing something; it is a series of actions or operations that people learn to do. For instance, children can draw, so *drawing* is a process; students can invent, so *inventing* is a process. Although children might learn about drawing and inventing by reading biographies of people like Michelangelo and Edison, process units call for them to actually draw or to actually invent. Like inquiry units, process units are extremely worthwhile for enrichment activities. Indeed, the two types often merge, so that children learn about a process while they are learning how to do it.

Making maps is a popular process unit. After children become familiar with surveying an area and representing it to scale on a piece of paper, they can produce their own maps. Locations such as children's houses, neighborhoods, cities, countries, and states can then be mapped out. Drama is another process. Children enjoy puppetry, pantomime, readers' theatre, and plays, so they can be guided in that direction. Pantomime might be performed to act out proverbs (e.g., "The early bird gets the worm"), titles of books and movies (as in charades), and figurative language (e.g., "strong as an ox").

Process Guide 5.2

Thematic units can use as an organizing theme literature or topics from content areas such as social studies and science. In pairs or small groups, investigate whether college methods texts in these content areas advocate a thematic approach. Are their suggestions for unit teaching, if offered, similar to or different from those presented in this chapter?

Informal Assessment

Assessment is a key component of all reading frameworks. As stated in Chapter 1, assessment guides instruction. The assessment techniques presented here can be adapted to fit all the reading frameworks and approaches discussed in this chapter. These techniques are means for tracking and documenting children's progress throughout the year. In addition, they are geared to providing information that is useful in planning instruction.

Informal Reading Inventories

The informal reading inventory (IRI), a set of graded passages and accompanying questions, is used to estimate children's oral and silent reading abilities. In the hands of a skilled examiner, the IRI is one of the best diagnostic instruments available. The major advantage of the IRI is that it enables the examiner to observe a child in the act of reading. Specifically, it yields information about both word recognition and comprehension that is not readily provided by standardized group tests. In addition to supplying valuable quantitative data, the IRI offers the opportunity to examine qualitative aspects of a child's performance. For example, behaviors such as a slow reading rate and word-by-word reading may be important indicators of difficulty. Also, by analyzing the types of errors the child makes when reading orally, the teacher gets a better insight into the strategies being used to interpret text.

Essentially there are three different types of IRIs. Some IRIs are made by the teacher, using regular classroom reading material. Although teacher-made IRIs are tied directly to the curriculum (a very desirable test characteristic), they are extremely time-consuming and difficult to construct. Since administrations of teacher-made IRIs tend to be limited, the appropriateness of the questions and the dependability of the instrument are hard to determine. A second type of IRI is provided with certain basal readers. These IRIs are used to place children in the appropriate level of the series. Sometimes this process will involve students who are new to the school; at other times students already in the system will be reevaluated. A third type of IRI is basically identical in format to the teacher-made and basal reader varieties; however, it has the advantage of having been normed. These standardized IRIs are generally more carefully constructed than the other two types. Most have been conceived and/or analyzed by noted reading professionals who are well versed in the area of measurement. The readability of each passage in these instruments has been thoroughly assessed both by conventional readability formulas and by field testing. Poorly written passages and questions are either revised or discarded and replaced with new ones having superior measurement characteristics. Because standardized IRIs have undergone rigorous examination, they tend to be of greater validity and reliability than the teacher-made or basal reader types. The primary question to ask before administering the standardized IRI is "How well do the passages represent the types of reading materials that children will encounter during the course of the year?"

Administering the Informal Reading Inventory.   Instructions for administering and interpreting an IRI will vary from instrument to instrument. For this reason, a generic description of the process will be presented. Although the guidelines are usually quite similar, the teacher will have to become thoroughly familiar with each IRI before attempting to administer it.

The basic informal reading inventory consists of a set of graded word lists, a book of reading passages for the student, and an examiner's recording booklet. The first step in administering the IRI is to have the child read orally from the word lists. This will allow the examiner to get a good idea of where to begin testing on the passages. Children should start with a list for a level that is two years below their current grade placement. If performance is satisfactory (usually 75 percent or better), they go on to the next higher lists until fewer than 75 percent of the words are recognized. If performance is unsatisfactory after the first list, the examiner drops to lower levels until 100 percent of the words are known. Many IRI manuals suggest that passage testing begin at the highest grade level at which 100 percent of the words on the list are correctly identified. This guideline should allow children to be successful on the first passage that they try.

It is usually recommended that the child read orally first. As the child reads, the examiner records any deviations from the text (errors) in the examiner's booklet. The booklet contains copies of the passages that are identical to those in the student's version. In the examiner's booklet, extra space is provided between lines to make it easier to mark the errors.

There are many types of errors, including reversals, omissions, additions, repetitions, mispronunciations, substitutions, and hesitations. The marking of oral reading errors is illustrated in Figure 5.3. Again, be sure to check each individual IRI to see which of these errors are counted toward the word recognition criterion.

When the child has completed the oral reading, comprehension questions are posed by the examiner. For the child to meet the instructional criterion, word recognition must exceed 95 percent (less than 1 error in every 20 words of text) *and*

FIGURE 5.3   Marking of Oral Reading Errors

Type of Error	Symbol
	Text: Mary saw a girl reading in the library.
Reversal	Mary saw a girl reading in the library.
	"Mary was a girl reading in the library."
Omission	Mary saw a girl reading in the library.
	"Mary saw a girl in the library."
Addition	Mary saw a girl reading in the library.
	"Mary saw a pretty girl reading in the library."
Repetition	Mary saw a girl reading in the library.
	"Mary saw a girl a girl reading in the library."
Mispronunciation or substitution	Mary saw a girl reading in the library.
	"Mary saw a girl reaching in the library."
Hesitation	Mary saw a girl reading in the library.
	"Mary saw a girl reading in the...library."
Word pronounced by examiner	Mary saw a girl reading in the library.
	"Mary saw a girl reading in the (5 seconds)..."
Self-correction	Mary saw a girl reading in the library.
	"Mary saw a grill a girl reading in the library."
Improper phrasing	Mary saw a / girl reading in the / library.
	"Mary saw a—girl reading in the—library."

comprehension performance must be 70 percent or better. Like the word lists, oral testing is continued until both independence (99 percent word recognition and 90 percent comprehension) and frustration (less than 90 percent word recognition or 50 percent comprehension) are achieved. Silent reading follows the same procedure, except that the only criterion considered is comprehension. Usually the examiner will alternate between oral and silent reading passages, trying to establish all three reading levels (independent, instructional, and frustration) for both oral and silent reading. In some cases, students will not score at all three levels. Young children or extremely poor readers may not obtain an independent level, and proficient readers might cover all levels of the IRI without reaching frustration. Other children will score at the independent level on one passage and at the frustration level on the next higher one. If this occurs, the instructional level is estimated to be at the midpoint between the two levels.

Process Guide 5.3

Examine the sample IRI passage in Figure 5.4. It has already been marked for a child's oral reading and responses to comprehension questions. Determine the child's word recognition and comprehension levels.

Determining Functional Reading Levels.   The IRI enables the teacher to determine how well children read. This information will aid in the selection of instructional materials. It also indicates what kinds of material can be given to children to read on their own and which materials may be too difficult.

FIGURE 5.4   A Sample IRI Passage—Grade 1

Plant Spiders

There are all kinds of spiders.

This black and ~~green~~ *gray* one is (called) a plant spider.

A plant spider has *very* small feet.
              ∧

All spiders have small feet.

Plant spiders live in nests.

They ~~soon~~ *shortly* learn to hunt for food and build new nests.

Comprehension Check

(Fact) **1.**   Is there more then one kind of spider? *Yes—many kinds* +

(Fact) **2.**   What two things do plant spiders quickly learn? *to hunt for food & build nests* +

(Fact) **3.**   What color was the spider in the story? *black & gray* ½

(Fact) **4.**   What size feet does a spider have? *little feet* +

(Inference) **5.**   At what time of year do we see more spiders? *in the springtime* +

Scoring Guide

Word Recognition Errors		Comprehension Errors	
Independent	0	Independent	0–1
Instructional	1–2	Instructional	1½–2
Frustration	4+	Frustration	2½+

Traditionally, the IRI is believed to yield three levels of reading performance: the independent level, the instructional level, and the frustration level. If passages are read aloud to the child, the inventory will also generate a capacity, or listening, level. These levels are briefly defined below.

Independent level. Achieved when the child reads with at least 99 percent word recognition and 90 percent comprehension. At this level, the child reads fluently with expression, and there are no signs of anxiety. Children should receive recreational reading materials that are written at this level of difficulty.

Instructional level. The highest level at which the child reads with at least 95 percent word recognition and 70 percent comprehension. It is expected that children can read materials of this difficulty with teacher assistance. Because this level is the focal point of instruction, its determination is most important. At this level, materials should challenge children without frustrating them.

Frustration level. The level at which reading is simply too difficult for the child. Word recognition accuracy is 90 percent or below and comprehension falls under 50 percent. Reading tends to be word by word, several errors are made, and the child exhibits signs of tension and apprehension.

Capacity level. A measure of the child's instructional listening level. It is the highest level at which 70 percent or more comprehension is achieved on passages that have been read aloud to the child. This level is assumed to represent the child's reading potential. By comparing the capacity level with oral and silent instructional levels, it can be determined whether a child is performing below what might be reasonably expected.

It is more meaningful to think of the instructional level as a range rather than as a fixed point. For example, take the performance of George, a fourth grader, on the oral reading passages in an IRI:

Passage	Word Recognition	Comprehension	Level
Second grade	100%	90%	Independent
Third grade	96%	90%	Instructional
Fourth grade	95%	70%	Instructional
Fifth grade	92%	60%	Frustration (Borderline)
Sixth grade	88%	40%	Frustration

Notice that George has scored at the instructional level for both the third-grade and the fourth-grade passages. As a result, it would be appropriate to supply him with materials at both levels of difficulty. Although his word recognition has slipped below the criterion for independent reading at the third-grade level, his comprehension remains high. George should be able to read third-grade material with a minimum of teacher aid.

For George, fourth-grade material is exactly at the traditional instructional level. He should be able to function nicely with materials at this level of difficulty, provided the teacher follows the directed reading lesson format. As long as conceptual background for the reading is developed, new vocabulary words are presented in meaningful contexts, and the purposes for reading are made clear, George should succeed regularly with fourth-grade materials.

By traditional standards, fifth-grade material falls into the questionable range for George (50–70 percent comprehension). It is not exactly instructional, nor is it frustrating. Since he did not recognize enough words or answer a sufficient percentage of comprehension questions, it would appear that this level of material should be avoided. But with a considerable amount of teacher guidance, George could be successful with fifth-grade material on a periodic basis. This would necessitate that the teacher provide numerous adjunct reading aids, such as anticipation guides, graphic organizers, or guided reading strategies, and that the material be of interest to him. If George is limited to fourth-grade material for instruction, his range of reading experiences may be unnecessarily restricted. In Figure 5.5, a framework is offered to assist teachers in assigning reading material.

Again, the IRI can be used only as a guide. The teacher must closely observe and analyze children's performance on the IRI in combination with normal classroom reading behavior. Be advised that it is not uncommon for the IRI to yield confusing results. A passage of great interest or one for which the child has no conceptual framework may not truly test what the child could otherwise accomplish. These passages will cause the child's profile to appear highly irregular. Teachers must consider all the factors that can influence children's responses,

FIGURE 5.5 Reading Levels and Types of Teacher Assistance

Level	Word Recognition/ Comprehension	Teacher Assistance	Usage
1. Independent	99% and 90%	None necessary	No restrictions (free reading)
2. Immediate instructional	Near independent criteria on at least one dimension	Minimal clarifications of words and concepts	Mostly free reading; may be used for reading lessons occasionally
3. Basic instructional	95–98% and 70–89%	Background vocabulary, purposes, skill training, reinforcement, evaluation	Daily
4. Periodic instructional	Near instructional criteria on at least one dimension	Same as for basic instructional, but including adjunct aids	Occasionally
5. Frustration	Below 90% or below 50%	Structured listening; provide easier material	Never

weigh them carefully, and integrate their conclusions with other assessments, both formal and informal, that have been made of the child.

Qualitative Word Recognition Analysis.   The quantitative data provided by the IRI are usually quite helpful in accurately identifying children's functional reading levels. There are, however, other ways to evaluate IRI performance, and these can significantly expand the utility of the instrument. By looking closely at the *quality* of word recognition responses, the teacher can gain a greater insight into the way a child processes written language concepts.

In examining word recognition performance, teachers need to look at the nature of oral reading errors in addition to the number of errors that are made. Goodman and Goodman (1994) suggest that children's errors (or miscues, as they call them) reflect the strategies they are using in trying to break the written language code. Some of the errors will indicate that the child is still making sense of the author's intended message, whereas others will indicate just the opposite. In this sense, some errors are "better" than others. The quality of the error can be determined by asking the question "Does this error limit the reader's comprehension of the text?" If it does not, it would be difficult to justify counting the error when attempting to specify independent, instructional, and frustration levels for word recognition. Perhaps a child who scored in the frustration range might have scored in the instructional range if the quality of the errors had been considered.

Suppose that a child reads the sentence "Boiling water is *likely* to burn you if you are not careful" as "Boiling water is *liable* to burn you if you are not careful." According to traditional scoring, a substitution has been made, which counts as one error. But clearly the child did understand the message. Not only is the substituted word the correct part of speech consistent with the pattern of the sentence; it makes perfectly good sense as well.

The error tells us something important about the way the child is approaching the reading task. It indicates that the child is reading for meaning rather than for precise word identification. Because the child was trying to make sense of the message, the error went by completely unnoticed. The response "liable" satisfied all of the child's criteria for moving onward; it sounded right, it fit the context, and it made sense. The child was probably cued by the combination of the initial letter-sound correspondence (*li*) and the constraints of grammar and meaning. When errors of this type occur, the teacher can conclude that the child is reading with the right purpose in mind; that is, the child is using information from more than one level of language to arrive at meaning.

Other errors are more serious. If the child says "Boiling water is *lively* to burn you if you are not careful," it is clear that obtaining meaning is not the primary goal of the reader. The child is responding only to the graphic similarity between the words *likely* and *lively*. If the child accepts this version blindly and forges ahead, the teacher can infer that the child is not making sense of the message. Instead, the child is attempting to solve words. If, on the other hand, the child recognizes the error, returns to the word, and tries to provide a meaningful response, it is apparent that the child is self-monitoring his or her understanding of the text. This self-correction strategy is desirable unless (1) the correction is motivated only by the wish to pronounce the word exactly, (2) corrections tend to be unsuccessful, or (3) there are so many self-corrections that fluent reading is disrupted and the meaning becomes lost.

Teachers need to look for patterns of errors. An oral reading sample should be examined as a whole rather than as a series of isolated errors. Y. M. Goodman and Burke (1972) indicated that a minimum of 25 errors must be identified before any conclusions may be drawn about the child's reading strategies. It is unlikely that any IRI passage will generate this many errors, so the teacher may wish to choose a longer reading selection. Unfortunately, locating and interpreting these reading samples tends to be a time-consuming process. We suggest that the teacher analyze the child's miscues over all of the passages that were administered during the IRI. From this larger sample, meaningful patterns may emerge. In particular, teachers should be looking to see whether the majority of the errors are meaningful or whether they tend to be only graphically similar to the desired response.

Process Guide 5.4

Go back to the oral reading passage you examined in Figure 5.4. This time examine the child's oral reading miscues from the standpoint of each one's effect on meaning. Do the miscues disrupt meaning? If you take into account the quality of the child's miscues and do not count those that preserve meaning, how is the child's word recognition level affected?

Sometimes the oral reading error itself does not directly indicate whether the reader's comprehension has been negatively affected. If a child read the sentence "When you first begin to run, limit yourself to a couple *hundred* yards" as "When you first begin to run, limit yourself to a couple *hunnerd* yards," the error might be attributed to dialect. Although this may seem appropriate, it is also possible that the child's response was purely phonetic. The child may not have assigned the meaning of the word *hundred* to the response *hunnerd*. A three-step procedure should be followed when an error is not immediately interpretable:

1. After the passage has been completed, direct the child back to the text and ask that the entire sentence be reread aloud.
2. Write the word on the board or a separate piece of paper, and ask the child to identify it.
3. Pose a question that requires an understanding of the term, such as "What do you mean by a couple hunnerd yards?"

More often than not, this procedure will help the teacher determine whether the reader's comprehension has in some way been limited. These probes are particularly necessary when none of the accompanying comprehension questions tap the child's understanding of the term or the concept it conveys.

For using the probes, two cautions are offered. First, great care must be taken in formulating the probe question. A statement like "How far is a couple hundred yards?" provides two extraneous cues. The word *far* gives away the notion of distance, and the correct pronunciation of the word *hundred* may elicit vocabulary knowledge that might not have been activated independently. If the child satisfactorily answers the question, the teacher may inappropriately conclude that the original miscue did not interfere with comprehension.

Second, many teachers are in the habit of having the child reread the sentence, but their approach is inadequate. The purpose of the rereading is to see if the error occurs again. If it does, the teacher may say "Now does that make sense to you?" Children quickly learn that the only time this question is asked is when the sentence does not make sense! Thus, the child will say that it doesn't, but cannot say why. For this reason, it is a good practice to ask the question even when no error occurs.

Only after the reader's comprehension has been determined can the full benefits of the qualitative analysis be realized. The idea of viewing oral reading errors as indicators of a child's reading strategies is not limited to performance on an IRI. Teachers can use the basic principles of qualitative analysis to interpret any instance of oral reading that occurs in the classroom. When a child makes an error, the teacher should attempt to understand why the error occurred and whether or not it restricts comprehension. Satisfactory answers to these questions will direct the teacher toward more appropriate instructional exchanges with the students.

Observation

Like other types of holistic evaluation (Farr, 1992), assessment by observation

1. Guides children's literacy development
2. Lends flexibility to teaching
3. Is performance-based
4. Facilitates decision making by providing multiple samples

Watching children carry out actual classroom reading assignments provides information about children that cannot be gained through traditional testing. Moore (1986) calls this process *naturalistic assessment* because it requires teachers to consciously observe children at work in the naturally occurring activities of the classroom. In using observation, teachers must make judgments about what they see. They view the whole spectrum of children's behavior and attempt to detect patterns that signal the onset of difficulty. These patterns are then interpreted to reach conclusions regarding children's strengths and weaknesses. This information can then be added to and compared with that gained from more traditional assessment tools.

Observation is not an easy task. It requires the ability to separate the important from the unimportant. This ability usually comes with experience, although it comes more readily to those teachers who persist in making a conscious effort to study children while at work in the classroom.

Teacher observations may be the most valid and reliable means of reading assessment. They are valid because (1) they occur as a natural part of the instruc-

*Teacher observations may be the most
valid means of reading assessment.*

tional lesson; (2) they are structured by the teacher's objectives, and thus children's
responses are viewed in an unbiased manner; and (3) they are conducted in the
context of real reading. This allows the teacher the opportunity both to assess what
has been learned and to observe how well children can apply what they know as
they read.

Reliability is achieved through the nature of assessment by observation.
Teachers can avoid the problem of lack of consistency associated with traditional
testing because their conclusions are based on numerous planned, purposeful observations over a period of time. The observed patterns have occurred time and
time again in real reading situations in the context of normal classroom activities.

Observations may be unstructured or structured, depending on how open-
ended teachers wish their information to be. If they are unstructured, teachers can
use *anecdotal records* (Rhodes & Nathenson-Mejia, 1992) to record children's interactions in reading, writing, class discussions, or other activities. The open-ended
nature of anecdotal records allows teachers to determine what details are important given the task, previous assessment data, and the particular literacy situations
being observed. If observations are structured, teachers use some form of predetermined observation guide to document specific literacy behaviors. These guides can
be used to augment the anecdotal records from unstructured observations. The
specific literacy behaviors that can be observed using a guide are many, but might
include the following (Rhodes & Nathenson-Mejia, 1992, p. 505):

1. Functions served in reading/writing
2. What aspects of text children attend to
3. Interactions with others about reading/writing

4. Interactions with materials
5. Hypotheses children are trying out in reading/writing
6. Misconceptions children have
7. Miscues children make while reading
8. How text is used before, during, and after reading
9. How a lesson affects children's reading/writing
10. Comparisons between what is said and what is done
11. How, where, and with whom children work
12. What children are interested in
13. What is said about reading/writing outside of school
14. How children use problem-solving in reading/writing
15. How children theorize about reading/writing

Running Records

Running records (Clay, 1985) are holistic recordings of young children's ability to read text material. They are similar to the qualitative analyses of the informal reading inventory discussed earlier in this section, but they do not require any technical knowledge on the teacher's part or any lengthy analysis. Clay (p. 17) suggests that teachers use running records for the following purposes:

1. Evaluating text difficulty
2. Grouping children
3. Accelerating a child
4. Monitoring progress of children
5. Keeping track of individual progress as different children move through different books at different speeds
6. Observing particular difficulties in particular children

A running record of text reading can be made easily and rather spontaneously. All the teacher needs to do is select a text of at least 100 words to be read by a child. Obviously, it is preferable to use materials present in the classroom for this purpose. Texts that are known to be easier or more difficult might be used if the teacher wishes to obtain insights into the child's strengths and weaknesses. No prepared script is necessary, as the recording can be done on any piece of paper. The child reads the text; the teacher records everything the child says. A check is made for each word the child reads correctly; errors are noted in full, as follows:

Bobby gave the baby her toy.   ✓   ✓   ✓   ✓   ✓   ✓   .
She screamed with delight.   ✓   *called*   ✓   ✓   .

When the record is complete, it can be analyzed for both error behavior and error rate. Specifically, the teacher can focus on the kinds of cues the child is using when reading:

1. *Is the reading making sense?* If the reading is meaningful, even if inaccurate, the child is probably making use of oral language knowledge.

2. *Is the reading grammatically correct?* If it is not, the child may have limited language skills or may be paying too much attention to detail and not using syntactical knowledge.
3. *Does the child make use of visual cues in the words and letters?* Fluent reading requires accurate recognition of visual cues in words, letters, and other details of print. For example, misreading *cow's* as *cow* or *con* or *row* will distort the meaning.
4. *Does the child read word by word?* The child may not understand that speaking and reading are similar processes and that oral language can be helpful in reading aloud.

To calculate the error rate, the teacher counts the number of errors made in the 100-word text. Using this guide, the teacher can evaluate the difficulty of the text for the child:

Error Rate	*Text Difficulty*
1:5 or less	Too difficult
1:10	Instructional
1:20	Too easy

When errors are plentiful, the child may become frustrated with the text; when the text is too easy, it may not provide enough of a challenge for the child. Those texts that are classified as instructional allow the child to use oral language knowledge in an attempt to make sense of his or her reading and thus are appropriate for developing reading abilities. The teacher should keep anecdotal notes about the child's running record and use them in combination with other assessment data to make appropriate instructional decisions.

When used continually throughout the year, the assessment techniques described above provide valuable information about children's reading abilities. IRIs can be administered at the beginning of the school year to furnish baseline information about children's needs and strengths, which can then be used to plan balanced instruction. Children's progress can be monitored during the year using running records, qualitative word analysis, and observations. This additional information keeps teachers informed and enables them to be thoughtful decision makers.

Creating Balance

The commonality among all the approaches presented in this chapter is that they give children opportunities to read and write for meaningful purposes, while allowing the teacher great autonomy in determining the essential strategies and skills to teach. These are requisite features of a well-balanced literacy program. Depending on your own beliefs and the grade level you teach, you may find one of these approaches more appealing than the others. However, keep in mind that, as we emphasized at the beginning of this chapter, there is no one best method. Informed teachers make curricular decisions based on the needs of the children with whom they are working. One multiage first- and second-grade teacher we know was very much committed to using a reading/writing workshop in her classroom. Yet, as she watched her emergent readers flounder in this context, she reexamined her beliefs and made some changes. She decided to use the language experience approach with them a few days per week in the workshop, thereby providing them with opportunities to feel successful as readers and to transition into conventional reading. This example illustrates the importance of creating balance, through an informed integration of educational philosophy, teaching strategies, and student assessment, all in an effort to best meet the needs of all children within the classroom community.

Summary

This chapter discussed balanced literacy and the features of an integrated language arts approach to reading instruction. Suggestions were made for organizing an integrated language arts classroom and using informal assessment to further thoughtful decision making. The importance of the teacher as a decision maker, empowered to nurture a community of literacy learners, was emphasized.

FOLLOW-THROUGH ACTIVITIES

Note: Level 1 activities may require limited access to children or classrooms. Level 2 activities should be completed using children and classrooms.

Level 1 Activities

1. Select one of the following authors, read a selection of his or her writings, and develop a short paper explaining the *historical role* of the author in the movement toward a balanced literacy approach.

Jeannette Veatch	Nancy Larrick
Dorris May Lee	Roach Van Allen
Roma Gans	Sylvia Ashton-Warnter

2. Select one of the following authors, read a selection of his or her writings, and develop a short paper explaining the *current role* of the author in the movement toward a balanced literacy approach.

Yetta Goodman	Kathryn Au
P. David Pearson	Marie Clay
Jerome Harste	Lucy Calkins

Level 2 Activities

1. Administer an IRI to one child. Interpret word recognition performance according to both traditional and qualitative analyses. Did the extended analysis provide any additional insights into the reading strategies that the child was using?

2. Working with a single elementary school student or a group of students, follow the guidelines for directing a language experience story or chart.

3. Arrange to observe in an elementary school classroom where thematic units are part of the classroom curriculum. Compare the processes children follow with the suggestions in this chapter. Are they similar? Different? Develop a two- or three-page paper summarizing your visit.

WORKING WITH PARENTS

An extra pair of hands and another adult language model can be of great help in any classroom, especially an integrated language arts classroom. Sharon Arthur Moore (1985), in the first edition of *Helping Children Learn to Read*, presented a practical way to solicit help. She wrote:

> As a first-year teacher, this writer was panic-stricken when a parent offered to help in the classroom. Thoughts of, Doesn't she think I'm doing a good job? and Whatever could I have her do? rampaged through my mind. Beginning teachers frequently experience pangs of insecurity when well-meaning parents offer to lighten those teachers' loads. By the second year, however, most teachers shed their anxiety and not only accept parental offers of help, but even solicit it. Perhaps you can even convince yourself to accept aid the first year.
>
> One way to determine the resources available to you is by sending home to parents a letter that explains, briefly, that you could use their cooperation to make this year special for their children. [See Figure 5.6.]

FIGURE 5.6   Letter to Parents

```
Dear ——————,

    The days are speeding by and I feel that we are all enjoying
an interesting and profitable education. As is always the case,
there are too few hours in the school day for all the things that
teaching entails. In addition, I know that many of you have special
talents or interests that you could share with my class. The
following checklist contains only some of the possible ways you
could help make this year a very special one for your children.
    The list is in two parts. Part I contains ways you can help
the class even if you are unable to come to school because of
family, work, or health. Part II suggests those ways we could use
you right here in the classroom. Please check all the ones you
feel you might be able to help with. Don't worry—you don't have
to do them all! I'll call on you for help as the need arises and
distribute the load fairly.
    Thanks so much for your support and help.

                              Sincerely,

                              Jane Doe
```

FIGURE 5.6   Continued

Part I

I cannot come to school, but I would be glad to help in the following ways:

_____ Word processing

_____ Cutting out pictures from magazines

_____ Making signs, labels, charts, etc.

_____ Canvassing my neighbors for discarded books for the classroom library

_____ Sewing up floor pillows with materials Ms. Doe provides

_____ Making puppets (material provided)

_____ Tape recording stories (tape recorder, books, and tapes provided)

_____ Making classroom games (materials provided)

_____ Other (list ideas here):

Part II

I am able to come to school and provide the following help:

_____ Teaching the class a language (French, Spanish, other _____)

_____ Teaching music to the class (appreciation, how to play an instrument, music theory, other _____)

_____ Teaching creative drama

_____ Teaching creative movement or dance

_____ Teacher's aide once a week for an hour

_____ Teaching cooking lessons

_____ Sharing my hobby or interest which is _____

_____ Story telling to the class

_____ Reading stories to the class

_____ Other (list your ideas here):

Name _____

Address _____

Phone _____

Letting parents help you is a way to let them share in the excitement of your classroom, as well as a way to further inform them about your classroom and how it operates. The more parents know about what you do, the better off you will be. Parents will be your greatest supporters when you need them. You will soon wonder how you ever managed without your corps of volunteers. (p. 332)

RESOURCES

Allen, J. B., Michalove, B., Shockley, B., & West, M. (1991). "I'm really worried about Joseph": Reducing the risks of literacy learning. *The Reading Teacher, 44,* 458–472.

This is a fascinating account of how supported risk taking, choice, time, and other features of a classroom full of language affected one very special child.

Atwell, N. (1998). *In the middle: Writing, reading, and learning with adolescents* (2nd ed.). Portsmouth, NH: Heinemann.

This new edition features Atwell's groundbreaking text on using a reading/writing workshop with adolescents, along with ideas for evaluation and for mini-lessons. The sections on workshops can be adapted for various grade levels.

Cullinan, B. (Ed.). (1992). *Invitation to read: More children's literature in the reading program.* Newark, DE: International Reading Association.

Genre studies, thematic units, and organizing literature-based instruction are major sections in this text, which is full of teaching ideas and suggestions.

Eeds, M., & Peterson, R. (1991). Teacher as curator: Learning to talk about literature. *The Reading Teacher, 45,* 118–126.

The authors discuss the possibilities of using dialogue in literature study groups.

Fowler, D. (1998). Balanced reading instruction in practice. *Educational Leadership, 55*(6), 11–12.

This short article describes one teacher's approach to implementing balanced reading instruction.

McMahon, S., & Raphael, T. (1997). *The Book Club connection.* New York and Newark, DE: Teachers College Press and International Reading Association.

Various articles in this edited book explain and explore Book Clubs.

Pappas, C. C., Kiefer, B. Z., & Levstik, L. S. (1990). *An integrated language perspective in the elementary school: Theory into action.* White Plains, NY: Longman.

With plenty of prototypes for classrooms, this text is an excellent source for ideas and practical suggestions on how to organize and implement integrated language classrooms.

Peterson, R., & Eeds, M. (1990). *Grand conversations.* Ontario, Canada: Scholastic.

Dialogue as teaching while children engage in reading and responding to literature is presented by the authors of this small, yet powerful, text.

Scharer, P. L., & Detwiler, D. B. (1992). Changing as teachers: Perils and possibilities of literature-based language arts instruction. *Language Arts, 69,* 186–192.

> This case study of the experiences of one author as a sixth-grade teacher trying to increase her use of literature for language arts instruction gives insight into the challenges and successes involved in making the transition from basal readers to trade books.

Short, K. G., & Burke, C. (1991). *Creating curriculum: Teachers and students as a community of learners.* Portsmouth, NH: Heinemann.

> Good things come in small packages—this short text discusses how curriculum is created in a classroom.

Smith, J. A. (1998). Mr. Smith goes to first grade. *Educational Leadership, 55*(6), 19–22.

> This article describes a university professor's experiences in returning to a first-grade classroom and implementing a balanced literacy program.

Strickland, D. S. (1998). What's basic in beginning reading? Finding common ground. *Educational Leadership, 55*(6), 6–10.

> In this article, Strickland describes the whole-part-whole method of reading instruction.

Thompson, G. (1991). *Teaching through themes.* New York: Scholastic.

> This text explores theme teaching—how to choose topics for study and the phases of implementing theme study. There are plenty of topics on which to model themes and units for teachers to experiment with, adapt, modify, or use as is.

Tompkins, G. E. (1990). *Teaching writing: Balancing process and product.* Columbus, OH: Merrill.

> Chapter 3 on the writing process and Chapter 10 on assessing students' writing are excellent sources of practical teaching ideas.

REFERENCES

Atwell, N. (1987). *In the middle: Writing, reading, and learning with adolescents.* Portsmouth, NH: Heinemann.

Atwell, N. (1998). *In the middle: Writing, reading, and learning with adolescents* (2nd ed.). Portsmouth, NH: Heinemann.

Au, K. H., & Carroll, J. H. (1997). Improving literacy achievement through a constructivist approach: The KEEP demonstration classroom project. *The Elementary School Journal, 97,* 203–221.

Clay, M. M. (1985). *The early detection of reading difficulties* (3rd ed.). Exeter, NH: Heinemann.

Duffy, G. G., & Hoffman, J. V. (1999). In pursuit of an illusion: The flawed search for a perfect method. *The Reading Teacher, 53,* 10–16.

Farr, R. (1992). Putting it all together: Solving the reading assessment puzzle. *The Reading Teacher, 46,* 26–37.

Freppon, P. A., & Dahl, K. L. (1998). Balanced instruction: Insights and considerations. *Reading Research Quarterly, 33,* 240–251.

Goodman, Y. M., & Burke, C. L. (1972). *Reading miscue inventory: Procedure for diagnosis and evaluation.* New York: Macmillan.

Goodman, Y. M., & Goodman, K. S. (1994). To err is human: Learning about language processes by analyzing miscues. In R. B. Ruddell, M. R. Ruddell, & H. Singer (Eds.), *Theoretical models and processes of reading* (4th ed., pp. 104–123). Newark, DE: International Reading Association.

Hall, M. (1981). *Teaching reading as a language experience* (3rd ed.). Columbus, OH: Charles E. Merrill.

McMahon, S., & Raphael, T. (1997). *The Book Club connection.* New York and Newark, DE: Teachers College Press and International Reading Association.

Moore, D. W. (1985). Gifted readers. In L. W. Searfoss & J. E. Readence, *Helping children learn to read* (pp. 354–369). Englewood Cliffs, NJ: Prentice-Hall.

Moore, D. W. (1986). A case for naturalistic assessment of reading comprehension. In E. K. Dishner, T. W. Bean, J. E. Readence, & D. W. Moore (Eds.), *Reading in the content area: Improving classroom instruction* (2nd ed., pp. 159–170). Dubuque, IA: Kendall/Hunt.

Moore, S. A. (1985). Parents as partners in reading. In L. W. Searfoss & J. E. Readence, *Helping children learn to read* (pp. 321–337). Englewood Cliffs, NJ: Prentice-Hall.

Pace, G. (1992). Stories of teacher-initiated change from traditional to whole-language literacy instruction. *The Elementary School Journal, 92,* 461–476.

Pearson, P. D. (1996). Reclaiming the center. In M. F. Graves, P. van den Broek, & B. M. Taylor (Eds.), *The first R: Every child's right to read* (pp. 259–274). New York and Newark, DE: Teachers College Press and International Reading Association.

Raphael, T. E., & McMahon, S. I. (1994). Book Club: An alternative framework for reading instruction. *The Reading Teacher, 48,* 102–116.

Rhodes, L. K., & Nathenson-Mejia, S. (1992). Anecdotal records: A powerful tool for ongoing literacy assessment. *The Reading Teacher, 45,* 502–509.

Routman, R. (1988). *Transitions: From literature to literacy.* Portsmouth, NH: Heinemann.

Routman, R. (1991). *Invitations: Changing as teachers and learners K–12.* Portsmouth, NH: Heinemann.

Seely-Flint, A. (in press). Know-it-alls and defenders: Examining interpretive authority within literacy events. *Reading Research and Instruction.*

Spiegel, D. L. (1998). Silver bullets, babies, and bath water: Literature response groups in a balanced literacy program. *The Reading Teacher, 52,* 114–124.

Strickland, D. S. (1998). What's basic in beginning reading? Finding common ground. *Educational Leadership, 55*(6) 6–10.

Thompson, G. (1991). *Teaching through themes.* New York: Scholastic.

Tompkins, G. E. (1990). *Teaching writing: Balancing process and product.* Columbus, OH: Merrill.

Viorst, J. (1972). *Alexander and the terrible, horrible, no good, very bad day.* New York: Atheneum.

CHAPTER

6　Decoding

INTRODUCTION

The most important goal of reading instruction is to produce children who *can* read and who *do* read. These children are accomplished readers who rapidly construct meaning and seem to be able to figure out what to do on their own when they lose meaning while reading. This independence is a crucial test of fluent reading ability. Without it, reading can become frustrating, time-consuming, and confusing. In this chapter we will introduce decoding strategies for helping children become fluent readers. The role of basic skills (context clues, phonics, and structural analysis) in acquiring those strategies will also be discussed.

GRAPHIC ORGANIZER

This graphic organizer summarizes the structure of Chapter 6:

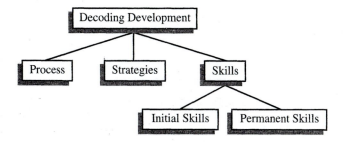

OBJECTIVES

When you finish this chapter, you should be able to understand and discuss each of these statements:

1. Fluent readers decode by translating print into meaning, shifting back and forth between immediate comprehension and mediated comprehension.
2. Fluent readers can apply decoding strategies as they attempt to regain meaning when it is lost.
3. Phonemic awareness plays an important role in initial decoding skill development.
4. Decoding skills serve as a foundation for decoding strategies.
5. Context offers a powerful clue to meaning found in print.
6. Phonics and structural analysis instruction should proceed analytically, be based on reliable generalizations, and involve oral practice.

The Decoding Process

Fluent readers comprehend by constructing meaning from print (Ruddell, Ruddell, & Singer, 1994). Comprehension is usually fast and immediate. Once in a while, even fluent readers lose meaning and find their smooth rapid comprehension interrupted. In this chapter we will discuss ways to help children learn what to do when their smooth reading is interrupted, strategies for figuring out what is causing meaning to be lost, and the role of decoding skills in these strategies.

Frank Smith's model of the comprehension process, presented in adapted form in Figure 6.1, has had a profound influence on our thinking and the development of teaching strategies to help children learn to decode. Smith (1988) distinguishes between *immediate* and *mediated* meaning identification (or comprehension):

Reading usually involves bringing meaning *immediately* or directly to the text without awareness of individual words or their possible alternative meanings. There

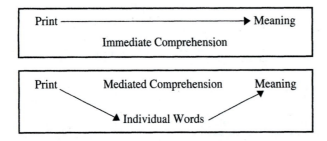

FIGURE 6.1   Immediate and Mediated Comprehension
After Smith, 1988.

are occasions, however, when the meaning of the text or of particular words cannot be immediately comprehended. On these occasions, mediated meaning identification may be attempted, involving the identification of individual words before comprehension of a meaningful sequence of words as a whole. (pp. 162–163)

A fluent reader, then, is one who is able to shift back and forth efficiently between mediated and immediate comprehension.

Decoding Strategies

Figure 6.2 presents one decoding strategy to guide readers in learning to focus their attention on meaning. The steps are simple, can be applied quickly, and are designed to assist readers in regaining lost meaning as rapidly as possible.

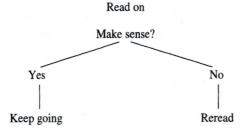

FIGURE 6.2   A Decoding Strategy for Regaining Lost Meaning

The decoding strategy in Figure 6.3 appears to be appropriate if the cause of lost meaning is an unknown word. It guides the reader's focus by direct application of decoding skills. As the reader comes to an unknown word that has caused loss of meaning, he or she can apply a sequential strategy by using the following steps:

1. *Skip/guess.* Skip the word, and guess its meaning on the basis of context clues.
2. *Sound out.* Sound out the word. If these steps fail…
3. *Ask/replace.* Ask someone for help, or replace the word with another one that makes sense. Any word will do as long as it makes sense.

Thus, children have a general strategy for seeking meaning and a specific decoding strategy based on applying decoding skills. The second strategy should be applied only if the center of confusion becomes an unknown word or two. Applying it *before* a general-meaning strategy is tried can lead children to believe that unknown words are the sole cause of loss of meaning. Of course, this is not true—meaning can be lost even when one knows (recognizes) every word.

The two decoding strategies are best taught in talk-through settings in which teachers model and demonstrate them for small groups of children. Individual reading conferences allow for reinforcement that is immediate and personal. Both the

FIGURE 6.3 A Decoding Strategy for Figuring Out an Unknown Word

small-group setting and the individualized conference allow for practice, too, when readers need it most—when they lose meaning during reading. Of course, instruction should be adjusted to the grade level of the children. It should begin in first grade.

For primary-grade children, the talk-through modeling and demonstrating done by teachers should be reinforced by large posters that provide visual reminders of the key steps in each strategy. They can be placed near the area where small-group instruction takes place. Additional posters can be put in any area in the classroom where children go to read quietly by themselves. In one classroom we observed, the teacher had placed a poster on the ceiling over the free-reading corner because children often stretched out on pillows to read and looked up at the ceiling when thinking about their story or a word they were having difficulty figuring out. In another classroom, a simple mobile was made and hung over the basal-reading group area. To make the steps as personal as possible, you might have children develop posters on their own to periodically replace those around the classroom. Placing a few posters in the school library is also a good idea.

What kinds of steps are found on decoding posters? We suggest that as few words as possible be used, regardless of the grade level. Children must be able to learn and practice these steps in as simple a form as possible. The posters should include key words for each strategy. Naturally, if you and the children in your classroom develop alternative words for each step, they will be even more meaningful. Pictures, either cut out of magazines or drawn in by the teacher, can be used initially to illustrate each step. Beyond the primary grades, posters may become smaller and may even be replaced by bookmarks or small cards taped to desks or tables.

Process Guide 6.1

Review the steps in the following decoding strategy, developed by the Tempe, Arizona, school district on the basis of the work of Marie Clay (1993).* Compare the steps in this strategy with those in the decoding strategies presented in Figures 6.2 and 6.3. How are they alike? Different? Are there alternative words you would use with first graders? Third graders? Seventh graders?

When You Get Stuck...
1. Look at the picture and think about the story.
2. Go back and read again (reread).
3. Try the beginning sound of the word and slide to the end of the word.
4. Read to the end of the sentence.
5. Now have another try.

   Does it make sense?
   Does it look right?
   Does it sound right?

6. Go on!

*The authors are indebted to Tempe Elementary School District #3, Tempe, Arizona, for this version of a decoding strategy.

Decoding Skills as a Foundation for Decoding Strategies

The decoding strategies presented in the last section require children to apply a series of steps for seeking and gaining comprehension. Underlying the application of the steps are the building blocks of any strategy—decoding skills. Decoding skills instruction is an essential part of any reading program. What do we mean by *decoding skills?* To help you understand the nature of these skills, we present in Figure 6.4 a model of decoding instruction. Decoding skills instruction can be roughly divided into two kinds: initial skills instruction and permanent skills instruction.

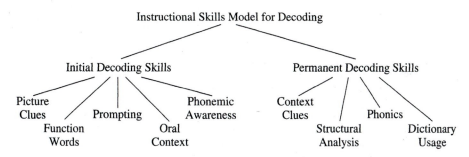

FIGURE 6.4   Initial and Permanent Decoding Skills

Initial Decoding Skills

Initial decoding skills are those presented as part of beginning reading instruction and functioning as bridges to permanent skills. They help children to get off to a rapid start in reading and to feel that reading is not difficult. They aid in making children's first encounters with print in school comfortable and rewarding. These initial decoding skills interact and offer children the opportunity to begin reading with ease. Although they are an excellent bridge to beginning reading, they must be replaced by skills and strategies children can use independently as print becomes more difficult. Initial decoding skills fall into five areas:

Picture clues. Beginning reading materials are dominated by pictures, in order to help children with comprehension.

Prompting. Until decoding strategies are acquired, teachers often tell children words they do not know.

Oral context. Using their listening ability, children hear others read words for them, are given help by peers, and acquire information about what is being read from oral discussions in reading groups.

Function words. These are "glue" words that hold sentences together, and they are best taught as whole words (e.g., *the, was, what, said, are*).

Phonemic awareness. Awareness of the phonemes (sounds) of our language and how words are segmented helps children to sound out words.

Function Words

Beginning teachers may be unaware of the controversy that has existed for many years over the teaching of function words. Experienced teachers have seen waves of often-contradictory research and methods come and go. The function words we refer to are those often called *structure words* or *sight words.* We use the term *glue words* to indicate that these words hold together the meaning-carrying words in beginning reading materials and appear with high frequency in those materials. Generally, they are also irregular in that they do not have a close correspondence between sound and symbol; that is, they do not sound out easily. Further, it may be difficult for children to learn some of these words, because they do not have sensory associations: Words such as *said, are, the,* and *is* do not smell, taste, feel, touch, or say anything!

We recommend observing the following guidelines for teaching function words to beginning readers:

1. *Go slowly!* Function words are usually a bit difficult for beginning readers to learn.
2. Teach function words when the children encounter them in print and need to know them.
3. Use simple, direct teaching steps that keep the focus on the words rather than on pictures or on the context in which the words appear. We suggest beginning direct instruction by calling attention to the word: point to it, or print it on a piece of chart paper, or print it on the chalkboard. Ask the children to pronounce the word for you before any teaching. If the response is correct, say "Right" and return to the reading. If, however, the children's response is not correct, then tell the word, making certain they all focus their attention on it. Have the children repeat the word several times. Then return to reading.

Function words that have been directly taught can be reinforced as they are encountered in reading. Any word that continues to cause difficulty can be placed on a special list of *stickers* or *demons* with which additional practice is given as time permits. However, isolated drills with piles of word cards should be avoided.

Phonemic Awareness

Phonics instruction, designed to teach children sound/symbol associations, assumes children are aware that speech is composed of a sequence of sounds, or phonemes. This understanding, called *phonemic awareness,* sets the stage for using phonics as one part of beginning reading instruction. Recent research indicates that children whose phonemic awareness is not fully developed encounter difficulty with beginning reading and beginning spelling instruction when that instruction is based on phonics (Ball & Blachman, 1991; Griffith, 1991; Snider 1997; Tangel & Blachman, 1992).

As Busink (1997) notes, two decades of research have shown that the ability to decode words is closely associated with phonological awareness (a term often used interchangeably with phonemic awareness). She also notes that phonological awareness can be taught both before and after reading instruction. Busink believes that the following should be part of any phonological training: (a) awareness that words may be thought of as sound objects apart from their meaning, (b) awareness that words consist of discrete sound segments, and (c) the ability to identify the same sounds across different words. Children learn these skills by listening to books, poems, and nursery rhymes and by joining in refrains and word plays. Stahl, Duffy-Hester, and Stahl (1998) suggest that by listening to alphabet books children come to understand that the letter *b* is for *b*ear because the first sound of bear is /*b*/. This understanding is the beginning of phonemic awareness.

Phonemic awareness is developed in preschool children through many and varied encounters with print, such as those described in Chapter 3. Kindergarten and first-grade teachers who provide a print-rich classroom environment encourage children to experiment with print, foster the development of phonemic awareness, and build on the awareness children have. Although some writers advocate using isolated exercises to develop phonemic awareness, we think such exercises are questionable. Drill or rote practice in exercises that have been designed to develop or assess phonemic awareness misses the point completely. Phonemic awareness is an insight into how sounds in a sequence combine to make speech. It develops slowly over time in language settings that have meaning as a central focus.

We believe that phonemic awareness is important for success in beginning reading and spelling instruction. It is developmental, and it is acquired by most children when they use language for genuine purposes before formal schooling begins. When children have difficulty with phonics or spelling, the teacher's first step should be to observe and informally assess their performance in language tasks that assume a high level of phonemic awareness. If children perform poorly, increased attention to activities similar to those that follow should be included as part of the classroom reading program. All of these activities initially require teacher modeling and group practice, as children become aware of sounds in spoken words.

1. *Rhyming.* Children recite nursery rhymes and then change words to make their own rhymes ("Hickory, Dickory, Dock./The mouse put on a *sock*."). Rhymes can also be made with their own names and those of classmates ("Ann has a fan.").
2. *Word matching.* Children use a thumbs-up or thumbs-down signal to indicate whether words have the same initial or final sounds. They can also indicate

which word is the "odd man out" (begins with a different sound than the other words in a group).

3. *Blending.* The teacher says the individual words in a compound word such as *snow + man* and asks students to blend the two small words into a longer word. Next, children are asked to blend onsets (beginning sounds) and rimes (patterns) such as *c + at = cat* to form words.

4. *Segmenting.* Children break sentences into words, then words into syllables, and finally words into sounds. They can clap each syllable as they break each word down.

5. *Manipulation.* Children are asked to remove a sound to make a new word (take the *b* off *b*oat) or to change a sound (change the *d* in *d*og to *l* in *l*og).

Permanent Decoding Skills

Instruction in permanent decoding skills begins early and builds during grades 1 and 2, usually tapering off by the end of grade 4. During the introduction and reinforcing of these skills, the decoding strategies discussed earlier can be taught simultaneously. As their skills improve, children should gain greater facility with decoding strategies. Figure 6.4 lists the major permanent decoding skill areas presented in basal readers and other supplementary materials. The three areas we will discuss in detail are *context clues, structural analysis,* and *phonics.* (Even though dictionary skills are included as part of decoding instruction in many materials for beginning readers, we do not believe that the dictionary is a valuable or efficient decoding tool for beginning readers.)

These three major skill areas form a foundation on which children build decoding strategies. Instruction in skills interacts with instruction in strategies. Each skill area interacts, too, with every other skill area. All three skill areas are really ways children gain meaning by making use of the language hints found in print. Good questions for teachers to ask about teaching decoding skills are "What's in print that I can use to show children how to get meaning?" and "What language clues, signals, or hints are found in print for readers to use as they read?"

To provide a language perspective for instruction in decoding skills, we want to relate each of the three skill areas to a cue system and show how three of the four cue systems discussed in Chapter 1 are interrelated. A *cue,* roughly speaking, is a language hint, signal, or clue that should trigger an "Aha! I got it!" reaction in children as they use it to gain meaning. The three cue systems are reviewed below:

Graphophonic cue system. The cue system in language that relates the sounds (phonemes) to the symbols (graphemes) of print.

Syntactic cue system. The cue system in language that governs the grammar of our language and how words are arranged, ordered, and structured.

Semantic cue system. The cue system in language that holds the meaning of what is being read.

The relation of these cue systems to the three skill areas can be explained by some simple examples. Read the sentence below, and then jot down on a piece of paper some words you think might fit in the blank.

Mary lives in the large white _____ at the end of the block.

We are willing to bet that you selected words in the noun class (such as *house*) and that, on the basis of your experience and the general sense of the sentence, you guessed places where people live. In other words, you used signals provided by the syntactic (order-of-words) cue system and the semantic (meaning) cue system in combination to predict the nature of the missing word and to narrow your choices. The skill area that helps you do this informed guessing is context clues. Instruction and practice in using context clues should provide children with the ability to use the syntactic and semantic cue systems in combination to unlock meaning.

Read the sentence again; this time we have supplied some additional language hints.

Mary lives in the large white t_____ at the end of the block.
Mary lives in the large white t_____h_____ at the end of the block.
Mary lives in the large white townh_____ at the end of the block.

This time the graphophonic cue system was used to further narrow your predictions or guesses and reduce the uncertainty to nearly zero. The two skill areas you could have used were structural analysis (to divide town/house) and phonics (*t*, *town*, *h* sounds). Instruction in both structural analysis and phonics should help children add more hints to those provided by the syntactic and semantic cue systems. *Working together, these three systems provide a combination of clues that aid children in predicting meaning and making accurate, informed guesses about meaning.*

First we turn our attention to teaching children to use context clues. Then we will discuss how to teach the skills involved in structural analysis and phonics.

Process Guide 6.2

The list of permanent decoding skills in Figure 6.4 is a composite from many sources. Select manuals from two or three basal reader series for grade 1 or grade 2, and find the list of decoding skills for each one. Then compare and contrast the terminology used by each series. Note identical terms, synonyms, and unique terms. Work in pairs or small groups, and divide the work. Present to the class a brief summary of what you find.

Teaching the Use of Context Clues

Teaching children to use context clues involves using *both* the syntactic and the semantic cue systems. These systems work together as powerful determiners of meaning. Instruction in using context clues is best accomplished by talking through with children how to use these clues to gain meaning of an unknown word. The basal reader group and the individual reading conference both offer opportunities for instruction. We suggest several techniques for introducing children to context clues:

1. Talk-through method
2. Context-strategy lessons
3. Cloze

Talk-Through Method.   The talk-through method is a strategy that utilizes children's experiences and teacher questioning to discover the meaning of unknown vocabulary in context. It is an informal technique and requires little teacher preparation. It also lends itself to normal classroom discussion and instruction.

The teacher presents new vocabulary to children in a sentence taken from a story or selection being read. Through questioning and discussion, the teacher *talks* children toward the discovery of the meanings of words. In this way, the teacher leads children to develop a habit of trying to discover the meanings of words through their own experiences and knowledge gained from the sentence.

When a teacher encounters a word that may present difficulty to children, the word with its surrounding context is pulled from the text and written on the chalkboard. After reading the sentence aloud, the teacher uses questioning strategies to enable children to discover the meaning of the word. An example of the talk-through method is provided below:

> Cats are endlessly, voraciously curious and seem to find their way to hidden treasures around the house, even when their owners cannot remember where to find them!

> TEACHER: What does the sentence tell you about *voraciously?*

> CHILDREN: It is something cats have to do.

> TEACHER: What do cats who are *voraciously* curious do?

> CHILDREN: Look everywhere and find things people can't.

> TEACHER: Are other animals *voraciously* curious? Are you?

> CHILDREN: Our dog did the same thing with my shoe.

> TEACHER: What do you think *voraciously* might mean?

The teacher could continue the discussion by having children list other examples of voracious behavior from their experiences. The talk-through method is easily implemented, and teachers need only remember to be certain to pull enough context from the selection to give children the maximum number of clues. Sometimes it is necessary to include two or three sentences.

Context-Strategy Lessons. The aim of context-strategy lessons is to systematically extend children's ability to use context clues and to develop independence in decoding unknown words. They are probably best introduced after the talk-through method has been used, because context-strategy lessons are more complicated and require children to make some decisions. They are appropriate for children beyond the beginning stages of reading (i.e., in grades 3 and above). Context lessons can also be easily adapted for use with content area vocabulary.

Context-strategy lessons help children discover what *direct* help is provided by context clues. If no direct help is available, children are then trained to search for *indirect* help through structural analysis or the dictionary. Note that we have included the dictionary as part of decoding, since context-strategy lessons are to be used with children who are beyond the beginning stages of reading and who would have had some instruction in using simple dictionaries. Emphasis is placed not only on strategies (looking for direct and indirect help), but also on skills (context clues, structural analysis, and dictionary skills).

When presenting a context-strategy lesson, the teacher should *walk* children through the strategies and skills needed to unlock the meaning of a new word in context. As an example, consider the target word *hydrophobia* in the sentence "John's mother has *hydrophobia.*" In analyzing this sentence with the children, the teacher should point out that no direct help is provided through the context, but that utilizing the strategy of indirect help may be profitable. Focusing on the structure of the word, in this case, provides a clue to the unknown word. *Phobia* means the fear of something, but what? Thinking about *hydro* and other words they have seen with that beginning, the children might think of *hydroplane* or *hydroelectric,* both of which relate to water. Putting *hydro-water* with *phobia-fear,* the children can derive *fear of water.* Here, structure was their best help in identifying the unknown vocabulary word.

Thus, each lesson stresses both strategies and skills, with the goal being to have children analyze the sentence to determine which strategy to use and then decide what skills within the strategy to apply. Schematically, the lesson format is as follows:

Strategy for Unlocking Meaning	***Skill(s) to Be Applied***
Author gives *direct* help.	Context clues of definition, synonym, comparison, and contrast
Author gives *indirect* help.	Structural analysis through affixes and root words; phonic analysis following structural analysis, if necessary
Author gives *no* help.	Dictionary skills to fit meaning to given context

Below are examples of sentences that teachers can use as models for constructing their own lessons on the various context strategies:

1. *Using context clues of definition.* The clue for the unknown word in this sentence is given by the author through a definition.

   The *ecologist,* a scientist who studies the environment, is usually quick to attack new sources of air pollution.

2. *Using context clues of synonym.* The clue for the unknown word in this sentence is given by the author through the use of a synonym—that is, through a repetition of the idea using another word.

   Although Alicia was a *novice,* or a beginner, on the slopes, she was fast becoming an expert.

3. *Using context clues of comparison and contrast.* The clue for the unknown word in this sentence is given by the author through an implied contrast with a known word, which enables the student to sense the meaning of the unknown word.

   Unlike Lyn, who was flattering in his actions with people, John was stubbornly *flippant.*

4. *Using structural analysis.* The clue for the unknown word in this sentence is not directly supplied by the context, but rather can be deduced by using the author's indirect help and one's own knowledge of root words and affixes.

   The American flag is *tricolored.*

5. *Using dictionary skills.* No help is provided by the author through context or structure. In such cases a dictionary may be needed to find a meaning of the word to fit the context.

   The candidate's aim was to *court* older voters during his election campaign.

In this example, context may be of no help to unlock meaning. The common meaning children might know (to go to *court*) is of no help either. Therefore, the dictionary is needed to find the meaning that best fits the example.

Cloze. In the classic cloze procedure, words are deleted randomly from a passage and readers are asked to supply the missing words. Cloze is thus useful as a procedure for teaching children how to use context clues to help determine the meaning of words. Using cloze as a teaching tool involves selecting a passage from a text and deleting words that have context clues. As a group, the teacher and the students decide on words that could replace the deleted words. Any word that retains the meaning of the sentence and the passage is considered correct. If a student gives a word that does not retain the meaning, the teacher or other students explain how they used the rest of the sentence or the meaning of the whole passage to come up with a better guess. Once students become familiar with using context clues, they can work independently and then come together as a group to share their responses. In the following sample sentence, we deleted words with strong context clues:

It was a _____, sunny day and we wanted to go for a _____ in the lake.

The teacher shows the students how to read ahead and then make guesses for replacement words. Correct choices for the first blank might be *bright*, *warm*, and *hot*; for the second blank, *swim* and *dip* would both be considered correct replacements.

Phonics and Structural Analysis:
An Overview

Before we discuss phonics and structural analysis, you should become familiar with the terminology associated with these skill areas. Study the following terms and their definitions carefully before you continue reading this chapter.

Phonics. Ways of teaching children phoneme/grapheme (i.e., sound/symbol) relationships to help them "sound out" words

Structural analysis. Ways of teaching children how to break up longer words into pronounceable units

Generalization. Statement that indicates the conditions under which a letter or group of letters stands for a particular sound or sounds. For example: "A final *e* at the end of a word usually means the preceding vowel has a long sound, as the *a* in *rate*." A phonic or structural-analysis generalization should help children predict the sounds that specific letters will signify.

Consonants. The letters

b	h	m	r	w
c	j	n	s	x
d	k	p	t	y
f	l	q	v	z
g				

Vowels. The letters

a   e   i   o   u

(and sometimes y and w)

Vowel sounds. In four major categories,

Long	Short	R-controlled	L-controlled
a—rate	a—hat		all—tall
e—he, she	e—set	er—her	al—calm
i—kite	i—hit	ir—fir	alk—walk
o—hope	o—stop	or—torn, doctor	
u—cute	u—cut	ur—turn	
(y—try)	(y—gym)		

Syllable. In reading, a unit of letters that represents a speech unit within a word. Each syllable has one vowel sound. For example:

1 2	1 2	1 2 3
u-nit	read-ing	ex-am-ple

Utility or reliability of a generalization. The consistency with which a generalization accurately predicts the sounds of the letters it covers. In other words, if children are taught to apply the generalization, does it work? Generalization 15 in Figure 6.5 of this chapter has a reliability of 100 percent, meaning that it is highly useful in predicting sounds. Generalization 32 in Figure 6.5 is less reliable, with its 46 percent.

Stressed or accented syllable. The syllable given the most emphasis when a word is pronounced. For example, in **talk**-*ing,* the syllable **talk** is given more stress than *ing;* in *con-***di**-*tion,* the syllable **di** is stressed.

Root or base word. A simple, basic form of word, usually one or two syllables, to which prefixes and suffixes are easily added. For example, *play,* play*ed, re*play.

Prefix. An affix (something added) placed *before* a root or base word to change the meaning of the word. For example: *re-* ("again"), *un-* ("not"), *anti-* ("against").

Suffix. An affix placed *after* a root or base word to change the meaning of the word. For example: *-s, -es* (plural), *-ed* (past tense), *-ful* (full of).

Consonant blend or cluster. Joining of two or more consonants in which each individual sound is still recognized. For example: b + 1 = *bl;* g + r = *gr.*

Consonant digraph. Joining of two consonants in which each individual letter sound is lost and a new sound is represented. For example: g + h = *gh* (rou*gh*); w + h = *wh.*

Segmenting. Breaking a word into sounds. For example: cat = /c/ + /a/ + /t/.

Blending. Putting sounds together to make a word; the opposite of segmenting. For example: /c/ + /a/ + /t/ = *cat.*

Onset. The consonant(s) preceding the vowel of a syllable. For example: *c* in cake, *br* in bring.

Rime (or *rhyme).* A vowel and any following consonants of a syllable. For example: *ike* in *like, ay* in *say.*

Phonics and structural analysis are the supporting skill areas that enable children to use the decoding strategy presented earlier in Figure 6.3. They both involve teaching children to use the graphophonic cue system of print by helping them learn phoneme/grapheme, or sound/symbol, relationships. This instruction usually means that children are taught phonic or structural-analysis *generalizations* that should help them reliably predict the pronunciations of phonemes, syllables, and words. Figure 6.5 lists these generalizations.

FIGURE 6.5   Reliability of Phonic Generalizations in Teacher's Manuals of Five Basal Series

Generalization	Number of Series	Reliability Percentage
1. In words in which the vowel is followed by a consonant and final *e*, the long sound of the vowel is usually heard (tak*e*; mic*e*; lon*e*).	5	77–87
2. If two or more consonants fall between two vowels in a word, divide the word between the consonants to make two syllables. The first vowel is usually short (ma*tt*er; sen*t*ence). *Note:* In the series with 88% reliability, the generalization was amended to teach children not to divide *th, sh, ck,* and *sh,* thus increasing the reliability.	5	78–88
3. If one consonant falls between two vowels in a word, try a long vowel first. If that sound doesn't suggest a word that make sense, try using a short sound of the first vowel (*va-por* or *vap-or; no-vice* or *nov-ice*).	5	24–52
4. When a single vowel falls between two consonants in a word or syllable, the vowel usually has a short sound (t*a*p; t*i*n-sel; st*o*p).	4	66–69
5. When the letter *r* follows a vowel, it changes the sound the vowel usually stands for (f*i*r; f*u*rther; t*i*re; c*a*r; f*o*r). *Note:* In one series, separate generalizations are stated for each *r*-controlled vowel:		
a. When *i* is followed by *r* (ir)	1	100
b. When *u* is followed by *r* (ur)	1	100
c. When *ire* occurs	1	100
d. When *a* is followed by *r* (ar)	1	74
e. When *o* is followed by *r* (or)	1	50
6. When *g* comes before *e, i,* or *y* in a word, the *g* stands for the sound of *j* (*g*em; *g*in; *g*ym).	3	70–81
7. A word that ends in a consonant followed by the letters *le* breaks into syllables before the consonant (ma-*ple*; sin-*gle*).	3	95–100
8. When a word of two or more syllables ends in a *y*, the *y* usually stands for a long *e* (cand-*y*; definite-l*y*).	2	91–94
9. When *e* comes at the end of a word and is the only vowel in the word, it has a long sound (m*e*; h*e*; sh*e*).	2	100
10. Two vowels together often stand for the long vowel sound of the first one (b*ai*t; b*oa*t; f*ee*t). *Note:* 78% is obtained by including *ai, oa,* and *ee,* but not *ea* or *ay*. If *ea* and *ay* are included, the lower reliability of 67% is calculated.	2	67–78
11. If a word ends in *ge*, the sound of *j* is heard (pa*ge*; ed*ge*).	2	100
12. Double consonants *at the end of a word* make one sound (mi*tt*; gra*ss*).	2	100

(continued)

FIGURE 6.5 Continued

Generalization	Number of Series	Reliability Percentage
13. Double consonants usually stand for a single sound in the middle or at the end of a word (se*tt*le; gro*ss*).	2	98–99
14. The letter *c* usually has the sound of *s* when followed by *e* or *i* (*c*enter; con*c*ede).	2	89–90
15. The letters *kn* at the beginning of a word make the *n* sound only (*kn*ow; *kn*it).	2	100
16. The letters *wr* at the beginning of a word made the *r* sound only (*wr*ite; *wr*ing).	2	100
17. The vowel sound in an unaccented syllable may be a *schwa* sound (**pen**-c*i*l; **tow**-*e*l; **gar**-d*e*n; **let**-t*u*ce).	1	49
18. When *y* appears at the end of a word, it is usually a vowel sound with a long *i* (tr*y*) or long *e* (cand*y*) sound.	1	85
19. When *-ed, -er, -ing,* or *-le* is added to a word with one vowel and one final consonant, the final consonant is doubled (tip to ti*pp*ed; hop to ho*pp*ing).	1	90
20. When a vowel comes before *nd* or *ld*, it can have a long or a short sound (b*e*nd; f*ie*ld).	1	88
21. One vowel at the end of a word usually has a long sound (cand*y*).	1	64
22. The letter *y* usually stands for the long *i* sound when it appears at the end of a one-syllable word (tr*y*).	1	55
23. The vowel *a* has the same sound when it is followed by *l, ll,* or *lk* (c*a*lm; c*a*ll; w*a*lk).	1	47
24. Two vowels together in a *stressed,* or *accented, syllable* usually stand for the long vowel sound (m*ee*t-ing).	1	57
25. Two vowels together in a *one-syllable word* usually stand for the long vowel sound (s*ee*k; s*oo*n).	1	59
26. When a word ends with *or* or with *or* followed by one or more consonants, the *or* usually sounds like the *or* in *torn*.	1	50
27. When a vowel is followed by final *re* (su*re*), the vowel does not have either the long, the short, or the *r*-controlled sound.	1	47
28. When *y* or *r* follows *er* (e*ry*, e*rr*), the vowel sound is similar to the one in *very*.	1	44
29. When a word ends with *er, ir, ur,* or with those letters followed by other consonants (*ern, irth, urn*), these letter pairs make the same sounds as *er* in *her*.	1	3

Generalization	Number of Series	Reliability Percentage
30. An *o* followed by *ld* makes a long sound (c*o*ld; s*o*ld).	1	100
31. An *i* followed by *ld* or *ght* makes a long sound (m*i*ld; l*i*ght).	1	75
32. When *g* appears at the end of a word, it makes a sound as in *tag*.	1	46
33. When *y* appears at the beginning of a word, it is a consonant with the same sound as the *y* in *yellow* and *yet*.	1	100
34. When *lk* occurs at the end of a word, the two letters have a single sound (ta*lk*).	1	100
35. When *mb* occurs at the end of a word, the two letters usually have a single sound (du*mb*).	1	100
36. When *x* appears at the end of a word, it has two sounds—*k* and *s* together (bo*x*).	1	100
37. When *gh* appears at the beginning of a word, it makes the *g* sound as in *ghost*.	1	100
38. When *x* appears at the beginning of a word, it makes the sound at the beginning of *xylophone*.	1	0 (no words in series)

Adapted from Sorenson, 1983, pp. 70–75. Used by permission of the author.

Should Phonic Generalizations Be Taught?

We advocate teaching phonic generalizations to children as part of decoding-strategy instruction. Phonics is a supporting skill area, along with context clues and structural analysis. When used together, skills in these three areas reduce the reader's uncertainty about the meaning of a specific word. Relying too much on phonics, on the other hand, creates an imbalance and results in inefficient decoding strategies. If a word is completely unfamiliar to the reader and is not part of his or her meaning-and-thinking vocabulary, then sounding out *by itself* will rarely result in discovery of the word's meaning.

As we mentioned earlier, phonics has been a controversial area of beginning reading instruction for many years. Most reading experts agree that there is value in teaching children sound/symbol generalizations directly or explicitly; debate has focused on how that teaching should be accomplished. It is not possible for us to discuss each individual method of teaching phonics or each phonics game or workbook currently on the market. At our last count, there were over 100 commercially published ways to teach phonics, plus hundreds of reinforcement games and workbooks.

Most reading experts agree that phonics should be taught directly.

Phonics instruction in schools traditionally has occurred as part of basal reader lessons. However, phonics is also learned and taught when commercial materials are not used, such as in literature-based, integrated, or holistic approaches to teaching reading (Dahl et al., 1999). As Freppon and Dahl (1991) state in an article titled "Learning about Phonics in a Whole Language Classroom," "The debate in this article is not about the usefulness of phonics in reading but about how phonics is learned and taught" (p. 190). They suggest some ways to incorporate teaching phonics into holistic classrooms:

1. Kindergarten programs should focus on providing children with daily reading and writing experiences to establish that print carries meaning. Repeated readings of children's literature, including predictable books in the classroom collection, practicing language through chants and songs, using written messages around the classroom, and writing in journals are a few of the experiences that help establish the idea that print is for communication.

2. Children can be nudged toward sound/symbol awareness through individual and small-group sessions in which the teacher helps them when they are selecting words to write. Teachers can demonstrate sound/symbol associations by helping children listen for sounds and make connections with letters. For example, if a child wants to write about *dinosaurs*, the teacher can model the sounds by pronouncing the word in syllables (di-no-saurs) and pointing out that you can hear a *D* as in David (or as in the name of a child in

the class whose name begins with the letter D). These demonstrations focus attention on sound/symbol associations.

3. Teachers can model writing by talking as they write messages and other written communications. As Kristen, a teacher observed by Freppon and Dahl, said, "It is not all right for me as teacher to write without talking. Children need to see me thinking through the process. I model my thinking, and I see them learning to think about letters and sounds" (p. 194).

Whenever anything is written for the class to read, whether it is the daily calendar, a group experience chart, or a list of daily chores, the teacher should talk through the message while writing it and model specific information about letters and sound/symbol associations. For example, if you were writing a list of classroom chores beginning with "Water the plants," you might say, "*Water* begins with the same letter as *Wendy*'s name and so does the day to water our plants, *Wednesday*."

What Phonic Generalizations Should Be Taught?

We suggest that you teach those generalizations that are honest and dependable— that is, those that will work when children try to use them. If children encounter a word to which a generalization could be applied, does it apply? With what degree of success? A high percent of utility is considered to be 75–80 percent. Through the application of computer technology, Sorenson (1983) updated Bailey and Clymer's classic 1960s studies with improved research design and data analyses. She developed a revised list of phonic generalizations taught in grades 1–3 in five leading basal series and then calculated reliability percentages for each one (see Figure 6.5). Some of the generalizations may seem to duplicate or overlap with some others because they are compiled from various series. Be sure to check the reliability of phonic generalizations in school district and state standards.

Is There a Sequence to Phonics Instruction?

Frankly, after a study of the research and an examination of commercial materials, it becomes apparent that there is no established sequence for teaching phonic generalizations. The sequence we suggest below is based on clustering widely accepted generalizations into broad categories and across phonics programs, especially those programs that are part of basal readers.

1. Phonemic awareness and letter-name knowledge
2. Consonant generalizations
3. Vowel generalizations

Our sequence of instruction cannot tell you if a specific generalization should be taught before or after any other generalizations, but it can serve as a rough guide.

What Is the Role of Letter-Name Knowledge in Phonics Instruction?

Knowledge of letter names has been the subject of much research and controversy. Although it has not been clearly demonstrated that such knowledge can predict success in learning to read, we believe that if children have quick recognition of letter names, phonics instruction will be easier for both teacher and child. When you are teaching the sound or sounds of a letter, children should have no difficulty recognizing the symbol they are to match with the sound(s). If they are not certain of the symbol, trying to add the task of matching a sound to that symbol will only result in confusion and slow down phonics instruction. A quick screening of letter-name knowledge is shown in Figure 6.6. If children fall below 80 percent correct on either the uppercase or the lowercase screening, then some instruction in letter names is indicated, along with an assessment of knowledge of *all* letter names.

Process Guide 6.3

Return to Chapter 1, and find Marissa's recipe for making a peanut butter and jelly sandwich. Working in small groups, examine and discuss her spelling of words. What evidence do you find that Marissa understands some sound/symbol associations? Discuss her knowledge of these associations—which ones seem secure and which seem to be undeveloped.

Teaching Phonic Generalizations

The authors of *Becoming a Nation of Readers* (Anderson et al., 1985) offer this advice to place phonics instruction in perspective:

> The right maxims for phonics are: Do it early. Keep it simple. Except in cases of diagnosed individual need, phonics instruction should have been completed by the end of second grade. (p. 43)

Stated even more bluntly in the words of the military: *Keep It Simple, Stupid,* or KISS! (with apologies to all, of course).

Phonics instruction should

1. Proceed analytically
2. Personalize lessons
3. Consider the reliability of each generalization
4. Include oral instruction and practice
5. Be taught in the context of authentic reading activities

Proceed Analytically. Most phonics methods can be placed on a continuum ranging from analytic to synthetic, according to the instructional sequence that dominates. Few methods are either/or, although most tend to lean more in one di-

FIGURE 6.6 Quick Screening for Letter-Name Knowledge

Directions:
1. Hand card with *uppercase* letters to child.
2. Say: "Say the name of each letter I point to."
3. Record child's response on a separate sheet of paper. Use + for correct and NR for no response. Record incorrect responses as accurately as possible.
4. Repeat for *lowercase* letters.

CARD 1 (UPPERCASE LETTERS)		CARD 2 (lowercase letters)	
1. A _____	6. S _____	1. b _____	6. d _____
2. C _____	7. W _____	2. e _____	7. h _____
3. F _____	8. O _____	3. r _____	8. n _____
4. K _____	9. Y _____	4. v _____	9. t _____
5. M _____	10. D _____	5. i _____	10. u _____

CORRECT/POSSIBLE

UPPERCASE   lowercase

_____/10   _____/10

rection than another. R. J. Smith and Johnson (1980) explain these two categories of phonics methods very concisely:

> *Analytic phonics.* After children have learned a number of sight words containing a particular letter-sound correspondence, they are taught or asked to discover the relationship. For example, after they have learned *dog, Dick, bad, weed,* and *dime,* they are asked what all those words have in common. Students might complete a workbook page on the sound represented by the letter *d.* Rarely are sounds isolated in analytic phonics; instead, they are referred to by sample words. "D" doesn't represent "duh" but refers to "the sound you hear at the beginning of Dick." The emphasis is on whole-to-part, whereas in synthetic phonics the emphasis is on part-to-whole.
>
> *Synthetic phonics.* The children are specifically taught certain letter-sound correspondences and are then asked to synthesize them—to blend them—into words. For example, once the children have learned the sounds of *s, n, p,* and *i,* they are asked to blend them to form *pin, sip, sin, nip, pins, spin.* In essence, this is a spelling approach to phonics and is of questionable value in the early grades. Children come to school wanting to learn to read, not wanting to memorize tiny sound segments. (p. 103)

We agree with Smith and Johnson in favoring an analytically oriented lesson sequence for phonics instruction. We believe that the less isolated the sound drill and instruction, the better. Pure synthetic methods or those leaning heavily in that direction often cause beginning readers confusion as they try to blend the sounds together to form whole words. They must learn to recognize that the sounds of a letter change, depending on its position in a word. Medial and ending sounds are different from beginning ones, such as the *d* in *dog, middle,* and *placed.* From a teaching view, it takes enormous amounts of teacher energy to keep beginning readers interested in isolated sound instruction and practice. Even though there is some isolated sound practice in even the most analytic method, it is brief, and sounds are quickly placed back into the context of whole words.

Personalize Lessons.   Phonics instruction should begin with children's own words. When a phonic generalization is being introduced, the words used for the initial instruction should be those that are personal to the children. From these words that children know personally, sounds can be identified and then transferred to other words not so easily recognized. Words from journals, experience charts, and other classroom experiences can be used. Though each child's words will be slightly different, holidays, school experiences, and community events supply enough key words common to all children. If a basal reader phonics lesson begins with whole words that are not personal ones for the children, save them; use personal ones when you introduce the phonic generalization. *Then* use the words suggested by the basal reader manual to provide practice in transferring the generalization. This sequence gives the children a personal anchor in their own vocabulary for the generalization:

1. Use the children's key, or personal, words to introduce the phonic generalization analytically.
2. Then move to the basal reader's suggested lesson sequence, if it is analytical.
3. Use basal reader words to show transfer of the phonic generalization to other words.

Consider the Reliability of Each Generalization.   The dependability or usefulness of the phonic generalizations you teach to beginning readers is important. We believe that only generalizations with a high reliability—75 or 80 percent and higher—should be taught to children. Check the phonic generalizations presented in Figure 6.5 for their reliability percentages. We recommend not teaching any generalization that has a low reliability percentage. Simply skip that portion of a basal reader lesson. Both teacher's and children's time can be better spent with other reading instruction and practice. If you encounter a generalization that is not on the list, decide whether it makes sense to teach the generalization in view of all you know about phonics instruction from reading this chapter.

Include Oral Instruction and Practice.   Children must *hear* the teacher say words and sounds, and they themselves must *say* those sounds and words for the teacher to hear. Using oral rhymes and chants helps children group words by spelling patterns. Keeping initial instruction and practice oral is not difficult.

When personal words are used, the teacher should pronounce each one for the children and have them repeat the words, just to be certain the children really do know the words. When worksheets and games are used, the directions should be read aloud to the children and be restated by them in their own words. If picture activities are part of phonics instruction and practice, children should say the name of each picture to be certain they all are using the same label. Calling the picture of a hat a "cap" while practicing the /k/ sound of the letter *c* will result in frustration and confusion for children. Checking the names of pictures with the children before beginning an activity will eliminate uncertainty. If phonic games that use whole words are substituted for some of the written worksheets in commercial programs, children will receive additional oral practice.

Be Taught in the Context of Authentic Reading Activities. By pointing out how phonic generalizations work in real print, the teacher makes them more meaningful to children. From reading books and poems aloud to composing a morning message or referencing environmental print, opportunities to teach phonics are everywhere. For example, after reading a book or poem aloud for enjoyment, the teacher can reread the selection, pointing out words that begin with the same initial sound. Children can then be asked to find other words beginning with the

Calling the picture of a hat a "cap" while practicing the /k/ sound will result in confusion for children.

same sound. How an *r* affects vowel sounds in words might be discussed. Irregularities in phonic generalizations also can be talked about in context: the *oo* combination makes a different sound in *school* than it does in *book*. Later—as students and teacher write and read a morning message about events in the school day, for example—opportunities should be sought to reinforce the generalizations that arose during the rereading of the story. Phonic generalizations also can be reinforced when children read environmental print such as labels in the classroom, name tags, and signs found around the school.

Phonics Beyond Beginning Reading Instruction

The issue of how long to continue phonics instruction, especially for those children who seem to have great difficulty, is of continuing concern to both classroom teachers and reading specialists. As Memory (1992) notes, for a variety of reasons content teachers are not able to help students learn or practice or apply decoding skills. He makes the following suggestions for helping weaker readers:

> Unfortunately, the teachers of content area classes are not in a position to provide much help in decoding those words. The large enrollment of most content area classes makes one-to-one assistance by the teacher difficult; and, in any case, much of the reading is assigned to be done outside of class, where the teacher is not present. These circumstances, however, do not absolutely prevent content area teachers from helping their weaker readers decode words or prevent them from providing other ways for that help to be obtained. This assistance may involve nothing more systematic and extensive than responding to raised hands when the students have been given a few minutes at the end of class to begin a reading assignment. If poor readers are reluctant to ask for teacher help in class, the assistance may have to be provided by "buddies," or peer tutors, either in class or in a study hall. Or if the teacher is fortunate, the aid may be given by an adult volunteer. In fact, it can be argued that the full potential of tutoring as an instructional strategy can be reached only if the peer or adult does a good job of assisting the weak student in decoding words. (p. 210)

But what kind of tutoring or assistance can peer and adult tutors provide? Memory gives specific tutoring tips in his article. We have listed a few of them below, along with some examples.

1. Give the reader obvious clues to pronunciation; for example, compound words can be divided.
2. Pronounce unknown words that cannot easily be sounded out; for example, *naive, fatigue.*
3. Point out context clues when they are obvious; for example, Bill was *petrified,* or scared silly.
4. Circle or print on separate paper familiar, regular clusters or syllables in unknown longer words to aid pronunciation; for example, *-ink, -ate, -ack.*
5. Point out root or base words and their affixes; for example, *underdeveloped.*

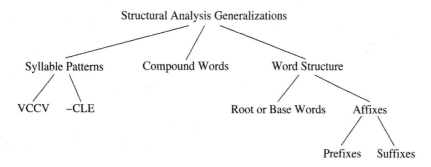

FIGURE 6.7   Categories of Structural Analysis Generalizations

Teaching Structural Analysis Generalizations

There is a widely held belief that phonics instruction should be completed by the end of second grade. As reading becomes more complex from grade 3 on, longer and longer words appear with greater frequency. What about the pronunciation and meaning of the 10,000 new words students will encounter each year, from fifth grade on (Cunningham, 1998)? How are students to deal with this load of new, longer words?

When, during reading, children encounter longer words that are unfamiliar, skills in structural analysis may help them divide these words into pronounceable units to which phonics skills can be applied. There are considerably fewer structural analysis generalizations than phonic ones. Instruction in structural analysis should also proceed analytically, beginning with children's personal, or key, words. The reliability of any generalization to be taught should be considered, and plenty of oral instruction and practice should be provided.

Promoting readiness for structural analysis instruction involves helping children hear segments or syllables in longer words. Simply clapping the syllables to a new longer word is an easy way to begin a structural analysis lesson. The clapping activity should be brief and should emphasize hearing the number of syllables in a word. When a longer word is being introduced within a basal reader story, as part of teaching the word you might have the children clap it in syllables and pronounce it aloud.

Reliability of structural analysis generalizations varies, but we recommend teaching only those with high reliability percentages (75–80 percent or higher). Burmeister (1968) determined the reliability percentages of a number of generalizations that are commonly taught. We present here only those that appear with great frequency in commercial materials, especially basal readers. The generalizations usually fall in two categories: those related to syllable division and those involving word structure. (See Figure 6.7.)

Generalizations	*Reliability Percentage*
Divide words between a prefix and a root, or base, word; for example, *trans-continental, sub-heading.*	95

Generalizations	*Reliability Percentage*
Divide words between two root, or base, words; for example, *cow-boy, some-time.*	95
Divide words between a suffix and a root, or base, word; for example, *bright-est, sail-ing.*	74
When two vowels are separated by two consonants in longer words, divide between the two consonants. *Pattern:* VC/CV, as in *mag-net; suc-cess. Note: ph, ch, th,* and *sh* are not separated.	94
Words that end in a consonant plus the letters *le* form a syllable with the consonant and *le. Pattern:* C + *le*, as in *tri-ple; ma-ple.*	93

The third generalization is mentioned not because we advocate its use, but rather because it is commonly found in beginning reading materials. Our rule of thumb about which suffixes (and prefixes) to teach is *When you, the teacher, must refer to the teacher's answer key for the meaning of a prefix or suffix, don't teach it to children.* For example, *-ic* and *-al* as suffixes carry little easily perceived meaning. On the other hand, prefixes such as *trans-, sub-, un-, post-, pro-,* and *anti-* have meanings that can be clearly established. When teaching the third generalization, teach only those suffixes (and prefixes) that clearly carry meaning, rather than teaching it as a blanket rule.

The following sequence of instruction in structural analysis can be adapted to fit almost any lesson found in commercial materials—both basal readers and content area textbooks—when it is necessary to preteach difficult vocabulary:

1. Write the word to be analyzed on the chalkboard or a piece of chart paper, pronouncing it several times for the children. Read the context from which the word was pulled and refer the children to that point in the text.
2. Divide the word into syllables and write them under or next to the whole word. Have the children clap or beat the syllables with you several times. Older children may simply repeat the syllables.
3. Discuss the clues you used to break up the word, such as a prefix, suffix, or syllable pattern.
4. Return to the context and discuss the meaning of the word, noting any clues from Step 3, such as a prefix or root word meaning, that helped with predicting the meaning.

Assessing Decoding Strategies and Skills

Formal testing of decoding strategies and skills is usually not necessary on a day-to-day basis. We suggest a functional approach; that is, while children are learning and practicing strategies and skills, the teacher should carefully observe their work and collect signs of progress and misunderstanding on the spot. Reteaching, increased practice, modeling, and demonstrations can be given as needed.

Periodically, though, and for children who seem to be having continual difficulty, formal assessment may be valuable. Use of the achievement tests provided as part of commercial materials (including basal readers) will give the teacher a record of progress. These tests, however, are usually contrived exercises and thus are not good indicators of whether children are using decoding skills and strategies in their reading and writing. If formal tests must be used, samples and observations of children's writing and responses to reading, such as running records, should be added to the test data before any conclusions are reached about children's decoding ability.

Summary

This chapter presented a combined view of instruction in decoding strategies and their supporting skill areas. Two strategies were explained. Suggestions and recommendations for teaching the supporting skill areas—the use of context clues, phonics, and structural analysis—completed the chapter.

FOLLOW-THROUGH ACTIVITIES

Note: Level 1 activities may require limited access to children or classrooms. Level 2 activities should be completed using children and classrooms.

Level 1 and Level 2 Activities
Locate a teacher's manual for a primary-grade level from a basal reader series. You may work in pairs to complete the following activities:

1. Find one story in the teacher's manual that appears to also teach a decoding skills lesson in phonics or structural analysis. Write down on paper the generalization that is the focus of the lesson and identify its reliability percentage using the lists of generalizations presented in this chapter. How reliable is the generalization?

2. List the lesson steps the manual suggests for teaching the generalization. Would you make any revisions on the basis of what you have learned in this chapter?

3. Apply the checklist below to the teacher's manual. Discuss your findings with others in your class.

   a. Is decoding defined in the series manual? If so, how?

   b. Is decoding instruction built into each story?

   c. Are the lesson steps designed to teach phonics and structural analysis skills analytically or synthetically?

   d. Does each story taught contain a balance of skills instruction and include context clue instruction as well as phonics and structural analysis?

   e. Are lessons skill-oriented and/or strategy-oriented?

Level 2 Activity
Visit a first- or second-grade classroom in which the teacher is not using a basal reader or other commercial materials to teach decoding, especially phonics. Interview the teacher about his or her approach to decoding. Observe reading and writing lessons and activities, and note how the teacher provides decoding instruction, modeling, and demonstrations. Compare your notes with the suggestions presented in this chapter. How similar to their suggestions are the activities you observed? How different? What additional ways of teaching decoding did you observe?

WORKING WITH PARENTS

Parent involvement includes parent education. Describing techniques you are using with children in school to help them become independent in using decoding strategies informs parents and gives them the opportunity to reinforce your teaching. For example, when children ask a parent to help them with a word they do not know, what would you like the parent to say? We hope your answer is "Encourage the child to guess a word that makes sense." Teachers can give parents concrete suggestions by developing a question-and-answer sheet that is sent home after a parents' meeting or individual conference. The information sheet might be arranged simply, as follows.

> QUESTION: *What should I do when my child asks for help with a word?*
>
> ANSWER: Have her or him first guess a word that makes sense.
>
> Why? The goal of reading is to make sense of print, to gain meaning from the written word. We stress that in school each day.
> You could also ask your child to look at the pictures for help, to read ahead and then go back, to try to sound out the word, and, if all else fails, to skip the word. These strategies provide the same kinds of guidance they get in school, so you are working together with us to emphasize getting meaning from the written word.

Fact sheets can be developed for other questions related to decoding instruction, too.

> QUESTION: *What can I do to help my child with phonics?*
>
> ANSWER: Relax--we are working hard in school with phonics instruction. You can, however, reinforce

some of what we are doing in two important areas:
helping your child with the rhythm of our language
and helping with knowledge of letter names.

1. Help your child keep his or her picture dictionary of
   the alphabet full of good pictures.
2. Read to your child whenever you can. Ask her or him to
   retell the story in sequence.
3. Label objects in his or her room or around the house
   until the words become familiar. No, not everything at
   the same time--just one or two objects until those
   words are learned!
4. Memorize favorite poems or nursery rhymes with your
   child, and recite them together for fun.

RESOURCES

Cunningham, P. M. (1998). The multisyllabic word dilemma: Helping students build meaning, spell, and read "big" words. *Reading & Writing Quarterly: Overcoming Learning Difficulties, 14,* 189–218.

The author summarizes research and presents practical teaching strategies for helping students read and spell multisyllabic words.

Eldridge, J. L. (1999). *Phonics for teachers.* Upper Saddle River, NJ: Prentice Hall.

This basic text for teachers covers phonics and phonics teaching.

Ericson, L., & Juliebo, M. F. (1998). *The phonological awareness handbook for kindergarten and primary teachers.* Newark, DE: International Reading Association.

This easy-to-read text offers entertaining ways to practice sound and word play in an integrated language arts environment.

Glazer, S. M. (1998). *Phonics, spelling, and word study: A sensible approach.* Norwood, MA: Christopher-Gordon.

This concise book shares sensible, logical, and meaningful approaches that guide students in using the written coding system to read and spell.

Griffith, P. L., & Olson, M. W. (1992). Phonemic awareness helps beginning readers break the code. *The Reading Teacher, 45,* 516–523.

The importance of phonemic awareness and whether it can be developed and assessed are discussed in this article.

Routman, R. (1991). *Invitations: Changing as teachers and learners K–12.* Portsmouth, NH: Heinemann.

Pages 147–157 offer excellent suggestions for placing phonics in perspective in holistic classrooms.

Stahl, S. A., Duffy-Hester, A. M., & Stahl, K. A. D. (1998). Everything you wanted to know about phonics (but were afraid to ask). *Reading Research Quarterly, 33,* 338–355.

Published as a theory and research-into-practice article, this piece suggests principles of good phonics instruction, especially on pages 339–344.

Wagstaff, J. M. (1997/1998). Building practical knowledge of letter-sound correspondences: A beginner's word wall and beyond. *The Reading Teacher, 51,* 298–304.

This article has suggestions for teaching phonemic awareness and letter-sound knowledge.

REFERENCES

Anderson, R. C., Hiebert, E. H, Scott, J. A., & Wilkinson, I. A. G. (1985). *Becoming a nation of readers: The report of the Commission on Reading.* Washington, DC: National Institute of Education.

Ball, E. W., & Blachman, B. A. (1991). Does phoneme awareness training in kindergarten make a difference in early word recognition and developmental spelling? *Reading Research Quarterly, 26,* 49–66.

Burmeister, L. E. (1968). Usefulness of phonic generalizations. *The Reading Teacher, 21,* 349–356.

Busink, R. (1997). Reading and phonological awareness: What we have learned and how we can use it. *Reading Research and Instruction, 36,* 199–215.

Clay, M. M. (1993). *Reading recovery: A guidebook for teachers in training.* Portsmouth, NH: Heinemann.

Cunningham, P. M. (1998). The multisyllabic word dilemma: Helping students build meaning, spell, and read "big" words. *Reading & Writing Quarterly: Overcoming Learning Difficulties, 14,* 189–218.

Dahl, K. L., Scharer, P. L., Lawson, L. L., & Grogan, P. R. (1999). Phonics instruction and student achievement in whole language first-grade classrooms. *Reading Research Quarterly, 34,* 312–341.

Freppon, P. A., & Dahl, K. L. (1991). Learning about phonics in a whole language classroom. *Language Arts, 68,* 190–197.

Griffith, P. L. (1991). Phonemic awareness helps first graders invent spellings and third graders remember correct spellings. *Journal of Reading Behavior, 23,* 215–233.

Memory, D. (1992). Guiding students to independent decoding in content area classes. In E. K. Dishner, T. W. Bean, J. E. Readence, & D. W. Moore (Eds.), *Reading in the content areas: Improving classroom instruction* (3rd ed., pp. 210–218). Dubuque, IA: Kendall/Hunt.

Ruddell, R. B., Ruddell, M. R., & Singer, H. (Eds.). (1994). *Theoretical models and processes of reading* (4th ed.). Newark, DE: International Reading Association.

Smith, F. (1988). *Understanding reading: A psycholinguistic analysis of reading and learning to read* (4th ed.). Hillsdale, NJ: Erlbaum.

Smith, R. J., & Johnson, D. D. (1980). *Teaching children to read* (2nd ed.). Reading, MA: Addison-Wesley.

Snider, V. E. (1997). The relationship between phonemic awareness and later reading achievement. *The Journal of Educational Research, 90,* 203–211.

Sorenson, N. (1983). *A study of the reliability of phonic generalizations in five primary-level basal reading programs.* Unpublished doctoral dissertation, Arizona State University.

Stahl, S. A., Duffy-Hester, A. M., & Stahl, K. A. D. (1998). Everything you wanted to know about phonics (but were afraid to ask). *Reading Research Quarterly, 33,* 338–355.

Tangel, D. M., & Blachman, B. A. (1992). Effect of phoneme awareness instruction on kindergarten children's invented spelling. *Journal of Reading Behavior, 24,* 233–261.

CHAPTER

7 Vocabulary

INTRODUCTION

Whether you're using a stinger at sunset or a pocket rocket at Malibu, surfing is a thrilling sport. Everyone enjoys getting tubed, but even hot-doggers occasionally go over the falls. Beginners usually start by catching soup before advancing to full-blown waves. Once they learn to catch the right wave and bottom-turn proficiently, surfers attempt rollercoasters and other intricate maneuvers.

Fluent reading means being able to move with ease through the wide variety of materials children encounter both in school and in nonschool activities. Fluent reading is intimately related to the ability to comprehend an author's message. If children possess a large stock of words to draw on, comprehension is certainly much easier. On the other hand, lack of a large reading vocabulary places children at a distinct disadvantage in getting meaning from print.

Possessing vocabulary might be better described as *owning* words. Ownership of words means that children feel comfortable with them and use them with facility in their daily language activities. As children expand the stock of words they own, they increase the opportunity to broaden their experiences. As Readence, Bean, and Baldwin (1998) have succinctly pointed out, all groups of people, whether surfers, carpenters, educators, or anything else, share special terminology peculiar to that group. *Insiders* are those individuals who use this vocabulary freely to communicate with members of a given group. *Outsiders* are those individuals who are ignorant of the special vocabulary and are, therefore, restricted in their communicative abilities. Ownership of an increasingly large number of words enhances children's ability to broaden their experiences by becoming insiders with new materials and new authors. This becomes even more important as children begin to read and learn in the content area subjects. Insiders will certainly have a better chance of success in academic learning than outsiders. If you were not an insider to the language of surfing, the opening paragraph was probably not particularly meaningful to you.

Research has shown that the most important factor in variability in reading comprehension is word knowledge (Ruddell, 1994). Words aid us in organizing our experiences, because they represent concepts in our environment and the interrelationships among those concepts. Words, acting as labels for concepts in our experience, facilitate our thinking processes; and since reading is a thinking process, vocabulary naturally is the prime contributor to reading comprehension. Anderson and Freebody (1985) concur, stating that it is probably safe to say that the number of word meanings a reader knows is an accurate predictor of his or her ability to comprehend text.

For these reasons, considerable attention to teaching children to own words is fundamental to instruction at all levels and is a key to children's success in reading and learning. This chapter will provide teachers with a repertoire of instructional strategies to foster children's ownership of words, as one step in becoming fluent readers.

GRAPHIC ORGANIZER

This graphic organizer summarizes the structure of Chapter 7:

OBJECTIVES

When you finish this chapter, you should be able to understand and discuss each of these statements:

1. Teaching children to own words is fundamental to their success in reading and learning.
2. Words are simply symbols that convey experiences and concepts.

3. As with all human experience, context is very important in vocabulary development.
4. Categorization helps children organize new concepts and learning in relation to previously acquired concepts.
5. Visual representations of information in text help children see relationships among words and concepts.
6. Activities designed to reinforce word definitions and meanings are necessary to make new words part of children's permanent vocabulary.
7. Direct instruction and practice with new words are essential to growth in children's vocabulary.

Guidelines for Developing Word Meaning

Vocabulary teaching in the schools traditionally has been accomplished through the following means:

1. Teaching phonic analysis in combination with teaching the meanings of structural elements
2. Teaching meanings from word lists found in commercial materials
3. Encouraging a habit of wide reading
4. Using workbook exercises to develop and reinforce word meanings
5. Leaving vocabulary to incidental learning—that is, assuming that vocabulary will grow without specific teacher attention

It can be argued that each of the above is a valid method of fostering vocabulary development, and it certainly can be said that any teaching method is better than no method at all. However, there are more effective strategies by which to build vocabulary. Accumulating evidence reveals that, for vocabulary learning, neither use of preselected word lists nor incidental teaching is well founded in research or practice. Although word meanings may be learned through wide reading, instruction is also needed to truly learn words of conceptual difficulty (such as those found in content textbooks) (Nagy, Anderson, & Herman, 1987).

Vocabulary is generally acquired in one of three ways. First, vocabulary may be learned through firsthand experience by interacting directly with the concept to be acquired. For example, children can learn the concept of *subtraction* by manipulating some type of counters such as straws or poker chips. Second, words may be learned through vicarious experience in which children are exposed indirectly to concepts represented by words. This can be accomplished through the use of videos, television, pictures, maps, and other associated audiovisual media. For instance, the difficulty of living in Antarctica may be learned by viewing a film or television program on the subject. Third, vocabulary may be acquired through the symbolic experience of a reader interacting with a text. The abstract concept *democracy* might best be learned this way. Therefore, vocabulary development strategies that capitalize on all of these ways are both psychologically and linguistically sound.

The following guidelines are recommended for teachers to consider as they develop vocabulary lessons:

1. *A word is not an object or idea; rather, it is a symbol for our experiences.* Experiences precede the generation of concepts. Words are simply symbols used to convey these concepts. In fact, words may be defined as a pattern of auditory or visual symbols that represent experiences or concepts (Readence, Bean, & Baldwin, 1998). This definition implies that word meanings are in an endless state of change, as the concepts that words represent are constantly being modified by daily experiences. Thus, words act as labels to enable children to communicate whatever is of immediate relevancy to them. The best learning of word meanings, therefore, takes place when words are taught from direct experiences.

2. *Words acquire meaning from the context in which they are used.* Knowing a word is not an all-or-nothing proposition. Words have multiple meanings, and children should be encouraged to work out those meanings as they appear in oral and written language. An experience of one of the authors provides an example of this principle. Feeling confident he knew the concept of *cat* and what it entailed, he encountered George, a cat without a tail. Upon asking the owner why the cat's tail was cut off, he received the following reply: "Its tail wasn't cut off; it's a Manx. They have no tail!" The author had to rethink his concept of cat and further modified his concept by reading a text about Manx cats and their relatives, the Rumpies and Stumpies, who are offspring of a mating between a Manx and a domestic shorthair cat. Of course, the author would not know cat as well as an individual who raises show cats! Knowing a general attribute or characteristic of a word is not the same as knowing the specific attributes of that word provided by the context in which it is encountered. Therefore, it is wise to present new words to children in an appropriate context rather than in isolation.

3. *Vocabulary learning should be situational.* Words to be learned should be drawn from children's experiences and from the materials they are using, such as basals, content texts, and trade books. These words are of immediate relevance. The use of commercial vocabulary development materials imposes additional new words on readers who already have enough new words to master during the course of regular classroom instruction.

4. *Vocabulary should be taught directly, not left to incidental learning.* Systematic and continual attention to vocabulary development is a necessary part of reading instruction. It is unwise to assume that children will learn words on their own as they encounter them in print. A habit of wide reading, closely akin to incidental vocabulary learning, will not necessarily cause vocabulary growth with difficult words unless it is coupled with specific instruction by the teacher. In fact, the authors believe that the best way to help children develop word meanings is to get them actively involved in the learning. Make the learning of new words more work for the children than for yourself—remember, you already know the words!

Knowing a word is not an all-or-nothing proposition.

5. *Using a variety of methods to teach meaning is better than using any one method alone.* Children can, and do, learn in a variety of ways; therefore, be eclectic. Develop a repertoire of instructional strategies that expose children to a combination of methods that will enhance their learning. This provides both you and the children with an opportunity to recognize which techniques work best and, at the same time, holds their attention and generates interest, because new words are not presented in the same way all the time. Doing the same thing daily can be tedious for everyone involved, both children and teacher.

6. *Developing word meanings requires practice.* Just as vocabulary development requires good, solid instruction, it also demands continual reinforcement. There is a tendency, especially in commercial vocabulary materials, to push the idea that practice by the children without prior instruction from the teacher will develop vocabulary. This assumption is false, and children will find this type of vocabulary development completely boring. Practice is reinforcement and should *follow* direct instruction. Long-term retention of new words by children is fostered through opportunities to use the words over and over, preferably in a variety of language settings. This relates directly to owning words. A child can acquire words at many levels of facility. (To review this concept, go back to Chapter 1 and review Principle 7: *Reading is one of the communication tools.*) There are words you feel comfortable with and use in daily speaking and writing. When you encounter these same words in reading and listening situations, you comprehend them quickly. Other words, however, may be understood only at the levels of reading and listening (receptive modes), where context exists as an aid to understanding. Some of these words are not firmly enough fixed that you will risk using them in speaking or in writing (expressive modes). Truly acquiring, owning, and using a word can take much time and practice. Such practice can be provided through individual work, by pairing children together to help one another, or by having them work in small and large groups. In any case, vocabulary development must include extensive practice involving reading, listening, speaking, and writing new words.

7. *One of the most significant factors in vocabulary development is teacher attitude.* A teacher's excitement about new words can be contagious. The interest a teacher can stimulate in words is a critical factor in vocabulary learning. Model words for your children; let them hear and see you using them. Let them see you using a dictionary to verify a word meaning. Don't be afraid to use a big word with children. After all, the interest you convey in words is directly related to the interest children will show in learning new words.

Getting Ready to Teach Vocabulary

Children are swimming in a sea of words each day in school—and some of them are drowning. Children bring to school a wealth of vocabulary from their everyday experiences, and on entering the school building, they are bombarded with words. There is no need to seek out a list of additional words children need to learn each week. Such lists are arbitrarily contrived by individuals who have little or no knowledge of the children in your classroom and their vocabulary needs. So where should the words you teach originate? Check the daily activities children are involved in for words they need to know. Start with important words children will need to know in their basal readers and in their content area subjects. Other sources of words may be their own free reading, the newspaper, or television. Both school and nonschool vocabulary should be considered.

Consider the difficulty of the words. First, do the children have an *anchor* for the new words? If they have had any prior experience with the word, you should utilize that knowledge in teaching the word by building a bridge between what children know and what they have to learn. Your task will be more difficult if an anchor does not exist. Second, are the new words technical in nature? That is, are they specific to a subject matter or area? If so, chances are that children will not have been previously exposed to the word, and the anchor may therefore be missing. Grasping the concept of *photosynthesis* in science will be more difficult than grasping a concept drawn from children's everyday experiences. Third, do the new words have multiple meanings? Is a cat a domesticated feline, a wild animal, a cool person, or a tractor? It depends on the context, and this possibility of multiple meanings requires tolerance of the relative degrees to which children may know a word. A child who knows just one of the meanings of a word may become confused in attempting to apply that meaning when another is required for understanding. Fourth, are you dealing with figurative language? Similes, metaphors, and other figures of speech present problems that other terms do not. The psychological processes involved in interpreting a metaphor or a simile are much more involved than those used to interpret a nonfigurative term. For example, knowing that cotton candy is sweet and comes on a stick will not help children interpret the sentence "the clouds in the sky were like cotton candy," unless they also know that both clouds and cotton candy can be fluffy. Finally, are you teaching or reinforcing the new vocabulary words? Teaching new words requires exposing children to the new words before they read, as well as monitoring their learning of the words during and after reading. Reinforcing new words requires practice. The tasks of teaching words and reinforcing words are different. Above all, considering the difficulty of teaching new words, have available a dictionary, a thesaurus, and a book of synonyms and antonyms to help in the teaching process.

Consider the time involved in teaching new words: How long will it take? That depends on the previous two considerations—the origin and the difficulty of the words. You need to consider your goal as well. The immediate goal of teaching a word to children to enable them to cope with a text is different from teaching a word that needs to become a permanent part of their language repertoire. Further, you must deal with the children's reasons for learning the word. They must sense that new words are relevant to their experiences, so that they can continue to gain facility with spoken and written language. It is imperative that children sense this, rather than feeling that they are learning new words only because the teacher dictates that they do so.

It is with the above guidelines and considerations in mind that we present a variety of instructional strategies for developing word meanings. In so doing, we distinguish between *initial vocabulary acquisition* and *subsequent vocabulary development*, as we maintain that the instructional focus for each of these is different.

Children enter school with vast oral language backgrounds; that is, their listening and speaking vocabularies are extensively developed. Beginning reading instruction can utilize this oral language background in acquainting children with the printed word. Activities designed to foster initial or early reading vocabulary growth must necessarily be child-centered.

On the other hand, beyond the initial stages of learning to read, subsequent vocabulary development becomes more materials-oriented and more teacher-oriented. As children mature and gain facility with the printed word in the middle grades, reading quickly becomes the vehicle to augment their listening, speaking, and writing vocabularies. Words acquire meaning from the context of the content area materials that a child uses, rather than from the personal meaning the child attaches to them. Through print, as well as other forms of communication, children can gain vast amounts of new experiences, learn new words, and acquire additional meanings for old words. That is, as children experience the printed word, an integration of the processes of learning to read and reading to learn begins—an integration that starts slowly but rapidly increases as children grow, learn, and experience print in its many forms.

The focus of the remainder of this chapter is on developing meaning vocabulary, or subsequent vocabulary development. For convenience, the strategies described in the next four sections of the chapter will be labeled (1) strategies emphasizing context, (2) categorization strategies, (3) strategies for visually representing information, and (4) extension activities.

Strategies Emphasizing Context

Chapter 6 discussed the use of context as a valuable decoding tool in unlocking the meaning of unknown words. In this section, that discussion will be expanded, since context can also be a valuable tool for increasing children's vocabulary. The *power* of context, indeed, cannot be underestimated; all human experience is dependent on it. Context dictates appropriate behavior and response. For example, having a beer might be appropriate at home after a long day at the office, but it probably would be considered highly inappropriate at a school board meeting.

It is difficult to think of reading without context, as it is a natural and necessary part of the process. Many reading authorities stress the importance of context in verifying and interpreting word meanings. Context is necessary for dealing with multimeaning words, word connotations, and other nuances of meaning inherent in language (Anderson & Nagy, 1991). The use of context enables children to make more informed predictions about the meanings of words in print and to monitor those predictions by checking them for syntactic and semantic appropriateness as reading continues. Frequently, writers provide clues to the meanings of words in sentences. Therefore, it is essential that children be able to use these clues to derive meaning from print. This section will describe three strategies that stress the importance of context:

- Contextual redefinition
- Vocabulary self-collection strategy
- Possible sentences

Contextual Redefinition

Contextual redefinition (Readence, Bean, & Baldwin, 1998) provides teachers with a format to communicate to children the importance of context in ascertaining meaning. It is simple to use, requires little extra teacher preparation for its presentation, and provides for transfer to other reading that children may undertake on their own. It is most effective when children encounter in their reading a few difficult words that may be defined by the context in which they occur. To demonstrate contextual redefinition, write a definition for each of the following words:

1. Hippophagy
2. Scabrous
3. Looby
4. Celerity
5. Nonplus

Children can be taught to use the power of context clues to construct meaning.

You may have found it difficult to provide definitions from your head for these isolated words. If so, read the sentences below, and try again to provide definitions for the words. See if the context helps you. After you write definitions, get a dictionary and check the meanings you wrote.

1. The drought had been long and severe. The cattle had died, and only the horses survived. The hungry natives had to resort to *hippophagy* to avoid starvation.
2. Since Waldo didn't want his wife to know he liked pornography, he kept his *scabrous* literature locked up in his desk.
3. Because Fred was awkward and not too bright, he often acted like a regular *looby*, knocking over and breaking things.
4. When Clarabelle accidentally brushed by the hornet's nest, she dashed away with uncharacteristic *celerity* to avoid multiple stingings.
5. After the material had been thoroughly presented, even bright students such as Hilda were unable to do the assignment. That would *nonplus* any good teacher!

Most likely, if you did not know the meanings of the words, the sentences helped you to infer their meaning. This use of inference is typical of fluent readers; they use context, often subconsciously, as a clue to meaning. Less efficient readers, however, may not use context as effectively. When faced with new words in text, some children focus on the word alone and do not make use of relevant contextual information. By using contextual redefinition, you can teach children the power of context in helping them to develop word meanings and effectively process print.

The following steps should be considered in teaching contextual redefinition:

1. *Select unfamiliar words.* Examine the text that will be read, in order to identify those words that may present trouble to children as they read and that are necessary to understand important ideas in the text.
2. *Write a sentence.* A context needs to be provided for each word so that children have appropriate clues to the word's meaning. If the text already has such a context, use the sentence(s); if not, create one.
3. *Present the words in isolation.* Using a chalkboard or transparency, ask children to offer definitions for each word. Children must defend their individual guesses and, as a group, try to come to some consensus as to what they believe the best meaning is. Some guesses may be downright humorous and off the wall. However, seeing this humor is a part of the process of learning about the power that context can provide. For example, some children could guess that *celerity* had some association with "celery" or that *nonplus* was the "opposite of adding."
4. *Present the words in context.* Using the text sentence(s) or the sentence you previously developed, show the word in its appropriate context. Again, children should be asked to offer guesses about each word's meaning and to defend those definitions. By doing this, less able children can experience the thinking processes involved in inferring a meaning from context. As a result, children model appropriate reading behavior for one another.
5. *Dictionary verification.* A child or group of children should then consult a dictionary to verify the guesses offered.

Through contextual redefinition, teachers should point out—or, even better, have children discover—that simply guessing at the meaning of a word in isolation is usually not accurate and can even be frustrating. Children should realize that context gives them much more information about the meanings of words and allows for better, more informed guesses.

Another benefit of this strategy is that children become active participants in the discovery of new word meanings, rather than passive receivers (particularly of new meanings that are teacher-provided). Finally, contextual redefinition has the potential to transfer to other reading situations. Children can independently apply a strategy of informed guessing through context when they encounter unfamiliar words in their own reading.

Process Guide 7.1

Before reading about the next vocabulary strategy, choose a partner and try to develop a lesson using contextual redefinition. Choose a selection from an appropriate grade-level text, and identify words that may present trouble to children at that grade level as they read—words that are necessary to understand important ideas in the text. Develop some appropriate contexts for each of these words. Try to predict what words students might use to complete the sentences.

Vocabulary Self-Collection Strategy

The vocabulary self-collection strategy (VSS) (Haggard, 1992) differs from contextual redefinition in that children, rather than the teacher, generate the words to be explored and learned. VSS capitalizes on children's experience and world knowledge as anchors for new learning.

One of the most interesting aspects of this strategy is its versatility. VSS can be used for general vocabulary acquisition by having children collect words they encounter in their daily lives. The words that children believe should be learned are brought in and presented to the class. The use of VSS with basal readers or content area textbooks, an aspect of subsequent vocabulary development, is central to the present discussion. In this case, words selected from the materials children are reading and learning from are presented to the class for further exploration and refinement. The vocabulary self-collection strategy is conducted using the following steps:

1. *Select the word.* Children are asked to go back through the assigned reading and identify one word that they think should be studied. If it is a content lesson, children are asked to select words that will help them acquire content knowledge. If the whole class is to be involved in lieu of a basal reading group, teams of two or three members can be used to save time and maximize participation. This also allows for discussion of the words and their meanings before the class considers them. The teacher should also select a word.
2. *Define the word.* Each child or team of children nominates one word. The teacher does likewise. These words are recorded on the chalkboard. As this is done, each word is defined in its original context, and reasons for choosing the word are given. The teacher leads a discussion geared to clarification and expansion of the word's meaning. Whatever information the children and the teacher have from personal experiences and the reading selection is added to obtain the appropriate definition. If desirable, the dictionary may be consulted to verify this definition.
3. *Finalize the word list.* After the discussion has been completed, the list of words must be narrowed down. This is accomplished by eliminating duplications, words already known, or words children do not wish to learn. Words that comprise the final list are redefined as children record the words and their definitions in their vocabulary journals. Words that have been discarded may be recorded on children's personal vocabulary lists, if so desired.
4. *Extend word knowledge.* Follow-up activities are used to enable children to refine and extend the meanings of the words on the final list. With the basal reader, suggestions in the teacher's guide or the basal workbook may be used if they pertain to the words selected. The teacher may need to design other activities if the basal activities do not deal with all the words. With a

content selection, the words should be incorporated into the study materials for the unit and can be tested as to how they apply to the text information.

VSS can also be used with content reading assignments before children actually read the text. In this case, the teacher asks the children to preview the text before they read it, with the purpose being to identify one or two words they feel are important. In this way, teachers might be able to identify the particular words that will cause children problems. Additionally, children get practice doing a text preview, an activity that can be helpful in the independent reading of text.

VSS is easy to implement, and the burden of most of the work falls on the children. As a consequence, the children become actively involved in the lesson, and they become more sensitive to new words. The discussions become lively as children draw from their own experiences and feel the enjoyment that can come from owning new words.

Possible Sentences

Possible sentences (Moore & Moore, 1992) is a strategy that helps children learn new vocabulary and, at the same time, engages them in predicting sentences that they might possibly find in a text. Children are provided with new vocabulary words they will encounter in their reading, along with some words with which they are familiar. From these words they generate statements. They then attempt to verify the accuracy of their sentences as they read. In essence, the vocabulary words and the sentences generated from them serve as a guide for their reading. The possible sentences technique creates interest in the text that will be read, as children become actively involved in learning and using the words to be found in it. Indeed, a study by Stahl and Kapinus (1991) indicated that possible sentences is effective in teaching vocabulary and promoting recall of text information.

In discussing this strategy, the following text passage will be used:

Bees and Honey

Bees are very important because they produce a delicious and healthful food, honey. But more important, they pollinate plants, trees, and flowers to produce food for people to eat.

While pollination is the chief job bees do for people, what really concerns them is gathering and storing nectar and pollen for their own food. There are scout bees who find the best sources of nectar and who show the worker bees by doing a "bee dance." The dance tells the other bees how far and in which direction to fly, so they won't waste time looking.

Bees work and fly as quickly as possible to the nectar source. Once there, they draw nectar from flowers and carry it to their hives in their "honey stomachs." In the hives they give this nectar to workers, who put it into a cell of the honeycomb. By fanning their wings rapidly, the bees set up a current of air. This evaporates and ripens the nectar and turns it into honey.

When the honey is ripened, the bees cover each cell with a wax fluid until it is ready to use. Bees eat only about half the honey they make. Beekeepers collect the leftovers. (Adapted from Surmach, 1981, pp. 77–83)

The possible sentences technique consists of the following five steps:

1. *List key vocabulary.* In order to lead children to an understanding of the story, the following vocabulary words are selected and listed on the board:

   Bees and Honey

Bees	Pollen	Worker bees
Pollination	Scout bees	Honeycomb
Nectar	Honey stomachs	Bee dance
Hive	Honey	

   Note that the teacher lists both the unfamiliar words to be learned and the words children already know. The teacher should pronounce each word as it is written on the board. Children may also volunteer words they associate with the topic.

2. *Elicit sentences.* Children are then asked to take at least two words from the list on the board and use them in a sentence. These *possible sentences* should be ones they think might possibly be in the text. The teacher should record these sentences as given and underline the words used from the list. It is important to write the children's sentences exactly as stated, even if the information in the sentence is incorrect. Children may use words already in sentences again, as long as a new context is created. This step of the strategy ends when children cannot produce any more sentences or after a specified period of time has gone by. Following are some sentences children might offer using the vocabulary words listed above:

   a. *Bees* use *nectar* to *pollinate* the *hive.*
   b. Scout *bees* help *worker bees* get *honey.*
   c. *Bees* get *pollen* from flowers.
   d. *Bees* do a *bee dance* when they find *honey.*
   e. *Bees* carry *honey* in their *honey stomachs.*
   f. A *honeycomb* is where *honey* is kept.

3. *Read and verify sentences.* Children are then asked to read the text for the purpose of finding out whether the possible sentences they have generated are accurate.

4. *Evaluate sentences.* When everyone has finished reading, each sentence is evaluated. Children may use the text as a reference. Sentences that are not accurate are omitted or refined according to what the text states. The discussion of each sentence calls for careful reading, and judgments of the accuracy of each sentence must be defended by children. Of the possible sentences above, Sentences c, e, and f are accurate as they stand. Sentence a will have to be refined, since bees do not pollinate a hive. It might be modified as follows: *Bees* use

nectar to make *honey* in the *hive*. Sentence b can be refined easily by removing *honey* from the sentence and putting *nectar* in its place. Sentence d also requires only slight refinement: *Scout bees*, rather than just *bees*, do the *bee dance*.

5. *Generate new sentences.* After the children's original sentences have been evaluated and refined, the teacher should ask the children for new sentences. These sentences are generated to further extend children's understanding of the text and its vocabulary. As these sentences are given, children again check them for accuracy and use the text for confirmation. All final acceptable sentences generated with this strategy should then be recorded by the children in their notebooks.

The possible sentences technique provides children with an opportunity to use listening, speaking, reading, and writing to learn new word meanings. Using their prior experiences, children think of ways to connect new vocabulary words to known words and evaluate them. They speak to express these connections and listen to other children's thoughts and connections. They read to verify the possible combinations and write the final versions in their notebooks. As a result, children become actively involved in new learning. Further, teachers are able to see the connections and modifications children make and can get an idea of how much additional reinforcement they may need in learning the words.

Categorization Strategies

Categorization of words serves as a means for children to organize new experiences and learning in conjunction with previously possessed concepts. It extends and improves on the way in which experiences are understood and remembered. Categorizing words also helps children improve their predictions, problem solving, and efficiency in processing conceptual information found in print. In essence, it aids children in making sense of their learning.

Categories can be drawn from personal observations and direct experiences in children's environment and from topics found in the text material that they will be reading and learning about. Using these sources, they are able to sort and group words on the basis of a recognition of the common characteristics those words share. From this classification, children can label a group of words and finalize their organization. Three categorization strategies are discussed in this section:

- Word fluency
- List-group-label
- Feature analysis

Word Fluency

Word fluency is an easily implemented vocabulary development strategy in which one of two participants attempts to name as many words as possible in 60 seconds. It is particularly appropriate for children in the primary grades and serves as an excellent means to increase verbal fluency. Readence and Searfoss (1986) recommend using word fluency as a lead-in to other categorization strategies. In word fluency, the teacher can model categories of words for children. The practice children gain in categorizing will be most beneficial in more structured categorization strategies such as list-group-label and feature analysis.

All that is needed for word fluency is a pencil, paper, and a clock or watch with a second hand. When first using this strategy, it is essential that the teacher demonstrate the technique with a child, so that the procedure and the directions are clearly understood by all children. In communicating the directions to the child, the teacher states:

> Now I want to see how many words you can name in one minute. Just any words will do, like *sky, cat, lamp,* or *happy.* When I say "Go," you begin saying the words as rapidly as you can, and I will count them. Counting numbers and using sentences are not allowed. You must use separate words. Go as rapidly as you can. Ready! Go!

The child goes first, and the teacher tallies the words on a sheet of paper. If the child should hesitate for 10 seconds, the teacher restates that any words will do. Those children experiencing difficulty in beginning this strategy may be motivated by pictures or by the teacher's suggestion, "Look around the room. What do you see?" or "Think of something we did today in school." The activity stops at the end of one minute.

Next, roles are switched. The child times and counts while the teacher names words. This is the key to the word fluency technique. It is here that the teacher can *model* categories of words for the children. Instead of randomly naming words as most children would do, the teacher gives words in categories so that the children can hear how the teacher is organizing the words (and how much more rapidly words can be given when they are categorized). Again, responses are tallied, and the activity is ended in 60 seconds.

The first step in scoring the responses is to count the words. All words are acceptable except (1) repetitions, (2) counting, and (3) sentences. Emphasis is placed on categorizing—for example, months, days of the week, proper names—by awarding participants extra points for categories of at least four words. The score for the activity is the total number of words named in one minute, plus the points awarded for categorizing. Graphs should be used so that children can chart their own progress with this activity. Line graphs, as shown in Figure 7.1, should be used to illustrate their advances in this categorization strategy. Visible, graphic signs of success should be reinforced. As children become accustomed to this technique, their scores will naturally rise, and the graph provides the incentive they need to continue with the activity.

The follow-up to the teacher's responses is particularly important. When the teacher's portion of the activity is completed, the teacher should ask the children, "How did the words I named go together?" (categories). It is here that many children see what the teacher was modeling with the categorization of words. Since extra points are given for such categories, the demonstration by the teacher can

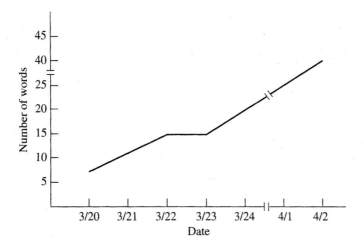

FIGURE 7.1   Charting Progress in Word Fluency

give the children the necessary incentive to want to do well with the word fluency activity and, thus, develop their vocabulary.

When children become familiar with this activity, the teacher can vary it by limiting the words named in one minute to a particular category or set of categories (things in a home, things we eat, and so on). As children begin to deal with content area subjects, word fluency can become a prime motivator for mastering the technical vocabulary of a particular subject. The teacher may begin this use of word fluency by stating "Today when we say words, let's think about the science lesson we had earlier and only say words we remember from that lesson." Then children will enumerate words associated with a particular lesson (that is, category) in a content subject and enhance their learning of that content vocabulary. Word fluency could be repeated frequently throughout the development of a unit of study to aid children in remembering and to reinforce new vocabulary relating to a particular category. The ease with which children recall technical vocabulary could be one measure of whether instruction in the use of new technical vocabulary has been effective. The authors have used word fluency at all levels—from primary grades through graduate classes—to reinforce new vocabulary.

List-Group-Label

List-group-label was originally conceived by Hilda Taba (1967) in her efforts to aid children in dealing with the technical vocabulary in social studies and science classes. Even though the foundation of this vocabulary development procedure is in the content areas, the concept of the lesson can be broadened to systematically improve the vocabulary and categorization skills of children in all elementary grades.

To implement a list-group-label lesson, a blackboard or large sheets of butcher paper, newsprint, or something comparable are needed on which to record the children's responses. A one- or two-word topic is selected by the teacher as a stimulus and is written at the top of the blackboard or paper. Topics may be drawn from a current event of the school year (Halloween, Christmas), places (kitchen, church, school), colors (white, blue), or content areas (science unit on nutrition— list protein foods). Almost any topic expressing an experience to which children can relate may be used.

Children are asked to think of words or expressions related to the topic. For instance, the teacher may state "Think of any word you know that reminds you of *growing things*." Responses are recorded. The teacher should accept all words, making no judgments (including tell-tale facial expressions) as to how good the responses are. The list of words given by the children should be kept manageable. Approximately 25 to 30 words is a good number, depending on the stimulus and grade level of the children. The teacher may add words identified as crucial to understanding a text selection if desired. After all the children have had an opportunity to offer words, the teacher should stop the listing by saying "I'll take two more words." Listed in Figure 7.2 are the words a second-grade classroom generated using the stimulus topic *growing things*.

Next, the teacher rereads the list orally, pointing to each word as it is pronounced. Older children may read the list of words by themselves. The children, individually or in small groups, are then instructed to construct smaller lists of words that have something in common, using only words from the large list that was just generated. Smaller lists created by the children should have at least three words. Words in the large list may be used in more than one small list, as long as the grouping is different. Children are instructed to give their group of words a label or title indicating the common characteristic they share. Children must verbally state why they have grouped their words in a particular way. In this way, all children can see other category possibilities.

flowers	animals	eating	food
water	seed	stem	bud
soil	rain	leaves	bloom
sun	roots	petals	insects
trees	garden	vines	lake
fruit	plants	mushrooms	fish
grass	vegetables	medicine	moisture
people	forest	cactus	pollution

FIGURE 7.2   **A List of Growing Things**

Using another part of the blackboard or another sheet of paper, the teacher records the words and category label from one child or group at a time. The large list must be visible for easy reference by the children. To personalize the activity, the teacher may choose to record beside the label the name of the child or group giving the small list of words. For the large list of words generated for *growing things*, the following categories were developed—though the outcome is not limited to the words mentioned by this second-grade classroom:

Growing Things
1. Fruit, vegetables, mushrooms, fish = things you can eat
2. Moisture, lake, rain = things made up of water
3. Roots, stem, leaves, petals, bloom, bud = parts of a flower
4. People, cactus, fish, insects = things without leaves
5. Sun, soil, water = things plants need to grow
6. Flowers, cactus, water, insects, people = words with two syllables
7. Mushrooms, medicine, moisture = words that begin with *m*
8. People, lake, moisture, medicine = words that end with *e*

As you can see, most of the groups the children generated are based on meaningful semantic associations. It should be noted, however, that groupings 6, 7, and 8 are based on surface-level spelling features, rather than meaningful features. This is not the intended outcome of list-group-label, even though such associations might serve as important mnemonic devices for some children as they deal with the task of the strategy. Teachers should accept surface-level groupings but should point out to children that meaningful associations are the type of groupings desired.

Since the grouping and labeling might present a problem for some children, the teacher may decide to *walk* the children through the list-group-label lesson before they do it by themselves, especially in the lower grades. Another suggestion is to construct the first category and title it, so children catch on to the procedure. Providing an initial list of words from the technical vocabulary of a specific content area under study and having children classify and label them is one variation. Another is making the categories and having children label them. The example below demonstrates the use of the list-group-label lesson with social studies vocabulary related to the organization of the United States government.

U.S. Government

Legislature	Senate	Speaker
Appeals	Executive	Cabinet
Veto	President	Majority Leader
Vice President	Override	Supreme Court
House of Representatives	Judiciary	Minority Leader

The teacher may have the children classify and label groups of words belonging to this list of social studies words. If a more structured approach is desired or needed, the teacher may create groups of words and have children label them. For instance, the teacher could group the following words together:

1. Legislature, executive, judiciary = ?
2. President, Vice President, cabinet = ?
3. Override, veto, appeals = ?

The reverse procedure may also be used—that is, the teacher can supply the label and have the children group words under the label. For example, the following labels may be given to children:

1. Branches of government = ?
2. Officers in the executive branch = ?
3. Checks and balances = ?

Finally, if children have words that they cannot fit into a neat category, tell them to start a *misfit* list. As categories are compared, children will learn that their own list of misfits is rarely like that of other children.

Experiencing and using the content vocabulary of social studies (or any other subject, for that matter) in this way will provide children with additional meaningful opportunities to master the vocabulary through active involvement. The list-group-label lesson can provide content teachers with a viable alternative to traditional vocabulary instruction that emphasizes memorization.

As with the word fluency technique, the authors have used list-group-label as a measure of how well children are learning technical vocabulary associated with a unit of study. List-group-label might occur at several points during the development of a content area unit in order to determine whether children are beginning to use and categorize the vocabulary introduced throughout the unit. Each time a list-group-label lesson has been completed, the categories may be placed on chart paper and compared. In this manner, children can see their progress in being able to recall and categorize the technical vocabulary associated with the unit of study.

It can be readily seen that the list-group-label strategy is a definite aid to vocabulary development as well as to organizing ideas. Children can both actively participate in this strategy and experience how other children conceptualize word categories. Words generated in the lesson can also be used on the vocabulary cards mentioned earlier in the chapter. The teacher must be sure to provide a context (phrase or sentence) for the words if they are to be used on vocabulary cards.

Process Guide 7.2

Before going on to the next strategy, break into small groups of four to six and do a list-group-label lesson. Select a topic from the news or a current event on the national, state, or local level that has generated some controversy. List at least 25 vocabulary words relating to the topic. Categorize the words, and provide labels for the groups. Be prepared to justify your categories.

Feature Analysis

Feature analysis (also called *semantic feature analysis* by Johnson & Pearson, 1984) is a categorization strategy derived from the theoretical construct of cognitive structure as the way in which human beings organize knowledge. As we process new information, (1) categories are established in our cognitive structure; (2) rules (feature analysis) are formulated to allocate objects (words, concepts) to these categories; and (3) category interrelationships are established in the cognitive structure so that we can ascertain how objects (words, concepts) can be related, yet also be unique.

In practice, feature analysis is a systematic strategy that enables children to see how words are related and, at the same time, to see how each word is still unique. Feature analysis can be used in all elementary grades and should begin with concrete categories within the experiential background of children before moving to categories of a more abstract nature.

Feature analysis is easy to implement. The key to this strategy is to *start slowly* and have children build on a basic structure. The authors have found that if teachers use word fluency and list-group-label with children until they are familiar with these two strategies, feature analysis is much easier for both the teacher and the children. The six steps that comprise this technique are described below:

1. *Select a category.* The teacher selects a category name to begin the lesson. The category should be something that is familiar to children, particularly when this procedure is first introduced. For illustration, we will use the category *animals.*

2. *List words in the category.* Once the category has been selected, the teacher or, preferably, the children supply words that name objects or concepts belonging to the category. In the case of the category *animals,* we can begin with a limited number of animal names. For purposes of illustration, we will use the words *dog, fish, bird, lion,* and *frog.*

3. *List features.* The teacher must now decide which features or traits are to be explored in the category. Possible features, which animals either have or do not have in common, are numerous. Start with only a few features; children will build on these at a later time. For our example, features to be explored are whether the animal (a) is a pet, (b) is a mammal, (c) flies, (d) swims, (e) breathes with lungs, or (f) breathes with gills.

After the first three steps of feature analysis have been completed, we have the following matrix.

Category: Animals

	Pet	Mammal	Flies	Swims	Lungs	Gills
Dog						
Fish						
Bird						
Lion						
Frog						

4. *Indicate feature possession.* Children are now guided through the matrix for the purpose of indicating whether or not, in this case, an animal possesses a particular feature. A simple +/– system can be used with primary-grade children to indicate feature possession. Children above the primary grades or those accustomed to feature analysis may use a more sophisticated system to indicate feature possession, such as a form of the Likert scale (always, most of the time, sometimes, a few times, never). Feature possession should be based on typical patterns; for example, though some fish may fly, flying is not typical of fish. Our matrix for the category of *animals* will look as follows, using a +/– system:

Category: Animals

	Pet	Mammal	Flies	Swims	Lungs	Gills
Dog	+	+	–	+	+	–
Fish	+	–	–	+	–	+
Bird	+	–	+	+	+	–
Lion	–	+	–	–	+	–
Frog	+	–	–	+	+	+

5. *Add words/features.* After children have indicated feature possession, they should be asked, first, to generate new names to be added to the matrix and, second, to suggest new features to be analyzed. The teacher may wish to set a limit on the number of words and/or features to be added to the matrix. However, as categories become more abstract or move outside of the children's experiential background, fewer words and features are usually generated.

Words such as *monkey, snake, octopus, penguin,* and *turtle* may be added to our example. Features to be added might include *reptile, hops, meat-eater,* and *two legs.* When children are generating additions to the matrix, they are expanding their vocabulary and developing concepts through categorization. The next and final step completes the feature analysis strategy.

6. *Complete and explore the matrix.* Children proceed now to complete the matrix by using the same feature possession system as before, along with the new words and features. Our final matrix looks like this:

Category: Animals

	Pet	Mammal	Flies	Swims	Lungs	Gills	Reptile	Hops	Meat-eater	Two legs
Dog	+	+	–	+	+	–	–	–	+	–
Fish	+	–	–	+	–	+	–	–	–	–
Bird	+	–	+	+	+	–	–	–	–	+
Lion	–	+	–	–	+	–	–	–	+	–
Frog	+	–	–	+	+	+	–	+	–	–
Monkey	–	+	–	–	+	–	–	–	–	–
Snake	+	–	–	+	+	–	+	–	+	–
Octopus	–	–	–	+	–	+	–	–	–	–
Penguin	–	–	–	+	+	–	–	–	–	+
Turtle	+	–	–	+	+	–	+	–	–	–

The final part of Step 6, exploration, completes feature analysis. Children are asked to analyze the matrix to see how words relate in a category, yet remain unique. For instance, it can be noted that no animal in the matrix possesses the same features as another—each is *unique.* Specifically, it can be noted that even though they are all animals, only certain ones can be pets, are meat-eaters, or have two legs. On the other hand, it can also be seen that members of a category (here, animals) do have certain things in *common.* A monkey and a lion have many things in common, as do a turtle and a snake.

Exploring the matrix is most effective when children, rather than the teacher, make these observations. If children wish, they may further expand the matrix on their own.

As can be seen, feature analysis is relatively easy to implement. It actively involves the children in categorization, conceptualization, and vocabulary expansion— and it can be fun!

Strategies for Visually Representing Information

Visual representations of information depict relationships among words and the concepts they convey so that children have a *map* of the upcoming text. In essence, this map acts as a guide to information to be presented and gives children a notion of what is important to learn and remember. Visual representations are frameworks for previewing and reading text. Their presentation usually requires teacher involvement, but teachers should encourage as much student involvement as possible through discussion. In this way, children can discover for themselves the relationships depicted in the representation. Two strategies for visually representing information are discussed in this section: graphic organizers and word maps.

Graphic Organizer

A graphic organizer is a schematic diagram that can be used to depict the vocabulary of a concept to be learned (Tierney & Readence, 2000). The diagram shows children the relationships that exist among the key vocabulary terms and gives them some idea of the concepts and vocabulary to be learned before reading a text selection. Using a graphic organizer is thus a way to organize text concepts and vocabulary into appropriate categories to enhance children's learning. It also serves as a frame of reference for children in their efforts to incorporate new words and concepts into previously acquired information.

The following steps are used in the design and construction of a graphic organizer:

1. *Identify key vocabulary.* Teachers need to make some decisions concerning the major concepts to be stressed during instruction. In this way, they avoid a haphazard search of new vocabulary in the text material and, instead, select those words that are necessary for understanding the important concepts. Additionally, selecting the major instructional concepts to be stressed aids teachers in defining their own course objectives. The vocabulary selected communicates only the key ideas in the material, thereby easing the vocabulary burden on students and the instructional burden on teachers. Following are the key concepts and vocabulary that might be used as the basis for constructing a graphic organizer for a selection on *fibers:*

Key Concepts
a. Fibers can either be synthetic or natural.
b. Synthetic fibers are chemically produced; natural fibers can be obtained from animals or vegetables.
c. Examples of synthetic fibers are acrylic, rayon, nylon, polyester, and acetate.
d. Examples of natural fibers are cotton, linen, wool, and silk.

Key Vocabulary
Fiber	Acrylic	Cocoon
Flax	Nylon	Silkworm
Fabric	Acetate	Yarn
Cotton	Linen	Rayon
Polyester	Wool	Silk

2. *Arrange words into a diagram.* Key vocabulary is arranged into a diagram, or graphic organizer, that shows children how the words interrelate. The graphic organizer may take many shapes, but generally the simpler it is, the better. The arrangement of the graphic organizer depends on the teacher, the number of concepts to be learned, and children's previous knowledge. If a large number of terms and concepts are to be depicted, it might be best to use more than one graphic organizer and to introduce them as needed in a series of lessons. Before presenting the graphic organizer to children, teachers are advised to evaluate the arrangement. Words can be added or deleted to depict more clearly the relations among the vocabulary items. Whatever choice is made concerning its arrangement, the important thing to remember is that the graphic organizer must *enhance* the children's understanding of the key vocabulary and concepts. For our example of fibers, one way to construct the graphic organizer might be as shown in Figure 7.3.

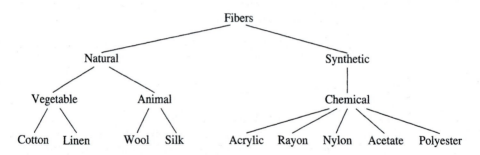

FIGURE 7.3   A Graphic Organizer on Fibers

3. *Present the graphic organizer.* The graphic organizer can be presented in the way most comfortable to the teacher—the chalkboard, a large poster board, or an overhead transparency. The teacher then proceeds to talk the children through the organizer, word by word. Children should be encouraged to apply knowledge previously learned by adding to the diagram any words that more fully complete it for them. Also, children should be directed through the presentation by teacher questions that further encourage their active participation. Mastery is not important at this point; rather, exposure and experience with the vocabulary are emphasized. After discussion of the graphic organizer, it should be left in full view. It will serve as a reference point for children as they read, and possibly they will add to it other words that they uncover in the reading. The graphic organizer will also serve as a reference for the teacher during follow-up discussion. Finally, it is emphasized that the graphic organizer is designed to acquaint children with the vocabulary rather than directly teach them the words. The use of vocabulary cards is recommended to enhance their mastery of the words.

The graphic organizer can also be useful for review and reinforcement after reading. Once teachers have selected the key vocabulary and concepts and have constructed the graphic organizer, the following steps should be used to adapt the strategy for review and reinforcement:

1. *Make multiple copies of individual words.* If, instead of being presented with the graphic organizer, children are to work cooperatively in small groups to construct their own diagrams, multiple copies of the words are needed, with one term per index card or slip of paper.

2. *Place children in small groups and explain the task.* Each group of children is provided a set of the terms and assigned the task of arranging the terms in a diagram to show how they are related. Blank slips of paper should also be provided, so that children can add new terms that will clarify the task for them. If children are not familiar with the graphic organizer concept, introduce the idea with a short example within their experiential background. Otherwise, an introductory example is not necessary. It should be made clear that children need not use all the terms, although they should make an effort to do so. Children will respond to the task more favorably in this way.

3. *Provide support.* Circulate around the room and become involved in the groups' task, particularly if help is requested. The first few times this technique is used, your support will be necessary and helpful. Use questions or comments to encourage children at their task, but do not dominate the activity.

4. *Provide feedback.* Judge when to end small-group activity. All groups will not finish simultaneously. Have the class as a whole develop a single graphic organizer at the board under your direction. Disagreements will occur, but use these positively. The additional discussion will clarify confusing issues.

There are several advantages to using the graphic organizer in a postreading situation. First, teachers are free to circulate among the children to see who is having difficulty, who needs assistance, and who needs additional teaching on the vocabulary. Second, the whole group discussion that focuses on developing a single graphic organizer provides an effective review as children share their perceptions and understandings from different perspectives. Finally, it actively involves children in the learning and review of the key vocabulary and concepts.

The same diagram that was used to introduce children to material to be read can also be used after reading, to aid in the recall of that material. Blanks can be left in the original graphic organizer for children to fill in by recalling the relationships among the key vocabulary items learned during reading and follow-up discussion. The words that were deleted are listed below the incomplete diagram in random order. For our fibers example, such a graphic organizer might look like the one in Figure 7.4. In order to complete the diagram, children are directed to either recall how the vocabulary and concepts are related or locate this information in the text material. This type of activity with a graphic organizer will also serve as an effective transition between teacher-presented graphic organizers and student-generated ones.

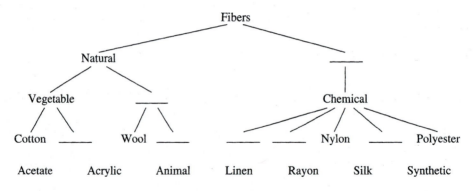

FIGURE 7.4   **A Graphic Organizer with Blanks**

Word Map

The word map strategy (Schwartz, 1988) is a systematic teaching procedure to develop children's concepts based on their existing conceptual background. Thus, this strategy centers around the notion of associating the new with the known in order to teach word concepts. The effective learning of new words requires knowledge of other words.

Showing children how concepts relate to one another in a hierarchy is an important step in helping them learn new concepts, but it might not go far enough. Certain concepts might require more in-depth processing, and children understand them better when they can generalize the concepts to new situations. A graphic organizer alone may not allow some children to fully grasp some concepts. Thus, the word map can become a useful alternative for attaining concepts.

A word map not only clarifies concepts by showing their relationships to other terms in a hierarchy but also improves the learning of new concepts by providing children with *examples* and *nonexamples* of each new concept, as well as *rel-*

evant and *irrelevant* attributes of that concept. In particular, it uses supraordinate, coordinate, and subordinate aspects of concepts, in addition to stressing the attributes, or characteristics, common to examples of that concept.

To facilitate the discussion of this strategy, a definition of terms is necessary.

A **supraordinate** aspect of a concept is represented by a term denoting a common, more general class, of which the target concept is a member. Thus, if the target concept is *quadrilateral,* the supraordinate concept would be *polygon.*

Coordinate aspects of a concept are represented by words that refer to members of the same general, or supraordinate, class. Concepts coordinate with *quadrilateral,* therefore, would include *triangle, pentagon,* and *hexagon.*

Subordinate aspects of a concept are represented by words referring to specific items or concepts that are part of the target concept but of a lower classification. For example, the concepts *square, parallelogram, rhombus,* and *trapezoid* are subordinate to *quadrilateral.*

Relevant attributes are those characteristics that belong to the target concept. Thus, *four-sided, closed figure,* and *made up of line segments* are relevant attributes of quadrilateral. (By examining relevant attributes of a concept, children can see not only what is an example of it, but also what is *not* an example of it. For instance, a triangle is not an example of a quadrilateral, because it is only three-sided. This gives children an opportunity to discover the likenesses and differences in terms when they attempt to define a concept.)

The following steps are recommended in creating and using a word map:

1. *Develop the target concept.* Construct a hierarchy that reveals the supraordinate, coordinate, and subordinate concepts of the target concept. Thus, if the target concept is *reptiles,* the hierarchy in Figure 7.5 might be constructed.
2. *Define the concept.* Be sure of the relevant attributes of the target concept for later discussion. Relevant attributes of reptile, for example, would be "a vertebrate, breathes air, has scales or bony plates, lays eggs, cold-blooded, lack of hair."

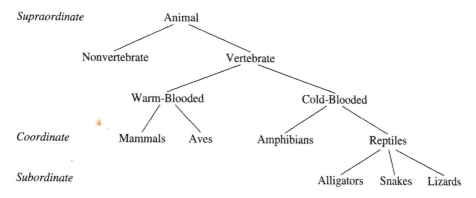

FIGURE 7.5   A Word Map of Reptiles

3. *Present the target concept.* Tell children the name of the concept they will learn and have them contribute examples of it, either individually or in small groups. List these on the board and begin to categorize these examples as they are offered. Children should be invited to challenge others' examples. With reptile, for instance, children may offer *snakes, turtles, alligators, crocodiles,* and *lizards,* all of which can be categorized as examples of the concept. If *frog* and *bird* are offered, other children could challenge them as nonexamples and properly categorize them under *amphibians* and *aves,* respectively.

4. *Finish constructing the hierarchy.* Provide children with your originally constructed hierarchy, making sure you explain why the terms are placed where they are. To enhance children's learning, you should strive through questioning to involve them as much as possible in naming terms in the resulting framework, or map.

5. *Guide children to relevant attributes.* Have children discover what characteristics all examples have in common. In this case, any confusions or misconceptions could now be cleared up as to what a reptile is.

6. *Guide children to irrelevant attributes.* Have children find differences among the examples previously offered. Finding differences that vary among the examples but that do not change the example into a nonexample will enhance their understanding of the concept. With *reptile,* some of these might be size of the egg laid, their habitat, and their size.

7. *Complete teaching of the concept.* Supply children with other examples, as well as nonexamples not previously mentioned. These could be concepts children will encounter in their reading assignment. For further reinforcement, direct children to make vocabulary cards on the concept. When teaching has been completed, children will have been supplied or will have discovered the hierarchy and a list of examples, nonexamples, and relevant and irrelevant attributes. With reptiles, this list may look like the following:

Concept: Reptiles

Examples	*Nonexamples*
Snakes	Frog
Turtles	Bird
Alligators	Fish
Crocodiles	Man
Lizards	Dog

Relevant attributes	*Irrelevant attributes*
Vertebrate	Where they live
Cold-blooded	Their size
Has scales or bony plates	Number of eggs laid
Breathes air	Size of eggs
Lays eggs	Their color
Lack of hair	

Using this strategy presents children with varied ways to think about the meaning of new vocabulary. Discovery learning is an integral part of the word map strategy. It allows teachers to find out what children already know and to use that knowledge to teach them. It also offers children the opportunity to see how new concepts are related to known concepts and to discover what a word represents as well as what it does not represent. Thus, it should help them generalize the concept and enhance their vocabulary development.

Process Guide 7.3

Break into groups of four to six people, and try this simulation. You are about to teach a health unit on nutrition and the basic food groups. The target concept is *carbohydrates.* Develop the target concept in a hierarchy, and come up with a list of examples, nonexamples, and relevant and irrelevant attributes. Share your final product with others, and discuss the differences among everyone's hierarchies.

Extension Activities

Extension activities are paper-and-pencil exercises designed to expand children's knowledge of vocabulary words. Their intent is to reinforce children's concepts about words that they have been previously told are important in their reading and learning. Thus, extension activities are constructed by the teacher as a final step in vocabulary teaching. Important words are introduced to children before they read. They use these words in their reading and any follow-up discussion. They then further practice with these words in an extension activity. These steps are all necessary to facilitate children's ownership of new vocabulary, since it is important to make these words part of their permanent store of vocabulary. Recall and memorization of definitions of words are involved in using extension activities; however, children must also be allowed to explore the relationships among words in a variety of ways. Therefore, extension activities should give children the opportunity to think about the meanings of the vocabulary words they are learning.

Before we move on to a discussion of various types of paper-and-pencil extension activities, readers are reminded that many of the strategies described previously in this chapter can also be used as vehicles for reinforcing and extending new vocabulary. The possible sentences technique incorporates, as part of the strategy, the refinement of initially constructed sentences and the generation of new sentences using the vocabulary under study. List-group-label and feature analysis can also extend and refine word concepts by allowing children to incorporate what they have learned from their reading and class discussion. Uses of a graphic organizer for reinforcement after reading include teacher support and whole-group discussion.

The extension activities discussed in the rest of this chapter are designed to focus on definitions or meanings or, in some cases, both. An extension activity that reinforces the definition of a word without requiring children to also consider the meanings of other words may be called a *definition activity*. A matching exercise reinforces word definitions. An activity that requires children to consider the meaning of a word in relation to the definitions or meanings of other words may be called a *meaning activity*. Categorization exercises and analogies reinforce word meanings.

Reinforcing Definitions

Extension activities designed to reinforce definitions of words may be used in a variety of ways in the classroom. They may be used by individual children, or children may be placed in small groups to work on them together. A combination of work formats may also be used. Children can work independently and then compare their responses in a small-group situation. Working in small groups will expose children to others' ideas and, therefore, enhance reinforcement. Using small groups rather than whole-group discussion increases opportunities to participate in the activity. Whether you have children work independently or in small groups will depend on children's ability levels and the extent to which they can function in task-oriented groups. In any case, whole-group follow-up is essential for final reinforcement and to clear up any confusions that may arise. Extension activities that reinforce definitions are matching exercises, word searches, and word puzzles.

Matching Exercises.   Matching exercises require children to recall and match words and their definitions. Such activities can be made more interesting and challenging by increasing the number of alternatives available in the matching process. In other words, instead of providing 10 words to match to 10 definitions, have children choose from a larger number of available definitions. For instance, children may be asked to match 10 words to 10 definitions when 12 or 13 are available. Another way to increase interest is to scramble the words that you are asking children to match. Of course, a combination of both of these variations would make the matching exercise even more challenging. Figure 7.6 presents a brief example of a matching exercise using these two variations.

Word Searches.   Word searches are easy to make, and children usually enjoy doing them. First, type or write the vocabulary words to be searched in an array. An initial array on the subject of U.S. presidents might look like Figure 7.7. Next, insert random letters to complete a rectangle. Allow sufficient space between letters to allow children to search for words.

Be sure to give clues to define each word used in the search. If no clues are used, the word search becomes only an exercise in word recognition, rather than a means to reinforce vocabulary. Our final word search for U.S. presidents might look like Figure 7.8.

Word Puzzles.   Word puzzles provide direct clues to the definitions of words. A word is embedded within the puzzle to give clues to children as they solve the

FIGURE 7.6   A Matching Exercise on Skin Disorders

Directions: Below are two lists. The numbered list on the left consists of types of skin disorders you have studied. Note that the words are scrambled. The list on the right consists of definitions for the words. First, unscramble the words, and write each one on the line next to its scrambled version. Then, find the definition of each word, and write the number of the word that matches the definition in the blank to the left of each definition.

1. selmo _____

2. rwtas _____

3. erfclkse _____

4. ncae _____

5. rwrgimno _____

___ **a.** Fungus infection characterized by ring-shaped patches; most common on the feet

___ **b.** Irritation of skin, usually due to the rubbing of clothing against some part of the body

___ **c.** Blemish, usually dark in color and often hairy, on body from birth

___ **d.** Small, usually hard, elevation of skin caused by a virus

___ **e.** Scaly sores or blisters that are very itchy and caused by bacteria

___ **f.** Skin lesion containing pus, caused by overproduction of oil by skin glands

___ **g.** Brownish spots on skin, usually caused by exposure to sunlight.

puzzle. The number of letters in each word is also indicated. Figure 7.9 shows a word puzzle.

Process Guide 7.4

Solve the word puzzle in Figure 7.9. This is a puzzle on what you have learned so far in this chapter—it should serve as a review for you.

Reinforcing Meanings

We will now examine extension activities that require the consideration of meanings of words in relation to meanings of other words. Like those activities designed to reinforce definitions, these exercises can be used by individual children or in small groups. In fact, in reinforcing meanings, there is actually more of a need to consider the use of small groups, because these activities are more challenging, and children may need the support of others to resolve them. As with

FIGURE 7.7 An Initial Array for a Word Search

```
        C   A   R   T   E   R
        L       E   N
        I       A   O
        N       G   S
        T       A   L       P
        O       N   I   X   O   N
        N           W       L
                J   A   C   K   S   O   N
                                    A
                                M
                        B   U   S   H
                        R
                    T
```

previous activities, whole-group follow-up is essential. Extension activities that reinforce meanings are categorizing, identifying relationships, and analogies.

Categorizing.   Categorization of words has been previously discussed as a valid means to help children focus on how words are related to one another. What will be discussed here is a suggested sequence of categorization exercises based on increasing task difficulty and level of abstraction. Use of the different types of categorizing activities will depend on the ability of the children and their familiarity with the notion of categorizing.

Which Doesn't Belong?   From a group of words, have children select one word that does *not* fit the category. Two simple examples follow:

1. Food
  a. Apple
  b. Pie
  c. Fork
  d. Cookies

2. Birds
  a. Parrot
  b. Duck
  c. Fireflies
  d. Chicken

FIGURE 7.8   A Word Search on U.S. Presidents

Directions: This is a word search involving U.S. presidents you have studied. Listed below the puzzle are brief descriptions of them. When you figure out each president's name, circle it in the puzzle. Their names may appear from bottom to top or top to bottom; they may also appear horizontally, vertically, or diagonally.

C	A	R	T	E	R	T	R	B
L	K	E	N	G	E	C	W	J
I	H	A	O	R	G	X	K	D
N	N	G	S	C	L	S	L	X
T	W	A	L	A	P	O	I	H
O	T	N	I	X	O	N	E	Q
N	A	C	W	Y	L	F	U	M
U	G	J	A	C	K	S	O	N
C	K	I	V	D	Q	P	A	S
H	O	B	F	R	S	M	J	E
L	P	K	I	B	U	S	H	Z
V	G	Y	Q	R	Z	Y	I	T
N	M	U	T	X	E	F	W	N

1. First president to visit Red China
2. President during World War I
3. He negotiated the Camp David Accords
4. Formerly a movie star
5. Eleventh president of the U.S.
6. Old Hickory
7. President during Korean War
8. President during the Gulf War
9. First Democratic president since Carter

Which One Fits?   From a group of words, have children select the one that best fits the category label. Two simple examples follow:

1. *Seasons*	2. *Fruit*
a. Spring	**a.** Hamburger
b. Easter	**b.** Wheat
c. Leap year	**c.** Banana
d. January	**d.** Caramels

FIGURE 7.9   A Word Puzzle on Vocabulary

Directions: Look at the clues below. Think of a word (or words) about vocabulary that has the same number of letters as spaces provided and that has the given letter in the same position. Write that word on the line having the same numerical position as its clue.

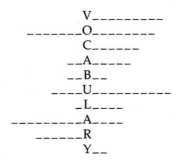

1. First word of a strategy emphasizing context
2. A hierarchically based strategy
3. All human experience is dependent on it
4. Precedes reinforcement
5. Last word in categorization strategy
6. Looks at likenesses and differences in concept
7. Reader with a large vocabulary
8. A major means of directly teaching new words
9. Someone who really owns a word
10. Key person in vocabulary teaching

The difficulty of this activity can be increased by telling children they must select *two* words that fit the category and by providing appropriate choices for them.

Words into Categories.   Give children a list of words and have them categorize the words according to labels you have provided. A simple example follows, with the labels to be used in boldface below each column:

Celery	Socks	Hats
Dogs	Cats	Cake
Shirts	Peanuts	Rats
Ice cream	Horses	Steak
Dresses	Shoes	Pigs
Foods	***Clothes***	***Animals***

The difficulty level of this task can be greatly increased by having children also provide the labels for categories, instead of using supplied labels.

Name the Category.   Provide children with a group of words and have them label the category. Two simple examples follow:

1. _____ .   2. _____
   a. Mother   a. Nickel
   b. Father   b. Dime
   c. Sister   c. Penny
   d. Brother   d. Dollar

To increase the difficulty of this task, add a word that does not fit the category and have children both name the category and circle the letter of one word that does not fit the category they named.

General to Specific. Supply children with groups of the same words, arranged in different order. Have them choose the group that is arranged from most general to most specific. This task probably presents children with the highest level of abstraction of all the categorizing activities mentioned. Two simple examples follow:

1. a. Dog, collie, animal, Lassie   2. a. City, county, country, state
   b. Collie, dog, Lassie, animal   b. County, country, state, city
   c. Animal, dog, collie, Lassie   c. Country, state, county, city
   d. Animal, collie, dog, Lassie   d. Country, city, state, county

It is essential to follow up these exercises by exploring children's reasons for selecting a choice or naming a category. This verbalization will allow children to listen to the thinking of others and clear up any confusion that may arise.

Identifying Relationships. Identifying relationships is closely tied to categorizing. Children are asked to perceive a relationship from among a group of words that includes distractors and then briefly describe that relationship. A brief example follows:

Science Relationships
Directions: In each group of words below, circle the three words that have something in common with one another. On the line provided, briefly state what the relationship is.

1. Intestines   Heart   Cells   Kidney   Muscles

   _____

2. Gastric juice   Milk   Water   Blood   Endocrine

   _____

3. Fibula   Spatula   Tibia   Clavicle   Medulla

   _____

4. Ligaments   Skin   Muscles   Fibers   Cartilage

   _____

Analogies.   Because analogies require children to draw inferences, they lend themselves well to creative thinking. At the same time, they may be difficult for children, particularly those who have not been previously exposed to analogies. Therefore, use simple analogies as models for children before moving on to more difficult ones. Relationships in the simple analogies should be verbalized. For instance, with the analogy "*Hard* is to *easy* as *cold* is to ___," the following should be verbalized: "Hard is the opposite of easy, so cold must be the opposite of something. What is the opposite of cold? Hot!" Analogies will be easier to deal with if choices are provided. For instance, with the example just discussed, the following choices might be supplied: *frozen, wet, hot, simple.* However, be reminded that only one correct answer can be provided for each analogy. If choices are not provided, the task will be more difficult, but it will allow for more divergence in response and, possibly, a more interesting discussion. Again, children's abilities need to be taken into consideration. A brief example, first with choices provided, then with the choices missing, follows:

Mathematics Analogies
Directions: The following analogies deal with some of the mathematics vocabulary you have just studied. In the first three, pick the answer that makes the most sense. In the last three, choose your own word to complete the analogy. Remember that in an analogy, the second set of words is related in the same way as the first set of words.

1. *Cube* is to *three* as *square* is to: two, four, six
2. *Angle* is to *triangle* as *curve* is to: rectangle, circle, octagon
3. *Sum* is to *addition* as *difference* is to: multiplication, division, subtraction
4. *Dividend* is to *divisor* as *numerator* is to:
5. *Midpoint* is to *median* as *average* is to:
6. *25* is to *5* as *16* is to:

The descriptions and examples discussed in this section provide a variety of means for reinforcing word definitions as well as word meanings. In no way do these exhaust the types of activities that might be used to extend and refine children's vocabulary. The possibilities are limited only by your time and creativity. Use these suggestions as points of departure for creating your own vocabulary-extension activities. It is important that some type of practice occur with the new words that children encounter, in order to help them move with more facility in their reading, writing, listening, and speaking.

Summary

This chapter discussed the importance of vocabulary in helping children become fluent readers. Children need to own words, so that they can move with facility in their daily language activities. They need to become insiders with new materials and new authors. Both direct teaching and practice are necessary in learning new words. Therefore, a repertoire of instructional strategies was presented to aid teachers in fostering children's ownership of words. Strategies utilizing context, categorization, and visual representations were discussed as means to teach students new vocabulary, and a number of extension activities were described to provide necessary practice with new words. We are now ready to explore the process of comprehension. Chapter 8 will explore a variety of comprehension strategies designed to help children glean essential information from text.

FOLLOW-THROUGH ACTIVITIES

Note: Level 1 activities may require limited access to children or classrooms. Level 2 activities should be completed using children and classrooms.

Level 1 Activities

1. Choose a text selection and design a vocabulary lesson using one of the context emphasizing strategies discussed in this chapter.

2. Choose a text selection and design a vocabulary lesson using one of the categorization strategies discussed in this chapter.

3. Design an extension activity to reinforce vocabulary that might have been taught from a text selection.

Level 2 Activities

1. From a text selection, design a possible sentences lesson and try it out with the children. What was their reaction?

2. Conduct a list-group-label lesson with your children, both before *and* after they have read the selection. What is your evaluation of the strategy? Did you see growth in the children's vocabulary usage?

3. Provide children with an extension activity to be used after they have read and discussed some material. Use small groups, if possible. Did the activity seem to reinforce the new vocabulary children were taught?

WORKING WITH PARENTS

The scene is an open-house meeting in the late fall of the school year in the fourth-grade classroom of Mr. Barry Wordy.

MRS. DOUTER: Mr. Wordy, my son Tommy comes home every day from school and tells me about the "word games" he plays. In the school he was in last year, he did do some word drills. However, the teacher didn't spend a lot of time on words, especially word games. Why is he spending so much time on them in your classroom?

MR. WORDY: Mrs. Douter, I'm glad you're taking an interest in your son's progress in school. Let me assure you that there is a definite purpose for what I'm doing. Long ago, before I became a teacher, I realized the power one possessed by having a well-developed vocabulary.

MRS. DOUTER: What do you mean by "power"?

MR. WORDY: Power? Let me explain. The larger a person's vocabulary, the more able he or she will be to cope with daily activities. Word knowledge also aids a child in school-related activities, because having a good command of words improves his or her ability to communicate successfully.

MRS. DOUTER: I guess I'm still concerned with how these word games will help Tommy read better. You know he had some problems at his last school.

MR. WORDY: One thing I learned last summer in my graduate course in reading was that word knowledge is an important factor in successfully understanding reading material. Words help us to more precisely express our thoughts. Since reading is a thinking process, word knowledge helps young readers, like Tommy, get the author's meaning when reading. Additionally, if his word knowledge is limited, he will focus on the author's words instead of the meaning. Increasing the size of Tommy's vocabulary will help him understand print, which is, after all, the important thing in reading.

MRS. DOUTER: Well, just how do your word games help Tommy read better?

MR. WORDY: Well, first of all, the vocabulary activities used in my classroom are not just word games, but strategies to foster vocabulary development, well founded in the psychological principles of learning. In many cases, I call them word games for the sake of the children, who seem to find playing games exciting and motivating.

MRS. DOUTER: Could you describe some of the word games—uh, vocabulary strategies—you use with Tommy and the other children?

MR. WORDY: Certainly, Mrs. Douter! Here's one of the word puzzles Tommy and the other children completed just yesterday to help them more fully develop their understanding of word meanings. This is just one of the strategies I use with the class. Let me give you some background on my vocabulary instruction. Much of what the children did in the primary grades, and some of what I have continued with this year, is concerned with helping children learn vocabulary in a way that will help them learn to read. The activities are centered on the child's own experiences. They build on the extensive speaking and listening abilities that children bring to school. This year, now that the children have developed some reading ability, the focus of vocabulary development shifts to reading in order to learn specific subject areas. In other words, word knowledge will become more materials-oriented and teacher-directed than before.

MRS. DOUTER: What exactly do you mean, Mr. Wordy, when you say your vocabulary strategies will become more materials-oriented and teacher-directed?

MR. WORDY: Well, children are ready to switch into textbooks and other formal reading materials now that they have already had experience examining words taken from their everyday language. Once this switch occurs, the teacher takes a much more active role in helping them develop their vocabularies, because this is crucial to their being able to cope with all the new material.

MRS. DOUTER: What specifically will you do?

MR. WORDY: Specifically? Categorization and context! Let me explain. Categorization aids children in seeing the likenesses and differences in their experiences—

the common attributes words share. Thus, categorization helps children organize and understand what goes on around them. Context fits right into the concept I explained before—using reading materials to learn. Using context not only helps children increase their vocabulary but also enhances their ability to read!

MRS. DOUTER: Well, you've convinced me! From what Tommy tells me, I'm sure it's exciting, too.

MR. WORDY: I'm glad you stopped in, Mrs. Douter. Do feel free to come again.

RESOURCES

Anderson, R. C., & Nagy, W. E. (1991). Word meanings. In R. Barr, M. L. Kamil, P. B. Mosenthal, & P. D. Pearson (Eds.), *Handbook of reading research: Volume II* (pp. 690–724). White Plains, NY: Longman.

The authors review theory and research on word meanings, giving general recommendations for instruction.

Brett, A., Rothlein, L., & Hurley, M. (1996). Vocabulary acquisition from listening to stories and explanations of target words. *The Elementary School Journal, 96,* 415–422.

This research study demonstrated that fourth graders who were provided with direct explanations of new vocabulary words learned more of the words than those students who just listened to stories containing the words.

Jensen, S. J., & Duffelmeyer, F. A. (1996). Enhancing possible sentences through cooperative learning. *Journal of Adolescent & Adult Literacy, 39,* 658–659.

This article discusses the use of cooperative learning as a means to enhance possible sentences.

Pittelman, S. D., Heimlich, J. E., Berglund, R. L., & French, M. P. (1991). *Semantic feature analysis: Classroom applications.* Newark, DE: International Reading Association.

The authors have provided a practical handbook for implementing feature analysis.

Rupley, W. H., Logan, J. W., & Nichols, W. D. (1998–1999). Vocabulary instruction in a balanced reading program. *The Reading Teacher, 52,* 336–346.

The authors describe a number of practical vocabulary development strategies.

Scott, J. A., & Nagy, W. E. (1997). Understanding the definitions of unfamiliar verbs. *Reading Research Quarterly, 32,* 184–200.

This study questions the efficacy of dictionary use when definitions are provided to elementary students without proper support.

Watts, S. M. (1995). Vocabulary instruction during reading lessons in six classrooms. *Journal of Reading Behavior, 27,* 399–424.

The author conducted a qualitative study of the kinds of vocabulary instruction given to upper elementary students and found that teachers most commonly gave word definitions rather than providing direct instruction in new word meanings.

REFERENCES

Anderson, R. C., & Freebody, P. (1985). Vocabulary knowledge. In H. Singer & R. B. Ruddell (Eds.), *Theoretical models and processes of reading* (3rd ed., pp. 343–371). Newark, DE: International Reading Association.

Anderson, R. C., & Nagy, W. E. (1991). Word meanings. In R. Barr, M. L. Kamil, P. B. Mosenthal, & P. D. Pearson (Eds.), *Handbook of reading research: Volume II* (pp. 690–724). White Plains, NY: Longman.

Haggard, M. H. (1992). Integrated content and long-term vocabulary learning with the vocabulary self-collection strategy. In E. K. Dishner, T. W. Bean, J. E. Readence, & D. W. Moore (Eds.), *Reading in the content areas: Improving classroom instruction* (3rd ed., pp. 190–196). Dubuque, IA: Kendall/Hunt.

Johnson, D. D., & Pearson, P. D. (1984). *Teaching reading vocabulary* (2nd ed.). New York: Holt, Rinehart & Winston.

Moore, D. W., & Moore, S. A. (1992). Possible sentences: An update. In E. K. Dishner, T. W. Bean, J. E. Readence, & D. W. Moore (Eds.), *Reading in the content areas: Improving classroom instruction* (3rd ed., pp. 196–202). Dubuque, IA: Kendall/Hunt.

Nagy, W. E., Anderson, R. C., & Herman, P. A. (1987). Learning word meanings from context during normal reading. *American Educational Research Journal, 24,* 237–270.

Readence, J. E., Bean, T. W., & Baldwin, R. S. (1998). *Content area literacy: An integrated approach* (6th ed.). Dubuque, IA: Kendall/Hunt.

Readence, J. E., & Searfoss, L. W. (1986). Teaching strategies for vocabulary development. In E. K. Dishner, T. W. Bean, J. E. Readence, & D. W. Moore (Eds.), *Reading in the content areas: Improving classroom instruction* (2nd ed., pp. 174–179). Dubuque, IA: Kendall/Hunt.

Ruddell, M. R. (1994). Vocabulary knowledge and comprehension: A comprehension-process view of complex literacy relationships. In R. B. Ruddell, M. R. Ruddell, & H. Singer (Eds.), *Theoretical models and processes of reading* (4th ed., pp. 418–447). Newark, DE: International Reading Association.

Schwartz, R. M. (1988). Learning to learn vocabulary in content area textbooks. *Journal of Reading, 32,* 108–118.

Stahl, S. A., & Kapinus, B. A. (1991). Possible sentences: Predicting word meanings to teach content area vocabulary. *The Reading Teacher, 45,* 36–43.

Surmach, M. (1981). A talk with a beekeeper. In *Sky climbers.* Glenview, IL: Scott, Foresman.

Taba, H. (1967). *Teacher's handbook for elementary social studies.* Reading, MA: Addison-Wesley.

Tierney, R. J., & Readence, J. E. (2000). *Reading strategies and practices: A compendium* (5th ed.). Boston: Allyn & Bacon.

CHAPTER

8 Comprehension

INTRODUCTION

One point on which educators might universally agree is that comprehension is the goal of all reading. Yet, at the same time, there is no universal agreement as to what exactly comprehension is. In fact, a certain mystique surrounds the notion of comprehension when one tries to pinpoint a definition. This may be due, in part, to the number of current taxonomies and skills hierarchies that attempt to account for the skills that comprise reading comprehension. Whose account is correct? Perhaps all of them, or perhaps none of them. The varied terminology that is used to describe comprehension is rampant with redundancies (Do we draw conclusions or make interpretations?) and fuzzy with dubious distinctions (Is there any difference between getting the main idea of a paragraph and that of a story, other than the size of the unit being dealt with?). One point to be made here is that, possibly, it is superfluous to pinpoint the correct, or best, account of comprehension skills. Such accounts are not blueprints for instruction; rather, they are classification systems that serve only as guides for the caring and well-informed teacher who must go about helping children learn to read and, therefore, comprehend.

We subscribe to the notion that comprehension is building connections between what children are to learn and what they already know—or, more simply, associating the new with the known. What we will describe in this chapter is an array of strategies that will help teachers deal with whatever taxonomy or scope and sequence they may be using. Teachers' choices of which strategy they use to help children comprehend will obviously be based on their beliefs about the particular skill they are teaching. Underlying all of that, however, should be the essence of comprehension: making connections between the new and the known.

One basic principle guides this notion: *Comprehension can be taught.* We believe that children can develop their comprehension abilities if strategies are used that allow one or more of the following to occur:

1. Teacher modeling of comprehension processes for children
2. Instruction and guidance in comprehension processes before, during, and after reading
3. Teacher feedback to children in their learning
4. Useful practice activities in a variety of materials to move children toward independence

In this way, teachers set up learning from text situations so that children interact with text, have a good chance of succeeding, and want to succeed.

Thus, the teacher is the key to helping children make connections between the new and the known. An effective teacher not only creates the proper instructional environment for meaning-making to occur but also has access to a repertoire of instructional strategies to help children comprehend before, during, and after reading. This chapter will describe a variety of strategies to teach children the process of comprehension and attempt to move them toward independence as they demand meaning of text.

GRAPHIC ORGANIZER

This graphic organizer summarizes the structure of Chapter 8:

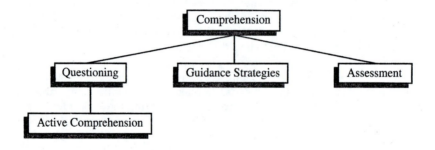

OBJECTIVES

When you finish this chapter, you should be able to understand and discuss each of these statements:

1. Comprehension can be taught.
2. Children learn best when the content to be learned is stressed alongside the processes needed to learn that content.
3. Using an approach based on levels of comprehension processes can develop children's understanding of text.
4. Getting children to ask their own questions about text is important if they are to achieve good comprehension.
5. Teacher-directed, but child-dominated, class discussions are essential for guidance strategies to be effective.
6. Retelling is a valuable aid for helping children comprehend as well as helping teachers assess children's understanding.
7. Perceived authority affects children's ability to be good critical readers.
8. Word association is an effective means of assessing prior knowledge.

Making Comprehension Strategies Work across the Curriculum

Before we launch into a discussion of individual strategies to help children comprehend, a discussion of some approaches to learning from text is necessary. There are a variety of ways to teach children the process of comprehension, but some seem to have more validity than others. Moore and Readence (1992) describe three possible approaches to providing comprehension instruction to children: (1) presenting isolated comprehension skills, (2) aiming children toward content, and (3) presenting content and skills concurrently.

Presenting isolated comprehension skills centers around the direct teaching of skills, free of content. In this approach, specific skills are presented to children regardless of the reading-and-learning task confronting them in their reading materials or assignments. For instance, teachers may present a lesson on finding main ideas, even though the comprehension task required of children in their reading assignment may be making inferences. The intent of such an approach may be to teach for transfer, so that children will become independent readers, but it is usually done with special materials or workbooks not related to the material at hand. Children need help and direction in transferring skills from one set of materials to another, and children may fail to see any purpose in learning skills that are removed from the materials they are attempting to learn.

Aiming children toward content differs from the previous method of teaching comprehension in that it focuses on acquiring text information rather than on *how* to acquire that information; thus, the total focus is on the content of the lesson and children's independent reading of it. Children are directed to read for certain purposes but are not told how they might acquire the information to fulfill those purposes. The problem with this approach arises from the fact that aiming children toward content does not necessarily teach them the skills needed to complete the task. Directing children to read for certain purposes may be necessary, but it may not be sufficient to improve their reading abilities.

Presenting content and skills concurrently is designed to do just that, by providing both direct skills instruction and guidance to selected text information. In this way, the product of the learning—that is, the text information—is stressed alongside the processes of the learning—that is, the skills needed to acquire that text information. Such an approach is based on *simulating, debriefing,* and *fading.* For instance, if the information to be learned is organized into a main idea/detail format, teachers first present a lesson on organizing information according to such a format; then they present to the children the content in which they will utilize that skill. Thus, attention is directed to processes of learning before attention is given to content to be learned, an approach that follows the notion of simulation. In a concurrent approach to comprehension instruction, teachers explicitly point out to children how to learn from text, first by modeling the processes necessary to comprehend and then by providing feedback to children in a debriefing session after they have learned the content to be acquired. Debriefing includes self-reports, introspection, and hindsight. Such feedback entails checking out with children the processes they used to comprehend the material in relation to what was modeled for them. Practice is also provided in a variety of materials, with teacher guidance. Finally, children can be moved toward independence in their reading and learning as teachers gradually fade, or withdraw, the instruction and guidance they provide. We believe that the concurrent approach to comprehension instruction, based on simulating, debriefing, and fading, is a workable approach; it is in this guise that a variety of instructional strategies will be presented.

Using Questioning to Develop Comprehension

Besides the techniques involved in the use of commercial materials, the technique most frequently used to promote children's reading comprehension is teacher questioning. Certainly, it is safe to say that teachers who are good questioners help children comprehend. Through effective questioning, teachers can (1) set children's thinking in motion by activating their prior knowledge about a topic, (2) focus children's attention by increasing their motivation to read or by directing their thoughts to selected aspects of text, (3) monitor children's comprehension by checking their understanding of those aspects of text, and (4) use children's responses in order to provide additional tailoring of the message. In other words, good questioning can lead to more effective learning.

Becoming a good questioner, however, is not a simple task. Teacher questioning can deteriorate into testing rather than instruction if care is not taken. The judicious use of questions requires patience, thoughtfulness, and a manageable system by which to generate questions. In our opinion, a simple hierarchy of comprehension processes serves as a practical means for ensuring that teachers ask questions at varying levels of understanding and children grasp the levels of text understanding required in their reading and learning.

Levels of Comprehension

Read the paragraph below and answer the questions that follow. Be prepared to defend your answers.

> Dave rode his horse slowly over the sand. The air was getting cool as the sun sank over the horizon. The horse kept up her search for a few blades of grass while Dave struggled to stay on her.
>
> 1. What was Dave riding?
> 2. What time of day is it?
> 3. What do you think will happen to Dave? Why do you think so?

By examining the responses you made to the above questions, we can describe the comprehension processes you went through in deriving your answers. For Question 1, your response of "his horse" was taken directly from the text. In fact, you were able to point to the answer in the text, because it was literally stated there. Such comprehension is called *text-explicit,* and it involves getting facts that are explicitly stated by the author of a text. The question is derived from the text, and no inference is required to arrive at an answer. In essence, you read the lines. Text-explicit comprehension requires you to tell what the author said, and usually there is only one correct answer. There is no gray area in answering a text-explicit question; that is, you are either right or wrong. Raphael (1986) uses the phrase *right there* to describe this type of comprehension.

In order to answer Question 2, you had to engage in a different type of comprehension process. Your response was not directly stated in the text; yet, obviously, your answer came from the text. You derived an answer by examining the facts: (1) the air was getting cool and (2) the sun was sinking. This examination led you to conclude that the answer was probably one or more of the following: dusk, early evening, 8 P.M., sunset, late afternoon, 7:00. When you infer an answer from the facts in a text, you are engaging in a process called *text-implicit* comprehension. You are required to think about your answer, and the number of answers to a text-implicit question may vary, depending on the experiential background of the respondents and the amount of prior knowledge each contributes to the act of reading the text. You are required to read between the lines of the text; the answer to the question is implicitly stated, rather than directly stated. This level of comprehension requires you to use the facts in a text in conjunction with your prior experiences to derive logical inferences. Raphael (1986) calls this type of comprehension *think and search.*

Finally, Question 3 engaged you in still another comprehension process. This time, your response was drawn from your head—that is, from your prior knowledge about scenarios similar to the one depicted in the example paragraph. In this case, a number of different responses may be appropriate, and the number of plausible responses is limited only by respondents' prior knowledge. Answers such as "Dave is probably tired and weak and will die if help doesn't arrive" or "Dave will die if he doesn't find food and water" are not derived from the text, and therefore the process of comprehension involved here is labeled *experience-based*. This process is akin to reading beyond the lines, or, as Raphael (1986) says, *on your own*. Figure 8.1 summarizes the distinctions among the three different comprehension processes.

Process Guide 8.1

Go back to the paragraph you previously read about Dave and his horse. Write two questions about the paragraph at each of the three levels of comprehension. Share your questions with the class and be prepared to defend your classification of each question.

Some Considerations about Questions

The suggestions that follow are designed to help you make the most of the learning opportunities that good questioning creates.

First, good questioning abilities develop over time, so patience and opportunities to practice are needed. Make sure not to ask too many text-explicit questions; children need to process text information beyond just what the author says. Questions need to be asked at all levels of comprehension, so that children have an opportunity to think about the text and are challenged to do so. However, in asking questions at higher levels, remember not to make them too diffuse. Questions such as "What is the main idea?" or "What kind of person is the main character of this story?" call upon children to synthesize the facts in a text selection in order to draw an inference; but whether they will actually do so and give appropriate responses is a different story. Even questions developed to stimulate chil-

FIGURE 8.1 Comprehension Processes

		Information Sources			
Process	**Alternative Definition**	*Question*	*Inference*	*Answer*	**Possible Answer**
Text-explicit	Right there	Text	No	Text	One
Text-implicit	Think and search	Text	Yes	Text	One+
Experience-based	On your own	Text	Yes	Reader	Many

dren's thinking at higher levels of comprehension should be specific enough to get them to respond. Several specific thinking questions, asked about major ideas or characterizations in a text, will probably get at the same information that a single diffuse question is intended to elicit; but the specific questions will do it more effectively, because there is more "structure" for responding.

Second, questions should be asked at all stages of the instructional lesson. There is not necessarily *only* one point in a lesson where questioning is appropriate. In the prereading stage, questions that activate children's prior knowledge will facilitate comprehension, particularly text-implicit comprehension (Pearson & Fielding, 1991). During reading, questions can be used to guide children to selected concepts in a text. In a postreading situation, questions can be used to stimulate a review process.

Third, children should be provided the right to be wrong and the freedom to respond. Children learn from the mistakes they make, and fear of failing cannot be construed as a healthy attitude to promote. Additionally, allowing children the freedom to respond connotes a tolerance for divergent responses. What you might expect to be given as an answer to a question might not be what is provided. In fact, children could give you plausible responses to questions at higher levels of comprehension than you might have even considered. To promote children's active involvement in learning, you have to learn to tolerate both mistakes and seemingly inappropriate responses to the questions you ask, because these responses are children's attempts at comprehending and figuring out the processes involved in doing so.

Fourth, children need time to think about their responses to your questions. Although rapid-fire questioning may be typical of most teachers, it appears that allowing think-time facilitates comprehension. Specifically, a minimum of five seconds should be given to children, both after you ask a question and after a child makes a response. Providing children more time to process a response to a question promotes longer responses, more accurate responses, and more speculative responses as children's risk-taking behaviors increase; thus, higher-level thinking is stimulated. Perhaps one of the most difficult things to cope with in question-asking is silence. Yet sustained silence seems to produce favorable results in promoting children's comprehension. Therefore, wait a little longer after asking a question before you repeat it, ask another question, or call on another child.

Fifth, the questions offered by instructional materials should be critically examined. Do not rely solely on questions provided by text authors. They cannot be cognizant of the special needs and abilities of your children, as you are. You are the only one who can ask questions that tailor the message so that the children become involved in comprehension at various levels. Questions written in your materials may not involve comprehension at all levels and may not even touch on the information you consider to be important.

Finally, almost any comprehension skill can be introduced, practiced, or reviewed under the rubric of an approach based on levels of comprehension. For instance, sorting out a main idea involves text-explicit comprehension or, more than likely, text-implicit comprehension. Making a prediction involves text-implicit comprehension. Critical reading behaviors, including the recognition of propaganda techniques, involve text-implicit and experience-based comprehension. Through teacher modeling, guidance, and feedback and through children's practice, such skills can be taught; but management problems are reduced when the approach is based on levels of comprehension, owing to the inherent simplicity of that approach.

Promoting Active Comprehension

Although we advocate the use of questioning as a means to promote children's comprehension, constant teacher-posed questioning does have a disadvantage. There is little evidence to suggest that teacher questioning alone leads children to develop mature, independent reading abilities. In fact, teacher questioning may cause children to become dependent on the teacher for understanding text material. In other words, children may be unable to process information beyond literal understandings because they have become dependent on external prompts. We know that children need to ask their own questions of text and should be able to evaluate text concepts on their own. When children become actively involved in their own comprehension through contributing their own knowledge to the text and through self-questioning, comprehension seems to improve (Pearson & Fielding, 1991). Thus, teachers need a plan to move children along a continuum from teacher-posed questions to child-generated questions. This plan is based on the notions of *active comprehension* and *fading,* as teachers and children work through a series of instructional strategies.

The goal of active comprehension is to have children learn to ask their own questions of text and guide their own learning before, during, and after reading. Children are guided through instruction in which their skill in asking questions is developed and responsibility for doing so is transferred from teachers to them. For the transfer of question-asking responsibility, a three-stage plan involving (1) modeling behavior, (2) phase-out/phase-in strategies, and (3) active comprehension is suggested. Modeling behavior essentially means demonstrating to children what good questioning behavior is. Children are walked through lessons and shown what is required in developing good questions while the thinking processes involved are modeled. At Stage 2, children are encouraged to ask their own questions; that is, we begin to phase in the children and phase out the teacher, with regard to question-asking. Teachers take less and less responsibility in formulating questions about text as children are guided through lessons and encouraged to ask their own questions in order to comprehend the text. Once children are able to ask their own questions about text without external prompting, they are engaging in active comprehension, the third stage of the plan.

As you can see, this plan is based on the notion of fading, or successive withdrawal, of teacher input and guidance. At first, responsibility for question-asking rests with the teacher. Through instruction and modeling, responsibility for this behavior gradually moves to children during the phase-out/phase-in stage. When teacher input becomes minimal and question-asking responsibility rests with children, the active comprehension stage has been reached. Using this notion of fading, Readence, Moore, and Rickelman (2000) recommend a series of instructional lessons that start with teacher-originated questions and progress through modeling and phase-out/phase-in strategies until questions originate mainly from children as active comprehension takes place. This set of instructional strategies is discussed here.

Modeling of Questioning by Teachers

The *directed reading activity* (DRA) is synonymous with the basal reader lesson. Also called the directed reading lesson, the DRA offers teachers a basic format for reading instruction on a group basis and has three stages: (1) preparation for reading, (2) guided reading, and (3) postreading skills development and enrichment activities.

The readiness phase of the DRA is designed to prepare children to read a story by relating it to their past experiences, developing interest in it, and setting purposes for reading. Although no order is implied and each may not be a discrete stage, four aspects of reading preparation are involved in this stage. One aspect is the development of concept background. Teachers try to make connections between the new and the known through a variety of language processes and media. Another aspect of readiness is creating children's interest in reading a text so that their comprehension and enjoyment may be maximized. A third aspect is the introduction of new vocabulary. Children are given oral familiarity with selected words that may be outside their reading vocabulary and word-recognition abilities. Finally, purpose is established so that children have explicit reasons for reading the text.

After children have been prepared for reading the text, they are directed to read silently to seek answers and fulfill the purposes set for reading. Once silent reading has been completed, a discussion follows in which the teacher checks to see whether the children have comprehended the text selection and read purposefully. Oral rereading can be used to clarify any confusion that may have arisen during silent reading, to set new purposes for reading, or to prepare for follow-up activities. In this final stage of the DRA, skills and concepts related to the text are extended and refined. Thus, review and reinforcement are provided for children in follow-up activities to enhance their future learning opportunities.

The use of questions posed by the teacher is central to the DRA. Questions are asked frequently in many components of the lesson, particularly in the comprehension-check and readiness phases. Readiness can be developed by using questions to make connections with previous learning or to create interest. Purposes may be set by posing questions to be answered during the text reading. Questions are probably most prevalent when the teacher checks comprehension in the discussion that follows reading. Finally, questions can be used in oral rereading, either for clarification or for preparation. Thus, in the DRA, children are dependent on the external prompts supplied by the teacher in order to comprehend. However, it is in this lesson format that the teacher can begin the modeling that children need in order to learn to ask their own questions. Children are given an opportunity to experience effective questioning behavior through the teacher's modeling. They must, however, also be given an opportunity to develop their own questions if they are to become active comprehenders. Therefore, children need instruction under a format that allows for a phase-out/phase-in strategy. The ReQuest technique (Manzo & Manzo, 1990) is one that provides such a format.

Reciprocal Questioning

ReQuest is an acronym for *reciprocal questioning*, and it is this reciprocity that distinguishes this strategy from the DRA or other teacher-directed lessons. ReQuest involves the children and the teacher in silently reading portions of a text and then alternately asking and answering questions concerning that material. The strategy is designed to help children

1. Develop their own questions about the text they are reading
2. Acquire purposes for their reading
3. Develop an inquiring attitude toward reading
4. Begin developing independent comprehension abilities

ReQuest can be conceived of as a phase-out/phase-in strategy wherein the teacher models good questioning behavior and also answers the questions children contribute from the text. As children become accustomed to the unique nature of this lesson, they will gradually take over more responsibility in the questioning sequence. Thus, ReQuest provides a format to fill the gap between instructional lessons in which the teacher directs children's comprehension processes by questioning and lessons that allow children to direct their own learning through active comprehension. The seven-step sequence for using ReQuest with children follows.

1. *Selecting appropriate material.* The teacher
   a. Chooses a text at the instructional level of the children
   b. Selects a fiction or narrative nonfiction text that contains a setting, characters, and an unfamiliar plot or story line
   c. Selects a text from which it is possible to predict what the story is about after reading

      A few paragraphs for a second- or third-grade book

      About four to six paragraphs for a fourth- or fifth-grade book

      About eight to ten paragraphs for a sixth-grade book

   d. Identifies the first point (P_1) in the text where prediction of the text content might be elicited from the children. The plot development, rather than the eventual outcome of the text, should be predicted
   e. Identifies a later point beyond which ReQuest will not be continued if children are unable to predict text content, usually after the section identified in (c) above

   f. Selects the amount to be read for each questioning sequence. It is best to begin one sentence at a time with *all* grade levels for the first few sentences of the text and then proceed

   One sentence at a time for grade 2

   A few sentences at a time for grade 4

   A paragraph at a time for grade 6

2. *Giving the rules.* The teacher

   a. Gives the rules for playing ReQuest
   b. Makes certain the children understand the rules

3. *Directing the questioning sequence.* The teacher

   a. Directs joint silent reading of the first sentence
   b. Closes the book after reading the first sentence
   c. Directs the students to keep their books open to ask questions
   d. Answers the questions asked by the students, asking for rephrasing of unclear questions
   e. Clarifies the students' questions only as a last resort
   f. Reinforces children for asking good questions
   g. Determines when the children have finished asking questions and has them close their books
   h. Asks the children questions

4. *Selecting appropriate questions.* The teacher

   a. Asks questions that sample all the levels of questioning

Type of Questions	Example
Text-explicit	What in the story says...?
Text-implicit	From these clues, what do you think...?
Experience-based	What has happened to you that makes you think...?

   b. Asks questions that are different from the children's questions
   c. Integrates information from sentences previously read

5. *Eliciting predictions of text content.* The teacher

   a. Elicits predictions of text content as soon as possible and asks the children to validate their individual predictions—"What have you read thus far that makes you believe this text is about...?"
   b. Makes a list of the suggested predictions of text content on the chalkboard or chart paper

6. *Directing the silent reading.* The teacher has the children read silently to the end of the text

7. *Comparing predictions.* The teacher

   a. Leads a discussion in which the children compare their predictions of text content with the actual text content

      b. Encourages the children to select, from *their* predictions, which ones might also have been logically used to complete the text

      c. Avoids labeling the actual text content as written as *right* and children's individual predictions as *wrong*. Children should see that the text could have had several plausible endings and might be encouraged to rewrite the text using their own individual predictions of text content

Questioning by Children

The directed reading activity and the ReQuest technique represent instructional strategies that allow the teacher to model effective questioning behavior and the children to begin to assume responsibility for asking questions of text material. We will now discuss two instructional strategies in which children take the dominant role in question-asking and the teacher takes on the role of facilitator. They are the directed reading-thinking activity and the survey technique.

Directed Reading-Thinking Activity.   The directed reading-thinking activity (DRTA) (Stauffer, 1969; Tierney & Readence, 2000) is based on the idea that children can use their own experiences to comprehend an author's message and can determine their own purposes for reading. The DRTA begins with the generating of hypotheses by children. As new information is extracted from further reading of the text, these hypotheses are continually refined. Thus, the children pose questions or make predictions about the text; test these questions, upon reading, to confirm, reject, or refine them; and generate new questions as reading progresses.

    Herein lies the essential difference between the DRTA and the DRA: The directed reading-thinking activity encourages children to develop their own reading and thinking processes by setting their own purposes for reading. In the directed reading activity, the teacher prescribes children's interaction with text material through questioning. Because these two strategies are otherwise fundamentally alike, the discussion of the DRTA will focus on the steps involved in the development of children's reading and thinking processes.

    Three steps are of concern in directing these processes: (1) predicting, (2) reading, and (3) proving. The text material is divided into appropriate segments for reading, and children proceed through each segment to define purposes for reading it and then to evaluate and revise these purposes as they acquire text information. To implement these steps, the following sequence is suggested. First, children read the title and examine any pictures that accompany the first segment of the text. The teacher should encourage children to make suggestions about what the text may be about or what might happen in it, using the title and pictures. The teacher then encourages children to discuss and evaluate these suggestions. Second, children read the text segment silently to verify their predictions. Third, children close their texts and examine the evidence. Previous predictions can then be evaluated in light of whatever information the children have acquired, and new predictions generated. When predictions are being examined and refined, oral rereading may be used to highlight particular pieces of evidence. After these three steps have been completed, children should be directed to read a new segment of the text, and the predicting, reading, and proving cycle continues. As the reading goes forward, the predictions, which at first may be quite divergent, will begin to converge as more and more text information is acquired. Once predictions about the text converge, it is recommended that children be directed to read the rest of the text on their own. From this point on, the steps of the DRTA are similar to those of the DRA.

If children encounter any new vocabulary in this predicting, reading, and proving cycle, they should be encouraged to use the context to figure out the word. Unlike the DRA, which introduces new words before any reading begins, the DRTA requires children to try to make an informed guess about the meaning of an unknown word by reading to the end of the sentence in which the word occurs. This gives children access to available syntactic and semantic clues as well as any graphophonic cues provided by the word itself. If children require help from the teacher, they are first encouraged to suggest what the meaning might be and explain how they arrived at that guess. Before providing the meaning, the teacher should model the thinking process for the children. Thus, emphasis is always placed on reading for meaning.

Survey Technique. The DRTA promotes active comprehension by having children initiate questions rather than just respond to them. The teacher acts as a facilitator as children move to analyze text on their own. The final strategy to be discussed in this section, the survey technique (Tierney & Readence, 2000), attempts to complete the cycle of active comprehension and, perhaps, epitomizes this notion. Children, on their own, formulate independent purposes for reading as they preview text material to be read, and teacher input into this process is further faded.

The survey technique is designed to have children systematically analyze the various aids present in text material in order to formulate their own purposes for reading. At first, this strategy is conducted with the whole class to familiarize children with the procedure before they are asked to do it on their own. The strategy consists of the following six steps:

1. Analyzing the title
2. Analyzing the subtitles
3. Analyzing other visual aids
4. Reading the introductory paragraph
5. Reading the concluding paragraph
6. Deriving the main idea

Specifically, children first read the title and speculate as to what will be included in the text. The same procedure is employed with any subtitles that may occur in the text. Children may be directed to construct questions to be answered in each of the various subsections. Next, any visual aids (pictures, charts, graphs, maps, etc.) in the text are analyzed to determine the kind of information they present. The introductory and concluding paragraphs are then read. Any post-reading questions in the text may also be skimmed. At this point, a general discussion should occur. Children should have a fairly good idea of the contents of the text by this time, and they are now asked to predict the ideas that will be discussed in the reading. These may be listed, and an overall main statement is derived that reflects the theme of the material. Children are then directed to read to verify their predictions.

Once children become familiar with the steps of the survey technique, they should be directed to survey the text on their own. A whole-group discussion can follow, which will allow children to pool the various ideas they have generated about the text, and formulation of a main idea statement can culminate the discussion. Allowing children to independently survey a text and then pool their acquired ideas initiates the process of withdrawing teacher guidance. As children become more proficient at conducting this strategy on their own, the whole-group discussion should be terminated. Independence of teacher direction and questioning has been achieved, with active comprehension the result.

In this section we have tried to provide a rationale for independent questioning by children and have suggested a sequence of instructional strategies to accomplish it. Teachers can use the technique of fading to gradually withdraw their direction and supplant it with increased input by children, so that children direct their own comprehension processes. We are not suggesting that this framework is quick or easy to implement. Nor are we saying that all the strategies should be followed exactly. Adapt the strategies to meet the needs and abilities of your children. Above all, remember that getting children to ask questions instead of just answering them is a move in the right direction—toward active comprehension.

Guiding Comprehension Before, During, and After Reading

The notion of providing guidance for children as they interact with text material is certainly not a new idea, but it has received great attention over the last 30 years or so. During this time, the strategies used to guide children have been refined, and new ones have been developed. Yet the reason for using guidance strategies remains essentially the same. Children sometimes need assistance in their reading, and the direction provided by a guidance strategy may be useful in helping children learn from text. Assistance can be provided for a multitude of reasons, primary among them being the importance of the information, the difficulty level of the text, and the abilities of the children.

Guidance strategies are not limited to one particular stage of an instructional lesson, though they are commonly associated with the reading stage. Before children read, guidance strategies may be used to focus their attention or activate their prior knowledge. During reading, guidance strategies may be used to simulate reading processes for children. Any guidance strategy used during reading necessitates a postreading follow-up, whose purpose may be to monitor comprehension or to debrief children on their comprehension. We will describe in this section a variety of strategies that provide guidance for children in their reading: anticipation guides, reading guides, and the guided reading procedure.

Anticipation Guides

The anticipation guide is designed to activate thoughts and opinions about concepts to be discussed in a text. It also focuses your attention on those concepts as you read. Sometimes the statements used in anticipation guides will be consistent with your beliefs and sometimes your beliefs will be challenged by the statements. One of the strengths of the anticipation guide is that misconceptions can be made to surface. Through the information you gain from reading, those misconceptions can then be rectified.

The anticipation guide is designed to stimulate children's curiosity and motivation to learn. Capitalizing on controversy and curiosity arousal has been established as a means to increase comprehension. The guide can be used any time children have some prior knowledge or preconceived ideas relating to the concepts that are to be presented. It can be used with children at any grade level and with most print and nonprint media, including videos, lectures, and field trips. Thus, any time new information is to be presented in some manner, the anticipation guide can be used to prepare children for that learning.

The role of the teacher in using the anticipation guide is critical to its success. Because the statements in the guide are experience-based and because a mismatch

Before children read, guidance strategies may be used to focus their attention.

may be created between children's experiences and the concepts to be learned, a variety of responses, both supporting and refuting the statements, may be elicited from the children. Some responses may even be wrong. You need to remember, though, that experiences vary, that children have a right to be involved and express their thoughts, and, most important, that children have a right to be wrong. The anticipation guide should be used without fear of failure. Therefore, the teacher should act as a facilitator who moderates any discussion of a guide statement and does not make judgments as to the worthiness of any response offered. All responses should be accepted; modification of any misconceptions children may hold in their initial knowledge base takes place through the instruction provided later. Though anticipation guides can be ideal springboards for discussion, this can be easily stifled if the teacher acts as a judge.

In discussing the steps in developing a guide, we will use the following example of an anticipation guide. It is designed for use in conjunction with a unit on cities drawn from a second-grade social studies text.

Cities
Directions: Below are some sentences about cities. Read each sentence. Do you agree with the sentence? If you do, place a check mark (✓) on the line before the sentence. We will talk about each one.

_____ **1.** Most people live in cities.

_____ **2.** It is better to live in a city.

_____ **3.** Only America has big cities.

_____ **4.** Cities are just the same as towns, only bigger.

_____ **5.** People live where they do because they want to.

The following steps are used in the construction of an anticipation guide (Readence, Bean, & Baldwin, 1998). We will relate these steps, wherever possible, to the example guide for the unit on cities.

1. *Identify the major concepts to be learned* from the text or whatever information source you may be using. This can be done by examining the teacher's manual (if one is available), reading or viewing the material, and deciding what deserves attention. This step is what teachers would normally do in lesson planning. In our example text about cities, children will read about these ideas:

    a. People live in cities because of the diverse facilities there.
    b. Cities are similar all over the world.
    c. Cities have different kinds of houses.
    d. Cities have problems because of so many people.
    e. There are different neighborhoods in a city.

2. *Determine how the main concepts support or challenge your children's beliefs.* In our example we need to take into consideration where our children live and,

possibly, their socioeconomic status. What might challenge a child living in the country or in a small town might not challenge an urban or suburban dweller. In other words, this determination must be based on your children's collective experiential backgrounds.

3. *Create three to five statements that support or challenge your children's beliefs and experiences* about the topic under study. These statements will be most effective when children's knowledge about a topic is neither too limited nor too extensive.

4. *Arrange the statements* on an overhead transparency, chalkboard, or work sheet in whatever order you think is most appropriate. This may correspond to the order in which the concepts are dealt with in the text. Add directions to the statements, and leave space to the left of each statement for responding. Obviously, the sophistication of the children who will be using the guide should be taken into consideration in designing it, particularly with the directions and statements themselves. If you examine the directions and statements in our example to be used with second-grade children, you will note that they are not very sophisticated. In fact, you might not even find our example guide challenging—but you aren't a second-grade child with second-grade experiences and knowledge.

5. *Present the guide to the children.* It is always best to read the directions and statements to them orally. Ask children to think about each statement, formulate a response to it, and be prepared to defend their opinions. Children may respond individually or work in groups to formulate a collective response.

6. *Discuss each statement briefly.* You might begin by asking how many children agree or disagree with each statement and then tallying children's responses. The short discussion of each statement should involve at least one response from each side of an issue. In this way children get to listen to others' thoughts about a topic, some supportive of their opinion and some not.

7. *Direct children to read the text,* keeping in mind their own opinions and the other opinions they have heard. By directing them to find out what the text has to say about each statement, you provide children with purposes for reading.

The anticipation guide offers an unusual and interesting way to activate children's prior knowledge and give them a preview of the text concepts they will encounter. Children become actively involved in the lesson through the discussion, which enables them to think about and defend their opinions before any actual reading takes place. The center of instruction shifts away from the teacher and onto each learner.

There are some other advantages to the anticipation guide. This strategy can be diagnostic in scope. Through the tallying and discussion of children's responses, you are in a position to assess both the quantity and the quality of their knowledge base about a topic. This will allow you to make appropriate decisions about how you will present the material, the kind of activities you will use, and possibly the amount of time you will spend on the topic. In other words, the guide allows you to tailor the message to your children. Another advantage of this strategy is that the guide can serve as the basis for the postreading discussion. After reading, children can be directed to respond again to the same statements, which now constitute a *reaction guide*. Children will be bolstered with the information gained from reading and may modify their initial responses to the statements. Again, a discussion ensues about each statement and specific parts of the text may be used to support or refute an opinion offered in the discussion. The reading guide also allows the teacher to get an idea of how well children have learned the text concepts.

Reading Guides

The term *reading guide* has been used loosely for many years to describe any supplementary activity given along with the text reading assignment. Most frequently, a reading guide takes the form of a series of questions designed by the teacher and intended to be answered by the children as a result of their reading assignment. Our use of the term is much more specific. We will define a reading guide as a series of statements that direct children's attention to the major ideas in a text and that help children acquire the comprehension strategies necessary to process the material.

The reading guide is based on the notion of simulation, wherein the comprehension processes necessary to assimilate text information are approximated. It serves as an adjunct to a text-reading assignment, and it is to be used *during* the reading to help children process the material. It also serves *after* the reading as the basis for discussion, wherein a teacher can monitor children's acquisition of both content and process. The following example of a reading guide is based on the Guidelines for Developing Word Meaning, found in Chapter 7.

> *Guidelines for Developing Word Meaning*
> **Directions:** Below are several statements relating to the information you will find in your reading. Place a check by the statements that contain the same information that is found in the text. Be prepared to give evidence to support your reaction.
>
> _____ 1. Vocabulary can be acquired through experience.
>
> _____ 2. Practice by children will develop their vocabulary.
>
> _____ 3. Word meanings change because words are labels for experiences.
>
> **Directions:** Below are some statements that ask you to think about what the authors meant by what they said. Check the statements that are reasonably supported by information in the text. Be prepared to give evidence to support your reaction.
>
> _____ 4. Using phonic analysis could build children's vocabulary.
>
> _____ 5. Direct teacher instruction is necessary if children are to grow in vocabulary knowledge.
>
> _____ 6. Knowing that *hot* means warm will help a child understand that word in any sentence.
>
> **Directions:** Below are some statements that ask you to apply what you already know about vocabulary development to information found in the text. Check the

statements that you think are reasonable and that you can support from your beliefs and the text information. Be prepared to give evidence to support your reaction.

    _____   **7.** Practice makes perfect.

    _____   **8.** A little guidance goes a long way.

    _____   **9.** Variety is the spice of life.

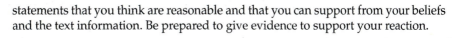

Process Guide 8.2

Complete the reading guide above. Break into small groups and discuss your answers and how you arrived at them. This exercise should serve both as a review and as a means to experience the comprehension processes involved in dealing with the guide.

The example above would normally be provided to you to use as you read the specified section in Chapter 7. Having completed a reading guide as an adjunct to reading, you are now in a position to take a retrospective look at the design of a reading guide. The above guide was designed to let you process the text information at all three levels of comprehension, giving you the opportunity to more fully understand the material. Note that the directions for each part were laid out to parallel the definitions of the three levels of comprehension. Let's look at each statement more closely.

In the first part of the reading guide, you probably placed a check by Statements 1 and 3. Statement 1 deals with how vocabulary is acquired. The text says that word meaning may be acquired in three ways, one of which is firsthand experience. Statement 2 was not checked because the text says that the idea that practice by itself develops vocabulary is a false assumption. Practice needs to be coupled with direct teacher instruction in order to build knowledge of word meanings. Statement 3 was checked because the text states that word meanings constantly change as one's daily experiences modify them. Words are simply labels for those experiences and the concepts they represent. Thus, in the first part of the guide, you engaged in the process of text-explicit comprehension in order to verify these statements.

In the second part of the reading guide, you probably placed a check by Statements 4 and 5. Statement 4 deals with one of the vocabulary-teaching methods traditionally used in schools. The text states that there are more effective strategies by which to build vocabulary, but it also states that any teaching method is better than no method at all. Therefore, it can be inferred that phonic analysis builds children's vocabulary—that is, the text implicitly meant this. Such is also the case with Statement 5. The text states that it is unwise to assume that children will learn new vocabulary on their own. Additionally, it states that practice with word meanings is necessary, but it should follow direct instruction. What we meant when we wrote the passage was that direct teacher instruction is necessary to help children build their vocabulary. Finally, Statement 6 was probably not checked, because it can be inferred from what was stated that just knowing one meaning of a word does not mean you will be able to interpret other meanings that word might convey.

In dealing with the last part of the reading guide, you engaged in experience-based processing. You had to put together what you already knew with information you picked up from the text. With regard to Statement 7, you more than likely have had the need or desire to become better at some task or recreational activity. To do so, you engaged in the activity or task with great frequency. Yet this practice may not have sufficed. Some instruction either was helpful to you or could have been helpful. So, practice is necessary but not sufficient. The text supports the same notion with regard to vocabulary development. Thus, Statement 7 was probably not checked. Statement 8 requires the same kind of text processing and experiential application that you performed in reacting to Statement 7. When you are supported in your endeavors to learn new tasks or activities and are guided toward your goal, your chances of success are enhanced. The text would support the same kind of thinking with regard to vocabulary development. Guidance provided to children in their attempts to learn new word meanings may be useful in later learning situations in which they are involved. Therefore, Statement 8 probably was checked. Finally, Statement 9 was probably also checked because you know that doing the same thing over and over again is monotonous. You also know that experiencing something in a variety of ways can be stimulating. The text supports this notion with its concern about eclecticism in helping children learn new word meanings. Thus, in all three cases in this part of the guide, experiences were juxtaposed with text information to process the statement.

Following are the steps in constructing and using a reading guide:

1. *Content analysis.* Decide what major ideas you wish the children to learn. There may be numerous ideas in a text selection, but children cannot be expected to learn everything. Ask yourself which major working ideas will be useful in later learning situations, and focus on those ideas.
2. *Construct statements.* Design statements that reflect those concepts. The statements that you construct should engage children in all levels of text processing, from text-explicit to experience-based comprehension. Make sure you use understandable vocabulary in your statements. Don't use vocabulary that will be learned in the text reading because children have not yet been exposed to that vocabulary; otherwise, the effectiveness of the guide will be reduced.
3. *Decide on assistance to be provided.* In constructing the statements you must also decide whether you need to provide any assistance to children in reacting to the statements. Assistance may be needed depending on children's abilities and the difficulty of the assignment, and it may be given in the form of an *information index* (a means to inform children where to find pertinent data about the statement). The information index usually takes the form of a numerical indication of the page and the paragraph where children can locate the information. Thus, a statement might be followed with an information index in this form: (49, 2). This indicates to children that they should

examine page 49, paragraph 2, to locate information to help them react to the statements. Gradually, the structure given by the information index should be faded until no assistance is provided and children react independently to the text.

4. *Give the assignment.* Assign the guide to children as an adjunct to their text reading assignment.

5. *Provide a follow-up discussion.* This is probably the most essential step in the development and use of the reading guide. Without a follow-up discussion, the reading guide can become just another meaningless worksheet. This discussion allows the teacher not only to check the comprehension of text concepts but also to monitor children's acquisition of strategies to process that information. Teachers can conduct a debriefing session to ascertain how children arrived at a particular answer. In debriefing, as children react to statements, they share their thinking and, thus, their comprehension processes. Any faulty thinking used in processing the statements may be clarified by the teacher through probing. In this way, the teacher can monitor children's comprehension processes and, at the same time, provide a vehicle for sharing these processes of comprehension with those children who experience difficulty in comprehending. In essence, children can act as models for others. This follow-up may be conducted by having small groups of children discuss and defend their responses to statements and then moving to the whole-group discussion—or the teacher may go directly to the whole-group discussion.

When reading guides are discussed, people often ask "Why use statements? Why not use questions?" First, using statements allows the teacher to focus on the meaning children bring to the text reading, rather than act as an authority figure checking to see whether the children have "gotten the right answer." Thus, the quality of the teacher's response to the discussion is enhanced. Additionally, statements *slice* the task placed on children—that is, they place fewer demands on children in the learning situation. It is easier to recognize a statement at a particular level of comprehension and react to it than it is to produce the response that is required by a specific question.

Guided Reading Procedure

The guided reading procedure (GRP) (Manzo & Manzo, 1990) was designed to help children develop some of the processes essential for independent growth in comprehension. The technique differs from the previously discussed guidance strategies in that statements are not used for children's reactions; rather, children read and recall text in a teacher-directed, but child-dominated, discussion. The GRP uses (1) a collaborative technique to recall information from text, (2) rereading to engage children in self-questioning and self-correction strategies so that they can fill in missing information and correct inconsistencies in their original recalls, and (3) organization to facilitate retrieval of the information from long-term memory. The GRP seems especially useful when the information to be read is fact-laden and the teacher deems the material important enough that children should remember it for subsequent learning situations. The length of the material used in conducting this strategy will depend on the difficulty of the concepts it contains and on the abilities of the children. Lengthier material may be broken into appropriate sections, and the GRP may be conducted over each section. The guided reading procedure has seven steps.

1. *Prereading purpose setting.* The GRP is designed to be a thorough reading and postreading guidance strategy. It is left to the teacher to activate children's prior knowledge about the topic before they read. Many of the strategies described thus far in this chapter and the strategies described in Chapter 7 on developing meaning vocabulary might be useful in accomplishing this. It may also be useful to employ a text survey (akin to the survey technique, discussed in this chapter) or to use brainstorming (akin to the list portion of the list-group-label lesson described in Chapter 7) as a means to activate and organize children's prior knowledge about a topic before the GRP is conducted. Children are directed to read the selection for a very general purpose: to remember everything about it. Of course, this is probably impossible, and it is only through a collaborative recall that the entirety of the text selection will be recalled. Nevertheless, the recall of much of the information read allows children to eventually sift through it and decide what is the most important information to remember as GRP proceeds.

2. *Reading the selection.* Children silently read the text to recall as much information about it as possible.

3. *Recalling the selection.* Children are asked to tell what they remember from their reading. Recalls are recorded on the chalkboard by the teacher or by volunteers selected by the teacher. Each bit of information is recorded exactly as the child gives it, regardless of its accuracy. At this time the focus is on unaided recall of as much of the text as possible; later the focus will shift to self-correction.

4. *Rereading for corrections and additions.* When children can recall no more information from memory, the teacher directs them to reread the text for the purposes of correcting inaccuracies in the recalls and adding information that was not remembered. The teacher may choose to have children examine the recalls first to see if there is any concern about the accuracy of the information or to see if there are any obvious gaps in what has already been recalled. This may help direct children's attention as they reread. Any inaccuracies that are found should be corrected, and new information should be added to the record of information already recalled.

5. *Organizing the information.* Children are now asked to organize the recalls in some form of outline, either main idea/detail or sequence of events, depending on the material. The teacher may ask questions to facilitate the organization of the information but should let children take as much of the responsibility as possible.

6. *Synthesizing the information.* During this step, the teacher makes sure that children understand how the information relates to what they have previ-

ously learned. The teacher may ask thought-provoking questions that require children to synthesize this new information. At first, the questions may need to be specific, but gradually they should become more general—for example, "How does this material relate to what we studied yesterday?" This, again, places more responsibility on the children for their learning.

7. *Testing comprehension.* At this point, it is necessary to check children's short-term memory because the GRP is designed to facilitate comprehension and recall. Thus, a short quiz is appropriate, and it may include matching, multiple-choice, true-false, and/or short-answer questions about the major ideas of the text. Since the focus of the GRP is comprehension and recall, the quizzes need not be graded. However, the results should be recorded, so that children can see how the strategy helps them with these tasks. In fact, we recommend that children graph their results, so that they can have a clear picture of how successful they are with the strategy. You might test long-term memory by quizzing the children on the same material a week later.

Two points need to be mentioned about the GRP. First, the strategy is not meant to be used frequently. It is an intense activity, and overuse of the strategy will lead to boredom, just as overuse of any activity would. Use the GRP no more than once a week. Second, adding a debriefing session to the strategy, perhaps in Step 6, is most beneficial for children's comprehension. Children should offer explanations of how they accomplished certain aspects of the lesson. Questions such as the following might be used to prompt children: How did you know this information was inaccurate? What made you decide this was a main idea? What alerted you to the fact some information was missing? If this is done and children share their thinking, all children will benefit and subsequent comprehension efforts may be enhanced.

In this section we have tried to provide you with a variety of guidance strategies that can be used before and during the reading of a text. All of these guidance strategies are most effective when you use a postreading follow-up to discuss or reexamine the information elicited by the guidance strategy. Additionally, any time you can get children to verbalize their thinking processes in dealing with text information, it is recommended you do so. In the long run, children will become better comprehenders, and your job of teaching will become less difficult. Now we will turn to other ways to develop children's comprehension.

Using Retelling to Develop Comprehension

Perhaps one of the simplest and most powerful ways to enhance children's comprehension and their desire to read is retelling. Retelling involves having children transform a text into their own words. It is a means to develop children's reading and writing across the curriculum as they recall a text after its reading. Brown and Cambourne (1987) and Glazer (1992) cite many advantages of the retelling strategy:

1. Its implementation requires little teacher preparation or involvement.
2. It can be flexible.

3. It develops a range of language abilities involved in reading, writing, listening, and speaking, as well as such literacy skills as organizing text information, recalling it, and reacting to what is recalled.

A child can retell orally, in writing, or by drawing a picture. Which way you choose to use retelling will depend on your children's familiarity and comfort with the procedure, their language sophistication, and their control of the reading and writing processes. Retelling may be conducted individually or in groups, spontaneous or planned, and unguided or guided. If it is done in a group setting, children must understand that they will each make mistakes and have a right to be wrong as they are developing their comprehension abilities.

Although unguided retelling may be a more natural means to ascertain what children recall from a text, some children need to be guided in their retelling. This guidance may be needed to initiate a retelling or to help them continue one. Eventually, the guidance can be faded as children become familiar with the procedures and forms of retelling. Glazer (1992) suggests that the easiest way to teach children retelling is in a small- or large-group setting where they are directed to retell the story in such a way that someone who has not read it will understand the story.

When guiding a retelling, you may need to prompt children with specific questions to encourage them to recall. Specific questions should be used only when children hesitate in their retelling, in which case questions should be used repeatedly until children begin to internalize them and can guide their own recall. Children's sense of story, discussed in Chapter 3, is used to guide a retelling; guiding questions revolve around the setting, plot, characters, time, and motives. Questions might take the following form:

Story Element	Question
Introduction	How did the story begin?
Setting	Where did the story take place?
Time	When did the story take place?
Characters	Who is the story mainly about?
	Who else is in the story?
Plot	What is the story mainly about?
	What happened first?
	What happened next?
Resolution	How does the story end?
Motives	Did you like the story?

Brown and Cambourne (1987) suggest that children be asked to make predictions about the text before it is read. These predictions should center on what the children think the story will be about but may even entail predicting some of the words they may encounter. As with other strategies that use prediction, the notion here is to activate prior knowledge and enhance the interaction between readers and the text. These predictions may be shared and discussed before reading to further engage the children. After the reading and retelling occur, the children can again share and compare what was recalled. In this way children can learn about each other's interpretations of the text and not only develop their knowledge about text but also learn that there may be more than one way to interpret it.

Critical Reading

> There are four kinds of readers. The first is like the hour-glass; and their reading being as the sand, it runs in and out, and leaves not a vestige behind. A second is like the sponge, which imbibes everything, and returns it in nearly the same state, only a little dirtier. A third is like a jelly-bag, allowing all that is pure to pass away, and retaining only the refuse and dregs. And the fourth is like the slaves in the diamond mine of Golconda, who, casting aside all that is worthless, retain only the pure gems.
>
> Coleridge

One aspect of reading instruction that educators at all levels seem concerned about is critical reading. We know our children are capable of critical thinking; they discuss topics of interest, question the arguments of others, and often produce their own logical responses to those arguments. Yet we are dismayed when we ask children to read critically and they aren't able to do so! What we think might be a naturally developing talent—a critical, questioning attitude toward speech and print—sometimes is simply turned off. Why is that?

Three factors seem to be involved in critical thinking and reading: (1) an attitudinal factor wherein the child suspends judgment and approaches the text with an open mind, (2) a problem-solving factor involving the use of logical inquiry, and (3) a judgment factor wherein the child is able to evaluate the text in terms of some standard. Possibly the most important of these factors is the attitudinal factor. From their first exposure to print, children begin to form the opinion that truth and print are the same. Society conditions us to accept authority, and, unfortunately, the use of a single text in the subject areas in our schools conditions children to accept that text as the authority. Readers will suspend judgment when faced with a perceived authority; and authority, we must remember, comes in many forms. The text, with its perfect spelling, its uniform margins, and clean-looking print, represents authority, which often encourages rote learning and discourages critical thinking, as can teachers and grading systems.

Wray and Lewis (1997) note that reading is not always conducted at a conscious level—that is, much of the decision making that takes place as one responds to text is done unconsciously. Readers are not always aware of how the language of a text affects them. Additionally, Wray and Lewis point out that all texts are biased, since their authors have made choices about words and language based on the view of the world they hold. We must remember that much of what children learn about the world comes from the use of socially approved texts in school. For example, they learn the texts' versions of what it means to be children and to be male or female in our social world, and they learn their teachers' definitions of success in reading.

We mentioned in earlier chapters that children will learn best in a classroom environment where they feel free to take risks because the penalty for being wrong is nonexistent. Children learn best in an environment where they have the right to be involved and express their thoughts and opinions and fear no consequences, because they know they have the right to be wrong. By making mistakes, children learn and grow. It is this same kind of environment that nurtures the critical thinker and reader. Such readers will suspend judgment, approach the text openly, and respond accordingly. Without this environment, children will try to second-guess the teacher in an effort to figure out just what it is the teacher wants them to get from the text. This is an all-too-common behavior, exhibited by students from elementary through college levels. To promote the type of classroom environment that will nurture critical reading, Wray and Lewis (1997) suggest that children be encouraged to discuss what their texts mean and talk about the purposes and choices behind the writing of the texts. They recommend the following guiding questions (p. 110):

- Who wrote this text? What are his/her qualifications for doing so?
- What is the text's purpose? Does the author tell you what the purpose is? Is there a hidden purpose?
- What choices were made during the text's production? What formats, structures, and vocabulary were rejected?
- Why were these choices made? What would be different if different choices had been made?

Children learn to solve problems and make judgments, as called for in critical reading, by engaging in text-implicit and experience-based responses to text. By engaging children in these comprehension processes, teachers both form the base for critical reading and increase children's meaning vocabulary. We recommend examining the following statements to get children on the road to critical reading:

1. My dog is good.
2. My dog is brown.

Which is a fact, and which is an opinion? Why? Obviously, this task is simple for you, but what about the beginning reader? With the beginning reader, start with sentence-level statements of fact or opinion, such as those above. For the primary grades, present the sentences orally. As children become older and more sophisticated, they can read the sentences and progressively move toward longer sections of text. Children need to judge which is a fact and which is an opinion and be able to defend their choices. The teacher can engage children in debriefing as they explain to others why they made their decisions. In essence, you should start slowly by slicing the task for children. Fact-or-opinion exercises, as described, can provide good starter statements for children for small-group or whole-group discussion. Justifications for children's responses are gathered from a variety of sources, both firsthand and text-based. The important thing to remember when engaging children in discussions requiring critical responses is to reward the process, *not* the product; otherwise, our purpose in doing the critical-reading exercise may be defeated. Remember—children will sometimes give unexpected responses.

Once children have become familiar with critical examination of fact-or-opinion statements, Wray and Lewis (1997) suggest confronting them with texts that take differing viewpoints about the world. In this way children will learn that different authors write differently about the same topic and that information is ever changing, not static. For instance, in reading about the Civil War, children might find that authors from the North and the South have written differently about the same battle. Similarly, in reading about space, they would see that material written 20 years ago is dated compared to material written today, because of scientific advances. Once children are able to recognize and deal with texts from differing viewpoints, Wray and Lewis suggest that they be asked to produce their own texts for a range of socially relevant purposes—for example, to complain about the trash on the playground or to promote the right to wear whatever teeshirts they want to school.

We think that critical reading is important, but we believe that teachers who engage in good comprehension-teaching behaviors will help children become good critical readers. If you model comprehension processes for children and engage them in the processes of debriefing, fading, and simulation, you will provide the help children need to respond critically to text.

Process Guide 8.3

Make a list of all the comprehension strategies in this chapter. Individually, and then in small groups, classify each strategy according to whether it enhances comprehension before, during, and/or after reading. Be prepared to justify your decisions.

Assessing Comprehension

Word Association

On numerous occasions in this text we have emphasized the importance of prior knowledge in the process of reading and understanding. The more prior knowledge children bring to the act of reading, the greater the chance of their successfully comprehending what they read. The converse is also true: The less prior knowledge children bring to bear, the greater the chance of their *not* understanding the text. Therefore, it behooves teachers to know how much knowledge their children bring to a learning situation before they actually encounter it. Teachers can then make informed decisions about how much guidance to provide their children before they read. If children know a lot about a particular topic, teachers can gear their instruction accordingly and spend less time providing background.

If children know little about a topic, it will prove beneficial to spend more time building background.

In this chapter and the previous one, we suggested a number of vocabulary and comprehension strategies (e.g., list-group-label, anticipation guide) that teachers can use to begin instruction. Although these strategies are instructional in scope, they can provide teachers with valuable diagnostic information concerning how much children know or do not know about a topic. We would like to suggest one other technique specifically designed to assess prior knowledge: word association. Word association is easy to implement and can provide teachers with information essential to their instructional planning and teaching.

Word association is suggested by Zalaluk, Samuels, and Taylor (1986) as a means of measuring children's knowledge about a topic by examining what words they associate with it. It is simple both to do and to score and can be given to an entire class. Children simply write down all the words they can think of that they associate with a key topic. In effect, this list is a gauge of children's knowledge base before reading. The rationale behind word association is that children will produce many words for topics about which they possess considerable knowledge; few associations will be made with topics that children know little about. Word association can be done in three steps:

1. *Preparing the stimulus material.* The selected key word is printed in the left margin on every line of a piece of paper. Unlike list-group-label, where newly elicited word associations may trigger additional words, this technique is designed to ensure that the key word alone cues the associations.
2. *Providing directions.* Children are informed that they will have three minutes to write down words related to the key word they will be given. They are told not to worry about filling in all the lines on the paper but to write whatever comes to mind when they see the key word. Children are told that the words they generate may be things, events, places, or ideas. As with other strategies, the teacher may model this activity if the task is new to children.
3. *Scoring.* After children record their responses, associations are scored by tallying the reasonable responses and awarding one point for each one. For example, if the key word is *solar system,* one point is given for "Earth" but none for "vegetables" since it is an unreasonable association. Points are awarded for word associations that are members of the same class as the key word (e.g., the name of another solar system), superordinate to it (e.g., the Milky Way), or subordinate to it (e.g., planets). However, no more than one point may be awarded for the same type of subordinate association. That is, one point may be awarded for Earth but no more for Mars or Pluto, since they are all examples of planets. This scoring system takes into account the fact that the generated word association, rather than the key word itself, may be cueing other words. The following key is suggested to score children's word associations:

0–2 points	low prior knowledge
3–6 points	average prior knowledge
7+ points	high prior knowledge

To illustrate, let's assume you were assessing a child's prior knowledge about animals, and the following list of words was generated:

mammals
birds
reptiles
cardinal
woodpecker
hawk

This child would be awarded four points—one each for mammals, reptiles, and birds as examples of animal types and only one additional point for the three types of birds. The child would be classified as having average prior knowledge, and you could plan to spend a normal amount of time building background.

Retelling

Earlier in this chapter we discussed how retelling could be used to develop children's comprehension. Retelling, however, can also be used instead of questions to assess children's understanding of what they read. On most informal reading inventories, for instance, comprehension performance is assessed by asking children questions about the story they have read. Often the question-and-answer format does not fully tap the extent of the children's understanding. An alternative method for determining passage comprehension is to require the children to retell the story in their own words. In doing so, they attempt to recall as much of the content as possible. Since the children are not limited to responding only to the questions, a more thorough assessment of their passage knowledge may be gained through retelling.

To initiate the retelling, make sure the child knows what he or she will be asked to do after the reading. Be prepared to tape the retelling, as taping will increase the accuracy of your assessment. After the reading, ask the child to retell the story as if he or she were telling it to a friend who had never heard it before. Morrow (1986, p. 141) suggests using the following prompts if the child has problems doing the retelling:

1. The following prompts are to be used only when necessary.

   a. If the child has difficulty beginning the story, suggest beginning with "Once upon a time…" or "Once there was…"
   b. If the child stops retelling, encourage continuation by asking "What comes next?" or "Then what happened?"
   c. If a child stops retelling and cannot continue with the prompts offered in (b), ask a question about the story that is relevant at the stopping point to encourage continuation. For example, "What was Jenny's problem?"

2. When a child is unable to retell the story, or if his or her retelling lacks sequence or detail, prompt the retelling, step by step, with the following dialogue.

   a. "Once upon a time…" or "Once there was…"
   b. "Who was the story about?"

c. "When did the story happen?" (Day, night, summer, winter?)
d. "Where did the story happen?"
e. "What was (name the main character) problem in the story?"
f. "How did she try to solve her problem? What did she do first/next?"
g. "How was the problem solved?"
h. "How did the story end?"

To score the retelling, we recommend using the holistic system developed by Irwin and Mitchell (1983). Since each child's retelling is unique with regard to personality, reaction, and understanding, assessment must be done as a totality and not by examining component parts. Only by judging the whole retelling can the essence, or richness, of the reader's comprehension be captured. For assessing a retelling, Irwin and Mitchell have developed five levels of richness, to characterize comprehension ranging from good to poor. These levels are given in Figure 8.2. Figure 8.3 is a checklist developed to compare principal qualities of each level of richness.

For an example of how you might score a retelling, first read the IRI passage on the next page, entitled "Plant Spiders."

FIGURE 8.2 Judging Richness of Retellings

Level	Criteria for Establishing Level
5	Student generalizes beyond text; includes thesis (summarizing statement), all major points, and appropriate supporting details; includes relevant supplementations; shows high degree of coherence, completeness, comprehensibility.
4	Student includes thesis (summarizing statement), all major points, and appropriate supporting details; includes relevant supplementations; shows high degree of coherence, completeness, comprehensibility.
3	Student relates major ideas; includes appropriate supporting details and relevant supplementations; shows adequate coherence, completeness, comprehensibility.
2	Student relates a few major ideas and some supporting ideas; includes irrelevant supplementations; shows some degree of coherence; some degree of completeness; the whole is somewhat comprehensible.
1	Student related details only; irrelevant supplementations or none; low degree of coherence; incomplete; incomprehensible.

5 = highest level, 1 = lowest level

FIGURE 8.3 Checklist for Judging Richness of Retellings

	5	4	3	2	1
Generalizes beyond text	X				
Thesis (summarizing statement)	X	X	X		
Major points	X	X	X	?	?
Supporting details	X	X	X	X	?
Supplementations	Relevant	Relevant	Relevant	Irrelevant	Irrelevant
Coherence	High	Good	Adequate	Some	Poor
Completeness	High	Good	Adequate	Some	Poor
Comprehensibility	High	Good	Adequate	Some	Poor

From Irwin, P. A., & Mitchell, J. N. (1983). A procedure for assessing the richness of retellings. *Journal of Reading, 26,* 391–396. All Rights Reserved. Reprinted by permission of the International Reading Association.

Plant Spiders[*]

There are all kinds of spiders.
This black and green one is called a plant spider.
A plant spider has small feet.
All spiders have small feet.
Plant spiders live in nests.
They soon learn to hunt for food and build new nests.

Then assume a child has read this passage and has retold it to you as follows:

> …Once there was a spider that lived on a plant. He lived in nests like birds and hunted for them. He was black and some other color and had small legs, too.…

An examination of this retelling reveals that the child did not generalize beyond the text or provide a thesis statement. A few major ideas and some supporting details are present, as is an irrelevant supplementation about birds. The child shows some degree of coherence, completeness, and comprehensibility. Thus, the child's retelling would probably be classified as level 2, indicating to the teacher that the child did not comprehend the passage very well. The teacher could add to these findings of the retelling by asking the questions that accompany the passage and getting a measure of probed recall.

Assessing comprehension through the use of retellings enables teachers to get a different look at how children comprehend. By examining retellings holistically, teachers can move away from the small details of recall based on questions and look at the effectiveness of the retelling as a whole. Additionally, teachers can see how children move beyond the story to evaluate it and relate it to their own lives. Finally, given the global nature of the assessment, examining retellings holistically allows teachers to be more consistent in their assessment of their children's comprehension.

[*]From N. J. Silvaroli, *Classroom reading inventory,* 4th ed., p. 53. © 1969, 1973, 1976, 1982, 1994, Wm. C. Brown Publishers, Dubuque, Iowa. All Rights Reserved. Reprinted by permission.

Summary

This chapter discussed the notion that comprehension involves associating the new with the known. We provided an array of strategies that we believe will promote this association in children. Central to our discussion of comprehension was the assumption that it can be taught. Emphasis was placed on teacher modeling and on the guidance and instruction children must be given in comprehension before, during, and after reading a text. The comprehension strategies described work best when reading skills and content are taught concurrently, using techniques that emphasize debriefing, simulating, and fading. A number of strategies that revolve around questioning and teacher guidance were described. We also examined retelling and critical reading, and we closed with a discussion of assessing comprehension. We are now ready to move on to the topic of studying; Chapter 9 will describe a variety of techniques for developing independent learning in children.

FOLLOW-THROUGH ACTIVITIES

Note: Level 1 activities may require limited access to children or classrooms. Level 2 activities should be completed using children and classrooms.

Level 1 Activities

1. Choose a short text selection, and construct a number of questions representative of each of the three levels of comprehension.

2. Design statements to be used in a lesson with children, following the directions for one of the guidance strategies, such as the anticipation guide or the reading guide.

3. Select any comprehension strategy from this chapter. Plan and teach a lesson in a simulation with a group of fellow students.

Level 2 Activities

1. Conduct a ReQuest lesson with some children. What is your evaluation of it? How did the children react?

2. Select one of the guidance strategies discussed in the chapter and try it out on some children. What is your reaction?

3. Using the criteria provided in this chapter for scoring retellings, evaluate two different sets of retellings provided by your instructor. What did you find out?

WORKING WITH PARENTS

The scene is a parent conference on the reading problems of Scott, a third grader, near the beginning of the year.

MR. REED: Scott's second-grade teacher said his main problem was comprehension. His teacher said that even though the skills list was followed closely, Scott still didn't seem to master the skills very well. I'm hoping that since we've moved and Scott has changed schools, you can help him with his problem.

MS. WRIGHT: I think we can help Scott. His problem doesn't seem to be any different from that of many other young children in learning to read.

MR. REED: I'm sorry, Ms. Wright. I don't understand what you mean.

MS. WRIGHT: My apologies, Mr. Reed. Let me clarify my comment. Sometimes beginning readers are so concerned with recognizing words that their comprehension suffers. What may complicate matters even more is that many of the instructional materials designed for beginning readers reinforce this by placing their emphasis on word recognition, too.

MR. REED: But isn't recognizing the words important?

MS. WRIGHT: Yes, it is, but comprehension is even more important! After all, what good is saying a word correctly if I don't know what it means?

MR. REED: Good point, Ms. Wright. So how do you help children comprehend?

MS. WRIGHT: Well, first of all, I believe in the direct teaching of comprehension.

MR. REED: Direct teaching?

MS. WRIGHT: Yes, I provide direct help in comprehension; I don't rely on the materials to do the teaching.

MR. REED: But aren't the materials useful?

MS. WRIGHT: Certainly they are! They're very useful to provide children practice in comprehension skills, but they don't do any teaching. That's where I come in.

MR. REED: Just how do you go about doing that?

MS. WRIGHT: Well, to begin with, I believe that the best way to learn something is to be shown how to do it. So, with the children, I model for them exactly what they should do in order to comprehend efficiently. To put it plainly, I think aloud so children can listen to what my thinking processes are. Then they know what they have to do themselves.

MR. REED: Sounds logical. Please continue.

MS. WRIGHT: Certainly, Mr. Reed. I also try to provide children with instruction and guidance before they read, while they're reading, and after they read. In this way, children are given a good chance of succeeding in their learning. Finally, I try to make sure the materials I use for practice are relevant to the children.

MR. REED: Relevant?

MS. WRIGHT: What I mean is that we don't have a set of materials only for reading and other sets of materials only for other things. I try to use the children's social studies and science texts, for instance, so children see that what we do in reading is useful in all the subjects.

MR. REED: Well, that makes a lot of sense to me.

MS. WRIGHT: Thank you. I appreciate your comment. I'll keep you posted on how Scott is doing, and I'm sure he'll do fine!

MR. REED: I think you're right, Ms. Wright. Thank you for your time.

MS. WRIGHT: No problem. Call me again if you have a concern.

RESOURCES

Barr, R., & Blachowicz, C. L. Z. (1993). Informal diagnostic procedures for classroom teachers. *Reading & Writing Quarterly: Overcoming Learning Difficulties, 9,* 51–80.

The authors describe how instructional strategies can be used diagnostically.

Dole, J. A., Duffy, G. G., Roehler, L. R., & Pearson, P. D. (1991). Moving from the old to the new: Research on reading comprehension instruction. *Review of Educational Research, 61,* 239–264.

The authors review the research on comprehension and teaching and offer instructional recommendations.

Durkin, D. (1978–1979). What classroom observations reveal about reading comprehension instruction. *Reading Research Quarterly, 14,* 481–533.

This classic research report reveals that comprehension assessment, rather than comprehension instruction, is predominant in elementary classrooms.

Glazer, S. M. (1992). *Reading comprehension: Self-monitoring strategies to develop independent readers.* New York: Scholastic.

This sourcebook contains practical techniques to help children develop and monitor their own comprehension.

Hoffman, J. V. (1992). Critical reading/thinking across the curriculum: Using I-charts to support learning. *Language Arts, 69,* 121–127.

The author presents the use of inquiry charts to teach critical reading and thinking.

Irwin, J. W. (1991). *Teaching reading comprehension processes* (2nd ed.). Englewood Cliffs, NJ: Prentice Hall.

This text presents practical strategies for teaching comprehension in grades K-12.

Olson, M. W., & Gee, T. C. (1991). Content reading instruction in the primary grades: Perceptions and strategies. *The Reading Teacher, 45,* 298–307.

The authors survey primary-level teachers for the strategies they find helpful in teaching content.

Readence, J. E., Moore, D. W., & Rickelman, R. J. (2000). *Prereading activities for content area reading and learning* (3rd ed.). Newark, DE: International Reading Association.

Numerous prereading strategies to begin lessons are suggested.

Tierney, R. J., & Readence, J. E. (2000). *Reading strategies and practices: A compendium* (5th ed.). Boston: Allyn & Bacon.

Units 1, 9, and 11 present a variety of practical comprehension strategies for classroom use.

Wray, D., & Lewis, M. (1997). *Extending literacy: Children reading and writing non-fiction.* New York: Routledge.

The authors describe a number of activities to use with nonfiction sources, including discussion of critical reading.

REFERENCES

Brown, H., & Cambourne, B. (1987). *Read and retell.* Portsmouth, NH: Heinemann.

Glazer, S. M. (1992). *Reading comprehension: Self-monitoring strategies to develop independent readers.* New York: Scholastic.

Irwin, P. A., & Mitchell, J. N. (1983). A procedure for assessing the richness of retellings. *Journal of Reading, 26,* 391–396.

Manzo, A. V., & Manzo, U. C. (1990). *Content area reading: A heuristic approach.* Columbus, OH: Merrill.

Moore, D. W., & Readence, J. E. (1992). Approaches to content area reading instruction. In E. K. Dishner, T. W. Bean, J. E. Readence, & D. W. Moore (Eds.), *Reading in the content areas: Improving classroom instruction* (3rd ed., pp. 52–57). Dubuque, IA: Kendall/Hunt.

Morrow, L. M. (1986). Effects of structural guidance in story retelling on children's dictation of original stories. *Journal of Reading Behavior, 18,* 135–152.

Pearson, P. D., & Fielding, L. (1991). Comprehension instruction. In R. Barr, M. L. Kamil, P. Mosenthal, & P. D. Pearson (Eds.), *Handbook of reading research: Volume II* (pp. 815–860). New York: Longman.

Raphael, T. E. (1986). Teaching question/answer relationships, revisited. *The Reading Teacher, 39,* 516–522.

Readence, J. E., Bean, T. W., & Baldwin, R. S. (1998). *Content area literacy: An integrated approach* (6th ed.). Dubuque, IA: Kendall/Hunt.

Readence, J. E., Moore, D. W., & Rickelman, R. J. (2000). *Prereading activities for content area reading and learning* (3rd ed.). Newark, DE: International Reading Association.

Stauffer, R. G. (1969). *Directing reading maturity as a cognitive process.* New York: Harper & Row.

Tierney, R. J., & Readence, J. E. (2000). *Reading strategies and practices: A compendium* (5th ed.). Boston: Allyn & Bacon.

Wray, D., & Lewis, M. (1997). *Extending literacy: Children reading and writing non-fiction.* New York: Routledge.

Zalaluk, B. L., Samuels, S. J., & Taylor, B. M. (1986). A simple technique for estimating prior knowledge: Word association. *Journal of Reading, 30,* 56–60.

9 Promoting Independent Learning

INTRODUCTION

Learning in school typically involves a variety of tasks such as following directions, setting purposes for reading, taking notes, completing written reports, and so on. Each of these tasks requires that children apply specific study strategies acquired in school to aid them as they attempt to learn independently. Study strategies become even more critical as children progress into the middle grades and high school and deal continuously with text material. For many children, however, strategies for independent reading and learning from text are never fully developed.

Research has indicated that high school and college students often possess a restricted range of independent learning strategies, and those they report are woefully inadequate (Simpson, 1984). In fact, the study technique most often cited by students turns out to be simple rereading. This may be because there is no systematic teaching of independent learning strategies in the early grades. Elementary teachers may neglect such lessons in the hope that secondary teachers will compensate for this deficit; secondary teachers may assume students have already been taught independent learning strategies. Either way, little or no attention is devoted to studying.

Complicating this matter further is the fact that, although instruction in independent learning begins in the elementary years, it usually is not developed until the middle grades, *after* children have been in school for five or six years. Instruction in independent learning strategies has traditionally been viewed as part of the *reading to learn* stage of instruction and placed in grade 4 and above, where learning from textbooks predominates. Below grade 4, the focus is on *learning to read,* or developing basic reading skills. As this line of reasoning goes, when children have learned the basic reading skills and learning becomes more directly related to textbooks, the focus of instruction should shift to the development of independent learning strategies. We reject this view of study instruction as too narrow and falsely based for three reasons.

First, instructional materials often contain a mixture of narrative and content selections, even at beginning levels. Second, many schools introduce content area texts in the primary grades. Third, some children select for recreational reading books whose contents not stories but factual selections similar to those found in subject textbooks. Thus, waiting until the middle grades to begin instruction in independent learning strategies ignores the reality of learning in the primary grades. Children, even in kindergarten, are continuously involved in tasks that require the application of independent learning strategies. For instance, children in the primary grades must listen to and follow teacher explanations; complete homework assignments; use textbooks to learn social studies, science, and other subjects, and use computer databases and the Internet to locate information. Since the development of independent learning strategies begins the moment children enter school, their teaching should be part of beginning reading instruction. Therefore, the purpose of this chapter is to make the point that instruction in independent learning strategies is basic, too, and to provide you with a notion of what independent learning strategies should be taught and how that teaching should be accomplished.

GRAPHIC ORGANIZER

This graphic organizer summarizes the structure of Chapter 9:

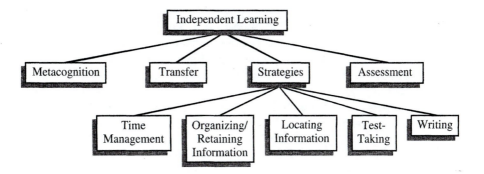

OBJECTIVES

When you finish this chapter, you should be able to understand and discuss each of these statements:

1. Instruction in independent learning strategies begins in the primary grades.
2. Learning to manage time and plan ahead is the basis for developing effective independent learning.
3. Sensing how a selection is organized is the basis for using a study system and taking notes.
4. Teaching locational skills begins with knowing how to use the parts of a textbook.
5. Knowing how to take tests should help children do better on them.
6. Writing research reports is an effective means for developing and reinforcing independent learning.
7. Study strategies should be assessed informally.

Metacognition

In order to effectively learn how to use independent learning strategies, children must already be establishing a foundation in the following areas: (1) listening and reading comprehension, (2) experiencing a wide variety of print, (3) general and content area vocabulary development, (4) following oral and written directions, and (5) questioning strategies.

Another area which helps provide a firm foundation for developing independent learning strategies is that of metacognition. Broadly defined, *metacognition* is an awareness of one's own mental processes—that is, knowing what you know (Paris, Wasik, & Turner, 1991). Although that may seem like doubletalk, metacognition is actually thinking about thinking; it is making an effort to manage your thoughts through conscious planning. Those who possess well-developed metacognitive abilities understand their own behaviors, use mental strategies they can verbalize, and can assess the quality of their thinking.

Young children, by and large, do not have good metacognitive abilities. Frequently, they do not understand or even try to monitor their own thought processes when they attempt to comprehend what they are reading. For instance, children rarely form good hypotheses about the meaning of a text before they read it or, for that matter, relate the prior knowledge they possess about the topic of the text. Children do not monitor how well they are comprehending as they read, nor do they know how to fix their difficulty when they encounter a comprehension problem.

Bergman (1992, p. 599) suggests that children should be asking the following kinds of questions as they read:

Task	*Questions*
To get the gist	What is the story about?
	What is the problem?

	What is the solution?
	What makes me think so?
To predict/verify	What is going to happen next?
	Is my prediction still good?
	Do I need to change it?
	What makes me think so?
To summarize	What has happened so far?
	What makes me think so?
To solve problems	Should I guess?
	Ignore and read on? Reread or look back?
	Why?

Since children who ask these kinds of questions as they read will comprehend better, helping children develop their metacognitive abilities is necessary if they are to develop effective independent learning strategies in later grades.

Perhaps the most effective way to begin helping children with metacognitive strategies is by modeling. Teachers can model their metacognitive strategies by using the *think-aloud*. As teachers describe their own thoughts about comprehending a text, children will see how and when to employ the identical strategies. That is, as children hear you verbalize how you used your prior knowledge about a text topic or what you did when you had a comprehension problem, they will begin to pick up the coping strategies a skilled reader uses to understand a text. The following procedure can be used to help children develop their metacognitive abilities:

1. *Selecting the text.* Select—or develop on your own—a passage that contains obvious problems. The passage should include points of confusion or difficulty, contradictions, or unknown words.
2. *Modeling.* As you read the passage, have children follow along silently, listening for how you think your way through the problems presented in it. Examples might include making a prediction (Since he fell off his horse, I predict he'll be hurt), using prior knowledge (This reminds me of when I accidentally left my fishing license at home and got caught by the game warden), or employing problem-solving strategies (That sentence was confusing so I'll reread it to see if it becomes clearer).
3. *Discussion.* After the reading, encourage the children to talk about what happened and why. Clear up any misunderstandings about the think-aloud and let them add their thoughts to yours.
4. *Practice.* After several modeling lessons, have children work in pairs to practice using the think-aloud. They should take turns reading and sharing their thoughts. The listening partner should add thoughts to the session and clear up any confusion. Children should also practice using the think-aloud silently as the final step in using the strategies independently.

It is also important that you give children the opportunity to practice their strategies with other forms of print besides the basal. In this way you will provide for transfer, which is another way to develop the foundation for independent learning strategies.

Transfer to Content Areas

Providing for *transfer* of reading skills to other forms of print is a key part of developing independent learning strategies. It is essential that children see the usefulness and function of reading skills in other parts of their lives and in other parts of the school day. We suggest that teachers build transfer activities into reading lessons. The activities and suggestions presented in this section should help children apply reading skills they have learned to other kinds of print.

At times, keeping one reading group busy will seem like a full-time job, without trying to keep the rest of the class productively occupied with learning. In addition, the activities suggested for keeping children busy who are not being instructed may not always seem exciting to either you or the children. Finally, teachers never seem to have enough time for science, social studies, health, or other content area subjects. The teacher's manuals to these texts are full of activities for which there never seems to be time. Using these activities provides children with relevant, meaningful, and interesting practice in using reading and other language tools. A quick survey of several teacher's manuals yielded a sample of truly exciting activities that could be completed with little or no teacher direction:

From a Science Text Teacher's Manual
1. Have children view a video as background or reinforcement for a lesson and prepare their own edited script for later presentation to the entire class.
2. As part of a unit on earth and space science, have children examine a weather map taken from the daily newspaper. From one map, they can forecast weather for today, tomorrow, and the next day in cities around the country. A single city may be selected by each child for long-term watching. A log or journal with other relevant climate and geographic facts about the city could also be part of this activity.

From a Health Text Teacher's Manual
1. Have children plan and carry out experiments on measuring changing pulse rates. They should record their rates before and after various experiences. Each individual chart can then be displayed and comparisons made. Some suggested activities:

    Record pulse standing, sitting, lying down (get the nurse's cooperation here).

    Record pulse before and after eating.

    Take a short walk down the hall; record pulse before and after your walk.

    Record pulse before and after gym class.

2. As part of a nutrition unit on balanced meals, tell the children they have a certain amount of money to spend for each lunch or dinner. They can plan the meal by shopping in newspaper and magazine ads, then cutting and pasting pictures of meals on individual posters. This activity can be completed individually, in pairs, or by a small group of children.

From a Math Text Teacher's Manual
1. For independent seatwork, use story problems or math riddles that are provided for extra practice or enrichment.
2. Have the children in pairs or triads create or rewrite math story problems in their own words and trade them with other pairs or triads for solving.

From a Social Studies Text Teacher's Manual
1. On a large sheet of poster board or paper, draw in the streets in the school neighborhood. Have children label them, draw signs, cut out shapes or pictures from old magazines, and add other print needed to create a sketch of the school neighborhood.
2. Have the children use classroom and library references to explore in greater depth a famous person who is being studied. They can prepare a bulletin board called "Little Known Facts About...."

Process Guide 9.1

Break into pairs. Examine the teacher's manuals from some content textbooks used in the elementary grades. Find at least two activities from two different content texts that could be used as transfer activities.

The above suggestions are only a sample of the kinds of transfer activities found in content area texts. To make maximum use of such activities teachers should try, *when possible,* to match a skill being taught in reading (such as using reference books) with skills required to complete an activity (e.g., "Little Known Facts About..."). This linking of skills taught in a reading lesson with a functional use of those same skills in another kind of print can be accomplished through what we call a *real-life reading lesson,* using the following steps:

1. A skill is selected.
2. Materials are selected for initial teaching. These materials are used in carefully controlled teaching in the reading lesson.
3. The skill taught in a carefully structured lesson, using controlled materials, is reinforced in the workbook.
4. Application lessons are taught using content area materials and real-life situations, with training for independence in the use of *real* materials.
5. Children work independently with real materials.

Skills such as using an index or a library's card catalog, reading maps, classifying things, establishing the sequence of events, and following directions (to name a few) can be taught in the setting of the reading group and then applied in other kinds of real-life print settings.

It should be noted that the basis of the real-life reading lesson—or, for that matter, any independent learning strategy discussed in this chapter—is the concurrent approach to comprehension instruction. That is, teachers model the processes necessary for performing the task and then provide guided practice for the children, with feedback as they perform the task. As children transfer what they have learned to other forms of print, teachers train for independent learning by gradually fading their guidance. It is with this kind of instruction in mind that we present our thoughts about what independent learning strategies should be taught to children.

Strategies for Independent Learning

Figure 9.1, a scope and sequence chart of strategies for independent learning, encompasses grades K–12 and offers teachers, administrators, and curriculum directors a guide for the infusion of independent learning strategies in the total curriculum. The specific strategies are clustered around five study strands: (1) time management, (2) organizing and retaining information, (3) locating information, (4) test-taking, and (5) writing.

It is cautioned that, as with any scope and sequence chart, individual teachers and schools should *not* apply the strategies rigidly. Rather, the chart should be modified to meet the local needs of the children and the school. Using this scope and sequence as a point of departure should make the infusion of any independent learning strategies program a successful one.

Time Management

Time management strategies are designed to produce children who can manage time, set goals, and complete short-term and longer-term assignments. Within this strand, the basic strategy to be introduced in the primary grades is that of getting ready and managing time. This strategy is reviewed and maintained throughout the grades.

Helping children learn to get ready to study and to manage their study time begins with showing them how to plan ahead and become responsible for their own learning. Teachers develop these insights by making children aware of the goals of each lesson or learning task. They also plan instruction with their children and encourage them to take responsibility for completing homework assignments. Some simple guidelines will help teachers accomplish these goals:

1. *Set purposes.* Make sure children know what is expected of them in each lesson you are teaching, through comments such as "Today we are going to read

**FIGURE 9.1 Scope and Sequence Chart of Strategies for Independent Learning,
with I = Introduce, R = Review, and M = Maintain**

Strategy	K	1	2	3	4	5	6	7	8	9	10	11	12
Strand 1—Time Management													
1.1 Goal Setting	I	R	R	R	M	M	M	M	M	M	M	M	M
—Daily schedule		I	R	R	R	R	M	M	M	M	M	M	M
—Long-term schedule				I	R	R	R	R	M	M	M	M	M
1.2 Completing Homework													
—Daily	I	R	R	R	M	M	M	M	M	M	M	M	M
—Weekly		I	R	R	R	R	M	M	M	M	M	M	M
—Long term				I	R	R	R	R	M	M	M	M	M
1.3 Estimating Time to Complete Tasks				I	R	R	R	M	M	M	M	M	M
—Managing tasks				I	R	R	R	M	M	M	M	M	M
—Breaking down tasks				I	R	R	R	M	M	M	M	M	M
1.4 Completing Assignments in School		I	R	R	R	M	M	M	M	M	M	M	M
1.5 Planning for Daily Study Time in School					I	R	R	R	M	M	M	M	M
1.6 Planning for Study Time Outside School					I	R	R	R	M	M	M	M	M
Strand 2—Organizing and Retaining Information													
2.1 Previewing													
—Simple narrative stories	I	R	R	R	M	M	M	M	M	M	M	M	M
—Complex expository/information texts					I	R	R	R	M	M	M	M	M
2.2 Setting Purposes for Reading	I	R	R	R	R	M	M	M	M	M	M	M	M
2.3 Predicting Story Sequence, Outcome(s)	I	R	R	R	M	M	M	M	M	M	M	M	M
2.4 Using Visual Aids	I	R	R	R	R	R	R	M	M	M	M	M	M
2.5 Taking Notes from Oral Presentations						I	R	R	R	R	M	M	M
2.6 Taking Notes from Text Materials					I	R	R	R	R	R	M	M	M
2.7 Mapping		I	R	R	R	R	R	R	R	M	M	M	M
2.8 Summarizing													
—Oral	I	R	R	R	R	R	R	M	M	M	M	M	M
—Written				I	R	R	R	R	R	M	M	M	M

(continued)

FIGURE 9.1   Continued

Strategy	K	1	2	3	4	5	6	7	8	9	10	11	12
2.9 PREP													
—Simplified formal				I	R								
—Complete system format					I	R	R	R	R	R	M	M	M
Strand 3—Locating Information													
3.1 Text Information													
—Book parts	I	R	R	R	R	R	R	M	M	M	M	M	M
—Glossary				I	R	R	R	M	M	M	M	M	M
—Table of contents		I	R	R	R	R	M	M	M	M	M	M	M
—Finding specific pages		I	R	R	R	R	M	M	M	M	M	M	M
—Alphabetical order		I	R	R	R	M	M	M	M	M	M	M	M
—Index			I	R	R	R	M	M	M	M	M	M	M
3.2 Using General References													
—Calendar	I	R	R	M	M	M	M	M	M	M	M	M	M
—Simple dictionary		I	R	R	M	M	M	M	M	M	M	M	M
—General dictionary				I	R	R	R	M	M	M	M	M	M
—Atlas, maps				I	R	R	R	M	M	M	M	M	M
—Encyclopedia				I	R	R	R	M	M	M	M	M	M
—Thesaurus				I	R	R	R	M	M	M	M	M	M
3.3 Using Specialized References													
—Reader's Guide						I	R	R	R	M	M	M	M
—Specialized dictionaries						I	R	R	R	M	M	M	M
—Specialized indexes						I	R	R	R	M	M	M	M
3.4 School Library Organization:													
Using card catalog or computerized retrieval system				I	R	R	R	M	M	M	M	M	M
3.5 Public Library Organization:													
Using card catalog or computerized retrieval system				I	R	R	R	M	M	M	M	M	M
3.6 Computers													
—Databases				I	R	R	R	R	M	M	M	M	M
—Internet				I	R	R	R	R	M	M	M	M	M

Strategy	K	1	2	3	4	5	6	7	8	9	10	11	12
Strand 4—Test-taking													
4.1 Getting Ready for Tests													
—Reviewing test material			I	R	R	R	M	M	M	M	M	M	M
—Reviewing notes					I	R	R	R	R	M	M	M	M
—Self-questioning: constructing sample questions and answers			I	R	R	R	R	R	R	M	M	M	M
4.2 Taking/Completing Tests													
—Pacing			I	R	R	R	R	R	M	M	M	M	M
—Types of tests													
True-false			I	R	R	R	M	M	M	M	M	M	M
Multiple-choice			I	R	R	R	M	M	M	M	M	M	M
Fill-in			I	R	R	R	M	M	M	M	M	M	M
Matching			I	R	R	R	M	M	M	M	M	M	M
Short answer				I	R	R	R	M	M	M	M	M	M
Essay				I	R	R	R	R	M	M	M	M	M
4.3 Managing a Test			I	R	R	R	R	R	R	R	M	M	M
Strand 5—Writing													
5.1 Types of Written Communication													
—Accurate copying		I	R	R	M	M	M	M	M	M	M	M	M
—Letters													
Personal		I	R	R	R	M	M	M	M	M	M	M	M
Business				I	R	R	R	M	M	M	M	M	M
—Summaries				I	R	R	R	R	R	R	M	M	M
—Short, single-topic reports				I	R	R	R	R	R	M	M	M	M
5.2 Writing Reports and Research Papers													
—Pre-writing stage: clarifying topic, setting time goals, locating references, organizing ideas					I	R	R	R	R	M	M	M	M
—Writing stage: first draft, in-process revision					I	R	R	R	R	M	M	M	M
—Post-writing stage: self-editing, peer editing, proofreading					I	R	R	R	R	M	M	M	M

Adapted from Christen, Searfoss, & Mateja, 1984, with permission of Kendall/Hunt Publishing Company.

Computers can be used to help students organize their notes and retain information.

about sharks" or "Today our task is to learn four new words." In this way, children see the beginning of the lesson and know what the end of the lesson will be. This will help them plan ahead and become responsible early on.

2. *Plan each day with the children.* Discuss what is scheduled for the day and what lessons are to be continued from the previous day. Record the daily plan on the chalkboard or on chart paper as a reminder. Using chart paper or a seldom-used corner of the chalkboard will allow the day's schedule to be saved and referred to while planning is done for the next day.

Set aside some time each day, even if it is only five minutes, for children to use on their own and for which they are responsible. Reserve such time at different points in the school day, not just at the end of the day. During the discussion of the day's activities at the beginning of school, take suggestions from the children as to their plans for their special personal time.

Return to the day's plan periodically and have children check how they are progressing. Ask children questions such as "Where are we now?" or "What will we do next?" Continue to ask those children who had not previously planned their personal time if they have now done so.

3. *Develop weekly and monthly plans.* As soon as children are capable of planning further ahead, begin developing weekly and monthly plans and posting them in the classroom. Preliminary plans for the next week can be made with the children on Friday afternoons by filling in activities previously scheduled, such as music or physical education. The remainder of the weekly schedule can be filled in on Monday morning. Make sure that the plan is visible all week. Such activities model planning and organizing behaviors for children. Encourage children to begin early on to keep their own calendars, date books, and notebooks to reinforce what you have modeled.

4. *Establish the foundation for good homework habits.* Conduct a brief discussion at the end of the school day to summarize the day's activities and to get a look at the next day. During this discussion, make sure to ask these two questions: (1) What's one thing you have learned today? and (2) What do you have to do to get ready for tomorrow? Such questions clearly place some responsibility on the children for evaluating what they have done and what they have to do. Parents can get involved in helping their children learn by also asking their children the same two questions when they get home from school.

Homework assignments can be as simple as reading a few pages of a pleasure book or as involved as reviewing a concept taught in science or another content area. Beginning in kindergarten, give children simple tasks to be completed before returning to school the next day. This develops the habit of planning independently and allows them to complete longer assignments as they come up in later grades.

Organizing and Retaining Information

Strategies for organizing and retaining information help children learn from oral presentations and text materials. Key to this strand is the ability to sense how something is organized. Comprehension and retention of what has been read are greatly facilitated when its organization has been sensed, regardless of whether it is a basal story or a content selection.

Several teaching strategies that have been previously discussed will help children learn to preview, predict, and/or sense organization of both stories and content selections. In the primary grades, group-experience dictation (Chapter 5) is helpful in teaching children what belongs in a story. Expectation outlines (Chapter 4) aid children in predicting and sensing what a factual selection is all about. In Chapter 8, you learned that ReQuest and the survey technique both help children make predictions about a text. Finally, writing can serve as an appropriate vehicle for developing a sense of organization. Once children have developed a sense of how a story or text selection is organized, they are ready to begin learning how to take and organize their notes and use them for retention purposes.

PREP System

PREP (Schmelzer, Christen, & Browning, 1980) stands for

Preview the selection.
Read the selection.
Examine by asking and answering questions.
Prompt yourself with memory aids.

It is a study system that can be used throughout the grades by children to organize and retain text information. The foundation for PREP lies in the preview step; therefore, by teaching children how to preview with factual basal selections, you will go a long way in helping them establish this study system as their own.

Use a simple brainstorming activity (the first part of list-group-label) before assigning any reading selection. If the topic of the selection is the moon, children might brainstorm by answering this question: What do I know about the moon? Record their responses before reading; after reading, compare them to what was learned about the moon. Once children understand the concept of brainstorming, have them preview the actual selection by examining the title and pictures. Again, follow up with a brainstorming session. Once children understand how to preview, it is time to teach them more of the steps involved in PREP.

Each step in the PREP system can be adapted to specific grade levels. With beginning readers, the first two steps of preview and read may be used and the last two steps omitted. As children develop their reading ability, the last two steps can be added. A brief explanation of each step is provided below:

1. *Preview.* Have the children read the title; look at any pictures, graphs, and charts; read the introduction or first paragraph(s); read the last paragraph(s) or summary; and use the headings and subheadings to detect major concepts to be found in the selection. A preview gives children a road map of the selection to be read and sets purposes for reading. Oral discussion should accompany the preview step. A brief list of questions or topics that the children expect to be discussed in the selection can be written down on the chalkboard or on chart paper.

2. *Read.* This second step involves reading the selection, keeping in mind the purposes set in the preview step. For older children, a simple system of note-taking, using a summary sheet, can be introduced as a means of recording, reviewing, and retaining information. This form of notes uses two columns on a sheet of paper. In the left column, or recall column, are recorded general headings or subheadings. In the right column, which is the wider one, the actual notes are recorded. An example of a summary sheet for one basal reader selection is reproduced in Figure 9.2. The sample summary sheet has these features:

- It is very brief; one page covers a number of pages of reading.
- The writer uses his or her own words to avoid rote copying.
- Abbreviations are used to save space and time.
- Indenting is used to record relevant facts related to main ideas or headings.

Notes taken in summary form can then be studied by covering either side and reciting. The cover sheet or card can be moved down the summary to check for accuracy of response. Of course, note-taking as part of reading would be omitted for beginning readers.

3. *Examine.* This step, like the final step (prompt), may be omitted for beginning readers in grades 1, 2, and 3; it is designed to be used with children reading at grade 4 and above. The examine step involves the children in constructing ques-

Cave Explorers

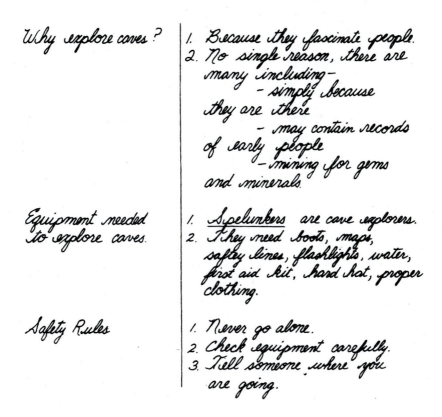

Why explore caves?
1. Because they fascinate people.
2. No single reason, there are many including—
   - simply because they are there
   - may contain records of early people
   - mining for gems and minerals.

Equipment needed to explore caves.
1. Spelunkers are cave explorers.
2. They need boots, maps, safety lines, flashlights, water, first aid kit, hard hat, proper clothing.

Safety Rules
1. Never go alone.
2. Check equipment carefully.
3. Tell someone where you are going.

FIGURE 9.2   Summary Sheet

tions about the selection, either during reading or after they have read. Children may need some guidance in asking questions; words such as *who, what, when, how,* and *why* may be given to them to get them started. As part of the follow-up discussion, individual children can lead the group by asking their own questions.

4. *Prompt.* This final step is designed to help children remember what they have read. One suggested technique is to show them how to quiz themselves. When convenient (e.g., at the end of a section covered by a heading), ask the children to stop and try to recite to themselves, aloud if possible, what they have read that is worth remembering. Recitation can be a group activity until children learn how to use it. The headings and subheadings, either taken from the selection or found in summary sheet notes, can be used as topics for recitation.

Although not as sophisticated as the original version, our adaptation of PREP should build a solid framework for the study demands of junior and senior high school, if begun early in children's reading instruction.

K-W-L

Another strategy for organizing and retaining information is K-W-L (Ogle, 1986). The acronym K-W-L stands for What We *K*now, What We *W*ant to Find Out, and What We *L*earned. K-W-L was developed as a three-step strategy for engaging children's prior knowledge and interest before they read a text. During their reading, children attempt to answer questions they have constructed about the text; after reading, they discuss what they found out about the topic of the text. K-W-L involves well-developed procedures for brainstorming, enumerating categories for organizing ideas, generating questions, monitoring what was learned, and guiding further reading and retention. Ogle suggests using some facsimile of the framework in Figure 9.3 to make the strategy more concrete.

FIGURE 9.3   K-W-L Strategy Framework

---

1. *K*—What We *K*now   *W*—What We *W*ant to Find Out   *L*—What We *L*earned

2. Categories of Information

  A.

  B.

  C.

---

1. *What we know.* The first step has two parts: (1) brainstorming to activate children's prior knowledge and (2) generating categories to organize ideas upon reading. Teachers begin by providing children with the specific topic of the selection to be read (e.g., sharks) and asking them to generate ideas about the topic. Teachers should use the chalkboard or an overhead to record children's responses while they are recording the same on their own copy of the framework. These responses are used as the basis for encouraging discussion and deepening children's thinking about the topic. With the topic of sharks, children might consider whether a particular idea (e.g., they are killers) pertains to all sharks or how they might verify such an idea. When prior knowledge has been activated, children are asked to generate categories of information they think they will encounter as they read. Teachers should ask children to examine the responses they have generated as a basis for naming some categories of information. For example, you might say, "From what we already know about sharks, let's think about what kinds of information are likely to be discussed in our reading. Do any of the ideas about sharks seem to fit together?" Teachers may need to model what it is that they expect children to do before children do it themselves. If list-group-label has been used previously, a reminder of the grouping step might be appropriate. Categories about sharks might include the various types, their enemies, and their eating habits.

2. *What we want to find out.* The rationale for the second step of the strategy is to develop a clear purpose for reading. Capitalizing on the interest that was generated in the first step of K-W-L, a desire to read the text, and any uncertainties that children may wish to clear up, teachers ask them to come up with questions that the text might answer. When this strategy is first used, the group might generate the questions to be answered. When children become accustomed to K-W-L, the group discussion of questions could become the basis for having children generate their own questions to be answered by the text. For sharks, possible questions might be as follows: Are all sharks killers? Just how dangerous are sharks? Where are they found? What are the sharks' enemies? Children then read to answer the questions generated.

3. *What we learned.* As children read the text, they use the questions to guide them and record possible answers in their framework. They also monitor their comprehension to see what questions still need to be answered or have not been sufficiently dealt with. At first, children should discuss their findings as a whole group; when they become more familiar with the strategy, they may discuss in small groups. The categories generated previously serve as the means for organizing and retaining the information learned; incomplete categories and unanswered questions can serve as the stimulus for additional reading or research.

When children have had enough practice with K-W-L, teachers should begin to fade their guidance. Children should be encouraged to use the strategy independently, particularly if they possess sufficient prior knowledge to guide their own reading.

Guided Lecture Procedure

Perhaps one of the most difficult of the independent learning strategies to master is that of taking effective notes. Beginning in the early grades, teachers need to model just what good note-taking involves. The children's experience charts provide an appropriate place to start. First have the children listen to an experience story. Then ask them to answer this question: In your own words, what was said? At first, small groups should work together to decide what was stated, reporting their conclusions to the whole class. Later, children may work alone. Teachers act as facilitators, giving the children feedback on what they decide has been said. Once children have become accustomed to the task, teachers can begin to use a more systematic strategy for listening and taking notes—the guided lecture procedure.

The *guided lecture procedure* (GLP) (Tierney, Readence, & Dishner, 1995) is designed for children who have problems (1) listening to and thinking about a text selection, (2) synthesizing what was stated, and (3) recording accurate notes. The

GLP dictates that children refrain from taking notes during the lecture and engage in intensive listening and thinking for the purpose of retaining all the information presented.

Prior to the lecture, children learn the purpose for listening by reading and copying the lecture objectives. These are stated as terminal objectives and should not exceed three or four, no matter what the age level. Younger children should get fewer objectives. This gives the children some idea of what to expect as the lecture proceeds.

The children then engage in purposeful listening as the lecture progresses. The amount of time the teacher lectures is dependent on the age and ability of the children; a teacher should lecture for only a short time when first using the GLP, and work up to longer times as children become accustomed to the task. When the allotted time for lecture has terminated, children are directed to write down in short form all they can recall. Children are encouraged to engage in a form of visual thinking, a mental perusal of the information presented, to see what relations can be formed with the material recalled. Children are given a maximum of five minutes for this task, the amount of time being dependent on the lecture information presented. This activity also allows children to become aware of what they did not understand.

Only lecture for a short time or children will tune you out!

Next, children work in small groups to summarize the lecture. Their summaries are discussed in terms of (1) putting notes into sequential order, (2) recognizing major concepts and details, and (3) drawing conclusions. The teacher acts as a guide, circulating among the small groups to answer questions and clarify their task.

At the conclusion of this part of the lesson or at some other time of the day, children are asked to reflect on what they have learned and the GLP activity itself. This is done in order to promote conceptualization and organization of the new knowledge and, subsequently, build long-term memory and motivate the children to participate in active study situations. Upon reflection, children are asked to write the lecture's major concepts, pertinent details, and conclusions, without referring to notes. This helps children to retain the most important information and enables them to self-appraise their knowledge level in particular areas.

The GLP enables children to interact with others to analyze lecture material until it has been comprehended thoroughly and accurately. Additionally, it allows children to participate cooperatively in a profitable learning experience. Finally, the GLP provides an instructional format that models for children what effective note-taking involves.

Locating Information

Information-locating strategies aid children in using book parts, general references, specialized references, and libraries as sources of information. The essential strategy involved in this strand is the ability to locate information in texts and other references when it is necessary for the fullest understanding of the material under study.

We believe one of the best beginnings to teaching locational strategies is to take the children on a *trip through the textbook*. This is simply a means to introduce a text to children by pointing out the various parts of the book, describing their purposes, and showing the children how and why they are used. For instance, you could point out the table of contents, tell the children that it is a means to locate particular sections of the book, demonstrate this for them, and then tell the children why it is a time-saving device. As you probably noted, introducing the text in this way has its beginnings in teacher modeling.

This approach can be used to introduce any important part of the text, such as the index, glossary, chapter title and subtitles, summaries, maps, and graphs. This initial familiarity will be helpful when children attempt to use the various textbooks parts. As with any independent learning strategy you teach, it is important to provide guided strategy practice and feedback with materials of relevance to the children. Teaching isolated skills, away from the materials of instruction, is not especially helpful in getting children to learn the strategy and apply it independently.

Once the foundation for locational strategies has been set by using the textbook, our point about relevance should be kept in mind as you begin to deal with other, more sophisticated strategies. For instance, teaching children how to use the card catalog in the school library will be most successful if it is done because they have to use the catalog to find information in the library for a class project, rather than just because the library is free or the librarian has the time to show children the card catalog.

Test-Taking

Test-taking strategies provide direct instruction in techniques for taking all types of tests. Though test-taking strategies will become increasingly important as children progress through the grades, children take tests from the moment they enter school. Therefore, any help that children are given in preparing for and taking tests will pay long-term dividends.

Make sure children are exposed to a wide variety of test formats when you check their comprehension from basals and content textbooks. Even more important, when you go over each exam, have children talk about how they arrived at the correct answers. Additionally, model your own thinking on why you constructed a particular question and what you expected children to do in the process of dealing with that question. Use the preparation kits that standardized test publishers provide to demonstrate to children the test-taking strategies that are recommended by the test makers. Again, a discussion of why these strategies are recommended would be helpful to the children.

Preparing for the Test

Children should be taught the necessity of review as a test-taking strategy. In particular, they should be taught that frequent, short review sessions are better than a few lengthy cramming sessions. Once children begin to take notes, they should be shown how to use them for study purposes. Additionally, teaching children to anticipate test questions by constructing potential test questions and answers on their own is important.

The night before the test, children should be encouraged to collect all the materials they may need to take the test—paper, pencil or pen, and whatever else. A light study session is better than a lengthy one. Advise children to get a good night's sleep so that they are refreshed. The importance of a good breakfast the day of the test should also be pointed out.

Taking the Test

Though there is no substitute for being knowledgeable and reviewing the material that they will be tested on, children will do a better job on classroom tests if they know how to take a test. In general, children should be taught to read all directions carefully before they begin the test. Failure to read directions is a major cause of poor test grades! Children must also learn to budget their time so they are certain to finish the test. Lingering on difficult items is wasteful; children should be told to skip these items and come back to them at the end of the test.

> **Process Guide 9.2**
>
> List the type of strategies you use when you take tests. Which of these strategies would you teach to elementary school children? Now compare your list to those that follow.

Below are some other, more specific guidelines that children should be taught for the most common types of tests they will take.

Multiple-Choice Tests.   Children probably take more multiple-choice tests than any other kind; therefore, it would be helpful to know the following strategies for taking such tests:

1. Always guess if you don't know the answer. Unless there is a penalty for wrong answers, never leave an item blank on a multiple-choice test.
2. If an obvious choice does not strike you right away, eliminate the choices that are obviously wrong, and guess from the choices that remain.
3. When two choices are identical (e.g., fifteen vs. 15), they are probably both wrong.
4. When two choices are opposites (open vs. closed), one is wrong and the other is often right.
5. An answer to one question may appear in the stem of another question.
6. When two choices seem equally good, select the one that is longest and seems to hold the most information.

True-False Tests.   Though tests are rarely composed of only true-false items, many teachers like to include a section of such items on their tests. True-false items can appear deceivingly simple. Here are some things children might remember about these test items:

1. Always guess. Unless there is a penalty for wrong answers, never leave a true-false item blank.
2. If part of an item is false, the whole item is false.
3. Be alert for the words *never* and *always*. Such absolutes often indicate a wrong answer.
4. Long statements are somewhat more likely to be true than short ones.

Essay Tests.   Because essay tests require recall of information, good writing skills, and organization, they are among the most difficult tests to take. These guidelines are helpful with essay tests:

1. In budgeting your time on an essay test, spend the most time on questions that are worth the most points.
2. Always give some kind of response, even if you don't understand the question.

3. Never give a minimal answer such as "no." On these tests, it is expected that you will elaborate and give full explanations.
4. Use the technical vocabulary of the course when writing an essay. Teachers want to know how much you know, which includes the vocabulary.
5. Proofread your answer. A careless presentation of your answer will reduce your grade.

Writing

Writing strategies develop proficiency in writing related to learning in content area subjects. Various types of written communication and strategies for writing reports and research papers are stressed. Throughout this book, we have emphasized the importance of writing as a primary literacy tool. One writing activity, the preparation of a research report, seems particularly well suited for developing independent learning strategies such as time management, organizing information, taking notes, and locating and using multiple sources of information. Thus, the research report is a useful vehicle for reinforcing many of the strategies that are important to know.

The Independent Writing Strategy (IWS) (Christen, Searfoss, & Bean, 1984) is a six-step procedure which integrates a number of study strategies that allow children to independently plan and complete written assignments such as research reports. Thus, IWS helps develop and improve study habits while at the same time providing a format for doing writing assignments. The steps in the procedure are described below:

1. *Brainstorm.* Once the topic is known, a few minutes spent generating ideas about the topic will go a long way in getting children started on the writing assignment. Brainstorming is the same procedure that is involved in the list step of list-group-label, described in Chapter 7.
2. *Preview reading material.* When information is to be used from a reference or a set of references, examining the material before it is read is a good first step in getting a general idea about its content and organization. (The first step of the PREP study system, described in this chapter, is a preview step.) Additionally, previewing serves as a warm-up for later, more careful reading of the material. In conjunction with the brainstorming step, previewing will enhance children's understanding of the material when it is read.
3. *Read and take notes.* In this step, children read the reference to ascertain what information will be useful in completing the assignment. The information should be recorded in the children's own words to make it more useful to them when they later integrate their notes into a draft of the report. Therefore, children will need to employ a good note-taking system to make maximum use of the reference.
4. *Write a first draft.* Once the materials have been read and the necessary notes taken, the next step is to develop a first draft of the report that integrates children's own ideas about the topic with what was gained from the reading. It

is not desirable at this time to attempt a finished product; at this stage children should be trying to organize their ideas in writing.

5. *Edit the first draft.* Children must examine their first draft carefully so that the second draft results in better content, style, and organization. Teachers can work with children so that they develop a sense of what to look for as they edit their own papers. To be truly independent in completing their writing assignments, children must be able to employ some type of writing checklist (like that used in the guided writing procedure in Chapter 10) to edit their papers. However, learning to be a good editor, like learning to be a good writer, takes time and patience.

   As an interim solution to the problem of editing, we recommend that children engage in some form of peer editing. This can be accomplished first in small groups and then faded to dyads. Children work cooperatively in editing one another's reports. Papers should be examined for content and organization as well as for spelling, capitalization, punctuation, and complete sentences. The point of using small groups of children first is to encourage a cooperative spirit, provide an environment where children can learn from one another, and pave the way for independent application of the editing skills the children learn as they work together.

6. *Write a second draft.* Children now use the comments gained from the editing in Step 5 to write a second draft. This should be a refinement of the first draft. The amount of revision will depend on the quality and quantity of comments made in peer editing.

Assessing Independent Learning Strategies

A substantial portion of the reading that children are expected to do in school occurs with content area textbooks. Success in each subject matter area requires not only a general ability to obtain meaning from print but also a facility in locating information, organizing and retaining information, and using that information in writing research papers. Although published instruments are available to assess children's independent learning strategies, we recommend that informal measures be used.

Informal assessment can be done functionally as children are taught independent learning strategies using their own classroom materials. If teachers observe how children put those strategies to use, they can get an immediate, relevant view of children's abilities to use the strategies. The instructional model we advocate— offering instruction that employs modeling, guided practice, and independent application—gives teachers a wonderful opportunity to assess whether or not children are successfully learning study strategies and to employ corrective feedback, if necessary. However, there are some other informal measures teachers can design that will help assess children's study strategies, particularly when children are applying them independently.

For instance, if you wanted to informally assess a child's ability to preview text material, the following approach might be used. Using a section of a text, give the child 5–10 minutes to get the main points of the material by doing a preview. Keep the time short enough to prevent word-by-word reading but sufficient for the text length. When the time is up, quiz the child using text-provided questions or questions of your own that can be answered by previewing. Be sure to ask questions that deal with headings and subheadings, introductions and summaries, italicized words, and any other graphic aids present. By such means, you will readily be able to tell whether the child knows what previewing is and is able to do it.

Similarly, a child's ability to take notes can be informally assessed. Choose a short section from a text chapter, and ask the child to take notes on the selection as if he or she were going to have a test or prepare a report. As the child is taking notes, examine whether the child (1) uses the text's organization as a guide for taking the notes, (2) is able to locate main ideas and supporting details, and (3) distinguishes between them by using an informal outline form.

A reasonable means for assessing locational skills is the *content reading inventory* (Readence, Bean, & Baldwin, 1998). This inventory is designed by teachers and measures children's knowledge of and ability to use the table of contents, the index, the glossary, pictorial information, and other aids specific to a particular textbook. It also can be used to assess the awareness and use of external learning aids such as the card catalog, the *Reader's Guide to Periodical Literature,* encyclopedias, and other reference materials. The content reading inventory is an informal group test, so it is easily administered and scored. Additionally, it has the advantage of identifying those locational skills that will require direct follow-up instruction. An example of a content reading inventory developed from a sixth-grade science textbook is provided in Figure 9.4.

Finally, if you wished to assess a child's ability to write a research paper, the following situation could be posed. Tell the child to suppose that he or she has been given three days to write a research paper in science (history), and the topic must be chosen from those you have listed. Ask the child which procedure he or she would use to choose the topic and prepare the paper. Make sure to state that books, magazines, and other appropriate special reference materials should be used. Obviously, the response given by the child would be limited by the research report–making strategies appropriate for his or her grade level, but you would essentially examine whether there was evidence of organization in the child's approach and then decide the amount of direction the child required. Specific responses by the child might include the following:

1. Find out which topic had the most available information.
2. Use the card catalog and/or *Reader's Guide.*
3. Examine special references such as atlases, almanacs, biographical dictionaries, and science encyclopedias.
4. Prepare a rough outline before beginning.
5. Set up note-taking procedures by reference.
6. Use the rough outline as a guide for writing the first draft.
7. Write a rough draft.
8. Revise the rough draft.

FIGURE 9.4   **Content Reading Inventory**

Part I
Directions: Use your textbook to answer the first 10 questions. Use your knowledge of sources of information to do the rest.

1. What part of the book could tell you on what page the chapter on weather begins? (*table of contents*)
2. What part of the book could tell you where to look in order to find out more about vitamins? (*index*)
3. In what section of the book could you locate a brief definition of a kilowatt? (*glossary*)
4. What do you think is the purpose of including the "Summing Up" section at the end of each chapter? (*chapter summary*)
5. Why is there a short passage before each chapter begins? (*chapter introduction*)
6. According to the diagram on page 209, which layer of the atmosphere is closest to the earth? (*using pictorial information*)
7. Turn to page 287. In the upper right-hand corner is a green box containing three words. Why do you think these words have been placed in the box? (*special vocabulary aids*)
8. How will the questions that appear in the margins of Chapter 13 help you learn about the properties of light? (*special comprehension aids*)
9. What is the purpose of the "Books You Can Read" section on page 203? (*reference information*)
10. What can reading the questions at the end of the chapter do for you before you read the chapter? (*study strategies*)

Part II
Directions: Answer the following questions without the use of your textbook or any other materials.

11. If you wanted to find the definition of a word that was not fully explained in the text, where would you look? (*dictionary*)
    a. An atlas
    b. The *Reader's Guide*
    c. The dictionary
    d. The thesaurus
12. What library guide could help you locate other books on oceanography? (*general library skills*)
    a. The *World Almanac*
    b. Guide to periodicals
    c. The Dewey classification chart
    d. The card catalog

(continued)

FIGURE 9.4 Continued

13. Where would you look to see where books written by Louis Pasteur could be found? (*specific library skills*)

    a. The author index
    b. The subject index
    c. The title index
    d. *Who's Who*

14. Between what two words would *carbohydrate* be found? (*dictionary—alphabetic order*)

    a. Carbolated and carbon
    b. Carbide and carbinol
    c. Carbocyclic and carbolated
    d. Carbazole and carbine

15. Which set of guidewords would be found on the page that *saliva* was on? (*dictionary—guidewords*)

    a. Safety and saintly
    b. Saintly and salmon
    c. Salmon and salve
    d. Salve and sanctuary

16. In reading about tornadoes, you learn that most occur in the midwestern states like Kansas. Where could you look to find out exactly where Kansas is located? (*atlas*)

    a. A dictionary
    b. An atlas
    c. *National Geographic* magazine
    d. *Statesman's Yearbook*

17. If you had to locate more information about the human body for an oral report to the class, what would be your best source? (*encyclopedia*)

    a. An encyclopedia
    b. A dictionary
    c. An anthology
    d. The newspaper

Note: The strategies being tested are given in the parentheses after each question. These would not be provided on the actual inventory given to children.

As can be seen from the examples given, independent learning strategies can be assessed without the use of published testing instruments. Informal assessment can provide teachers with the information necessary to ensure that children are aware of and can use independent learning strategies.

Process Guide 9.3

Design your own content reading inventory from a content text of your choice. In small groups examine and critique each other's inventories for the study strategies they are attempting to test.

Summary

This chapter made the point that instruction in independent learning strategies should begin in the primary grades and continue throughout children's schooling. The foundation for study strategies instruction begins with the implementation of the print-rich classroom described early in the text. It was recommended that teachers provide for transfer of basal reading skills to other forms of print through the use of teacher's manuals from content textbooks and the real-life reading lesson. Strategies for independent learning were delineated in a suggested scope and sequence chart. Specific strategies were described in the areas (strands) of time management, organizing and retaining information, locating information, test-taking, and writing. Finally, suggestions were offered for assessing children's independent learning strategies.

FOLLOW-THROUGH ACTIVITIES

Note: Level 1 activities may require limited access to children or classrooms. Level 2 activities should be completed using children and classrooms.

Level 1 Activities

1. Select a strategy from Figure 9.1 and design a real-life reading lesson for teaching that strategy.

2. Using library resources and the computer, work in pairs or triads to collect sources of information about the hurricane seasons on the Atlantic and Pacific coasts. Compare the tracks, sizes, and resultant damage of hurricanes over the last three years. Be prepared to share the results of your research with the whole class.

Level 2 Activities

1. Teach a real-life reading lesson based on a time management strategy.

2. Conduct a lesson using the PREP system or the guided lecture procedure. What is your evaluation of the strategy? What is the reaction of the children?

3. Have children do a research report using the independent writing strategy. Did the lesson seem to reinforce children's study strategies?

WORKING WITH PARENTS

The scene is a parent conference with Mr. Penn early in the school year in the second-grade classroom of Ms. Sill.

MR. PENN: Ms. Sill, my daughter Kathy tells me that she is learning a lot in your classroom about how to be an independent learner. Kathy doesn't seem to be a good enough reader yet to be taught study skills. After all, she's only beginning second grade.

MS. SILL: I appreciate your concern, Mr. Penn, but teaching children how to study should be the concern of all teachers, no matter what the grade level.

MR. PENN: I don't understand. Studying was something my teachers dealt with when I had to learn from science, history, and other textbooks.

MS. SILL: Well, that may be so, but I teach my children that independent learning is basic to all that they will do in my classroom.

MR. PENN: Basic?

MS. SILL: Yes, let me explain. Even in kindergarten, children are involved in working with a daily schedule, doing homework, or predicting how stories will end. At this grade level, we do all those things and many more. They all involve some aspect of studying or independent learning. From my point of view, it would be inappropriate to neglect this part of the curriculum.

MR. PENN: Please go on.

MS. SILL: Well, today I introduced the children to some of the things they need to do to prepare themselves to take a multiple-choice test. Tomorrow, I'll give them such a test. After I have graded the tests, I'll use them as a vehicle for further teaching the children about multiple-choice tests. Since they will be taking such tests for the rest of their school lives, I want to begin teaching them now about making themselves better test takers.

MR. PENN: That makes sense. What other aspects of studying will you teach Kathy this year?

MS. SILL: Oh, a number of things. I'll teach them about taking other kinds of tests and writing letters. Plus, I'll be reinforcing the study strategies they learned last year, like using the parts of our textbooks appropriately and finding words in the dictionary. By mastering these skills, my children will be well on their way to developing effective independent learning habits that they will use the rest of their lives.

MR. PENN: That sounds good to me. I wish I had had a teacher like you when I was in elementary school. That might have helped me with a lot of problems I had studying when I got to high school!

MS. SILL: Well, thank you, Mr. Penn. Come again if you have other questions about what Kathy is doing in my classroom this year.

RESOURCES

Bergman, J. L. (1992). SAIL—A way to success and independence for low-achieving readers. *The Reading Teacher, 45,* 598–602.

The notions of metacognition are used in a program designed to help low achievers succeed in reading.

Miholic, V. (1994). An inventory to pique students' metacognitive awareness of reading strategies. *Journal of Reading, 38,* 84–86.

This article describes the use of an inventory to help students think about what they do when they read.

Paris, S. G., Wasik, B. A., & Turner, J. C. (1991). The development of strategic readers. In R. Barr, M. L. Kamil, P. Mosenthal, & P. D. Pearson (Eds.), *Handbook of reading research: Volume II* (pp. 609–640). New York: Longman.

The authors discuss strategic reading and independent learning.

Readence, J. E., Bean, T. W., & Baldwin, R. S. (1998). *Content area literacy: An integrated approach* (6th ed.). Dubuque, IA: Kendall/Hunt.

Chapter 12 describes useful strategies for locating, organizing, and retaining information, as well as test-taking.

Simpson, M. L. (1984). The status of study strategy instruction: Implications for classroom teachers. *Journal of Reading, 28,* 136–142.

The author examines what children are currently taught about studying and suggests ways that might be more effective.

Stahl, N. A., King, J. R., & Henk, W. A. (1991). Enhancing students' notetaking through training and evaluation. *Journal of Reading, 34,* 614–622.

A four-stage instructional sequence (modeling, practicing, evaluating, and reinforcing) is described for developing student-directed note-taking strategies.

Tierney, R. J., & Readence, J. E. (2000). *Reading strategies and practices: A compendium* (5th ed.). Boston: Allyn & Bacon.

Units 9 and 12 present a number of practical strategies for students' independent learning.

REFERENCES

Bergman, J. L. (1992). SAIL—A way to success and independence for low-achieving readers. *The Reading Teacher, 45,* 598–602.

Christen, W. L., Searfoss, L. W., & Bean, T. W. (1984). *Improving communication through writing and reading.* Dubuque, IA: Kendall/Hunt.

Christen, W. L., Searfoss, L. W., & Mateja, J. A. (1984). *Study skills scope and sequence chart: K thru 12.* Dubuque, IA: Kendall/Hunt.

Ogle, D. (1986). A teaching model that develops active reading of expository text. *The Reading Teacher, 39,* 564–570.

Paris, S. G., Wasik, B. A., & Turner, J. C. (1991). The development of strategic readers. In R. Barr, M. L. Kamil, P. B. Mosenthal, & P. D. Pearson (Eds.), *Handbook of reading research: Volume II* (pp. 609–640). New York: Longman.

Readence, J. E., Bean, T. W., & Baldwin, R. S. (1998). *Content area literacy: An integrated approach* (6th ed.). Dubuque, IA: Kendall/Hunt.

Schmelzer, R. V., Christen, W. L., & Browning, W. G. (1980). *Reading and study skills: Book one.* Rehoboth, MA: Twin Oaks.

Simpson, M. L. (1984). The status of study strategy instruction: Implications for classroom teachers. *Journal of Reading, 28,* 136–142.

Tierney, R. J., Readence, J. E., & Dishner, E. K. (1995). *Reading strategies and practices: A compendium* (4th ed.). Boston: Allyn & Bacon.

10 Writing and Reading

THOMAS W. BEAN

University of Nevada, Las Vegas

INTRODUCTION

This chapter provides an array of strategies to help elementary- and middle-grade students write effectively. Moving into the realm of nonfiction material, the chapter views writing as an important means of extending reading comprehension across the curriculum. As students progress to the middle grades, they read and respond to ever more complex texts in content areas such as science and social studies. Writing can form an important bridge from students' thoughts and prior knowledge to ideas expressed in a text. Thus, the chapter begins with a discussion of the integrated reading and writing process.

Writing is always a risk-taking process, much like plucking notes on an electric guitar for all to hear. Fledgling writers need opportunities to explore ideas without simultaneously worrying about all the conventions of writing. The forms of writing considered in this chapter range from journal writing for oneself, which frees a child to explore ideas without fear of making blatant transcribing errors, to more public writing for peer and other audiences. The discussion of writing to learn delves into specific strategies for integrating expository reading and writing assignments. The section on imaginative writing delves into poetry and song lyrics.

Finally, the chapter describes various approaches to guiding students' writing through multiple stages of composing and transcribing. Ways of assessing students' writing that involve peer editing, analytical checklists, and individual conferences are discussed, with the intent of helping you manage the increasing paper load in classrooms where students write.

GRAPHIC ORGANIZER

This graphic organizer summarizes the structure of Chapter 10:

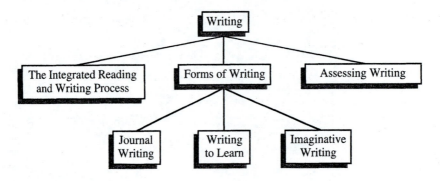

OBJECTIVES

When you finish this chapter, you should be able to understand and discuss each of these statements:

1. Composing in writing involves the exploration and development of ideas and feelings.
2. Journal writing fosters a personal link between a student's inner self and the often distant ideas of a textbook.
3. Writing helps students think like the authors of expository text, and as a result, students read expository text with more insight.
4. Writing to learn implies more than just outlining or jotting down notes after reading.
5. Writing activities that accompany otherwise dull texts make static ideas come alive.
6. Writing is *not* a one-shot, one-day process.

7. Imaginative writing stretches students' thinking about ideas they encounter in their reading.

8. There are many ways to evaluate students' writing.

The Integrated Reading and Writing Process

In third grade, Kristen wrote the following poem after reading about sunflowers:

> **Sunflower**
> *Sunflower, sunflower, where are you?*
> *In the wild, running away from you.*
> *Sunflower seeds, sunflower seeds, where are you?*
> *I'm in the chicken and cattle food it's true.*
> *Sunflower leaf, sunflower leaf, how big are you?*
> *I'm about 6 inches long and wide too.*
> *Sunflower stem, sunflower stem, how thick are you?*
> *I'm very thick and very strong too.*
> *Sunflower, sunflower, how tall are you?*
> *I'm 8 feet tall and I thank you.*

Kristen's poem was designed to be one part of a large mobile she was creating to illustrate her developing knowledge of sunflowers. The mobile would be hung overhead in the classroom along with other children's creations. Thus, her multimedia creation based on her reading and studying about sunflowers would have an interested audience, and she worked hard to make it attractive.

Well before third grade, children need many opportunities to experience writing and reading as integrated social practices, which offer mutual support in the early developmental stages of literacy growth. In the early grades, writing allows students to mimic material they read or listen to and experiment with its structure (Dahl & Farnan, 1998). Writing can be defined broadly as "composing and expressing ideas through letters, words, art, or media and print" (Dahl & Farnan, 1998, p. 5). This definition acknowledges children's playful interest in language in all its various forms. Reading and writing are transactional processes, each one influencing the other (Dahl & Farnan, 1998). They need to be taught together in classrooms where literature and nonfiction materials provide good rhetorical models, as well as stimulating topics that children can use as launching pads for their own unique explorations in journals, poetry, musical lyrics, and other forms.

Reading and writing are similar in that they have corresponding instructional stages in the classroom (Tompkins & Hoskisson, 1995). For example, prereading and prewriting precede the reading stage and the drafting stage, respectively. Then reading has a responding stage, while writing has a revising stage. Finally, reading often involves shared responses in literature circles, while writing may conclude with a publishing stage.

In addition to having a transactional relationship with reading, writing offers children a means of reflecting on difficult concepts in content area materials. Kristen's multimedia sunflower creation also included a number of concepts about the functions of sunflowers, again in the form of a poem:

Nectar for bees
Oil for cooking
Seeds for birds
A yellow daisy
Big and round
Dark seeds center
Tall as dad
Like a sun
In my garden
I'm a sunflower

The back of her sunflower mobile included a bibliographic reference to the nonfiction book she had consulted about sunflowers. By establishing a supportive climate for multimedia reading and writing displays, Kristen's teacher helped her to effectively link reading and writing, seeing them as integrated activities. The teacher clearly viewed reading and writing as a means to share ideas with others.

Bloome and Katz (1997) have proposed that teachers adopt a new perspective on the processes of learning to read and write: "Instead of viewing learning to read and write as the acquisition of decontextualized skills, learning to read and write can be viewed as becoming socialized into particular social practices in particular social settings. From this perspective, teaching students to read and write is not a technical matter, but a cultural matter" (p. 216). In one effective application of this approach, Kotlik Alaskan kindergarteners were encouraged to link their natural interest in animals and wildlife with the strong oral tradition of their home culture (Akaran & Fields, 1997). First a letter from the teacher went home, explaining the project. Then the children interviewed family members about personal adventures involving animals. Next the children dictated and illustrated the stories, which were bound into books and shared in class and at home. Some of the stories included photos of boats and other cultural artifacts.

Children need to exert some power and autonomy over their writing, while getting plenty of feedback and editing support from peers and the teacher. Because reading and writing are social practices, it is important that the teacher pay attention to the classroom climate. Even very young children may apply pressure on each other that can influence the content of their writing. For example, Phinney (1998) found that a group of kindergarten girls who regularly met to work on their stories often included themselves as characters, taking this opportunity to engage in status marking by making the youngest character the most important or the prettiest. In fact, writing was secondary in importance to status marking, and the girls often altered their stories because of this function.

Contemporary classroom research shows that highly successful first-grade classrooms across the country have seamlessly integrated reading and writing

(Wharton-MacDonald & Boothroyd, 1998). Children in these classrooms wrote for authentic purposes, such as keeping observational journals of plant growth or chick development. They wrote get-well cards, thank-you notes, letters to parents and pen pals, menus, memos, and announcements, and they created multiple forms of journals to record their thoughts. Children's literature authors strongly influenced their writing styles, as the children imitated the rhythms and diction of the stories they encountered in class. Wharton-MacDonald and Boothroyd also found that scaffolding of students' writing was a characteristic of the best first-grade classrooms they observed; writing models and conferencing helped guide children toward successful writing experiences. These classrooms provided large blocks of uninterrupted time for reading and writing. At least 45 minutes were available, and teachers modeled the reading and writing processes by participating with children (Allington et al., 1998). Students read to themselves and did buddy reading. They all wrote about their reading every day, in journals. They also wrote letters to authors and main characters of stories they read. They wrote in groups and alone. Through thematic topics, their reading and writing were related to their content learning in science, social studies, and other subjects.

Giving further support to the movement to integrate reading and writing in our classrooms, the International Reading Association and the National Association for the Education of Young Children issued a joint position statement in *The Reading Teacher* (1998). The statement asserted that reading and writing are best developed through creative approaches that involve song writing, poetry, environmental print, language experience charts, and a variety of other material. "Children's ability to read words is tied to their ability to write words in a somewhat reciprocal relationship. The more opportunities children have to read and write, the greater the likelihood that they will reproduce spellings of words they have seen and heard" (p. 204). The statement cautioned that no single approach is best for all children—good teachers use a variety of approaches.

Journal Writing

One of the best ways to help students capitalize on the reading-writing connection is to engage them in various forms of journal writing. Many elementary teachers make journal writing a natural part of their teaching. Journal writing lets students explore ideas, concepts, and experiences on their own terms, as artists, scientists, and authors do. Ideas are fleeting, and a journal is an ideal place for students to explore their own thoughts in an unstructured way. Journals can be used to share personal experiences and feelings or to keep a log of natural phenomena such as plant growth or stages of the moon. In the following passage from his travel journal, James records his thoughts on a family vacation to the southwestern desert:

> Finally we are in the car and on our way. I can hear the wind blow against the car. I see tall mountains. I smell the fresh sent of dirt. I feel the strong hot wind blow onto my hair. Now I can see lots of yuccas out the window. There a sort of cactus. I also see a large clear dirt land.

Journals are a place to stretch out in writing. James's journal entry focuses on his feelings about crossing the dry, hot desert. He is free to explore language, and he experiments with words like *scent*, which he spells "sent."

Journals offer a powerful way to connect classroom content learning and students' home-based interests. For example, for math class you might have students count points in a Nintendo game or measure the weight of their dogs, recording the results in a journal (Brown, 1997). Then, based on their journal entries and models you provide, they create their own word problems. After exchanging problems, they attempt to solve each other's problems in class.

The following guidelines should help you get students started on journal writing:

1. *Make journal writing a regular part of your teaching; students need to write in their journals on a daily basis.* Consider using journal writing as a way to enter and exit topics in various content areas. For example, in a science unit on evaporation and particles of matter, you might present students with a familiar situation such as the following, to stimulate some prereading reflection in their journals:

> It was a rainy day, and the teacher said, "When it rains heavily at Golden School, puddles of water form in the playground outside our classroom. What happens to the puddles when the sun comes out again?"

Presented with the above prompt, Emerald wrote in her journal:

> *The puddles get dry. Not all at once. A little bit at a time. The small puddles first. Then the big puddles. Soon we can play.*

At this prereading stage, Emerald has an idea of what happens, but she does not yet know why the puddles dry out. Later, after she had read and talked about a text passage discussing evaporation, her postreading journal entry reflected her new knowledge:

> *The sun makes the puddles <u>evaporate</u>. You can't see it. Tiny particles in the water go into the air. Then we can play.*

Emerald can draw puddles in her journal. She can talk about how she feels on a rainy day. Most important, Emerald can take risks in her journal. Her reflections are unrestricted by spelling and grammar conventions.

2. *Model journal writing by keeping your own journal and sharing entries aloud with students.* Much like sustained silent reading sessions, reflective journal writing sessions work best if you actively participate and share your thoughts. At times your journal entries may range from thoughts about how a lesson is going to reflections about how today's weather makes you feel. Sharing diverse entries with students gives them a sense of the far-reaching ideas and feelings they can explore in their journals.

3. *Look at students' journals and respond to their thoughts.* Try to keep your dialogue journal responses brief and encouraging. One way to include journal writing in your grading scheme is with a simple page count. A more qualitative reading might take into account the development of a student's understanding of a topic. For example, Emerald progressed from a basic to a more technical view of evaporation. Alternatively, you may decide to use some of the material dealt with in journal writing as the basis for a quiz question.

4. *Allot 5 to 10 minutes each day for journal writing.* On some days, you may decide to use journal writing as a way of entering and brainstorming about a topic. On other days, you may want to interrupt a lecture, lab, or activity and have students reflect on what they have been doing. Use journals as flexibly as you see fit, but make them a regular part of your classroom. The benefits reaped in student creativity, enthusiasm, and depth of thought will be worth the few extra minutes you devote to this important process.

Process Guide 10.1

Write a journal entry reflecting on your feelings when you read a children's book aloud to students. Then, exchange entries with a colleague in class and discuss your views on using children's literature in teaching.

Writing to Learn

When students explore a topic through writing, they develop ownership of new concepts. More important, unexpected ideas and insights sometimes emerge through the act of writing. The five strategies that follow will help students reconstruct ideas expressed in expository texts.

Semantic Mapping

A semantic map can be defined as "a categorical structuring of information in graphic form" (Heimlich & Pittelman, 1986, p. 1). Semantic maps are generally more free-flowing than graphic organizers. They are less tied to the hierarchical text structure pattern of an author. Rather, they represent the reader's individual approach to reconstructing text concepts. Children in the first grade can learn to construct a semantic map. They often enjoy embellishing their maps with illustrations.

Most maps should have three levels of information:

1. The main topic in a central hub
2. Branches labeled to indicate major ideas or categories
3. Branches containing specific supporting details

Unlike graphic organizers, which should be brief, semantic maps may contain a substantial number of lower level supporting details. Thus, at the postreading stage, they serve as an ideal basis for summarizing or reacting to ideas expressed in a text. Maps serve equally well as a way of clustering students' brainstorming before they read a text.

The semantic map in Figure 10.1 represents a postreading reconstruction of an informational article about koalas (Burt, 1987). The map forms a foundation for fifth grader Hilary Fox's summary of the article. Hilary's map of the article contains four category labels, which she created to organize the information. Mapping is an especially powerful strategy with texts that fail to offer adequate subheadings or are disorganized.

The article provided all the information Hilary listed with the exception of the statement "doesn't like tourists," under the category "How They Look and Act." Hilary based this "fact" on Qantas Airways advertisements showing a disgruntled koala having his day ruined by gawking tourists. Students need to know

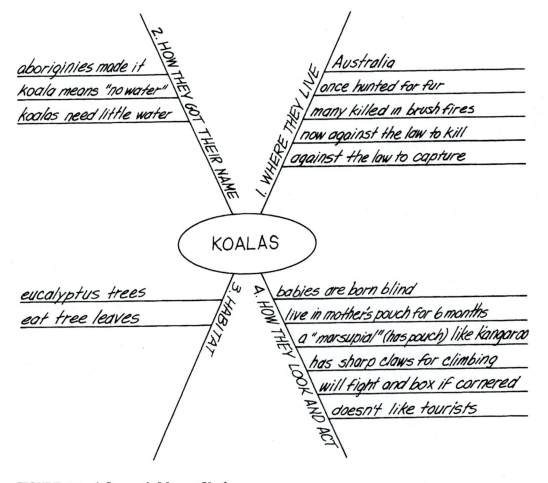

FIGURE 10.1   A Semantic Map on Koalas

through your modeling that, much like journals, semantic maps can include information from prior knowledge or personal reactions to an author's ideas. These reader-based notions can be coded with brackets to distinguish them from information actually present in the article.

Hilary used her map to construct the following summary:

All About Koalas

Koalas live in Australia. They used to be hunted. Fur coats were made from their fur. A lot of Koalas were killed in fires. They almost became instinct. Now there is a law. People cannot kill or capture Koalas.

The name Koala means "no water." Aborignies made up the name because Koalas don't need much water.

Koalas live in trees and eat the leafs. They get water from the leafs.

The babies are born blind. They live in the mom's pouch like a kangaroo. Koalas are nice if people don't bother them. They have sharp claws. They can fight and box if you scare them. Koala bears do not like tourists! If you go to Australia, leave them alone!

By Hilary Fox

Hilary's summary of the article contains a few unusual spellings for difficult words like "extinct." Most important, though, her summary is a well-structured, cohesive, and comprehensive rendering of key ideas in the article. She is well prepared to answer test questions about koalas or to conduct further research into their reclusive personalities. She might use her summary to generate questions she would like to have answered about koalas. She could visit a zoo where koalas are kept and find out more about their habits.

In teaching mapping, you should start with well-constructed reading selections and model the process for students. Begin by placing the topic in a central hub, and then elicit major category labels. Have students search the selection to identify supporting details important enough to be included in the map. With younger students, you may want to supply a prestructured map with empty slots for them to fill as you guide a discussion of the material. Older students can eventually use mapping as an independent approach to prewriting, much as Hilary did in this example.

Probable Passages

Another writing-to-learn strategy that helps students actively think like an author is probable passages (Wood, 1984). Probable passages was originally developed for use with predictable story patterns, but it can work equally well with the expository text patterns (i.e., information, cause-effect, compare-contrast, and problem-solution). Indeed, probable passages can help sensitize students to these various text structures through writing. Much like possible sentences (discussed in Chapter 7), this strategy capitalizes on prediction and verification using a student-authored text passage evaluated against the original text.

The steps involved in developing a probable passages lesson are as follows:

1. Analyze the selection for the most significant concepts or for vocabulary that may need extra emphasis. Present those words on the board or overhead projector. The words and sample lesson below are from "Beach Oil Spills" (adapted from Mickadeit, 1987). This article follows a cause-effect structure. Thus, the words are listed under those category labels. The lesson is from the area of current events.

Cause	*Effect*
oil spills	crude oil
pollution	shoreline
Grunion	eggs
	polluted
	died

2. Explain the text structure categories that encompass the key words. You may want to introduce the concept of cause and effect, using a cartoon or some other more concrete visual.
3. Give students a copy of an incomplete selection. The first part of the selection should introduce the cause. Leave out only those key words that are listed. The second part of the text frame should include only an opening sentence leading into the effect of, in this case, the oil spill. The following incomplete text frame illustrates this step:

Beach Oil Spills
The ocean is a fragile place. Sea creatures need an unpolluted home if they are to survive. When we drill for oil off our beaches, _____ may cause high levels of _____. Toxins in oil such as gasoline and benzene are dangerous to fish like the California grunion. _____ are small, silvery fish that come ashore on spring evenings to lay their eggs in the wet sand.

   A recent oil spill near Seal Beach, California [*use the words from the "effect" side of your list to write the rest of this passage the way you think an author might*].

4. Read the list of key words to students and discuss their definitions.
5. Tell the students to use the words to construct a probable passage. The following probable passage was written by Shane Ingram, a sixth grader:

Beach Oil Spills

The ocean is a fragile place. Sea creatures need an unpolluted home if they are to survive. When we drill for oil off our beaches, oil spills may cause high levels of pollution. Toxins in oil such as gasoline and benzene are dangerous to fish like the California grunion. Grunion are small, silvery fish that come ashore on spring evenings to lay their eggs in the wet sand.

   A recent oil spill near Seal Beach, California dumped lots of crude oil on the shoreline. The thick, gloppy crude oil polluted the beach. Grunion eggs died from the poisons in the oil.

6. Next, have students read the original selection, noting how close their probable passage came to the original passage. Shane's second paragraph paral-

leled the overall message in the original selection. Now, he simply needs to note the facts and supporting details in the original, which follows. Students can also share their probable passages with others in the class.

Beach Oil Spills (Original Passage)

A recent oil spill near Seal Beach, California dumped 420 gallons of crude oil into the ocean. Over 84 gallons were carried on the tide into the shoreline where grunion leave their eggs. Biologists who studied thousands of eggs from the oil spill area found that 24 percent of the eggs from the polluted sand at Seal Beach died.

There are so many other grunion spawning that they will survive this disaster. But the effect of oil spills on sea life could wipe out even larger areas of our fragile ocean environment.

7. After they have read and considered the original passage, advise students to modify their first draft to include this new information.

These student-authored passages help establish a framework for the plethora of facts and supporting details students encounter in content area texts.

Cubing

Cubing helps students explore topics from various dimensions using the concrete visual of a cube with its six sides (Tompkins, 1990). Cubing can serve as a prewriting brainstorming activity before text reading and research. It can then be used to collect and organize research information from reading, interviews, videos, and other sources. Multiple dimensions of topics in nutrition, science, social studies, mathematics, art, music, and other content areas can be examined through cubing. You should introduce cubing with a familiar topic before embarking on more difficult selections. For example, you might have students explore the various dimensions of potato chips, ice cream, hamburgers, or other familiar foods as a whole-group activity to get a sense of how cubing works. Cubing consists of the following steps:

1. Construct cubes either on paper or from milk cartons or other material.
2. Instruct students to use the six sides of the cube to

   Describe it. (Include its colors, shapes, and sizes.)

   Compare it. (What is it similar to or different from?)

   Associate it. (What does it make you think of?)

   Analyze it. (Tell how it is made or what it is composed of.)

   Apply it. (What can you do with it? How is it used?)

   Argue for or against it. (Take a stand, and list reasons for supporting it.)

In the example that follows, paired fourth-grade students selected particular animals that they wanted to write about. Other students in the class comprised the

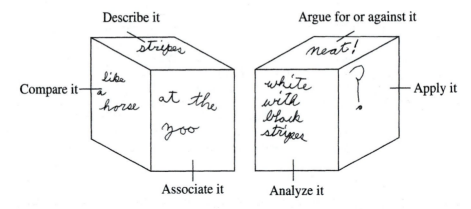

FIGURE 10.2   Initial Cube on Zebras

audience for this project. The cubes in Figure 10.2 show the efforts of two students, Felicia and Halley, before they completed any research reading about zebras.

Felicia and Halley's cube demonstrates a grasp of how cubing works, but their understanding of zebras at this prereading stage is limited. They know from visits to the city zoo that zebras have stripes and look like horses, but they have little in-depth knowledge of zebras.

During the next few days, Felicia and Halley visit the library and locate a good article about zebras and their stripes in *Ranger Rick* magazine (Donahoe, 1991). They discover that not all zebras have white backgrounds and black stripes. Some have brown, red, or tan stripes. They also learn that there are three kinds, or species, of zebras: plains zebras, Grevy's zebras, and mountain zebras. Surprisingly, they discover that each zebra has its own individual stripe pattern, much like human fingerprints. The zebra is related to the horse, but it is shorter than a horse, with bigger ears and no mane. The stripes are thought to confuse enemies and help zebras stay in a herd when they are traveling across the African landscape.

Felicia and Halley then revise their cube. The revised cube in Figure 10.3 forms the basis for organizing a research paper around the six categories expressed on the six faces.

Once Felicia and Halley have arranged the information from the article on the cube, they write a short research paper summarizing what they learned. The paper in Figure 10.4 is Felicia and Halley's final draft, to be shared with other class authors and published for future classes.

Writing Roulette

Writing roulette was originally developed as a free-writing strategy in which students could write about anything at all for a set period of time, usually monitored with a kitchen timer (Shuman, 1979). They would then pass their writing on to a

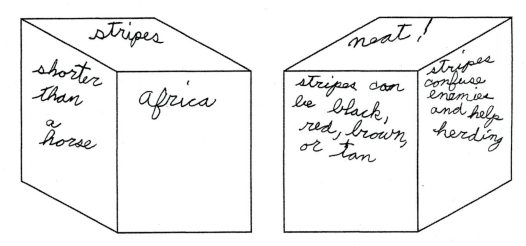

FIGURE 10.3   Revised Cube on Zebras

peer, who would continue developing the passage for an additional five minutes or so. Much like sustained silent reading, writing roulette helped students break out of a plodding, transcribing approach to writing and move into a rapid-fire, free-association form of composing.

Bean (1992) added two dimensions to the writing roulette strategy to improve its power as a writing-to-learn experience. First, rather than simply write anything down, students are asked to use a simple three-part story structure for the activity such that three different students participate in writing each part of the story. Second, they explore content material within the framework of this story by selecting key vocabulary words from their expository reading and including these words in whatever section they are writing.

The procedure for a writing roulette session is as follows:

1. Provide a simple structure for the story consisting of three major elements or divisions:

   a. A setting or characters
   b. A problem or goal for the main character
   c. A resolution

2. Advise students that each section of the story must use at least *one* word from their content unit. These words should be underlined.
3. Set a specific time limit for the first story section (e.g., five minutes for the setting). You can use a kitchen timer for this.
4. When time is up, have students exchange papers or collect and shuffle them so that a second author writes the problem or goal section. Set a time limit, and advise students to read the paper they receive and continue the story.

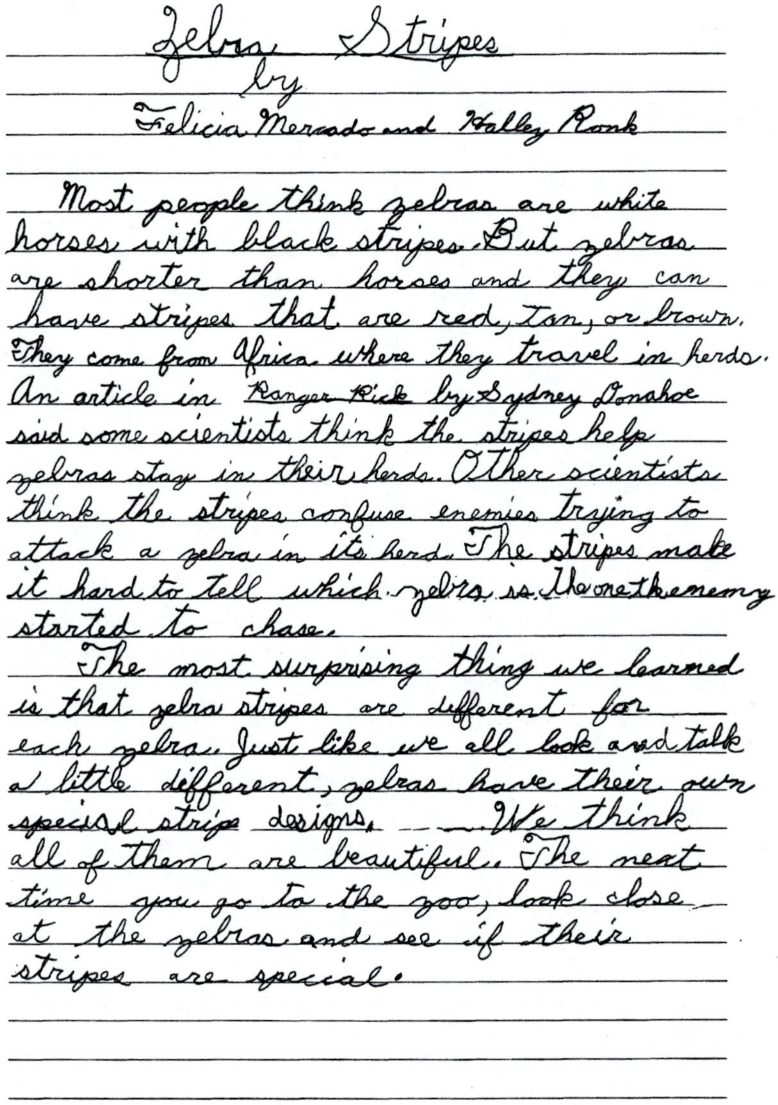

Zebra Stripes
by
Felicia Mercado and Halley Rook

Most people think zebras are white horses with black stripes. But zebras are shorter than horses and they can have stripes that are red, tan, or brown. They come from Africa where they travel in herds. An article in *Ranger Rick* by Sydney Donahoe said some scientists think the stripes help zebras stay in their herds. Other scientists think the stripes confuse enemies trying to attack a zebra in its herd. The stripes make it hard to tell which zebra is the one the enemy started to chase.

The most surprising thing we learned is that zebra stripes are different for each zebra. Just like we all look and talk a little different, zebras have their own special stripe designs. We think all of them are beautiful. The next time you go to the zoo, look close at the zebras and see if their stripes are special.

FIGURE 10.4   Research Paper on Zebras

5. Exchange papers one last time so that the third author can provide a resolution for the story. Have students return the story to the original author and share aloud those stories that are particularly interesting or that use content vocabulary in creative ways.

Writing roulette is an excellent review strategy before a quiz. It is best introduced when students have a good grasp of content vocabulary.

Process Guide 10.2

Form groups of three students, and appoint one member of each group to be the teacher. Conduct a writing roulette session using vocabulary terms from your book and class notes. Each section of the three stories your group cooperatively writes should contain two words from your methods course. Share your stories with the rest of the class when they are complete.

The final writing-to-learn strategy, the guided writing procedure, is a more elaborate approach than those introduced thus far. It takes students through pre-reading and postreading stages of a lesson using writing as a means of exploring content.

Guided Writing Procedure

The guided writing procedure (GWP) is designed to help students achieve written fluency in content areas (Smith & Bean, 1980; Searfoss, Smith, & Bean, 1981). The GWP taps students' prior knowledge of a topic and helps them modify or add to this knowledge through speaking, listening, writing, and reading. Unlike the writing-to-learn strategies explored up to this point, the GWP emphasizes editing, writing for content, and form. The GWP focuses on four major teaching objectives:

1. To activate and sample students' prior knowledge of a topic before they do any text reading
2. To sample and evaluate students' written expression in a content area
3. To improve students' written expression through guided instruction
4. To facilitate the synthesis and retention of content area material

Recent research exploring the impact of the GWP on students' content learning and writing suggests that the GWP significantly improves the quality of students' writing. Specifically, those students receiving GWP instruction are better able to integrate information from various sources in writing that is carefully edited and readable (Martin, Konopak, & Martin, 1986; Konopak, Martin, & Martin, 1987).

The GWP involves a series of ten steps spanning three days of content instruction:

1. Write the topic of study on the board, and ask students to brainstorm words or phrases they associate with the topic. The example below demonstrates the GWP for the topic "Why Did the Dinosaurs Vanish?" (adapted from Granger, 1982).
2. List any student responses verbatim on the board. Have students discuss their terms and explain why they are related to the topic under consideration.

Students generated the following list for the topic of the dinosaurs' disappearance:

too cold	grew too much
no food	killed by bigger animals
storms	abominable snowman
too hot	big foot

3. Have the class construct an outline or graphic organizer of these ideas with category labels. For example:

Why Did the Dinosaurs Vanish?

   I. Climate Causes
      A. too cold
      B. too hot
      C. storms
  II. Physical Causes
      A. grew too much
      B. no food
III. Predator Causes
      A. killed by bigger animals
      B. abominable snowman
      C. big foot

4. Have students individually write a short paragraph or two as a first draft, using the outline as a guide to content and organization. It is important to specify a peer audience for this information. Students can write for another class member or a class member who is absent during this activity.

5. Collect these first drafts, and quickly analyze the paragraphs using the GWP checklist in Figure 10.5. Do *not* make any marks on students' papers. The checklist illustrates analysis of the following first draft, written by sixth grader Rudolfo Padang:

Why Did the Dinosors Vanish?

Dinosors went away cause of tree things; The climate causes, psychical causes, and predator causes.

    I think it was Big Foot chase them away.

Rudolfo began with a clear topic sentence, and his brief composition flows logically. Since his background knowledge about dinosaurs is limited at this stage of the lesson, he includes no supporting details. He seems to handle sentence structure reasonably well. However, in the area of mechanics, he needs to edit for punctuation and spelling.

6. The next day, return these student drafts and checklists. Have students edit and polish their first drafts using the guidelines on the checklist. You can provide extra help by walking around the room to assist individual students. This is also a good time for individual conferences with those students in need of more attention. You may want to display some sample drafts on the overhead to model the process of editing for organization of ideas, style, and mechanics.

FIGURE 10.5   GWP Checklist

Name: _Rudolfo Padanz_	✓ = Okay
Date: _3/15_	0 = Needs revision
	? = Can't tell

Organization of ideas

Clear topic	✓
Supporting details/examples	0
Logical flow	✓

Comments: _____

_____

Style—Shows variety in

Word choice	✓
Sentence length	✓

Comments: _____

_____

Mechanics

Complete sentences	✓
Capitalization	✓
Punctuation	0
Spelling	0

Comments: _____

_____

7. Collect these second draft efforts, and simply record any comments, especially praise, at the bottom of the original checklist.
8. Assign text reading, such as the following passage, advising students that the purpose of this assignment is to find additional information they can include in their compositions:

Why Did the Dinosaurs Vanish?

What happened to these giant creatures that ruled the earth for nearly 200 million years? Why did they disappear? Why did they become extinct? There are many theories, or ideas, about what may have happened to them.

One theory is that a dreadful disease swept through the world of the dinosaurs.

Another is that smaller animals ate the unprotected dinosaur eggs.

Still another theory is that the climate of the earth changed. From being very warm and comfortable for the giant reptiles, the climate grew cold and dry.

The swamps dried up and the seas grew smaller. The dinosaurs could not survive these changes.

Another theory is that new kinds of plants began to grow on earth, replacing the old ones. If the plant-eating dinosaurs could not adapt, or change, their eating habits, they would die out. Without the plant-eating dinosaurs as food, the meat-eating dinosaurs could not survive either.

No one knows for sure why the dinosaurs vanished from the earth. Scientists have been wondering for years. All we have left of the dinosaurs are the fossils they left behind. Someday, by studying these fossils and by making new discoveries, we may learn why the dinosaurs disappeared.

9. Together in class, revise the original outline (in this case, about dinosaurs) to reflect ideas gleaned from the previous day's reading of the text. The passage students read about the disappearance of the dinosaurs emphasized four theories about the cause of this catastrophic event. Unlike the students' fantastical and certainly more exciting explanations of the dinosaurs' disappearance, the text makes no mention of Big Foot or the Abominable Snowman. However, the text does mention a change in climate as a possible cause of their demise. It also talks about predators, albeit in a different vein. Thus, the new outline will contain some old, prior-knowledge information and the new information gleaned from the text.

Why Did the Dinosaurs Vanish?

I. Climate Causes
   A. changed from warm to cold and dry
   B. swamps dried up and seas grew smaller
   C. new plants grew that plant-eaters didn't like
   D. meat-eaters didn't have plant-eaters to eat
   E. (storms)
II. Physical Causes
   A. disease killed them
   B. (grew too much)
III. Predator Causes
   A. small animals ate dinosaur eggs
   B. (killed by bigger animals)
   C. (big foot or abominable snowman)

It is important to note that the integrity of students' theories about the dinosaurs' disappearance remains intact. Since the last paragraph of the text implies that scientists are still exploring this question, students' ideas should be given consideration.

10. Have students revise and expand their compositions in light of this new information from the text. They may work in pairs or small groups while you

circulate to help them integrate text and prior knowledge. Have students turn in these final drafts for a grade, or give a quiz on this information. You may wish to use their compositions as a lead-in to a unit—in this case, on dinosaurs. Rudolfo's final draft shows a marked improvement in writing and content.

Why Did the Dinosaurs Vanish?

The dinosaurs vanished. Maybe they are extinct because the climate changed. It got to be cold and dry instead of warm and nice. Maybe new plants grew that dinosaurs did not want to eat.

Maybe a awful sickness killed them. Or small animals ate their eggs.

No one knows for sure why this happened. I know. It was Big Foot!

Rudolfo's new version contains supporting details from the text and echoes the tentative tone of the passage, at least until his final statement. He chooses to staunchly maintain his own theory that Big Foot wiped out the dinosaurs. It would be interesting to have him expand on this notion with arguments supporting his theory.

The GWP is an intense but worthwhile approach to integrating text reading and writing. Since it relies on prior knowledge, reserve its use for units in science, math, and history that feature topics of general interest.

Imaginative Writing to Learn and Inform

There are countless exciting and imaginative ways to share information in writing. The Resources section of this chapter lists books and articles that feature a dizzying array of teaching strategies you can adopt. In this section, five imaginative writing strategies are introduced.

Poetry

Poetry is one of the most enjoyable forms of writing for children to read, listen to, and creatively imitate. Luce-Kapler (1999, p. 298) said: "Poetry is the rhythm of our living, the connective tissue between our sensory experiences and the language we rely on to remember those experiences. We find that rhythm in the ending of a line, a single word following on the next that returns us to the breathless moment, the tightening of muscles, the wary eye."

You can introduce children to poetry writing by providing a model or poetry framework (Luce-Kapler, 1999). Select a poem and reproduce it line by line, leaving a large space between each line. Have students read the first line and write one or two lines in response, without worrying too much about the content. The goal here is to help students get into the rhythm of the poem. Once all the lines have new lines following them, take away the lines of the original poem; a new-found poem, with its own unique voice but slightly resembling the original poem, will remain.

A traveler to the Great Sand Dunes, just below the Sangre de Cristos mountains in southern Colorado, wrote this free verse poem:

> **Wind and Mountains**
> The wind here makes mountains with its hands
> Picking up sand and dust
> On its daily journey across the Rio Grande
> Wind like a sculptor
> An artist in nature
> But not alone
> It builds a 700 foot high mountain of sand
> But not alone
> It needs the 14,000 foot tall Sangre de Cristos mountains
> And the low passes where the wind is funneled
> Back into the San Luis Valley
> Together, wind and mountains make the Great Sand Dunes
> But not alone

Fourth-grade Hector came up with the following creative responses:

> **Wind and Mountains**
> The wind here makes mountains with its hands
> *On our farm wind rustles my hair*
> Picking up sand and dust
> *Tossing my hat across the fields*
> On its daily journey across the Rio Grande
> *Every afternoon when I go out to play*
> Wind like a sculptor
> *Wind like a friend*
> An artist in nature
> *Comes over to my house*
> But not alone
> *So I'm not alone*
> It builds a 700 foot high mountain of sand
> *We move everything in my yard*
> But not alone
> *Together*
> It needs the 14,000 foot tall Sangre de Cristos mountains
> *The afternoon brings the wind in summer*
> And the low passes where the wind is funneled
> *So we can fly my kite*
> Back into the San Luis Valley
> *Into the potato field behind my house*
> Together, wind and mountains make the Great Sand Dunes
> *Together me and the wind*

But not alone
  So I'm not alone

The result is this new-found poem:

> *Wind and Me*
> *On our farm wind rustles my hair*
> *Tossing my hat across the fields*
> *Every afternoon when I go out to play*
> *Wind like a friend*
> *Comes over to my house*
> *So I'm not alone*
> *We move everything in my yard*
> *Together*
> *The afternoon brings the wind in summer*
> *So we can fly my kite*
> *Into the potato field behind my house*
> *Together me and the wind*
> *So I'm not alone*

Students can exchange their new-found poems and use these as models or frameworks to create yet other poems. The class can engage in bookmaking once a collection of poems has been assembled (Johnson, 1996). In this way children will develop a sense of book layout and artistry. They can illustrate their poetry and share their work with a larger audience.

Music

Music is a natural extension of poetry and, like poetry, offers a fun medium for integrating reading, writing, and content learning. The ReWrite strategy allows students to learn concepts through music writing and performing (Bean, 1997; Readence, Bean, & Baldwin, 1998). Music comes in many forms, and you do not need to be an experienced musician to use ReWrite in your classroom. Many elementary teachers use ReWrite with rhythmic clapping, rap song writing, and familiar folksongs. The lyrics that students write are the crucial ingredient in a ReWrite lesson, but children genuinely enjoy performing their musical creations too.

ReWrite typically spans two to three days and includes prereading, reading, and postreading/writing stages. First you do a task analysis of a topic and select the key concepts you want students to grasp. You then create one or two opening verses of a song. These verses should contain some basic, minimal knowledge about the topic. You can even include some misconceptions that will be resolved as students acquire more accurate knowledge of the topic being introduced. The lesson that follows was designed for a group of fourth graders, who were studying insects in their Southern Colorado area.

Music is a natural extension of poetry and another way to integrate reading, writing, and learning.

ReWrite: Day One.   In preparation for a field trip to the Great Sand Dunes, where students would acquire new knowledge about an unusual bug that lives only in the dunes, their teacher introduced them to the following song about the Circus Beetle. This beginning song, with a single verse containing only naïve knowledge about the Circus Beetle, was the starting point for the ReWrite lesson. The song follows a simple 12-bar blues rhythm pattern in the key of E.

> **Circus Beetle Blues I**
> E
> *The circus beetle dances for you cause it seems like it likes to perform*
> A   E
> *It stands on its head…just like it won't do you no harm*
> B7   A
> *It seems so cute you want to take it home*
> E
> *It seems so cute you don't want to leave it alone*

The first day students enjoyed singing and chuckling about this funny creature.

ReWrite: Day Two.   The following day the class set out for their field trip to the Great Sand Dunes, looking forward to finding out more about the Circus Beetle. Before they embarked on their hike up the 700-foot dunes, the ranger at the dunes gave a brief talk on some of the insects in this beautiful area. In particular, he showed them a glass box with a Circus Beetle in it and explained that it stands on its head as a warning to potential enemies. It performs this cute act just before emitting a stream of foul-smelling fluid, much as a skunk does. Everyone laughed and got excited about returning to the song with this new, somewhat disturbing news about the Circus Beetle.

ReWrite: Day Three.   Back in class, the students consulted a book their teacher had, *Insects and Other Arthropods of Great Sand Dunes National Monument* (Weissmann, Clement, & Kondratieff, 1993). They then gathered in small groups and wrote new verses, reflecting more accurate knowledge of the Circus Beetle which they had gained from reading and consulting sources on the Internet.

> ### Circus Beetle Blues II
> E
> *The circus beetle dances for you cause it seems like it likes to perform*
> A   E
> *It stands on its head...just like it won't do you no harm*
> B7   A
> *It seems so cute you want to take it home*
> E
> *It seems so cute you don't want to leave it alone*
>
> E
> *This hairy little dude isn't cute at all*
> *Its little black hairs make me creep and crawl*
> A   E
> *It tips its butt up into the air and squirts and struts it's just not fair*
> B7   A
> *Oh Circus Beetle don't do me no wrong*
> E
> *You go your way and I'll move along*
>
> E
> *The Circus Beetle has hair on his back and lifts his smelly behind*
> A   E
> *He looks real cute but he's not very kind*
> B7   A   E
> *His favorite snack is grasshoppers, beetles, and ants*

Once the verses from a ReWrite lesson have been completed, you can assemble them into a complete song and each group can perform its own lyrics. The song can then be put up in the classroom, performed for other classes, audiotaped, or added to a collection of ReWrite songs. At the reading stage of the lesson, you may wish to supplement ReWrite with other material such as study guide questions, anticipation-reaction guide statements, and whatever level of scaffolding you feel your students need to learn the new concepts (Readence, Bean, & Baldwin, 1998).

ReWrite is an entertaining way to make concepts accessible and memorable, using blues, folk music, familiar children's songs like "Row, Row, Row, Your Boat," or contemporary music forms like rock 'n' roll and rap. Southern Colorado teachers Jean LaTourette and Janet Rogers used the following adaptation of

Aretha Franklin's "Chain of Fools" to teach the concept of the food chain to fourth graders at Crawford School.

> **Chain of Food**
> *Chain, chain, chain (Chain, chain, chain)*
> *Chain, chain, chain (Chain, chain, chain)*
> *Chain, chain, chai-ai-ai-ai-ain*
> *Chain of food*
>
> *[Predator:]*
> *For all these years, I thought you were my meal.*
> *But I found out that I'm just a link in a chain.*
>
> *[Prey:]*
> *You got us where you want us, we're nothing but your prey,*
> *We have to use camouflage to make it through the day.*
>
> *Chain, chain, chain (Chain, chain, chain)*
> *Chain of food*
>
> *Carnivores eat meat, herbivores eat plants,*
> *You give us nutrients.*
> *You're in our habitat.*
>
> *[Predator, with back-up singing fish:]*
> *You tell me to leave you alone but in the world it's how it's done.*
> *Bigger animals eat the smaller ones*
> *It's the system of survival.*
>
> *[Prey:]*
> *We're added to the—*
> *Chain, chain, chain (Chain, chain, chain)*
> *Chain, chain, chain (Chain, chain, chain)*
> *Chain, chain, chai-ai-ai-ai-ain*
> *Chain of food*
>
> *[Prey:]*
> *We try to hide in coral, we try to hide in sand.*
> *We even try to sting you, but you end our life span.*
>
> *Chain, chain, chain (Chain, chain, chain)*
> *Chain, chain, chain (Chain, chain, chain)*
> *Chain, chain, chai-ai-ai-ai-ain*
> *Chain of food (Repeat chain, chain)*

Familiar pop songs, blues, oldies, country music, rap, hip-hop, and simply clapping a rhythm all offer a way to weave music into reading and writing in a fashion that is engaging, as well as likely to build students' knowledge.

Who Am I?

The "who am I?" form of imaginative writing gives students a chance to project themselves into topics in science, social studies, and other content areas (Readence, Bean, & Baldwin, 1998). In science, for example, a "who am I?" paper might focus on "I am your stomach" and discuss what the world would be like from the stomach's point of view. In social studies, a paper on "I am the President" would explore this topic in the first person. Virtually any topic can be approached from a "who am I?" frame of reference. You will need to carefully model the process of developing this paper.

Process Guide 10.3

Develop a brief "who am I?" sketch using a topic related to your academic major, a favorite food, or a hobby you enjoy. Exchange sketches with another class member, and see whether that person can determine who you are.

Student-Authored Math Problems

Writing forms an excellent foundation for unlocking word problems in math. Winograd (1992) describes a project in which fifth-grade students wrote their own math word problems and shared these problems with peers in small cooperative groups. They had to pay close attention to writing clear problems that would translate into the appropriate mathematical operations. The following is an example of a fifth-grade student's word problem focusing on multiplication.

"Who am I?" "I am your stomach!"

My older brother runs 5 miles each day on his high school cross-country team. He usually runs at an average pace of 8 minutes for each mile. How long does it take him to run the 5 miles?

Winograd found that generating word problems helps students become more receptive to problem-solving instruction. Student-authored problems tap day-to-day issues and capture students' interests.

"Choose Your Own Adventure" Stories

Students in the middle grades are fond of "choose your own adventure" books, which allow the reader to chart a course through a story that has multiple pathways. In a "choose your own adventure" book, each chapter or part is followed by two choices of direction. You can capitalize on students' enthusiasm for this story type by having them treat nonfiction topics using the "choose your own adventure" format (Sargent, 1991). The following steps culminate in the creation of a team-authored story with multiple pathways throughout:

1. Consider the characteristics of typical "choose your own adventure" books. Also consider the nonfiction content and structure of books like Joanna Cole's (1987) *The Magic School Bus: Inside the Earth.* Although not a "choose your own adventure" book, *The Magic School Bus* series deals with nonfiction topics in an exciting fashion.
2. Decide which member of the team will write each story section.
3. Make a map or flow chart of story parts and branches that take the story in different directions.
4. Develop a draft version of the story, and try it out.
5. Create the final version of the story to print and bind.

A "choose your own adventure" story might consider racing a solar car, skating on roller blades, acting in a play, dancing in a musical, fishing, horseback riding in the hills, finding an old shack, or whatever students' imaginations reveal.

Assessing Writing

As you engage students in a process approach to writing for real audiences over multiple drafts, you naturally increase the volume of papers to be graded. In this last section of the chapter, some guidelines and strategies are offered that should help you respond to students' writing without becoming catatonic in the process.

When students produce longer compositions in the form of science, history, or math reports, guiding them toward success becomes paramount. Thus, you need to acquire some teaching strategies to guide the first and final draft stages of an expository report.

Checklists that analyze writing for content and form (such as the GWP checklist) offer a means of guiding revision without littering a student's paper with red marks (Heller, 1991). Perhaps the best form of responding is the individual conference, guided by a checklist. Students can also engage in evaluation of their own and others' writing, using a series of generic questions.

Although holistic scoring of compositions can be a powerful evaluation tool to manage the paper load, a teacher who lacks adequate practice and training in its use is better off using straightforward checklists. Holistic evaluation of papers relies on a quick impression in which a paper is compared to a template piece of writing that represents a particular score along a scale of 1 to 4, 1 to 6, and so on. Reliable scoring of papers in this fashion requires at least two raters. Thus, for most teachers, a more analytical scheme like the GWP checklist is preferable.

The three assessment schemes considered in this final section—individual conferences, self evaluation, and peer evaluation—can all be incorporated in your classroom with relative ease. Each of these approaches will make a significant difference in the quality of students' writing and provide them with strategies they can use as they advance through the grades.

Individual Conferences

You can organize individual conferences according to a sign-up sheet or a first-come, first-served system, or you can simply rove about the room meeting with various students. Newkirk (1986) describes an individual conference as a conversation between teacher and student. Dahl and Farnan (1998) recommend that writing conferences strive for shared ownership of writing rather than too many teacher recommendations. When students are writing for real audiences, they need some focused revision suggestions that they can manage. A series of generic questions can serve to guide your conversations with students. Newkirk offers the following questions (1986, p. 121); you may wish to compose your own.

1. What do you like best about this draft? What do you like least?
2. What gave you the most trouble in writing this?
3. What kind of reaction do you want your readers to have—amusement, anger, increased understanding?
4. What surprised you when you wrote this? What came out different from the way you expected?
5. What is the most important thing you learned about your topic in writing this?

Amidst these important questions, Newkirk cautions that the major pitfall in any individual conference is that the teacher will do all the talking. It is particularly important to avoid monopolizing the conversation, as the act of talking about writing sometimes triggers an idea that may help reshape a composition. If students have a series of questions that they respond to beforehand and bring to the individual conference to share, self evaluation rather than teacher direction may guide the conversation.

Self Evaluation

Self evaluation using an instrument like the GWP checklist can provide a basis for constructive suggestions from the teacher. Or a series of questions like the following may serve to guide this process:

1. What makes you happy about this writing?
2. Do you excite your reader with a good beginning?
3. Is there a clear topic sentence?
4. Do you back up your ideas with details and examples?
5. Do you use a variety of words to express your ideas?
6. Are your sentences different lengths?
7. Do you use complete sentences?
8. Did you check your writing for correct capitalization, punctuation, and spelling?

One element that may be difficult to pinpoint on a checklist or series of questions is the writer's unique voice. A piece of writing that has the individual stamp of a student's personal interest in the topic has a quality that makes it fun to read. For example, Rudolfo's insistence that Big Foot wiped out the dinosaurs displays this quality. Unfortunately, most expository texts students read are devoid of this crucial element. Hence, students reading these texts need models of writing, often found in trade books rather than texts, that display the author's enthusiasm and individuality.

Peer Evaluation

Although self evaluation is an important part of the writing process, peer evaluation offers an even more powerful approach. Evaluating one's own writing is always difficult. We know what we meant to say, even if on paper the message is garbled. Inconsistencies and incoherent passages are more readily apparent to another reader.

Teams of two students can accomplish the task of reviewing each other's work if they have adequate practice and clear guidelines. As a means of giving students some practice in peer editing, use some writing samples from a lower grade level, and model the process of applying a writing guide checklist to these samples. Since the writing belongs to anonymous students from another grade level, you offer a nonthreatening context in which your students can practice their peer-editing skills. Once students have a good grasp of how to respond to a peer's writing, they can begin exchanging papers and working collaboratively to improve each other's drafts.

To ensure that peer editing is a positive activity, you should supply some specific guidelines. For example, once students have read a peer's paper and are ready to begin filling out a writing guide checklist like the one for the GWP, they should begin at the top of the checklist with a compliment such as

"I thought the most interesting part of your paper was..."
"You gave the most complete information about..."

Any negative comments should be posed as questions. In particular, the generic question "Can you tell me more about..." seems to allay any defensive feelings.

Finally it is important that the "editor" not simply find problem areas in a peer's paper. Rather, the reader should offer some solutions in the form of alternative organizational structures, revised sentences, correct spellings, and so on. The reader needs to enter the peer-editing process with the idea that this is not an opportunity to do a passive reading of a paper and take a few potshots at the writer, who is left in a quandary about how to remedy these problems.

These strategies will help you manage the paper load in a class where students write a great deal, and they should help students produce high-quality papers that are enjoyable to read. However, the intense processes of producing a first draft, peer editing, and revision should be reserved for major projects, which you will need to take time to evaluate. Much of the writing described in this chapter calls for more informal responses. Thus, one way to manage the paper load is to grade selectively. Spot-check all but the major compositions students undertake.

Summary

This chapter introduced recent thinking about the integration of reading and writing. Three forms of writing were considered in some detail: (1) journal writing, (2) writing to learn, and (3) imaginative writing to learn and inform. Within the writing-to-learn section, five teaching strategies were introduced and demonstrated: (1) semantic mapping, (2) probable passages, (3) cubing, (4) writing roulette, and (5) the guided writing procedure. The section on imaginative writing suggested five enjoyable vehicles for writing to inform, as well as to learn: (1) poetry, (2) music, (3) who am I? (4) student-authored math problems, and (5) "choose your own adventure" stories. Finally, the chapter discussed responding to students' writing through individual conferences, self evaluation, and peer evaluation. By integrating these lessons into the classroom, a teacher can help students see that expository text really is not so elusive. Once students begin to create their own expository passages, they will learn to look at texts from the inside out, thinking like authors.

FOLLOW-THROUGH ACTIVITIES

Note: Level 1 activities may require limited access to children or classrooms. Level 2 activities should be completed using children and classrooms.

Level 1 Activities

1. Observe a classroom where journal writing is an integral part of the curriculum. Summarize your observations of children's journal writing and discuss these observations with another student in your class.

2. Visit an elementary classroom for at least a week. Keep a log of writing activities you observe. Categorize these activities according to the headings on the graphic organizer

for this chapter: Journal Writing, Writing to Learn, and Imaginative Writing. Compare your findings with those of other students.

3. Examine commercial materials aimed at engaging children in writing. Using the headings from this chapter, decide what forms of writing are being emphasized. Compare your findings with those of other students.

Level 2 Activities

1. Collect some examples of children's writing to learn or imaginative writing, and discuss these writing samples.

2. Select one of the writing-to-learn strategies, and conduct a lesson on it with children. Respond to children's writing using the writing guide checklist, and conduct at least one individual conference, following the guidelines in this chapter.

3. Design an imaginative writing assignment, using one of the strategies from this section of the chapter (e.g., poetry or music). Try it out with a group of children, and evaluate your experience with this lesson.

WORKING WITH PARENTS

The scene is a parent conference early in the year centering on Mrs. Burack's concerns about the writing of her fourth-grade son Brett.

> **MRS. BURACK:** Brett's always had trouble with grammar and spelling, Mr. Spenser. I notice the paper he just brought home is filled with errors, but you haven't marked them as my teachers used to. Why is that?
>
> **MR. SPENSER:** That's a good question, Mrs. Burack, and I'll be glad to explain what we have learned in recent years about teaching writing. You'll notice on Brett's paper that there are comments about the ideas he has expressed. Brett isn't hamstrung like some writers his age by anxiety about getting each word perfect in an early draft. I guide my students through a series of drafts in writing they intend to share with other students. This early in the year, Brett has written a draft of what he knows about snakes.
>
> **MRS. BURACK:** Brett loves snakes!
>
> **MR. SPENSER:** Now that everyone has written a draft about a topic that is special in his or her life, we are going to edit these drafts together, paying attention to how clearly the ideas are communicated, but also to the concerns you raise. When you see Brett's next draft, I think you'll be pleased at the progress he's made in expressing his ideas with accurate grammar and spelling.
>
> **MRS. BURACK:** Now I see where you are going. But can you show me how you manage to get someone Brett's age to edit his work?
>
> **MR. SPENSER:** Sure. Here's a writing guide checklist that students use to evaluate each other's work. I have them team up and exchange papers. It's called peer editing. With enough guidance, they get to be pretty good at helping each other out. Here, let me show you some of the books written by last year's students.

Here's one on whale sharks, another one on dinosaurs, and this student had her own horse so she wrote about that. Here's one explaining how to skateboard on a ramp, with photos of the author showing us how to do it.

MRS. BURACK: These are great! I am glad I visited your classroom today. School was never like this. I remember countless grammar drills, diagramming sentences. We didn't write any books. It was like signing up for the rowing team, then spending all your practicing on a rowing machine by the side of the dock. Your class gets students off the dock and into a boat, learning to write by writing.

MR. SPENSER: Yes. I remember diagramming sentences and rowing machines. We've come a long way since those days.

MRS. BURACK: Brett's really excited about your class. Now I am too. Thank you, Mr. Spenser.

MR. SPENSER: Come again and visit, Mrs. Burack.

RESOURCES

Bromley, K. (1999). Key components of sound writing instruction. In L. B. Gambrell, L. M. Morrow, S. B. Neuman, & M. Pressley (Eds.), *Best practices in literacy instruction* (pp. 152–174). New York: Guilford Press.

This selection is a good resource for Internet web sites that both foster student writing and provide opportunities to share it.

Dahl, K. L., & Farnan, N. (1998). *Children's writing: Perspectives from research.* Newark, DE: International Reading Association.

This monograph offers excellent strategies for introducing writing to young children. Guidelines for teacher-student writing conferences are included.

Hart, K., & Hart, M. (1997). *Old songs made new.* Alamosa, CO: HartLine Press.

This collection of songs and three CDs, organized by content area and concept, is an ideal resource for the nonmusician and musician alike. Included are song sheets, chords, and notes for familiar folk tunes, with lyrics devoted to content-area ideas.

Iannone, P. V. (1998). Exploring literacy on the Internet: Just beyond the horizon: Writing-centered literacy activities for traditional and electronic contexts. *The Reading Teacher, 51,* 438-443.

This article offers a collection of teacher resources for writing on the Internet. Projects, lesson plans, and places where children can publish their work online are included.

International Reading Association and the National Association for the Education of Young Children. (1998). Learning to read and write: Developmentally appropriate practices for young children. *The Reading Teacher, 52,* 193–216.

This position paper provides a view of various stages of children's reading and writing development. Specific strategies are included.

Searfoss, L. W., Bean, T. W., & Gelfer, J. I. (1998). *Developing literacy naturally.* Dubuque, IA: Kendall/Hunt.

This book is a good resource for reading and writing activities that are developmentally appropriate for children from preschool to second grade.

REFERENCES

Akaran S. E., & Fields, M. V. (1997). Family and cultural context: A writing breakthrough? *Young Children, 52,* 37–41.

Allington, R., Morrow, L. M., Wharton-MacDonald, R., Collins Block, K., & Pressley, M. (1998, Spring). Effective early literacy instruction: Complex and dynamic. *English Update,* 1–8. Albany, NY: The Center on English Learning and Achievement.

Bean, T. W. (1992). Combining writing fluency and vocabulary development through writing roulette. In E. K. Dishner, T. W. Bean, J. E. Readence, & D. W. Moore (Eds.), *Reading in the content areas: Improving classroom instruction* (3rd ed., pp. 319–323). Dubuque, IA: Kendall/Hunt.

Bean, T. W. (1997, May). ReWrite: A music strategy for exploring content area concepts. *Reading Online.* Online journal of the International Reading Association. Available: http://www.readingonline.org

Bloome, D., & Katz, L. (1997). Literacy as social practice and classroom chronotypes. *Reading and Writing Quarterly: Overcoming Learning Difficulties, 13,* 205–255.

Brown, S. (1997). First graders write to discover mathematics relevancy. *Young Children, 52,* 51–53.

Burt, D. (1987). Koalas. *Cricket: The Magazine for Children, 14,* 13.

Cole, J. (1987). *The magic school bus: Inside the earth.* New York: Scholastic.

Dahl, K. L., & Farnan, N. (1998). *Children's writing: Perspectives from research.* Newark, DE: International Reading Association.

Donahoe, S. (1991, February). Razzle-dazzle zebra stripes. *Ranger Rick,* 19–28.

Granger, J. (1982). *Amazing world of dinosaurs.* Mahwah, NJ: Troll Associates.

Heimlich, J. E., & Pittelman, S. D. (1986). *Semantic mapping: Classroom applications.* Newark, DE: International Reading Association.

Heller, M. F. (1991). *Reading-writing connections: From theory to practice.* New York: Longman.

International Reading Association and the National Association for the Education of Young Children. (1998). Learning to read and write: Developmentally appropriate practices for young children. *The Reading Teacher, 52,* 193–216.

Johnson, P. (1996). Page consciousness: The development of writing with illustrations. *Language Arts, 73,* 493–505.

Konopak, B. C., Martin, S. H., & Martin, M. A. (1987). An integrated communication arts approach for enhancing students' learning in the content areas. *Reading Research and Instruction, 26,* 275–289.

Luce-Kapler, R. (1999). White chickens, wild swings, and winter nights. *Language Arts, 76,* 298–304.

Martin, M. A., Konopak, B. C., & Martin, S. H. (1986). Use of the guided writing procedure to facilitate reading comprehension of high school text material. In J. A. Niles & R. V. Lalik (Eds.), *Solving problems in literacy: Learners, teachers, and researchers,* Thirty-fifth Yearbook of the National Reading Conference (pp. 66–72). Rochester, NY: National Reading Conference.

Mickadeit, F. (1987, June 10). 24% of grunion eggs destroyed by oil spill. *The Register,* Santa Ana, CA.

Newkirk, T. (1986). Time for questions: Responding to writing. In T. Newkirk (Ed.), *To compose* (pp. 121–124). Portsmouth, NH: Heinemann.

Phinney, M. Y. (1998). Children "writing themselves": A glimpse at the underbelly. *Language Arts, 75,* 19–27.

Readence, J. E., Bean, T. W., & Baldwin, R. S. (1998). *Content area literacy: An integrated approach* (6th ed.). Dubuque, IA: Kendall/Hunt.

Sargent, B. E. (1991). Writing "choose your own adventure" stories. *The Reading Teacher, 45,* 158–159.

Searfoss, L. W., Smith, C. C., & Bean, T. W. (1981). An integrated language strategy for second language learners. *TESOL Quarterly, 15,* 383–389.

Shuman, R. B. (1979). Writing roulette: Taking a chance on not grading. In G. Stanford (Ed.), *How to handle the paper load* (pp. 3–4). Urbana, IL: National Council of Teachers of English.

Smith, C. C., & Bean, T. W. (1980). The guided writing procedure: Integrating content teaching and writing improvement. *Reading World, 19,* 290–294.

Tompkins, G. E. (1990). *Teaching writing: Balancing process and product.* Columbus, OH: Merrill.

Tompkins, G. E., & Hoskisson, K. (1995). *Language arts: Content and teaching strategies.* Englewood Cliffs, NJ: Merrill.

Weissmann, M. J., Clement, L. P., & Kondratieff, B. C. (1993). *Insects and other arthropods of Great Sand Dunes National Monument.* Tucson, AZ: Southwest Parks and Monuments Association.

Wharton-MacDonald, R., & Boothroyd, K. (1998, December). *When first-graders write: Contexts, forms, and characteristics of student writing in five states.* Paper presented at the annual meeting of the National Reading Conference, Austin, TX.

Winograd, K. (1992). What fifth graders learn when they write their own math problems. *Educational Leadership, 49,* 64–67.

Wood, K. D. (1984). Probable passages: A writing strategy. *The Reading Teacher, 37,* 496–499.

CHAPTER

11 Assessing Reading Abilities

INTRODUCTION

The assessment of reading skills and abilities is an important part of the teaching-learning process. It enables teachers to make informed decisions about the nature of the instruction they are providing for their children. *Before* instruction begins, assessment helps teachers choose materials and techniques that offer the greatest likelihood of success. *During* instruction, assessment directs teachers toward the kinds of adjustments that will make the lesson flow more smoothly. *After* instruction is completed, assessment indicates how much children have learned. Taken as a whole, assessment is not a one-time undertaking but, rather, an essential component of all phases of the instructional sequence.

Assessment provides focus for instruction. As teachers gain a reasonable picture of children's abilities, they can begin to bridge the gap between what students know and what they need to know. For example, there is no question that children react differently to various modes of instruction. Using several sources of diagnostic information, teachers can determine the best way to present material. Without some form of assessment, teachers have no way of knowing how to approach instruction.

It must be remembered, however, that assessment information is useful for audiences other than teachers—for example, parents and the general public. Farr (1999) suggests that, when thinking about assessment, we need to consider how the information gained from testing will be used. He describes assessment as a puzzle; in order to sort out the pieces, we need first see the whole picture—that is, determine the intended audience and what type of information they need. On the one hand, teachers need information that will help them with instructional decision making about their students. On the other hand, parents need information that will allow them to monitor their children's progress and examine the effectiveness of the school. The general public also is concerned about accountability. As the needs of assessment vary depending on the audience, so must the assessment tools used.

Assessment is not always easy. It can be complicated by a wide range of factors, none of which is more prevalent than the notion of individuality. Each student in a class can be described in many ways. To the eye, features of appearance such as height, weight, hair, and clothing are most prominent. Rarely are any of these external features relevant to reading instruction. The most important features reside *within* the learner. How motivated is this child? What life experiences has the child had that can be parlayed into additional learning? What is the child's capacity for learning? How well can the child read? Does the child read all materials with proficiency, or are there certain types of materials that the child can read with greater ease than the child's general level of functioning indicates? What types of materials appeal to the child's interests? These are all important questions, but they represent only the tip of the iceberg. The range of pertinent questions that might be asked about any child is infinite. For this reason, obtaining a perfect measurement is nearly impossible.

Does this mean that attempts to assess children's reading abilities will prove futile? On the contrary, it merely reinforces the idea that assessment should not be taken lightly. Teachers must make every conceivable effort to keep apprised of each child's growth. Information must be integrated from a wide variety of sources, including standardized tests, informal measurements, observation, anecdotal records, parent reports, and school histories. To avoid the tendency to jump to diagnostic conclusions, a teacher should view all sources of information in relation to one another. Each source alone is only a crude indicator of performance; in combination, however, multiple sources can provide a more accurate and reliable picture of a learner.

In previous chapters we discussed many types of assessment tools that teachers can use to guide their instruction. In this chapter we will look at assessment techniques that provide information about the results of instruction and can be useful in disseminating achievement information to parents and the general public. We will begin our discussion by examining the guiding principles and beliefs that underlie assessment in general.

GRAPHIC ORGANIZER

This graphic organizer summarizes the structure of Chapter 11:

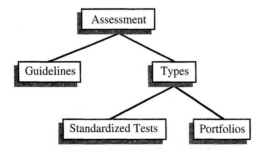

O B J E C T I V E S

When you finish this chapter, you should be able to understand and discuss each of these statements:

1. Reading assessment is a daily, ongoing process.
2. A test is really only an estimate of a child's performance at one particular point in time.
3. Teachers should have a general knowledge of the various types of tests, their purposes, and their limitations.
4. Different audiences require different information regarding children's reading development.
5. Standardized tests provide general information about children's reading abilities.
6. Portfolios provide information about the progress of reading/language instruction.

Guidelines for Reading Assessment

Purposes of Reading Assessment

Reading assessment should be a dynamic, ongoing process. It is not sufficient to assess children only at the beginning of the school year. Teachers must closely monitor children's reading progress throughout the year. This does not mean that times must be set aside to conduct formal diagnoses but, rather, that teachers must pay careful attention to children's performance on a day-to-day basis in individual and small-group situations. A surprising amount of valuable diagnostic information is available to the teacher who is adequately prepared to look for it while children are involved in normal classroom reading activities.

The importance of reading assessment is not limited to reading as a subject area. Other subjects will depend on reading assessment to the extent that reading is fundamental to that particular discipline. Subjects such as language arts, social studies, art, and mathematics all require reading-related operations. If materials are provided to children without some consideration of their reading ability, there is likely to be an instructional mismatch between readers and texts. This mismatch will no doubt negatively affect children's performance. Since teachers are responsible for seeing that children reach their full academic potential, they cannot afford to rely on incidental learning alone. They must know precisely what should be taught and how to teach it.

Principles of Reading Assessment

Because assessment directly influences instruction, it is necessary that clear and consistent principles guide teachers' thinking. Generally, assessment should be based on the following beliefs:

1. *An assessment is only as good as the individual who interprets the data.* There is no substitute for the sensitivity and perceptiveness of an experienced teacher. Since teachers deal with children directly, hour after hour, day after day, no one is in a better position to make judgments about the learning needs of their children.

2. *Assessment is a continuous process.* Regular classroom activities are rich sources of diagnostic information. Careful observation of children while they are engaged in routine reading tasks is more meaningful than results from a single test administered at the beginning of the school year. Children change markedly over relatively short amounts of time. For this reason, teachers must try to keep abreast of significant changes in performance, attitudes, and interests through close supervision of instructional activities. The only way state-of-the-art knowledge about children can be gathered and maintained is by treating assessment as an ongoing practice.

3. *A test is only a small sample of behavior.* Tests are designed to obtain information that might normally require more time to discover. They provide an expedient, but not always thorough, measure of performance. Since no test can ever estimate the full range of children's reading capabilities, test results must always be viewed with some degree of caution.

4. *Any single test or observation in isolation is insufficient grounds for drawing meaningful diagnostic conclusions.* Because all tests are prone to some amount of error, there is a distinct liability in hazarding guesses based on any one piece of information. It is preferable to synthesize test results on the same factor (such as reading comprehension) across several measurements of the factor. It is not at all uncommon for reading tests to yield very different pictures of a child's performance. When the scores are examined in combination with one another, more dependable instructional decisions can be made.

5. *Reading difficulties are rarely attributable to a single cause.* A child's reading profile is generally influenced by a number of factors interacting in an extremely complex way. Although one factor may be primarily responsible for a reading problem, secondary factors as a group may significantly impede learning. Each factor must be evaluated in conjunction with all other factors and as part of a total pattern.

6. *Assessment is far more than determining children's weaknesses.* An awareness of children's strengths (in addition to their weaknesses) allows teachers to base their instruction on a solid foundation of already acquired skills. This approach promotes a much more positive image of the diagnostic process because children are viewed as having abilities as well as weaknesses.

Process Guide 11.1

Following is a matching test designed to determine how much you do and do not know about testing terminology. The column on the left is a list of measurement terms. In the space before each term on the left, enter the number of the appropriate definition from the column on the right. Be prepared to defend your choices.

How Much Do You Know About Testing?

_____ Raw score

_____ Norms

_____ Stanines

_____ Norm-referenced test

_____ Standardized tests

_____ Mean

_____ Standard error of measurement

_____ Validity

_____ Diagnostic test

_____ Reliability

_____ Standardized scores

_____ Achievement test

_____ Criterion-referenced test

_____ Standard deviation

_____ Percentile rank

1. The degree to which a test gives consistent results when administered repeatedly; usually expressed by some form of coefficient.
2. Administered and scored according to a uniform procedure and measured against a norm.
3. Expected variation in test scores if the test were to be given repeatedly to the same person. It is both added to and subtracted from an individual's score to obtain the range within which the individual's true score really lies.
4. A test typically containing many subsections and designed to analyze an individual's specific strengths and weaknesses.
5. The statistics that describe the test performance of the groups on whom the test was standardized, groups considered representative of those for whom the test is intended.
6. A general term for referring to a variety of transformed raw scores that can be compared across other individuals and tests.
7. A test whose results are meant to be compared with previously established norms.
8. The degree of accuracy with which a test measures what it is intended to measure.
9. The number of items answered correctly.
10. Compares one score with other scores of individuals on that level.
11. A measurement of the mastery of certain skills.
12. Normalized standardized scores with a mean of 5 and a standard deviation of 2.
13. A test of specific content, measuring individual performances without comparison to the entire group.
14. The arithmetic average of a group of scores.
15. A measure of the variability, or dispersion, of a group of scores. The closer the scores cluster around the mean, the smaller the measure will be.

How Test Types Differ

Before teachers can begin to assess children's reading ability, they need to become familiar with many different types of tests and their uses. As the distinctions among the tests become clearer, teachers will be able to choose instruments that more closely meet their diagnostic needs. They will also be able to put the results of the instruments in proper perspective. By virtue of the sheer numbers of tests that are currently available, it is unreasonable to expect teachers to possess a thorough and specific knowledge of each individual instrument. Instead, they should have a general knowledge of the various types of tests, recognize their purposes and limitations, and be able to apply this knowledge in classroom situations. In this way, children become the ultimate beneficiaries of their teachers' test awareness.

Generally, tests can be characterized as either *formal* or *informal*. Formal tests have been standardized; that is, a standard set of directions has been provided for administering the test, and the instrument has been given to large groups of children at several grade levels. The purpose in giving the test to so many children is to establish a standard to which the performance of individuals can be compared. These statistical standards, referred to as *norms,* are computed by averaging the scores of children at each respective grade. To determine the meaning of a child's score, one simply compares it with the performance of the norming group. This is why standardized tests are often called *norm-referenced.*

Although it is generally standardized, a *survey test* differs from other formal instruments in that it measures general performance in a given area, rather than yielding precise measures of each individual's performance. Typically, survey tests are intended to assess the status of a group. Survey tests are most useful when given at the beginning of the year to identify children who are having problems in global areas such as word analysis, vocabulary, and comprehension. Although a survey test is capable of identifying these children, it cannot indicate specifically what a particular child knows or has difficulty with. Examples of survey tests are the CAT (California Achievement Test) and the ITBS (Iowa Test of Basic Skills).

Informal assessment instruments do not use norms as a means of interpreting the quality of an individual's score. A child's performance is judged solely on the basis of whether or not it meets a predetermined *criterion* of success. In informal testing, the teacher is not at all concerned about how the child's score will compare with other children's scores. Rather, the teacher wishes to know if the child has attained a level of skill mastery that justifies progressing to the next higher level of instruction. Most informal tests are made by teachers themselves and, as a result, can be specifically tailored to the scope and sequence of the local school's reading curriculum. Some informal tests are published, and many of these are now computer-scored. The resulting printouts give the teacher a more exact picture of each child's skill profile and often provide specific suggestions and activities for corrective teaching.

In choosing a test, several factors must be considered. Three of the most important considerations are self-evident. First, tests may be given to either *individuals* or *groups;* second, tests may be *oral* or *silent,* and third, tests may be *timed* or *untimed.* Each of these factors is directly tied to the purposes for testing and, therefore, should not be taken lightly. Children may respond quite differently to a silent-group-timed test than they would to an oral-individual-untimed test. By combining all the factors acknowledged in this section, one begins to see that tests appear in a wide variety of forms. Even more overwhelming is the fact that tests can be characterized in many more ways than those mentioned. Additional distinctions might involve factors of *test construction* (including specific content, item types, and answer-recording format), methods of *test validation,* and the nature of *test scoring, interpretation,* and *reporting.*

Since the selection of tests tends to be difficult, the following question framework is offered to simplify the task:

1. Are there distinct reasons why a standardized test would be more appropriate than an informal one?
2. Does a particular standardized test sufficiently measure the specific content, skills, and abilities relevant to the scope and sequence of the curriculum?
3. Will a general test tell me all I need to know, or should a more specialized instrument be used?
4. Is this a test I will give at the beginning of the year for screening purposes or one I will use at the end of the year to measure how much children have learned?
5. Is an individual test necessary to measure what I want, or will a group test suffice?
6. Would an oral or silent test yield the most important information for my purposes?
7. Is it absolutely necessary that the test be timed, or could I learn more about the children if it were not?
8. Will the time invested in the testing result in improved instruction?

Standardized Tests

After a test has been selected, administered, and scored, the serious business of interpreting the results comes into play. In criterion-referenced testing, this is usually just a matter of determining whether or not the criterion has been reached. The interpretation of standardized tests is a good deal more complicated. Because statistical comparisons will be made between the norming group and an individual child, somewhat complex mathematical operations are involved. The intricacies of standardized testing can be confusing to teachers, let alone parents. If they expect to communicate the results of formal measurements to parents, teachers will need to have a fundamental grasp of the basic concepts and be able to translate this knowledge into a form that is understandable.

All standardized test scores are based on the normal curve, the bell-shaped distribution appearing in Figure 11.1. In a normal distribution, scores are distributed symmetrically about an average score known as the *mean.* There are as many

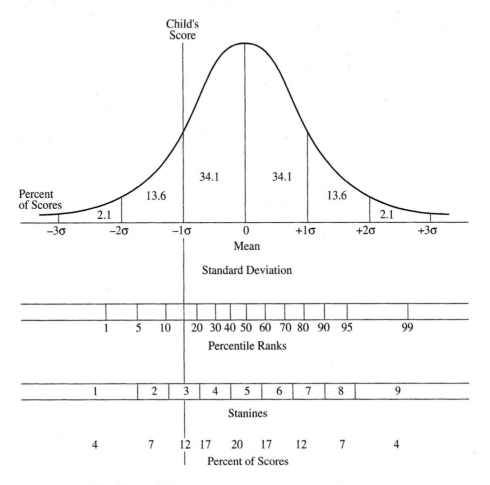

FIGURE 11.1   The Normal Curve

scores up to various distances above the mean as there are down to equal distances below it. Notice that the scores are concentrated near the mean and decrease in number the farther one departs from it. Most of the scores (approximately 68 percent) occur within 1 *standard deviation* above and below the mean. The standard deviation is a measure of the variability, or dispersion, of a group of scores. It can be used as a general guide for interpreting an individual child's performance. By examining a score in relation to the standard deviation, one can determine how well the child performed on the test. For example, if a child scored more than 1 standard deviation below the mean on a reading test, there would *probably* be cause for concern.

Why probably? All tests are prone to a certain amount of error. The term *standard error of measurement* is used to refer to the degree to which the obtained score differs from the true score; the higher the standard error of measurement, the less reliable the score. If a test were to be given repeatedly to the same child, a certain amount of variation would be expected. The standard error of measurement helps define how broad the range of possible scores might be. It is calculated by finding the obtained score on the normal curve, subtracting the standard error of measurement from the obtained score, and adding the standard error of measurement to the obtained score. The distance between the two extreme points establishes a range in which the child's score will occur two-thirds of the time. When the standard error of measurement is not considered in test interpretation, there is a greater possibility that any instructional decisions based on the test score may be suspect.

Test score interpretation is further complicated by the fact that a child's score may be expressed in many different, yet equivalent, ways. The score may be expressed as a percentile rank, a stanine, or a grade equivalent. Although these different scales allow for flexibility in score reporting, they are also a source of confusion to both teachers and parents. If the particular scale that is used to express the score is unfamiliar, then the score cannot be interpreted.

In formal testing, the term *standard score* is applied to any score that can be transformed to another scale. Each representation is equivalent, but the units of the scales differ. The relatedness of standard scores can be demystified somewhat by drawing the analogy between a child's test score and (of all things) a pot of boiling water. To determine how hot the water is, we must measure the temperature. On the Fahrenheit scale the temperature would read 212 degrees. However, on the centigrade (Celsius) scale it would measure 100 degrees, and on the Kelvin scale it would measure 373.16. The temperature of the water has not changed—only the scale used to express it. The same holds true for a test score. The score itself does not change, but the scale does. So to fully understand what a child's score means, one needs to know how the scales differ from one another.

The most common scores used in standardized testing are defined as follows:

Raw score. The total number of correct items on a test. The raw score is the first result obtained in scoring. It is a direct measurement that has not been converted or otherwise interpreted.

Percentile rank. The position of a score within the entire group of scores. The percentile rank is the percent of scores equal to or lower than the obtained score. A child who achieves a percentile score of 75 has scored as well as or better than three-fourths (75 percent) of the individuals who took the same test. Percentile scores are misinterpreted more than any other standard score; they do *not* represent the percentage of correct answers.

Grade-equivalent score. The grade level for which an obtained score is the estimated average. Usually expressed in years and months of school (for example, 3.4), the grade equivalent is the grade level for which the raw score is the middle score, or median. Grade-equivalent scores may be misleading because they may not be based on actual testing at those particular times of the year and, therefore, should be used with great caution.

Stanine score. The score on a standard 9-point scale with a mean of 5 and a standard deviation of 2. Stanine scores are often reported because they represent a range of performance rather than a single point on the normal curve.

To get an idea of how the standard score scales relate to one another, refer back to Figure 11.1. Assume that a child correctly answered 12 of 40 items on a standardized reading comprehension test. How does this score compare with the scores of other children who have taken the test? Through mathematical computation, it might be determined that this score falls exactly 1 standard deviation below the mean. By locating the score on the normal curve and drawing a vertical line through it, one can see how this score could be expressed using different standard scales. This child achieved a percentile rank of approximately 16 and a stanine of 3. (Since the grade equivalent is not a standard score, it cannot be determined directly from the position of the score on the normal curve.) Like the temperature of boiling water, the score does not change; only the means of expressing it does.

As teachers and parents gain a greater awareness of the various scales of measurement, it is likely that the lines of communication between school and home will improve. This knowledge will reduce the possibility that misunderstanding will stand in the way of a child's progress.

When properly interpreted, standardized tests provide one means of obtaining information. However, standardized tests are not without their disadvantages. Listed below are important factors that must be considered before teachers make instructional decisions based on formal test scores:

Norming. It is absolutely essential that norms be based on children like those in your class. If the norms are inappropriate, any comparisons of performance will be tentative at best.

Guessing. The majority of standardized tests use objective items (such as multiple-choice questions) to allow for machine scoring. As a result, the possibility exists that a correct answer on any item will occur as a result of chance factors alone. A child's score could be unduly inflated by good guessing. When this happens, teachers may expect the child to perform up to a level that was not truly achieved in the first place.

Content. Standardized tests of reading comprehension often assess literal understandings only. Higher-level thinking skills give way to the recall of details. Another important consideration is that the content of the standardized measure should be similar to that used in the classroom. If it is not, the test scores will be of limited utility.

Passage dependence. In many tests of reading comprehension, it is not even necessary to read the passage in order to answer certain questions. If an item can be answered without the aid of the passage, it is said to be passage-independent. Such items are of little use in determining how well children gain information from reading.

Floor and ceiling effects. If an inappropriate-level test is administered, it is possible that the results will be misleading. Ceiling effects occur when the test does not challenge the child. Because there is a limit to how high the score can go, the ability of better readers may be underestimated. Floor effects occur when less able readers can score no lower than a particular level, by virtue of

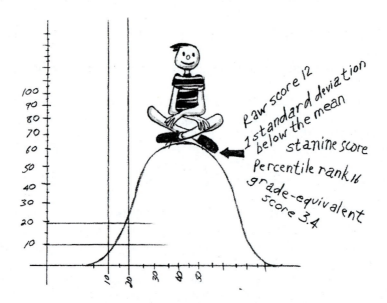

To understand what a child's test score means, one needs to know how the scales differ.

signing their names or guessing. These effects will overestimate the ability of a poor reader.

Timed versus untimed tests. The fact that standardized tests are timed works against those children who are methodical. The slow but accurate reader will be penalized on such a test.

Appeal. It is a well-known fact that children will perform better on materials that are of interest to them. The extent to which the material appeals to the children will no doubt influence their scores.

There is no question that standardized tests offer some advantages. They are easily administered to groups and allow the achievement of students to be compared with that of other students nationwide. However, standardized tests may not always provide the type of information about individual performance that enables teachers to make meaningful instructional decisions. For information about the results of instruction over time, a more appropriate assessment tool is the portfolio, discussed next.

Portfolios

Portfolios are systematic collections of children's work over time (Tierney, Carter, & Desai, 1991). Portfolios allow teachers to document children's progress and to share that information with the children, their parents, other teachers, and administrators. In essence, they are a display of what children are learning and have learned, but they are more than a sum of end products. Portfolios should be the means to document children's development over time with a single reading or writing task as well as a history of their progress in multiple literacy events.

Selection of the items to be placed in a portfolio must be a collaborative effort between the child and the teacher. It is important for the child to have a sense of ownership of the contents of the portfolio. However, this is not to suggest that anything goes. The teacher and child must work together to establish criteria for the contents of the portfolio (Wiener & Cohen, 1997). In addition to the child's selections, the portfolio can contain various assessments, observations, and anecdotal records contributed by the teacher. The portfolio can also contain communications between the parents and the teacher, as well as those between the child and the teacher.

Along with selecting the items to be placed in portfolios, children need to reflect on the importance or significance of these items. This can be accomplished through portfolio conferences. During these conferences, children should have the opportunity to look at their work and decide why certain work should be included in the portfolio or, perhaps, deleted from it. In this way portfolios also provide assessment information to the children, allowing them to review their work and explore their development as literacy learners.

Tierney and associates (1991, p. 44) cite the following benefits of assessment through portfolios:

1. It represents the range of reading and writing in which children are engaged.

A portfolio allows children to display what they have learned.

2. It engages children in assessing their progress and/or accomplishments and establishing ongoing learning goals.
3. It measures each child's achievement while allowing for individual differences between children.
4. It represents a collaborative approach to assessment.
5. It has as a goal child self-assessment.
6. It addresses improvement, effort, and achievement.
7. It links assessment and teaching to learning.

Gillespie, Ford, Gillespie, and Leavell (1996) report the following advantages for children of using portfolios:

1. Portfolios allow students to reflect on their development and to explore their strengths and weaknesses as readers and writers over time.
2. Portfolios help children to understand the relationship among reading, writing, and thinking.
3. Portfolios allow for children to assume responsibility for their learning.

In order to get children started, the teacher may have to stimulate the reflective process. Perhaps the best way to help children reflect on their own learning is through metacognition. We introduced this concept in Chapter 9, stating that "those who possess well-developed metacognitive abilities understand their own behaviors, use mental strategies they can verbalize, and can assess the quality of their thinking." The guidance teachers give children in developing their independent learning abilities through metacognition will support the children's participation in the assessment process.

Virtually anything teachers can do to get children to think about—and ask questions of—a text before, during, and after they read it will be useful in developing their abilities to assess their own progress. The think-aloud strategy, also introduced in Chapter 9, is one technique. Another is to have children maintain a book log, which is a record of books they have read and their responses to them. Children can record why they chose a particular book, what they liked or did not like about it, and what they learned from it. Glazer and Searfoss (1988) have formalized this suggestion by recommending the use of the chart in Figure 11.2 to record children's thoughts about a book. Teachers can also use the book log as a means of engaging in a dialogue with children during portfolio conferences.

Gillespie and her colleagues (1996) also point out the advantages for parents of using portfolios:

1. Portfolios document their children's acquired knowledge and growth over time.
2. Portfolios can serve as concrete foundations for communication between teachers and parents.

This is not to suggest, however, that there are not some weaknesses in the portfolio system. For one thing, constructing and reviewing portfolios is very time-consuming and therefore requires a commitment on the part of the teacher and the children. For another, portfolios can lead to the one-best-assessment-tool

FIGURE 11.2   Book Log

Title: _____

Author: _____

Reader's Name: _____

Before Reading	**After Reading**

Before Reading

What do you already know about this book without having read it? Make a list below:

_____

_____

_____

_____

_____

_____

_____

Read your list again. Now, because you know these things, what do you think this book will be about? What will you find out about when you read this book?

_____

_____

_____

_____

_____

_____

After Reading

Why did you like this book?
What did you like about it?

_____

_____

What did you not like about it?

_____

_____

Tell what the book is about.

_____

_____

_____

Was your prediction right?

_____ yes _____ no

What is your "kid's rating" for this book?

1   2   3   4   5   6   7

terrible ◀━━━━━━━━▶ terrific

Look at your list again. What was in the book and what was not?

_____ _____

_____ _____

_____ _____

_____ _____

From Susan M. Glazer and Lyndon W. Searfoss, *READING DIAGNOSIS AND INSTRUCTION: A C-A-L-M AP-PROACH,* © 1988, pp. 171–172. Reprinted by permission of Allyn and Bacon, Inc.

mentality. While portfolios do have the advantage of permitting the documentation and assessment of literacy learning in an authentic fashion, they are not THE assessment tool. They are one of several means of assessment that can provide a full, rich image of children (Tierney et al., 1998). Another feature of portfolios is that they take away from traditional instructional time because of the need for portfolio conferences. However, Valencia (1999) suggests that, because of the benefits to the children, these conferences constitute valuable instructional time. They allow children time to reflect on their own literacy learning and to plan with the teacher. Thus the children are also using assessment to guide instruction.

Just how individual teachers organize the information that goes into the portfolio can be left to their discretion, as there is no one prescribed system. We suggest using a three-ring binder with dividers and tabs so that you can easily locate and access work in the portfolio. Following is a list of items that might be included in a portfolio. It covers items the teacher may want to include from other assessment tools, as well as suggestions for children's inclusions. As we noted earlier, although the children must have the freedom to decide what goes into the portfolio, this freedom exists within the context of a collaborative effort between the children and the teacher.

Reading	*Writing*
Literature response activities	Free choice writing
Lists of books read	Assigned compositions
Story maps	Journals
Book reviews	Science observations
Book conference summaries	Various drafts on a topic
Lists of favorite poems/authors	Informal writing tests
Running records	Checklists of mechanics
Questionnaires	List of writing topics
Standardized test results	Ways to write without a pencil
Oral reading on audio tape	

One way of encouraging feelings of ownership of their portfolios is having the children design their own covers.

Children's assessment portfolios are like the portfolios artists develop to display their work to potential buyers. In this case, however, the buyers are those individuals interested in knowing about and providing any necessary instructional assistance with children's artwork.

Process Guide 11.2

Reflect back on the teaching and learning strategies you have read about in this text. What other strategies might you use to help children develop their abilities to assess their own progress? Compare your list with those of other students. Be prepared to explain your choices.

Some Cautions and Comments

The assessment techniques presented in this chapter should be viewed in proper perspective. No single indicator is sufficient grounds for drawing conclusions about a child's abilities or interests. The information obtained from diagnosis should be integrated in order to establish a profile of performance and attitudes. Taken as a whole, the data can be extremely revealing. Of course, how revealing the data prove to be will depend on the individual who interprets the emerging patterns, because assessment is a process requiring decision making by people, not tests.

Our experience is that teachers tend to underestimate their diagnostic potential. More often than not, they will call on an outside source, such as a school psychologist or reading teacher, to confirm suspicions that they have about a child. The irony of this tendency is that, through working with the child on a day-to-day basis, the teacher probably knows more than a brief diagnostic session can hope to reveal. By always appealing to authority in the form of standardized tests or learning specialists, teachers fail to give themselves credit for their own powers of perception. In yielding to the advice of the specialists against their better judgment, teachers run the risk of harming or cheating the child in the process.

There are other ways in which children can be harmed by assessment. One of the most damaging is the practice of labeling. From the first day that children enter school, they are evaluated. Initially, there is a readiness test, then later a wide assortment of achievement and diagnostic measures. Children are expected to keep pace with a nonexistent standard known as *the average*. Heaven help the child who dares to dip below the criterion of acceptable performance! The child may spend the remainder of his or her school experiences trying to escape from the label. Even worse, some children just quit trying altogether. For them, the label becomes a self-fulfilling prophecy: They perform according to the expectations that are held of them. They are told that they are slow, or poor learners, or dyslexic; any number of terms may be used to indicate that they are seriously different from their peers. If these children did not have an irreconcilable problem before they were labeled, they probably do afterwards.

Why are children labeled at all? When a child does not keep pace, all the adults associated with the child begin to look for answers. They feel an obligation to try to do what is best. When the adults are unable to solve the learning problem, panic sets in and labels start to flow. They assume that by attaching some label to the problem they have begun to correct it. After all, that is precisely what occurs in the medical community. Doctors examine the symptoms, apply various diagnostic tests, label the disease, and prescribe appropriate treatment. Although this paradigm works well for physical ailments, it cannot always be applied to the way children behave and think. In education, we tend to label children as a means of explaining and justifying our inability to help them. If a label results in improved achievement and no long-lasting emotional stigma is attached to the child, then the label has served its purpose. However, if labels merely help adults cope with their own frustration, they should not be used at all.

Summary

In this chapter, the importance of assessing children's reading skills and strategies was examined. Assessment is the foundation of instruction. It allows teachers to determine what concepts need to be taught and the best ways to go about doing so. Standardized tests were discussed as a means of identifying children's levels of functioning, and portfolios were recommended for collecting performance data. With this knowledge, teachers can select, utilize, and interpret the results of instruments that most closely meet their diagnostic goals and needs. As teachers gain increased facility with reading assessment, children will be assured of more meaningful instruction.

FOLLOW-THROUGH ACTIVITIES

Note: Level 1 activities require limited access to children or classrooms. Level 2 activities should be completed using children and classrooms.

Level 1 Activities

1. Interview a parent and a teacher. Ask them about their thoughts on testing and how they use—or what they think about—test information. Share your results with a small group of students in your class.

2. Interview both a primary- and an intermediate-level teacher. What types of assessment tools do they use? What kinds of information do they get from each tool that helps them with their instructional decision making?

Level 2 Activities

1. Observe a teacher who uses portfolio assessment. How does the teacher use the information in the portfolios to communicate the effectiveness of his/her classroom?

2. Select two children and begin to develop a portfolio of their reading and writing performance. Use both child and teacher assessments in developing the portfolio. After a two- to three-week period of data gathering, write a report on their progress in their reading/writing interactions. What did you find out? Are the children making progress?

WORKING WITH PARENTS

```
Dear Parent,
Rather than just send your child's standardized test
results home, we have decided to write this letter to
give you an explanation of what those scores mean.
```

First of all, you will see that there are separate scores for vocabulary and comprehension, as well as a score for total reading. The total reading score is simply an average of your child's scores on the vocabulary and comprehension subtests.

Second, you will see two types of scores reported. One is called a percentile score; the other is a grade-equivalent score. Both are indications of your child's performance in relation to that of other children of the same age and grade level. For example, if your child had a percentile score of 78, it means that your child scored as well as or better than 78 percent of the children in that grade who took the test. The grade-equivalent score, on the other hand, is a little different. For instance, if your child had a score of 3.8, it would indicate that your child probably performed the same as the average third grader taking that test in the eighth month of the school year.

We use "probably" because your child's test results are just an estimate of your child's ability. They are an estimate because many factors can affect your child's performance, such as time limitations, interest, etc. Therefore, if we are concerned about your child's performance, we will give your child an individual examination designed to diagnose any reading difficulties that might be affecting your child's ability to read successfully. In this way, we can provide the kind of instruction required to help your child become a better reader.

The reason we give the children a standardized test is twofold. First, we can report to the parents how well the children as a group are performing in reading, compared with other groups of children across the state and country. Additionally, the tests allow us to evaluate our instructional program. By examining the performance of all children at a particular grade level, we can adjust our program to better meet the needs of children not doing as well as other children who took the test.

We hope this letter has helped you better understand the test, your child's scores, and why we give this test.

Please feel free to visit or call if you have any
questions about our testing program.

Thank you.

Sincerely,

John S. Fair, Principal
Haven Elementary School

RESOURCES

Barrentine, S. J. (Ed.). (1999). *Reading assessment: Principles and practices for elementary teachers*. Newark, DE: International Reading Association.

This collection of articles from *The Reading Teacher* covers theory and practice in literacy assessment.

Calfee, R. C., & Hiebert, E. H. (1991). Classroom assessment of reading. In R. Barr, M. L. Kamil, P. B. Mosenthal, & P. D. Pearson (Eds.), *Handbook of reading research: Volume II* (pp. 281–309). New York: Longman.

This article reviews the literature on literacy assessment.

Hiebert, E. H., & Calfee, R. C. (1992). Assessing literacy: From standardized tests to portfolios and performances. In S. J. Samuels & A. E. Farstrup (Eds.), *What research has to say about reading instruction* (2nd ed., pp. 70–100). Newark, DE: International Reading Association.

The impact of standardized tests is examined, and alternative forms of assessment are discussed.

Tierney, R. J., Carter, M. A., & Desai, L. E. (1991). *Portfolio assessment in the reading-writing classroom*. Norwood, MA: Christopher-Gordon.

This text is designed to provide teachers with a framework for implementing portfolios in their classrooms.

Tierney, R. J., & Readence, J. E. (2000). *Reading strategies and practices: A compendium* (5th ed.). Boston: Allyn & Bacon.

Unit 14 presents a discussion of assessment strategies.

Wiener, R. B., & Cohen, J. H. (1997). *Literacy portfolios: Using assessment to guide instruction*. Upper Saddle River, NJ: Prentice Hall.

The authors provide a framework for setting up literacy portfolios, ideas for using portfolios to guide instruction, and classroom examples of teachers who use portfolios.

REFERENCES

Farr, R. (1999). Putting it all together: Solving the reading assessment. In S. J. Barrentine (Ed.), *Reading assessment: Principles and practices for elementary teachers* (pp. 44–56). Newark, DE: International Reading Association.

Gillespie, C. S., Ford, K. L., Gillespie, R. D., & Leavell, A. G. (1996). Portfolio assessment: Some questions, some answers, some recommendations. *Journal of Adolescent and Adult Literacy, 39,* 480–491.

Glazer, S. M., & Searfoss, L. W. (1988). *Reading diagnosis and instruction: A C-A-L-M approach.* Englewood Cliffs, NJ: Prentice Hall.

Tierney, R. J., Carter, M. A., & Desai, L. E. (1991). *Portfolio assessment in the reading-writing classroom.* Norwood, MA: Christopher-Gordon.

Tierney, R. J., Clark, C., Fenner, L., Herter, R. J., Simpson, C. S., & Wiser, B. (1998). Portfolios: Assumptions, tensions, and possibilities. *Reading Research Quarterly, 33,* 474–486.

Valencia, S. (1999). A portfolio approach to classroom reading assessment: The whys, whats, and hows. In S. J. Barrentine (Ed.), *Reading assessment: Principles and practices for elementary teachers* (pp. 113–117). Newark, DE: International Reading Association.

Wiener, R. B., & Cohen, J. H. (1997). *Literacy portfolios: Using assessment to guide instruction.* Upper Saddle River, NJ: Prentice Hall.

12 Adapting Instruction for Children with Disabilities

KYLE HIGGINS

RANDALL BOONE
University of Nevada, Las Vegas

INTRODUCTION

The ability to read is essential for social and economic success in our society and has been identified as necessary for competitiveness in a technological society (Snow, Burns, & Griffin, 1998). As a society we have long recognized the importance of successful reading; however, only recently have we begun to understand the profound and enduring consequences of not learning to read (Juel, 1988; Lyon & Chhabra, 1996). The lack of proficient reading skills has been identified as a risk factor associated not only with academic failure and school dropout but also with unemployment and trouble with the law (Cornwall & Bawden, 1992; Werner, 1993). Whitman (1995) found that individuals who test in the least proficient literacy levels are often unemployable, as even low-skilled jobs demand adequate reading abilities. Thus a vicious cycle begins. If you cannot read, you do not practice. If you do not practice, you do not become automatic and fluent in your ability to recognize words. And if you do not read, you do not succeed in today's world.

Although experts do not agree on the exact number of poor readers caught in this cycle, a report from the Department of Education (National Center for Education Statistics, 1993) indicates that 90 million of the 191 million adults in the United States either are illiterate or can perform only simple literacy tasks. National longitudinal studies suggest that one in six school-age children will encounter a problem in learning to read (National Center to Improve the Tools of Educators, 1996) and that reading failure is the most "significant reason that children are retained, assigned to special education, or given long-term remedial services" (Learning First Alliance, 1998, p. 52).

Particularly affected are those students with disabilities. These children are given a variety of labels by the educational system—students with learning disabilities, students with mental retardation, students with communication disorders, at-risk students. Regardless of the label, most of these students have one characteristic in common: They struggle to read. Among the millions of Americans who have learning disabilities, at least 75 percent have been identified as having a reading disability (National Institute of Child Health and Human Development [NICHD], 1994). The viciousness of this cycle is exemplified by recent research indicating that the problem emerges during the first three years of school (National Center to Improve the Tools of Educators, 1996) and that 74 percent of those who are unsuccessful readers in the third grade are still unsuccessful readers in the ninth grade (Lyon, 1995).

Thus Stanovich's (1986) application of the *Matthew effects* concept—the rich get richer and the poor get poorer—is very true for students who struggle to read. The ramifications of not learning to read on the lives of these children are profound. Not only are the paths to subject matter blocked, but social and personal relationships are affected as well. We live in a society that places much value on literacy—a person who does not learn to read suffers greatly (Lerner, 1997).

GRAPHIC ORGANIZER

This graphic organizer summarizes the structure of Chapter 12:

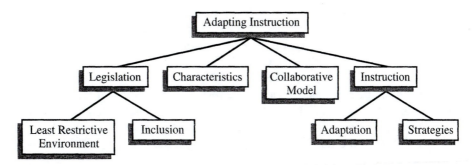

O B J E C T I V E S

When you finish this chapter, you should be able to understand and discuss each of these statements:

1. For most children with disabilities, reading is the first problem identified by classroom teachers, leading to referral and eventual delivery of special education services.
2. Special education is a service, not a place, and involves individualized instruction for children with disabilities.
3. The least restrictive environment for learning for many children with disabilities is the general education classroom.
4. Public Law 94-142 provides for free, appropriate public education for all children.
5. Reauthorization of the Individuals with Disabilities Act (IDEA-1997, P.L. 105-17) places greater emphasis on the inclusion of children with disabilities in the general education curriculum.
6. Reauthorization of the Individuals with Disabilities Act (IDEA-1997, P.L. 105-17) mandates greater participation by general educators as members of the individualized education program (IEP) writing team.
7. Instructional modifications can be made in the general education classroom to help children with reading disabilities achieve success in school.
8. General education teachers, special educators, and educational assistants must work together to plan instruction for students with disabilities within the general education community.

Legislation and the Least Restrictive Environment

Today in the United States all children have a right to attend public school. Each state has a legal obligation to provide a free, appropriate education to all children regardless of their race, economic level, ethnic group, gender, skill level, or disability. For children with disabilities, this right came later than it did for other groups. With the passage of the Education for All Handicapped Children's Act (EHA, P.L. 94-142) in 1975, a free, appropriate education for all children with disabilities became a right and a reality.

The Education for All Handicapped Children's Act guarantees children with disabilities and their parents certain rights, and it places specific responsibilities on people who deliver services to children with disabilities. This law is the foundation on which current special education practice is built. It mandates that children be placed in the least restrictive environment (LRE). It states that, to the extent appropriate, children with disabilities should be educated with children without disabilities; furthermore, removal from the general education environment should occur only when the nature or the severity of the disability is such that education cannot be achieved satisfactorily in the general education environment with the use of supplementary aids and services. EHA requires that each child with a disability have a written individual education program (IEP) plan developed in a meeting attended by a representative of the school, the child's current teacher, the parents/legal guardian, the child, and the special educator or counselor. It also defines the procedures for identifying a student as needing special education services, outlines the rights of parents to disagree with the educational services provided by the school, clarifies related services to which a child might be entitled (e.g., speech therapy, transportation, physical therapy, and occupational therapy), and describes the categories of disabilities that make a child eligible for special education services.

In 1986, a series of changes to EHA began with the passage of P.L. 99-457. Congress authorized expansion of the provisions of special education law to children from 3 to 5 years of age and encouraged states to provide services to infants and toddlers. The focus for services is the entire family, with the law mandating an individualized family service plan (IFSP) for families with children age 5 and under.

In 1990, the Act was renamed the Individuals with Disabilities Education Act of 1990 (IDEA, P.L. 101-476). The intent was to reaffirm the commitment to support appropriate education for all children with disabilities. IDEA has more contemporary person-first language, and it substitutes the preferred term *disability* for the term *handicapped*. IDEA upholds the major provisions of EHA, but it adds significantly to the provisions for very young children with disabilities and for students preparing to leave secondary school. The law mandates that a description of transition services for students with disabilities be provided at age 16 (age 14 for students with more severe disabilities). The categories of *autism* and *traumatic brain injury* were added at this time, and Congress welcomed further public comments on defining *attention deficit disorder* in the law.

The Individuals with Disabilities Education Act Amendments of 1997 (P.L. 105-17) were signed into law in June, 1997. The law reauthorized IDEA and added a number of new provisions. Several provisions are important for educators involved in providing services to students with disabilities in the general education environment. Recognizing that most students with disabilities spend the majority of their time in the general education classroom, IDEA-1997 mandates that a general education teacher be a part of the IEP writing team. Acknowledging that students with disabilities have often been excluded from local and state assessments, the law also adds a requirement that all students with disabilities be assessed in the same manner as typical students, using the same assessment tool or an alternative tool. In order to prepare students with disabilities for life after school, the age for transition planning was lowered to 14 for all students. The law also mandated the training and supervision of educational assistants who participate in the provision of services to students with disabilities.

IDEA-1997 places greater emphasis on student participation in the general education curriculum than did the past laws. It required reconceptualizing the IEP as a much broader document, encompassing student goals and objectives for general education as well as special education services.

Not only have federal laws made it illegal not to include all children with disabilities in our public school system and provide them with an equal education;

they have become much more specific concerning the type of education offered and where that education should occur. The law is reemphasizing the concept of the least restrictive environment and is pointing educators more and more in the direction of general education.

Current Trends in Special Education

Over the past 15 years, the movement in special education has been toward providing educational services for students with disabilities in the general education classroom. This trend toward serving students with disabilities in more inclusive programs has been motivated by a number of factors, the primary one being the least restrictive environment (LRE) clause of IDEA (U.S. Department of Education, 1998). In fact, IDEA-1997 mandates that the placement of students with disabilities in settings other than general education classes be specifically justified. The law goes on to state that placement in a setting other than the general education classroom may occur only after intensive supports have been provided to keep the child in the general education classroom.

The U.S. Department of Education's 20th Annual Report to Congress (1998) indicates that in the 1995–96 school year more than 95 percent of students ages 6–21 with disabilities attended schools with their peers without disabilities. The data indicate a gradual increase in the percentage of students with disabilities who are educated in general education classes for at least 80 percent of the school day. Approximately 46 percent of all students with disabilities are removed from their general education classes for less than 21 percent of the school day. Conversely, the data reflect a decrease in the number of students who are removed from general education for 21 to 60 percent of the school day. Overall, there has been a clear decrease in resource room use by students with disabilities.

The concept of providing special education services in the inclusive community of the general education classroom has its basis in the philosophical ideology that favors normalization of children with disabilities and elimination of labels for these children (Lerner, 1997). The underlying belief is that all students have the basic human right to attend their neighborhood school with their typical peers (Edgar, 1987; Ferguson, 1996; Sawyer, McLaughlin, & Winglee, 1994). This philosophy holds that moving students with disabilities away from their typical peers highlights their disabilities, disrupts or fragments their education, and teaches them to be dependent (Friend & Bursuck, 1999). The goal is to provide education in a setting that more closely approximates the real world that the students will live in once they leave school.

The emphasis on including students with disabilities in the general education classroom also reflects growing recognition that many students with disabilities complete high school without the knowledge and skills necessary for adult independence (U.S. Department of Education, 1997; Wagner et al., 1992). For all students with disabilities, the major factor predicting successful high school graduation is the ability to read at a fourth-grade level (U.S. Department of Education,

1998). Yet data collected by the National Longitudinal Transition Study (NLTS) indicate that three to five years after leaving high school fewer than 25 percent of youth with disabilities were enrolled in postsecondary education, those who were employed were engaged in low-wage jobs with few opportunities for promotion, and more than half continued to live with their parents (Wagner et al., 1992)—all factors that have been correlated with lack of reading proficiency (Cornwall & Bawden, 1992; Werner, 1993; Whitman, 1995).

The Debate about Inclusion

Few professionals question a student's human right to interact in a heterogeneous society. However, the field of special education continues to debate which students with disabilities should be included in general education classes and exactly how much time they should spend there. On one side of the debate are those educators who seriously question the assumption that students in need of special education services should receive those services in a segregated setting—that is, a special education room (McLeskey & Waldron, 1996; Sailor, 1991; Skrtic, Sailor, & Gee, 1996). On the other side are those who maintain that only students who can meet certain performance standards and rate of academic performance standards should be included in a general education classroom (Fuchs & Fuchs, 1995; Kauffman, 1995). Most educators fall somewhere between the two groups (Chalmers & Faliede, 1996). Regardless of one's beliefs about this debate, however, it is important to remember that the placement or setting is not a treatment; what goes on in the setting is the treatment (Zigmond, 1995). In short, special education is not a place; rather, it is a service and as such can be provided in any appropriate environment.

Advocates for inclusion have described the benefits of educating students with disabilities in the general education environment. These researchers have examined the impact on students with disabilities and their peers without disabilities.

Benefits for Students with Disabilities

The benefits to students with disabilities of being integrated into general education classrooms include the following:

1. Children with severe disabilities experience more social interaction when they are in the inclusive environment of a general education classroom (Brinker, 1985).
2. Students with disabilities, both mild and more severe, in the general education classroom work more on academic tasks than their peers in special classes do (Hunt et al., 1994).
3. Students who are included in general education classrooms make greater gains in academic skills than do students who receive special education services in separate settings (Giangreco et al., 1993; Ryndak et al., 1995).

4. Students with disabilities receive a fuller range of instruction in the general education classroom than they do in special education pull-out programs (e.g., exposure to social studies and science) (Simpson & Myles, 1990; Wang & Reynolds, 1996).
5. When they are included in the general education classroom, students with disabilities spend more time with other students and less time alone (Hunt et al., 1994).
6. The stigmatization that so often occurs when students with disabilities are segregated is lessened (Lilly, 1992), and the students learn that they are full class members, not second-class citizens who are somehow inferior to their peers (Hahn, 1989).
7. When they are included in the general education classroom, students with disabilities form more friendships with students without disabilities. (Evans et al., 1992; Hendrickson et al., 1996).

Benefits for Students without Disabilities

Students without disabilities can likewise derive benefits from being part of a class that includes peers with disabilities:

1. Students without disabilities exhibit increased acceptance and understanding of students with disabilities and are more likely to acknowledge their similarities (York et al., 1992).

Students without disabilities learn that people with disabilities are more like them then they are different.

2. Students without disabilities exhibit increased tolerance for diversity (McLeskey & Waldron, 1996) and indicate that they have become more comfortable around people who differ from them (Peck, Carlson, & Helmstetter, 1992).
3. The academic grades, test scores, and ratings of social behavior of the children without disabilities do not decrease as a result of being in classrooms with children with disabilities (Sharpe, York, & Knight, 1994).
4. Middle school students without disabilities indicate that they feel personal satisfaction as a result of their interactions with peers with severe disabilities. Areas of benefit identified by the students include improved self-concept and social cognition, reduced fear of differences, greater tolerance of others, development of personal principles, and the opportunity to experience nondemanding friendships (Peck, Donaldson, & Pezzoli, 1990).
5. The flexibility and social and emotional development of students without disabilities increase as a result of their frequent interaction with students with disabilities (Giangreco et al., 1993).
6. Students without disabilities learn that they live in a heterogeneous world and that disabilities are simply one type of diversity. This leads to the understanding that people with disabilities are more like them than they are different (McLeskey & Waldron, 1996).

Those who support the inclusion of students with disabilities only under certain circumstances offer these concerns:

1. Treating all students alike may deny some students with disabilities their right to an individualized education and may be a violation of the federal special education law (Council for Exceptional Children, 1993).
2. Teachers will continue business as usual and will not make appropriate modifications for students with disabilities (Zigmond & Baker, 1990).
3. General education classrooms and the teachers who work in them are not always prepared to meet the needs of students with disabilities (Vaughn et al., 1996).
4. The supports needed to make inclusion work properly often are not in place in a school (Vaughn & Schumm, 1995).
5. For students with disabilities who need a more specialized, structured environment than the general education classroom, alternative placements may no longer be provided (Kauffman, 1995).

Regardless of where one stands on this debate, the reality is that the scope of services for students with disabilities is changing rapidly (U.S. Department of Education, 1998). For more and more students, the least restrictive environment is being defined as the general education classroom. In this time of change, all those involved in education are in the position of having to reevaluate their roles in the educational process. It is important that teachers learn about the special education services in their schools and define their roles in teaching students with disabilities in the general education community (Friend & Bursuck, 1999). The goal of this redefinition of roles is for all who work in public education to work together to create a cooperative interdisciplinary team that supports each member, as well as all of the students—with and without disabilities—who reside within their care.

Process Guide 12.1

Break into small groups. Each group should select one item from the benefits listed previously and one item from the concerns listed and compare and contrast the two items.

Characteristics of Children with Disabilities

Just exactly who are these students with disabilities? In education we have arbitrarily divided children into three groups: those with disabilities, those without disabilities, and those at risk for school failure. We discuss these groups of children as if they were distinctly different from one another, and we place them into educational environments—general education and special education—as if those differences were distinct enough to warrant separating the groups from one another. The reality is that all children differ from one another in individual characteristics and backgrounds along a continuum. Because the differences among most children are relatively small (e.g., some are taller than others, some wear glasses, some are better at spelling), most children can benefit from the general education program. Inclusion of students with disabilities in the general education program maximizes the potential of most students, ensures their rights, and is the preferred option whenever possible (Friend & Bursuck, 1999).

Children who require special services to reach their potential are more like their typical peers than they are different from them. But just as all the children in a classroom are unique individuals, so are children with disabilities. It is important not to generalize—assigning the characteristics of one child with a particular disability to another child with the same disability. A key to working with students with disabilities is recognizing that they are a heterogeneous group and that even students with the same disability (e.g., learning disability, mental retardation) and the same level of a disability (e.g., mild, moderate, severe) are individuals with unique learning needs.

No two children with a disability experience their disability in exactly the same way. Some children have problems in a very specific area, such as the fine motor skills involved in handwriting. Some children have obvious physical disabilities, such as blindness. Other children have less obvious yet just as pervasive disabilities, such as difficulty in reading, conceptualizing, and/or organizing their work. Still others may experience no academic problems but have difficulties with their social relationships. While students with disabilities are a diverse group of individuals, they do share one characteristic—they do not learn in the same manner or as efficiently as their peers without disabilities. These students differ from typical students in the intensity, frequency, and sophistication of their behavioral or academic repertoires (Choate, 1997). Because of this, special considerations must be taken into account when developing instruction for these students.

Although the problems of children with reading disabilities may originate from a variety of factors (e.g., physical, environmental, psychological) (Kirk, Kliebhan, & Lerner, 1978), they often produce similar behavioral characteristics when the child reads. Mercer (1991) categorizes the characteristics that teachers may observe into four problem areas (see Figure 12.1).

The behavioral characteristics of students who experience difficulty with reading have been identified by Hallahan, Kauffman, and Lloyd (1999). These characteristics, while less overt than those cited by Mercer, nonetheless have a profound effect on the child's reading proficiency and how individualized instruction is developed for the child. Students may experience a problem in only one area or in several areas (see Figure 12.2). It is important to consider both the reading problem area and the behavioral characteristics when planning instruction for these students. Such instruction must be comprehensive and thorough.

Process Guide 12.2

Break into small groups and discuss the following questions: (1) How are children with disabilities similar to children without disabilities? (2) How are children with disabilities different from children without disabilities? (3) How should a classroom teacher address the issue of providing appropriate instruction to all children in a classroom?

Collaboration among Educators

In the past, teaching—whether general education or special education—was characterized by autonomy. Teachers most often worked in isolation, consulting with each other infrequently if at all (Little, 1982). A typical teacher's day was spent alone with students in the classroom. Teachers were expected to possess all the skills needed to deal with whatever problems might arise in that classroom—behaviorally and academically. They rarely had the opportunity to discuss problems or concerns about students, ask for advice from others, or seek help from others. This atmosphere of isolation in schools is changing. Teachers often meet in grade-level teams to share and problem solve, and they create interdisciplinary teams to work on curricula (Friend & Bursuck, 1999). With the inclusion of students with disabilities in the general education classroom, more and more collaboration between general education teachers and special education teachers is occurring. General education teachers

FIGURE 12.1   Behavioral Characteristics of Students with Reading Disabilities

Problem Area	Behavioral Characteristics Observed
Reading habits	■ Tension movements—appears tense when reading (e.g., frowns, bites lip) ■ Insecurity—refuses to read or cries when asked to read ■ Loss of place—frequently loses place when reading or engages in frequent repetitions ■ Lateral head motion—jerks head when reading ■ Holds material too close
Word recognition errors	■ Omissions—frequently omits words when reading orally ■ Insertions—frequently inserts words when reading orally ■ Substitutions—frequently substitutes words that change the meaning when reading orally ■ Reversal—reverses letter order in words, changing the meaning of the words (e.g., "no" for "on") ■ Mispronunciations—frequently mispronounces words when reading orally, changing their meaning ■ Transpositions—often transposes word order when reading orally ■ Unknown words—hesitates (pausing for 5 seconds or more) on words he/she cannot pronounce ■ Slow, choppy reading—reads slowly, without fluency (e.g., 20–30 words per minute)
Comprehension errors	■ Inability to recall basic story facts—experiences difficulty with specific questions about the story ■ Inability to recall items in a sequence—has a difficult time telling the sequence of occurrences in a story ■ Inability to recall the main idea(s)—has difficulty identifying the main idea of a story
Miscellaneous symptoms	■ Word-by-word reading—reads in a slow, halting manner ■ Strained, high-pitched voice—reads in a voice higher than his/her regular voice tone ■ Inadequate phrasing—pauses inappropriately when reading aloud, affecting meaning ■ Ignoring or misinterpreting punctuation—runs phrases, clauses, and/or sentences together

Adapted from Mercer, 1991, p. 498.

and their special education colleagues are forming interdisciplinary teams to support one another, develop appropriate instructional plans for students with disabilities within the general education classroom, and ensure the success of students with disabilities in the inclusive community.

FIGURE 12.2   **Behavioral Characteristics of Students with Reading Problems**

Problem Area	Behavioral Characteristics Observed
Problems with aspects of language Because reading and writing are both language-based tools, students with reading disabilities often manifest written language problems.	■ Messy handwriting ■ Poor spelling ■ Simple and disorganized sentences
Problems with phonological awareness For students with reading problems, phonological skills are intimately linked to reading skill. Students may not understand that words can be broken into syllables or phonemes.	■ Lack of understanding of the system ■ Lack of fluency when reading orally ■ Comprehension difficulties ■ Mispronunciation of words ■ Poor spelling
Problems with syntax Students may not use word clusters to guide their reading, or they may confuse the relationship of the words read.	■ Difficulty with syntax ■ Comprehension difficulties
Problems with semantics Students struggle to understand the meaning of passages read.	■ Slow in reading unknown words ■ Reading mistakes that change the meaning of the passage ■ Inefficient reading strategies ■ Poor decoding skills ■ Poor vocabularies ■ Overreliance on context clues to compensate for deficits in decoding skills ■ Poor reading comprehension ■ Inability to understand the gist of the information read (e.g., the theme of a narrative) ■ Focus on minor details of a reading passage, caused by overreliance on background knowledge ■ Provision of idiosyncratic information in response to comprehension questions

Adapted from Hallahan, Kauffman, & Lloyd, 1999, pp. 333–338.

Collaboration describes how the general educator and the special educator work together, not what they do (Friend & Bursuck, 1999). Collaboration is a process, not a product. It is an intangible, based on the style professionals use to accomplish the goal they share (Cook & Friend, 1993). A collaborative relationship between the general educator and the special educator is a key element in the success of the child with disabilities within the general education classroom.

Creating a collaborative relationship requires effort by all involved. This interactive process enables professionals with diverse expertise to contribute to a common solution to problems shared by the group (Idol, Paolucci-Whitcomb, & Nevin, 1986). For the process to be successful, the participants must be aware of and nurture the components of successful collaboration (see Figure 12.3).

It is important to remember that effective collaboration encompasses the belief that all students can succeed in school (Olson & Rodman, 1988) and that, regardless of current barriers, all students have the right to an appropriate education. It is through collaborative efforts that the responsibility to provide these opportunities to all students within all classrooms and within all schools is met (Goldring & Rallis, 1993).

Collaborative Consultative Model

The term *collaborative consultative model* has become popular in the effective school literature and in special education literature. In this model, special educators work collaboratively with general educators as instructional consultants. This process of collaborative consultation has been described as "an interactive process that enables professionals with diverse expertise to generate creative solutions to mutually defined problems" (Idol et al., 1986, p. 1). The collaborative approach greatly enhances the likelihood of success because the proposed solutions or strategies are generated from a wider knowledge base than is possessed by any single person (Wood, 1992).

The collaborative consultative partnership may include other general education teachers, special education teachers, educational assistants, speech therapists, counselors, parents, and others. All participants in the collaborative consultative model work together in a specialized problem-solving process. Consultation is most effective when it is based on the principles of collaboration discussed earlier; however, it has a more direct purpose than collaboration. Its goal is to help the general education teacher to resolve a problem or concern that exists in the classroom (Friend & Bursuck, 1999). Thus the crucial role of the general educator in the consultative model is to ask the right questions and relay critical information in a timely manner to the special education teacher or consultant.

The collaborative consultative process usually begins with the general education teacher's completion of a written request form indicating a behavioral or academic concern about a particular student. It is important that the teacher's concern be carefully described in observable terms (e.g., "student cannot answer inferential comprehension questions," not "student cannot remember anything"). The consultant in the school (e.g., special educator, counselor, speech therapist) then contacts the teacher to arrange a meeting. At the meeting they discuss expectations for students in the teacher's classroom and how this particular student is not meeting these expectations in the area of concern. This meeting allows the teacher and the consultant to further clarify concerns and to target exactly what the consultant should look for on a visit to the classroom.

The consultant arranges a time to visit the classroom and observe the child in the activity of concern (e.g., reading). The consultant gathers information on the

FIGURE 12.3   Components of Effective Collaboration

Component	Suggestions
Goals are shared Philosophies concerning the goal, resources, and knowledge must be discussed.	■ Work on establishing a personal relationship ■ Respect one another's philosophies ■ Listen to one another
Participation is voluntary Collaboration cannot be forced; participants must make a personal commitment to be involved.	■ Invite participation ■ Nurture those who choose to participate ■ Do not overburden those who participate
Parity is valued All who participate must truly believe that each person has valuable knowledge and expertise to contribute to the process.	■ Recognize that all participants are well-trained professionals ■ Recognize that there exists more than one solution to a problem ■ Rotate and share leadership roles
Equity is valued All who participate are responsible for contributing to the common goal. Everyone is an equal partner in the process.	■ Use names, not titles, when interacting ■ Volunteer for activities ■ Be aware if one person is assigned or takes on more duties than others
Responsibility is shared All who participate must share the responsibility for participation and decision making.	■ Delineate clearly all agreed-upon actions and follow-up activities ■ Communicate frequently—in writing or in person ■ Create a balance between coordination of tasks and division of labor—divide work equally ■ Spend time brainstorming solutions before decision making
Accountability for outcomes is shared All who participate must share accountability for the results of their decisions—positive or negative.	■ Adopt a learn-from-failure-or-success mind set ■ Do not fear acknowledging risks or potential failure ■ Celebrate successes together ■ Support one another through difficult times
Resources are shared Each participant must be willing to share his or her resources (e.g., time, expertise, equipment, materials).	■ Identify personal resources for the group ■ Make joint decisions concerning resource allocation ■ Adopt a group mind set concerning resources
Collaboration is seen as an emergent entity Each participant must understand that the process of collaboration grows and matures over time.	■ Nurture relationships ■ Work on building trust ■ Respect one another ■ Share in decision making

Adapted from Friend & Cook, 1996; Vandercook, York, & Sullivan, 1993.

child's behavior before and after the area of concern, as well as academic data concerning the child's performance. Often the consultant makes several observations, to ensure advice or modifications take into consideration all variables affecting the child's progress; it is important to ascertain whether the problem might be an environmental one, lying outside of the child (e.g., time of day, day of the week).

After the observations have been completed, the teacher and the consultant meet again to discuss what was observed. At this meeting they work together to (1) clarify understanding of the problem; (2) generate strategies or modifications for dealing with the problem; (3) select and prioritize strategies or modifications for dealing with the problem; (4) create a plan to implement the strategies in the classroom; (5) identify resources, personnel, or other supports needed to implement the plan; (6) establish a time line for putting the strategies into effect in the classroom; and (7) schedule another meeting to evaluate the plan. Typically, it is the responsibility of the general educator to implement the plan in the classroom.

At the evaluation meeting, the consultant and the teacher determine whether the strategies or modifications have alleviated the identified problem. If the problem has been taken care of satisfactorily, the strategy or modification may be continued for increased results or eliminated if it is no longer needed. If the problem has not been alleviated, the next strategy on the prioritized list may be implemented or the consultant and the teacher may begin the problem-solving process all over again (Friend & Bursuck, 1999).

Wood (1992, p. 87) suggests that general educators use the following self-evaluation questions to assess their contributions to the consultative process.

1. Do I give the suggested adaptations a fair trial before concluding that they are inappropriate or ineffective?
2. In the consultant's absence, do I keep a running log of questions, observations, and comments regarding mainstreamed children to share with the consultant at a later time?
3. If a recommended approach is not feasible for use in my classroom or conflicts with my professional values, do I clearly make the consultant aware of this instead of carrying it out inconsistently or not at all?
4. Do I make a conscientious effort not to treat the children with disabilities as too special, particularly during activities when adaptations are not necessary?
5. Do I and staff members under my supervision maintain confidentiality pertaining to the identification of and issues related to the individual needs of mainstreamed children in our classroom?
6. If there are unresolved issues or questions regarding any aspect of the consultative relationship, do I share them with the consultant before discussing them with other teachers and administrators?

Friend and Bursuck (1999) suggest that special educators and general educators work together to apply a systematic approach to identifying areas of concern or need for students with disabilities in the general education classroom. They believe that this approach will facilitate the identification of reasonable accommodations for all students. The INCLUDE strategy (Friend & Bursuck, 1999) is based on the assumptions that student performance is the result of the interaction between the student and the classroom environment and that by carefully observing the student and the environment teachers can reasonably accommodate most students with disabilities in their classroom. The strategy is designed to maximize student success without taking a large amount of teacher time, and it is founded on the premise that the accommodations made for students with disabilities are often appropriate for other students in the classroom who do not have disabilities. The INCLUDE strategy for accommodating students with disabilities in the general education community involves seven diagnostic steps (Friend & Bursuck, 1999, p. 109):

Step 1: Identify classroom environmental, curricular, and instructional demands. Typical classroom demands that affect student learning and behavior are classroom organization, grouping of students, lighting, noise level, instructional materials, student evaluation, and instructional methods.

Step 2: Note student learning strengths and needs. Because students with disabilities are such a heterogeneous group, one cannot assume anything about their learning profile. Students with disabilities have strengths and weaknesses in a variety of learning areas, and these must be considered when developing instruction for them. Important areas to consider are basic skills, learning strategies, survival skills, social-emotional development (e.g., interpersonal skills, self-concept), and physical development (e.g., motor skills, vision).

Step 3: Check for potential areas of student success. This step involves focusing on what the student can do well and building the student's strengths into instructional planning. For example, if a student has trouble reading but has good handwriting, the student would be assigned the role of notetaker of a group. Building in opportunities for students to feel successful and work in an area of strength enhances self-concept.

Step 4: Look for potential problem areas. This step involves assessment of the student's disability in terms of the instructional context to ascertain whether there is a potential discrepancy between teacher expectations and student ability.

Step 5: Use the information gathered to brainstorm instructional adaptations. If a discrepancy exists that might keep a student from succeeding, the special educator and the general educator need to brainstorm solutions to eliminate or minimize the effects of the discrepancy. This is where accommodations and adaptations within the general education classroom are identified.

Step 6: Decide which adaptations to implement. In this step the general educator and the special educator select adaptations to implement within the general education classroom. Considerations when selecting adaptations are

(a) Adaptations should be age-appropriate (e.g., no blue bunnies for high school students).

(b) Adaptation ideas should be prioritized and the easiest one implemented first. (Keep in mind that any adaptation selected will often be appropriate for other students in your classroom, too.)

(c) Adaptations should be based on student needs, not teacher convenience (IDEA-1997 is clear that the student takes precedence).

(d) Adaptations should promote the active participation of the child with the disability with her/his general education peers.

(e) Adaptations used should be those that the research literature has shown to be effective for students with disabilities.

Step 7: Evaluate student progress. Once the adaptation has been implemented, its effectiveness should be evaluated regularly. You may evaluate effectiveness through grades, observations, charting and graphing, portfolios, performance assessments, and ratings (e.g., teacher, student, parent). Gathering this information on a regular basis will provide important guidance on whether the adaptation should be continued or changed.

Working with Educational Assistants

A key component in working with students with disabilities in the general education classroom is the educational assistant. A variety of job titles are used throughout the United States to refer to school personnel who assist in the education of students with disabilities. These titles include paraeducator, educational aide, instructional assistant, paraprofessional, teacher's assistant, and educational assistant. Pickett (1988) defined educational assistants as school employees "whose position is either instructional in nature or who deliver other direct or indirect services to students and/or parents; and who work under the supervision of a teacher or other professional staff member who is responsible for the overall conduct of the class, the design and implementation of individualized educational programs, and the assessment of the effect of the programs on student progress" (p. 2).

Educational assistant is one of the fastest growing educational positions in the United States today. The number of these personnel working in public schools has grown from approximately 10,000 in the early 1960s to between 300,000 and 500,000 currently (Green & Barnes, 1988–1989; Logue, 1993). Employment projections for the next 10 to 20 years indicate an increased need for skilled educational assistants to help with many instructional and noninstructional tasks in public education (Doyle, 1997).

One reason for the increase in the number of educational assistants working in public schools is an increase in the number of students with disabilities receiving their education in the general education classroom. Educational assistants have to be hired to provide assistance to the students in the classroom, as well as to provide assistance to the general education teacher both directly (e.g., facilitating teacher-developed instruction with a small group of students) and indirectly (e.g., making curricular adaptations according to teacher instructions). Two of the most common ways educational assistants are used are (1) to provide assistance to a single student who needs ongoing individual support (e.g., a student who cannot move her arms may have an assistant to take notes for her) and (2) to assist several students who need less support for shorter periods of time (Jones & Bender, 1993; Palma, 1994). The educational assistant who works with several students simultaneously may be in a classroom for short periods of time (e.g., only during reading) rather than all day and may, as time permits, help students without disabilities or the teacher.

It is important to remember that educational assistants are considered non-certified staff, and thus their responsibilities for decision making and instructional planning are limited. Their role necessitates that they work with certified educators to apply information, strategies, or interventions in the most appropriate manner (Doyle, 1997). IDEA-1997 mandates that educational assistants and other similar personnel be trained for the work they do with children with disabilities and that they be appropriately supervised. For example, the teacher may be expected to prepare the materials the educational assistant will use with a group of children or to train the educational assistant on a particular educational method. Often, the teacher will be given a written description of the assistant's job responsibilities.

A good partnership with an educational assistant, however, is based on achieving an equal status. Everyone working in an inclusive community must work within the constructs of equity and parity. Although the teacher has some supervisory responsibility over the educational assistant in the partnership a teacher forms with an educational assistant, everyone has valuable skills to contribute and everyone should have equivalent responsibilities (Wadsworth & Knight, 1996).

Doyle (1997) suggests that the general educator, the special educator, and the educational assistant meet regularly to clarify their roles and responsibilities in planning for the success of the child with a disability in a general education reading program. Palma (1994) maintains that holding the first of these meetings at the beginning of the school year sets a positive tone for the year-long partnership and ensures that all involved are informed about expectations, roles, and responsibilities. Friend and Bursuck (1999) suggest that the following questions be addressed at this meeting:

1. Whom might the educational assistant help in the classroom? Should the assistant work only with a targeted student, or is it permissible for the assistant to help any student in the classroom?
2. Who is responsible for evaluating the educational assistant's job performance?
3. Are there any limits on the types of duties the educational assistant can be asked to perform?
4. What expectations does the educational assistant have concerning the work in a particular classroom?

5. What other job components (e.g., other duties, break time) must be considered when planning the educational assistant's day?
6. What type of communication system will be used to facilitate the resolution of concerns or problems among the team members?

A variety of factors are involved in determining the educational assistant's specific responsibilities in a classroom. These factors range from the severity of the child's disability to the context of the classroom to the teaching style of the general education teacher. It is important to remember that educational assistants are hired to fulfill student-specific needs first. Their primary responsibilities and duties must relate to providing support to students with disabilities in the general education classroom. Here are some general guidelines for working effectively with an educational assistant:

1. Establish a set time when you, the special educator, and the educational assistant will meet to discuss the academic and social progress of the student(s) with a disability.
2. Provide the educational assistant with a copy of his/her daily and weekly schedules. These schedules should document the roles and responsibilities of the educational assistant in your classroom, as well as serve as a form of communication between you and the assistant. The educational assistant should have input into the schedules. Remember that the educational assistant may be working in several classrooms with different teachers.
3. Orient the educational assistant to the organization of your classroom. Explain the essential rules and policies for the classroom, clarify where you want the assistant to work, explain your behavior management program, etc.
4. Provide the educational assistant with his/her own personal space (e.g., desk, place to put personal belongings). This person needs to feel as if she/he is a member of your classroom.
5. Make your learning priorities for the student clear to the educational assistant. Provide the assistant with a good view of how to support the student in moving toward any learning goals or benchmarks that have been established.
6. Orient the educational assistant to the noninstructional tasks that are his/her responsibility (e.g., record keeping, photocopying, maintaining bulletin boards) and when you expect these tasks to be completed (e.g., before school, during recess).
7. Provide the educational assistant with appropriate information from the student's IEP in a workable format. Doyle (1997) suggests an IEP matrix in which the goals and benchmarks for a particular student are expressed in the form of a checklist to be used during the day.
8. Clarify the educational assistant's roles and responsibilities in relation to the delivery of instruction for the specific student or group of students.
9. Remember that it is your responsibility to plan for the educational assistant while the assistant is in your classroom. The role of the special educator is to suggest accommodations and modifications that will help the student with a

disability deal with a particular lesson—not to plan for the assistant during that lesson.

10. Nurture your relationship with the assistant. He/she will be a valuable asset.

Process Guide 12.3

Break into small groups, and discuss the changing roles of all educators within a school. Identify the positive aspects of (1) working in a collaborative team, (2) working with a special education consultant, and (3) working with an educational assistant.

Instructional Adaptations

Reading is probably the most important academic skill children learn during their years in school (Mastropieri & Scruggs, 1994). The ability to read forms the foundation upon which most school-related instructional activities and learning rest. Fortunately, most children learn to read and are successful in school. According to Liberman, Shankweiler, and Liberman (1989), 75 percent of students intuitively discover the relationships between spoken and written words and learn to read, regardless of the instructional method. However, that leaves 25 percent of students who do not possess such strengths.

Reading is identified as one of the main difficulties for students with disabilities (Mercer, 1991), as well as for students who are at risk for school failure but who have not been identified as having a disability (Carnine, Silbert, & Kameenui, 1990; Simmons & Kameenui, 1998). In this section we will discuss some approaches that a general education teacher can take to address the specific reading difficulties experienced by children with disabilities.

General Management of a Reading Program

The creation of a successful reading program for children who have difficulty reading involves more than just the selection of curricular materials at the appropriate level. It is important to remember that students who struggle to read are often anxious and frustrated. Many have experienced years of reading failure and as a result have little motivation to read. These students truly wish that they could read and are often angry that they cannot. A key to the general management of a reading program for these students is the creation of a psychologically safe reading environment—one that is designed around the individual student's learning needs and is age-appropriate. Strategies or instructional materials that are appropriate for other students in the classroom may not be suitable for these students. This is where collaboration with the special educator can prove to be invaluable.

In structuring the general management of your reading program for students with disabilities keep in mind that the amount of time spent reading is a critical factor (Leinhardt, Zigmond, & Cooley, 1981). Increasing the amount of time children spend actively engaged in reading may require examining the organization of the classroom. You might ask the special educator or the educational assistant to observe how many children are off-task when (1) you give instructions, (2) they move from one activity to another, and (3) they work independently. This information will help you and the special educator plan for the students in your classroom. Figure 12.4 provides general management suggestions for use in structuring a reading environment suitable for students with disabilities.

General Adaptations to a Reading Program

Adaptations are defined as "any adjustment or modification in the curriculum, instruction, environment, or materials in order to enhance the participation of a member of the classroom community" (Udvari-Solner, 1992, p. 3). Many students—

FIGURE 12.4   General Management Suggestions for Increasing Reading Achievement

Goals	Management Suggestions
Increase the amount of time children are on-task reading.	Spend less time delivering instructions and transitioning between reading activities.
Ensure that the children hear (or read) and understand instructions.	Make instructions clear and simple, have children repeat instructions to you, present instructions in more than one modality (e.g., orally and visually), use the buddy system, and have a place on the board for the day's assignments or instructions.
Reduce wait time and transition time.	Use individual contracts or work folders, have a learning center set up for use during such times, and provide each child with an independent reading selection for use during such times.
Allow extra time to reteach a skill before going on to additional concepts.	Use peer tutors or small-group instruction provided by an educational assistant, a special education parent co-teacher, or a parent tutor.
Enhance or focus a student's attention.	Use cues, prompts, acronyms, and highlighting of key concepts or words.
Increase the amount of time students spend working independently.	Make sure that independent seatwork is at the student's academic level. The student should be able to read and understand the instructions for the seatwork, or a buddy should be designated to provide explanations.

with or without disabilities—can benefit from reading adaptations to accomplish their reading tasks more efficiently and to participate more fully in classroom reading activities.

Doyle (1997) identified three general categories of adaptations: (1) adaptations that are constant over time, (2) adaptations that are short term and preplanned, and (3) adaptations that are developed on the spot. These adaptations can be developed by the general educator, by the collaboration team, or by the special education consultant.

Adaptations that are constant over time are those used frequently by the student in a variety of situations during the day. Examples of this type of adaptation are the use of computers, cue cards, and assignment schedules. Adaptations that are short term and preplanned are usually developed for a specific instructional unit or activity. Examples of this type of adaptation are the use of modified worksheets, a tape-recorded reading passage, or a reading buddy. Adaptations that are developed on the spot arise in response to a child's need at a specific point in time. The general educator or educational assistant has to make the instructional modification as instruction is occurring. On-the-spot adaptations must be chronological age–appropriate, promote active participation and interaction by the child with disabilities, build on the child's strengths, take into account the child's self-esteem, and be nonintrusive in nature (Doyle, 1997).

The National Center to Improve the Tools of Educators at the University of Oregon has developed six curriculum design principles central to planning a reading program that will respond to the instructional needs of students with diverse disabilities. These principles are derived from current research focused on identifying the features of high-quality educational tools and strategies for diverse learners (Carnine, 1994). They address the acute instructional needs of learners who are vulnerable to reading failure—the 25 percent of children who need intensive and systematic methods to learn the complex rules and strategies involved in reading. Figure 12.5 outlines these six principles.

Assessment

Reading assessment should be viewed as a process of learning each child's strengths and weaknesses so as to determine instructional program needs. As such, it should be not an isolated event but rather an ongoing process and an integral part of the child's educational program. When direct and regular assessment is implemented in a reading program, teachers can make changes in instruction in response to individual student needs.

When students with disabilities come into the classroom, they usually bring with them assessment information. This information generally takes the form of standardized test results, including percentile ranks, grade equivalents, and stanine scores. While this information will provide some general insights into the reading abilities of the student, it will not give you the most critical component of assessment—the information you need to place the student along a continuum of instruction or within a scope and sequence of objectives.

FIGURE 12.5   Six-Principle Curriculum and Instructional Design Framework
for Reading Instruction

Principle	Definition	Considerations
Big ideas	Big ideas are those that contribute most to a child's reading success. Focusing on big ideas involves defining and teaching what is important in a curricular area. The basic assumption is that some ideas are more critical than others to the acquisition of reading skills, and it is the teacher's responsibility to prioritize what will be taught, from most important to least important.	■ Consider what information or knowledge is fundamental and what is simply not essential. ■ Remember that students with disabilities are often playing catch up and simply do not have the time for information that does not contribute directly to their reading success.
Conspicuous strategies	Conspicuous strategies are sequences of teaching events and teacher actions that make explicit to the learner the steps required to complete the task. It is the teacher's responsibility to outline the steps or strategies needed to complete the task and directly teach them to the student.	■ The strategies should be conspicuous. ■ The strategies should be easy to apply. ■ The strategies should be applicable to a variety of learning situations.
Mediated scaffolding	Mediated scaffolding is the external personal guidance, assistance, and support provided to a student by teachers, instructional materials, peers, or assignments. Scaffolding may be constant over time or short term. It is always designed to meet individual student needs.	■ Scaffolding may be substantial in the beginning learning stages and gradually removed as the student gains fluency and knowledge. ■ Scaffolds range from simple (e.g., a procedure prompt) to complex (e.g., a conceptual framework for studying).
Strategic integration	Strategic integration involves the integration of new information with previous knowledge. Integration must be strategic so that it produces a more generalizable and higher order thinking skill.	■ Strategic integration results from careful planning on the part of the teacher. ■ Tasks must be carefully sequenced so that new information relates to information already mastered by the student. ■ Previously learned skills must be integrated with new skills and practiced over time.

Principle	Definition	Considerations
Primed background knowledge	Priming involves practicing a known strategy as a before-the-learning activity. A brief reminder, task, or exercise requires the learner to retrieve or use known information prior to beginning a new task.	■ Always practice what a student knows and can do independently before teaching new information. ■ If a student experiences difficulty retrieving an already mastered skill, this may be an indication that you need to go back and reteach that skill before moving forward.
Judicious review	Judicious review is more than simple practice; it is a carefully planned system of review that is embedded within the presentation of new material. The teacher must make a conscious effort to design a review schedule that ensures retention while extending the student's understanding of the skills, concepts, and strategies to be used in the reading process.	■ Review should be designed to develop fluency and automaticity. ■ Review should be varied to promote wide use of the skill. ■ Review should occur daily. ■ Review may involve guided practice (e.g., help that is faded over time).

Adapted from Simmons & Kameenui, 1998, pp. 7–9.

Children need to become aware of the building blocks of language.

Curriculum-based assessment is a procedure used to determine a student's level within a reading program, as well as to monitor a student's progress over time. Tied to the reading material used by a teacher, curriculum-based assessment provides up-to-date information concerning a student's reading achievement. Should the information collected indicate that the child is not achieving, the teacher can change the material or instructional intervention immediately. Because children with disabilities are often behind their peers in the general education classroom, constant monitoring is needed to ensure that valuable instructional time is not wasted. Fuchs and Fuchs (1986) found that students whose teachers use curriculum-based assessment to monitor progress have higher reading scores than about two-thirds of the students whose teachers do not use curriculum-based assessment. The power of curriculum-based assessment is that it allows general educators to assess children in terms of acquisition of the skills included in their own school's curriculum rather than relying on standardized test scores to measure learning and achievement (Heward & Orlansky, 1992). In addition, it is an accountable assessment procedure that displays the student's performance changes over time (Lerner, 1997).

Working with a special education consultant, the teacher can design a curriculum-based assessment system to meet the individual learning needs of a student with disabilities. The area of reading that is the focus of the child's IEP must be determined so that the assessment can be developed with the individual child in mind. The system will take into consideration the teacher's reading strategies and the materials used to teach reading. Curriculum-based assessment can be designed to measure oral reading rate (e.g., how many words read correctly and incorrectly in a set time period), reading comprehension (e.g., types of comprehension questions answered correctly or incorrectly), vocabulary development, and so on. Because curriculum-based assessment is responsive to the child's reading strengths and weaknesses, it can make instruction more efficient and can optimize the learning of students with disabilities (Howell, Fox, & Morehead, 1993).

Teaching Reading to Students with Disabilities

When students struggle to learn to read, both general education and special education teachers face a difficult task. Often these students are the victims of poor reading instruction, or they have been passed along while teachers and parents waited for them to mature (Hallahan, Kauffman, & Lloyd, 1999). Engelmann (1997) tells teachers to remember when planning instruction for these students, that they (1) differ from their peers in some very important ways, (2) often suffer from declining self-confidence because of their reading failure, (3) may apply some faulty reading strategies from previous instruction, and (4) must learn to read at an accelerated rate if they are to catch up.

To overcome these obstacles to reading, teachers must adopt an attitude of "no more business as usual." There is an extensive research base that identifies the most effective approaches to teaching reading to children with disabilities. This research base must be strategically applied in the classroom to optimize children's potential to acquire reading skills. Research indicates that children with disabilities benefit from reading programs that include many diverse elements.

Direct instruction. Specific skills should be targeted and explicitly taught to the child. To understand the rules and mysteries of the printed word, most children with reading disabilities need direct teaching and intensive instructional intervention (Carnine, Silbert, & Kameenui, 1990; Mather, 1992; Pressley, Harris, & Marks, 1992; Pressley & Rankin, 1994). For these children, reading is not an intuitive process.

Direct instruction in language analysis. Children need to become aware of the building blocks of language. They need to be taught sound segmentation— that is, how to orally break words down into their component sounds. They should play with the sounds of language until they can pull words apart into syllables and pull syllables into individual phonemes (Friend & Bursuck, 1999; U.S. Department of Education, 1996).

A highly structured phonics program. The program should teach the alphabetic code directly and systematically. The program should move from simple to complex activities, teach regularity before irregularity, and discourage guessing (Adams, 1991; Beck & Juel, 1995; Mather, 1992; Simmons & Kameenui, 1998; U.S. Department of Education, 1996). A systematic program implemented correctly does not allow children to practice their errors; it corrects errors immediately and provides corrective instruction and practice.

A combined reading and writing program. Children need to write the words they learn to read (Bos & Vaughn, 1998; Friend & Bursuck, 1999; U.S. Department of Education, 1996). Writing lends another dimension to an otherwise one-dimensional activity, and it promotes generalization of skills by the student. Suggested tasks include writing stories, writing reports, keeping journals, and writing letters.

A literate environment. Children with disabilities profit from a literate environment that includes an in-class library, wall charts, access to multimedia instructional materials (e.g., CD-ROMs, books on tape), and displays of student work (Pressley & Rankin, 1994).

Strategy instruction to increase reading comprehension. Strategy instruction is designed to involve the learner actively in the learning process. The goal is to get students with disabilities to apply strategies such as (1) planning before reading, (2) monitoring their understanding during reading, and (3) reviewing what they know after reading. The application of learning strategies helps students become active, involved learners who direct their own learning (Chan, Cole, & Barfett, 1987; Lenz, Ellis, & Scanlon, 1996). Research indicates that regardless of the reading strategy taught, the feature that is critical to student success and lasting benefit is that *the teacher directly taught the strategy to the students* (Billingsley & Wildman, 1990). Direct teacher instruction includes

1. modeling (e.g., teacher models out loud the steps in performing the strategy) (Billingsley & Wildman, 1990)
2. interaction (e.g., discussions, cooperative learning activities, peer conferences) (Palincsar, David, Winn, & Stevens, 1991)
3. guided practice; that is, students practice the strategy under the watchful eye of the teacher, who provides corrective feedback and praise and fades the strategy as the students become more proficient (Harris & Pressley, 1991)
4. systematic feedback (that is, feedback that is specific, carefully planned, and timed) (Billingsley & Wildman, 1990)

Fluency building activities. Students must be given enough practice that their reading becomes accurate and fluent (Felton, 1993; Hasbrouck, 1996; La-Berge & Samuels, 1974). Strategies for building fluency include reading aloud (Trelease, 1995), repeated reading of short passages (O'Shea, Sindelar, & O'Shea, 1987), and providing books on tape (Carbo, 1978).

Vocabulary development. Vocabulary development is crucial to academic development (Baker, Simmons, & Kameenui, 1998). Children need a rich vocabulary to succeed in the basic skill areas; but as they progress in school, specialized vocabulary becomes vital to learning content material. A vocabulary development program that meets the needs of children with disabilities should (1) teach words that are important for academic success and not typically learned independently and (2) teach systematic procedures to make children independent vocabulary learners (Anderson & Nagy, 1991). Examples of strategies recommended in the literature are the keyword method (Mastropieri, Scruggs, & Fulk, 1990), semantic mapping (Sinatra, Berg, & Dunn, 1985), and semantic features analysis (Anders & Bos, 1986).

Word recognition activities. Word recognition refers to the ability to link the printed word with its meaning (Stanovich, 1991). The ability to link words and meaning is critical for mastery of reading, as it enables readers to concentrate on the meaning of the text (Lerner, 1997). While word recognition is often described as a lower-level reading skill, it does provide support for the higher-level cognitive skills (Chall, 1991). If a student must concentrate all of his or her effort on simply recognizing words, there will be little cognitive-processing capacity left for comprehension. Direct instruction in word recognition provides a tool for the development of automaticity (quick, automatic response) in reading for students with disabilities. This instruction may incorporate words from the Dolch Sight Word List (Johnson, 1971) or frequently found words from the student's reading material.

Whatever reading intervention program is implemented for children with disabilities in the general education classroom, it is important that they receive intensive instruction (Friend & Bursuck, 1999). These children must be given many opportunities to practice a skill they are learning, with materials that contain words they are able to decode and recognize on sight.

Process Guide 12.4

In small groups, compare and contrast reading instruction for students with disabilities and reading instruction for typical learners. Make a list of the similarities and differences in the reading programs for the two groups of students.

Summary

Reading is a very complex process. For those of us who are proficient readers, reading appears to be simple—it is something we do without thinking. For those who struggle to read, however, reading is anything but simple, and the opportunities to catch up diminish over time (Simmons & Kameenui, 1998; U.S. Department of Education, 1998). Early, direct intervention is needed as soon as signs of reading failure appear. Children with disabilities likely have failed to benefit from conventional educational practices. Fortunately, the fields of special education and reading have amassed a plethora of research that points teachers in the direction of teaching practices effective in preventing and intercepting reading failure for many children. For children with disabilities, more than one key is needed to unlock the meaning of the written word (Heymsfeld, 1989), and educators need to use every key at their disposal. The ability to read remains the door to the future.

FOLLOW-THROUGH ACTIVITIES

Note: Level 1 activities require limited access to children or classrooms. Level 2 activities should be completed using children and classrooms.

Level 1 Activities

1. Describe how you would go about forming a collaborative team in a school setting.

2. Obtain a copy of IDEA-1997 and interview a special educator about the changes in the law and how they are being implemented in schools.

3. Using suggestions in this chapter, make a list of ideas for increasing reading instruction time for students with disabilities in the general education classroom.

4. Observe a special education classroom and a general education classroom during reading instruction. Compare and contrast the types of reading activities employed. Pay particular attention to time on task, directions given, and feedback provided.

5. Observe a general education classroom in which students with disabilities are included for reading instruction. Interview the teacher about the modifications and adaptations he/she has made for the students.

Level 2 Activities

1. Read orally with a typical third grader and with a third grader with a reading disability. Compare and contrast their word recognition abilities, fluency rates, comprehension abilities, and decoding skills.

2. Spend five consecutive days in a general education classroom, observing a student who is having difficulty reading. Keep observational notes, and list the activities the teacher requires of the child that involve reading.

3. Read orally with a typical tenth grader and with a tenth grader with a reading disability. Compare and contrast their word recognition abilities, fluency rates, comprehension abilities, and decoding skills.

4. Attend an IEP meeting for a child with a disability who is included in the general education classroom for reading. Pay particular attention to the types of assessment results, the goals developed for the child, the instructional benchmarks developed for the child, and the materials and activities suggested for use in the general education classroom.

5. Interview an educational assistant who works in a general education classroom with students with disabilities. Ask about the duties the assistant performs for (a) the student with disabilities, (b) other students in the classroom, (c) the general education teacher, and (d) the special educator.

WORKING WITH PARENTS

A good working relationship with the parents or guardians of a child with a disability in the general education classroom is a key ingredient in the child's academic success. The quality of the interactions with parents is important for all children in a classroom, but it is vital for children with disabilities (Sileo, Sileo, & Prater, 1996). The parents and teacher who work together form a powerful team to ensure the success of the child with a disability in the general education environment.

Parents often see their child's experiences in a classroom—both academic and social—in a way that teachers cannot. The information and insights that they share can be valuable in designing appropriate instruction, as well as in dealing with the child as a whole individual. It is important to listen to and apply the suggestions offered by parents. Most teachers simply do not understand what it is like to be the parent of a child with a disability. These parents have stresses and concerns that are different from those of other parents in the classroom. Because of their unique stresses and concerns, they may have requests and suggestions that differ from those made by other parents.

The working relationship that develops between the teacher and the parents will depend on the student's needs, the involvement of the parents, and the teacher's efforts to make the parents feel that their input is valued. A critical factor in the development of a strong working relationship with the parents of children with disabilities is sensitivity to their point of view (Grossman, 1995). Educators must remember that parents know the child much better than they ever will. By making the parents feel welcome in the classroom, listening carefully to their thoughts and concerns, recognizing that they play a significant role in the education and development of their child, working with them and the special educator to meet their child's needs, and always keeping them informed of their child's progress, a teacher can forge a collaborative relationship with parents.

Regular communication between teachers and parents is the foundation of an effective collaborative relationship. Communication can be accomplished through parent-teacher conferences, informal notes sent home, telephone calls, and formal school newsletters. Always remember that parents of students with disabilities tend to hear only negatives about their child. A good rule of thumb is that for every negative communication you have with parents you need to have at least five that are positive.

Parents have a specific role to play in the educational planning for their child. They have input at the IEP meeting, and they must be kept informed of any program changes that involve their child. They act as advocates for their child and can work with you to ensure that adequate supports are provided to meet the child's learning and social needs in your classroom.

There has been much debate about encouraging parents to provide tutoring at home for their child. Often, home tutoring by parents results in frustrated parents and child. Any reading homework assigned should be carefully planned to ensure the success of the child. All homework should be work that the child can complete independently and should involve material already mastered by the child. The homework should be for review only, providing practice with a skill already introduced and practiced at school. Homework adaptations to be considered include

- Giving fewer items to complete
- Tape-recording instructions
- Providing two nights to complete an assignment instead of one
- Verifying the clarity of the assignment with the child before he/she leaves for the day
- Allowing the child to begin the assignment in class so that you can identify any problems before the child takes the assignment home
- Communicating regularly with the parents about the role they should play in the completion of the homework

RESOURCES

All books listed below will provide the general educator and the special educator with a wealth of information concerning the process of collaboration, as well as working with students with disabilities within the general education environment. As education becomes more and more inclusive, it is incumbent upon both the general educator and the special educator to expand their levels of knowledge beyond their current level of expertise—to do any less creates an environment that is inhospitable to children with diverse learning needs.

Choate, J. S. (1997). *Successful inclusive teaching: Proven ways to detect and correct special needs.* Boston: Allyn & Bacon.

Doyle, M. B. (1997). *The paraprofessional's guide to the inclusive classroom: Working as a team.* Baltimore: Brookes.

Friend, M., & Bursuck, W. D. (1999). *Including students with special needs: A practical guide for classroom teachers.* Boston: Allyn & Bacon.

Schmidt, M. W., & Harriman, N. E. (1998). *Teaching strategies for inclusive classrooms: Schools, students, strategies, and success.* Ft. Worth, TX: Harcourt Brace College Publishers.

Simmons, D. C., & Kameenui, E. J. (Eds.). (1998). *What reading research tells us about children with diverse learning needs: Bases and basics.* Mahwah, NJ: Erlbaum.

Stainback, S., & Stainback, W. (1992). *Curriculum considerations in the inclusive classrooms: Facilitating learning for all students.* Baltimore: Brookes.

REFERENCES

Adams, M. J. (1991). Why not phonics and whole language? In W. Ellis (Ed.), *All language and the creation of literacy* (pp. 40–52). Baltimore: Orton Dyslexia Society.

Anders, P. L., & Bos, C. S. (1986). Semantic feature analysis: An interactive strategy for vocabulary development and text comprehension. *Journal of Reading, 29,* 610–616.

Anderson, R. C., & Nagy, W. E. (1991). Word meanings. In R. Barr, M. L. Kamil, P. B. Mosenthal, & P. D. Pearson (Eds.), *Handbook of reading research: Volume II* (pp. 690–724). New York: Longman.

Baker, S. K., Simmons, D. C., & Kameenui, E. J. (1998). Vocabulary acquisition: Research bases. In D. C. Simmons & E. J. Kameenui (Eds.), *What reading research tells us about children with diverse learning needs: Bases and basics* (pp. 183–217). Mahwah, NJ: Erlbaum.

Beck, I. L., & Juel, C. (1995). The role of decoding in learning to read. *American Educator, 19*(2), 7, 10–20.

Billingsley, B. S., & Wildman, T. M. (1990). Facilitating reading comprehension in learning disabled students: Metacognitive goals and instructional strategies. *Remedial and Special Education, 11*(2), 18–31.

Bos, C. S., & Vaughn, S. (1998). *Strategies for teaching students with learning and behavior problems.* Boston: Allyn & Bacon.

Brinker, R. P. (1985). Interactions between severely mentally retarded students and other students in integrated and segregated public school settings. *American Journal of Mental Deficiency, 89,* 587–594.

Carbo, M. (1978). Teaching reading with talking books. *The Reading Teacher, 32 ,* 267–273.

Carnine, D. (1994). Introduction to the mini-series: Diverse learners and prevailing, emerging, and research-based educational approaches and their tools. *School Psychology Review, 23,* 341–350.

Carnine, D., Silbert, J., & Kameenui, E. J. (1990). *Direct instruction reading* (2nd ed.). Columbus, OH: Merrill.

Chall, J. S. (1991). American reading instruction: Science, art, and ideology. In W. Ellis (Ed.), *All language and the creation of literacy* (pp. 20–26). Baltimore: Orton Dyslexia Society.

Chalmers, L., & Faliede, T. (1996). Successful inclusion of students with mild/moderate disabilities in rural school settings. *Teaching Exceptional Children, 29*(1), 22–25.

Chan, L. K. S., Cole, P. G., & Barfett, S. (1987). Comprehension monitoring: Detection and identification of text inconsistencies by LD and normal students. *Learning Disabilities Quarterly, 10,* 114–124.

Choate, J. S. (1997). *Successful inclusive teaching: Proven ways to detect and correct special needs.* Boston: Allyn & Bacon.

Cook, L., & Friend, M. (1993). Educational leadership for teacher collaboration. In B. Billingsley (Ed.), *Program leadership for serving students with disabilities* (pp. 421–444). Richmond, VA: Virginia Department of Education.

Cornwall, A., & Bawden, H. (1992). Reading disabilities and aggression: A critical review. *Journal of Learning Disabilities, 25,* 281–299.

Council for Exceptional Children. (1993). *CEC statement on inclusion.* Reston, VA: Author.

Doyle, M. B. (1997). *The paraprofessional's guide to the inclusive classroom: Working as a team.* Baltimore: Brookes.

Edgar, E. (1987). Secondary programs in special education: Are many of them justifiable? *Exceptional Children, 53,* 555–561.

Engelmann, S. (1997). Theory of mastery and acceleration. In J. W. Lloyd, E. J. Kameenui, & D. Chard (Eds.), *Issues in educating students with disabilities* (pp. 177–195). Mahwah, NJ: Erlbaum.

Evans, I. M., Salisbury, C. L., Palombaro, M. M., & Hollowood, T. M. (1992). Peer interactions and social acceptance of elementary-age children with severe disabilities in an inclusive school. *Journal of the Association for Persons with Severe Handicaps, 17,* 205–212.

Felton, R. H. (1993). Effects of instruction on the decoding skills of children with phonological-processing problems. *Journal of Learning Disabilities, 26,* 583–589.

Ferguson, D. L. (1996). The real challenge of inclusion: Confessions of a "rabid inclusionist." *Phi Delta Kappan, 77,* 281–287.

Friend, M., & Bursuck, W. (1999). *Including students with special needs: A practical guide for classroom teachers.* Boston: Allyn & Bacon.

Friend, M., & Cook, L. (1996). *Interactions: Collaboration skills for school professionals* (2nd ed.). White Plains, NY: Longman.

Fuchs, D., & Fuchs, L. (1995). What's "special" about special education? *Phi Delta Kappan, 76,* 522–530.

Fuchs, L. S., & Fuchs, D. (1986). Curriculum-based assessment of progress toward long-term and short-term goals. *Journal of Special Education, 20,* 69–81.

Giangreco, M. F., Dennis, R., Cloninger, C., Edelman, S., & Shattman, R. (1993). "I've counted Jon": Transformational experiences of teachers educating students with severe disabilities. *Exceptional Children, 59,* 359–372.

Goldring, E. B., & Rallis, S. F. (1993). *Principals of dynamic schools: Taking charge of change.* Newbury Park, CA: Corwin.

Green, J. E., & Barnes, D. L. (1988–1989, Winter). Do your "aides" aid instruction? A tool for assessing the use of paraprofessionals as instructional assistants. *The Teacher Educator, 24*(3), 2–9.

Grossman, H. (1995). *Special education in a diverse society.* Boston: Allyn & Bacon.

Hahn, H. (1989). The politics of special education. In D. K. Lipsky & A. Gartner (Eds.), *Beyond separate education: Quality education for all* (pp. 225–241). Baltimore: Brookes.

Hallahan, D. P., Kauffman, J. M., & Lloyd, J. W. (1999). *Introduction to learning disabilities* (2nd ed.). Boston: Allyn & Bacon.

Harris, K. R., & Pressley, M. (1991). The nature of cognitive strategy instruction: Interactive strategy construction. *Exceptional Children, 57,* 392–404.

Hasbrouck, J. (1996, April). *Oral reading fluency: A review of literature with implications for use with elementary students who are difficult to teach.* Paper presented at a meeting of the Council for Exceptional Children, Orlando, FL.

Hendrickson, J. M., Shokoohi-Yekta, M., Hamre-Nietupski, S., & Gable, R. (1996). Middle and high school students' perceptions on being friends with peers with severe disabilities. *Exceptional Children, 63,* 19–28.

Heward, W. L., & Orlansky, M. D. (1992). *Exceptional children* (4th ed.). Columbus, OH: Macmillan.

Heymsfeld, C. R. (1989). Filling the hole in whole language. *Educational Leadership, 47,* 64–67.

Howell, K. W., Fox, S. L., & Morehead, M. K. (1993). *Curriculum-based evaluation: Teaching and decision making* (2nd ed.). Pacific Grove, CA: Brooks/Cole.

Hunt, P., Farron-Davis, F., Beckstead, S., Curtis, D., & Goetz, L. (1994). Evaluating the effects of placements of students with severe disabilities in general education versus special classes. *Journal of the Association for Persons with Severe Handicaps, 19* , 200–214.

Idol, L., Paolucci-Whitcomb, P., & Nevin, A. (1986). *Collaborative consultation.* Austin, TX: PRO-ED.

Johnson, D. D. (1971). The Dolch list reexamined. *The Reading Teacher, 24,* 455–456.

Jones, K. H., & Bender, W. N. (1993). Utilization of paraprofessionals in special education: A review of the literature. *Remedial and Special Education, 14*(1), 7–14.

Juel, C. (1988). Learning to read and write: A longitudinal study of fifty-four children from first through fourth grade. *Journal of Educational Psychology, 80,* 437–447.

Kauffman, J. M. (1995). Why we must celebrate a diversity of restrictive environments. *Learning Disabilities Research & Practice, 10,* 225–232.

Kirk, S. A., Kliebhan, J. M., & Lerner, J. W. (1978). *Teaching reading to slow and disabled learners.* Boston: Houghton Mifflin.

LaBerge, D., & Samuels, S. J. (1974). Toward a theory of automatic information processing in reading. *Cognitive Psychology, 6,* 293–323.

Learning First Alliance. (1998). Every child reading: An action plan of the Learning First Alliance. *American Educator, 22*(1 & 2), 52–63.

Leinhardt, G., Zigmond, N., & Cooley, W. W. (1981). Reading instruction and its effects. *American Educational Research Journal, 18,* 343–361.

Lenz, B. K., Ellis, E. S., & Scanlon, D. (1996). *Teaching learning strategies to adolescents and adults with learning disabilities.* Austin, TX: PRO-ED.

Lerner, J. W. (1997). *Learning disabilities: Theories, diagnosis, and teaching strategies.* Boston: Houghton Mifflin.

Liberman, I. Y., Shankweiler, D., & Liberman, A. M. (1989). The alphabetic principle and learning to read. In D. Shankweiler & I. Y. Liberman (Eds.), *Phonology and reading disability: Solving the reading puzzle* (pp. 1–33). Ann Arbor: University of Michigan.

Lilly, M. S. (1992). Labeling: A tired, overworked, yet unresolved issue in special education. In W. Stainback & S. Stainback (Eds.), *Controversial issues confronting special education: Divergent perspectives* (pp. 85–95). Boston: Allyn & Bacon.

Little, J. W. (1982). Norms of collegiality and experimentation: Workplace conditions of school success. *American Educational Research Journal, 19,* 325–340.

Logue, O. J. (1993, April). *Job satisfaction and retention variables of special education paraeducators.* Paper presented at the Twelfth Annual Conference on the Training and Employment of the Paraprofessional Workforce in Education, Rehabilitation, and Related Fields, Seattle, WA.

Lyon, G. R. (1995). Research initiatives and discoveries in learning disabilities: Contributions from scientists supported by the National Institute of Child Health and Human Development. *Journal of Child Neurology, 10*(Suppl. 1), S120–S126.

Lyon, G. R., & Chhabra, V. (1996). The current state of science and the future of specific reading disability. *Mental Retardation and Development Disabilities Research and Reviews, 2,* 2–9.

Mastropieri, M. A., & Scruggs, T. E. (1994). *Effective instruction for special education* (2nd ed.). Austin, TX: PRO-ED.

Mastropieri, M. A., Scruggs, T. E., & Fulk, B. J. (1990). Teaching abstract vocabulary with the keyword method: Effects on recall and comprehension. *Journal of Learning Disabilities, 23,* 92–107.

Mather, N. (1992). Whole language reading instruction for students with learning disabilities: Caught in the cross-fire. *Learning Disabilities Research & Practice, 7,* 87–95.

McLeskey, J., & Waldron, N. L. (1996). Responses to questions teachers and administrators frequently ask about inclusive school programs. *Phi Delta Kappan, 78,* 150–156.

Mercer, C. D. (1991). *Students with learning disabilities* (4th ed.). New York: Merrill Publishing.

National Center for Education Statistics. (1993). *Adult literacy in America: A first look at the results of the National Adult Literacy Survey* (Survey No. 065-000-00588-3). Washington, DC: U.S. Government Printing Office.

National Center to Improve the Tools of Educators. (1996). *Learning to read/reading to learn information kit.* Reston, VA: Council for Exceptional Children.

National Institute of Child Health and Human Development (NICHD). (1994, August). National Institute of Child Health and Human Development Conference on Intervention Programs for Children with Reading and Related Language Disorders, Washington, DC.

Olson, L., & Rodman, B. (1988, June 22). The unfinished agenda: Part II. *Education Week,* 17–23.

O'Shea, L. J., Sindelar, P. T., & O'Shea, D. J. (1987). The effects of repeated readings and attention cues on the reading fluency and comprehension of learning disabled readers. *Learning Disabilities Research, 2,* 103–109.

Palincsar, A. S., David, Y. M., Winn, J. A., & Stevens, D. D. (1991). Examining the context of strategy instruction. *Remedial and Special Education, 12*(3), 43–53.

Palma, G. M. (1994). Toward a positive and effective teacher and paraprofessional relationship. *Rural Special Education Quarterly, 9*(1), 53–59.

Peck, C. A., Carlson, P., & Helmstetter, E. (1992). Parent and teacher perceptions of outcomes for typically developing children enrolled in integrated early childhood programs: A statewide survey. *Journal of Early Intervention, 16*(1), 53–63.

Peck, C. A., Donaldson, J., & Pezzoli, M. (1990). Some benefits nonhandicapped adolescents perceive for themselves from their social relationships with peers who have severe handicaps. *Journal of the Association for Persons with Severe Handicaps, 15,* 241–249.

Pickett, A. L. (1988). *The employment and training of paraprofessional personnel: A technical assistance manual for administrators and staff developers.* New York: City University of New York, National Resource Center for Paraprofessionals in Education and Related Services, Center for Advanced Study in Education.

Pressley, M., Harris, K. R., & Marks, M. B. (1992). But good strategy instructors are constructivists! *Educational Psychology Review, 4,* 3–31.

Pressley, M., & Rankin, J. (1994). More about whole language methods of reading instruction for students at risk for early reading failure. *Learning Disabilities Research & Practice, 9*(3), 157–168.

Ryndak, D. L., Downing, J. E., Jacqueline, L. R., & Morrison, A. P. (1995). Parents' perceptions after inclusion of their child with moderate or severe disabilities in general education settings. *Journal of the Association for Persons with Severe Handicaps, 20,* 147–157.

Sailor, W. (1991). Special education in the restructured school. *Remedial and Special Education, 12,* 8–22.

Sawyer, R. J., McLaughlin, M. J., & Winglee, M. (1994). Is integration of students with disabilities happening? *Remedial and Special Education, 15,* 204–215.

Sharpe, M. N., York, J. L., & Knight, J. (1994). Effects of inclusion on the academic performance of students without disabilities: A preliminary study. *Remedial and Special Education, 15,* 281–287.

Sileo, T. W., Sileo, A. P., & Prater, M. A. (1996). Parent and professional partnerships in special education: Multicultural considerations. *Intervention in School and Clinic, 31,* 145–153.

Simmons, D. C., & Kameenui, E. J. (1998). Issues and challenges in reading achievement. In D. C. Simmons & E. J. Kameenui (Eds.), *What reading research tells us about children with diverse learning needs: Bases and basics* (pp. 1–17). Mahwah, NJ: Erlbaum.

Simpson, R. L., & Myles, B. S. (1990). The general education collaboration: A model for successful mainstreaming. *Focus on Exceptional Children, 23*(4), 1–10.

Sinatra, R. C., Berg, D., & Dunn, R. (1985). Semantic mapping improves reading comprehension of learning disabled students. *Teaching Exceptional Children, 17,* 310–314.

Skrtic, T. M., Sailor, W., & Gee, K. (1996). Voice, collaboration, and inclusion: Democratic themes in educational and social reform initiatives. *Remedial and Special Education, 17,* 142–157.

Snow, C. E., Burns, M. S., & Griffin, P. (Eds.). (1998). *Preventing reading difficulties in young children.* Washington, DC: National Academy.

Stanovich, K. E. (1986). Matthew effects in reading: Some consequences of individual differences in the acquisition of literacy. *Reading Research Quarterly, 21,* 360–407.

Stanovich, K. E. (1991). Word recognition: Changing perspectives. In R. Barr, M. L. Kamil, P. B. Mosenthal, & P. D. Pearson (Eds.), *Handbook of Reading Research: Volume II* (pp. 418–452). New York: Longman.

Trelease, J. (1995). *The new read-aloud handbook* (4th ed.). New York: Penguin.

Udvari-Solner, A. (1992). *Curricular adaptations: Accommodating the instructional needs of diverse learners in the context of general education.* Topeka, KS: Kansas State Board of Education.

U.S. Department of Education. (1996). *Learning to read, reading to learn: Helping children with learning disabilities to succeed.* Washington, DC: Author.

U.S. Department of Education. (1997). *Nineteenth annual report to Congress on the implementation of the Education for All Handicapped Children's Act.* Washington, DC: Author.

U.S. Department of Education. (1998). *Twentieth annual report to Congress on the implementation of the Education for All Handicapped Children's Act.* Washington, DC: Author.

Vandercook, T., York, J., & Sullivan, B. (1993). True or false? Truly collaborative relationships can exist between university and public school personnel. *OSERS News in Print, 5*(8), 3.

Vaughn, S., & Schumm, J. S. (1995). Responsible inclusion for students with learning disabilities. *Journal of Learning Disabilities, 28,* 264–270, 290.

Vaughn, S., Schumm, J. S., Jallad, B., Slusher, J., & Saumell, L. (1996). Teachers' views of inclusion. *Learning Disabilities Research & Practice, 11,* 96–106.

Wadsworth, D. E., & Knight, D. (1996). Paraprofessionals: The bridge to successful full inclusion. *Intervention in School and Clinic, 31,* 166–171.

Wagner, M., D'Amico, R., Marder, C., Newman, L., & Blackorby, J. (1992). *What happens next? Trends in postschool outcomes of youth with disabilities.* Menlo Park, CA: SRI International.

Wang, M. C., & Reynolds, M. C. (1996). Progressive inclusion: Meeting new challenges in special education. *Theory into Practice, 35*(1), 20–25.

Werner, E. (1993). Risk, resilience, and recovery: Perspectives from the Kauai longitudinal study. *Development and Psychopathology, 5,* 503–515.

Whitman, D. (1995, January 16). Welfare: The myth of reform. *U.S. News & World Report, 118,* 30–33, 36–39.

Wood, J. W. (1992). *Adapting instruction for mainstream and at-risk students* (3rd ed.). Columbus, OH: Macmillan.

York, J., Vandercook, T., Macdonald, C., Heise-Neff, C., & Caughey, E. (1992). Feedback about integrating middle-school students with severe disabilities in general education classes. *Exceptional Children, 58,* 244–258.

Zigmond, N. (1995). Models for delivery of special education services to students with learning disabilities in public schools. *Journal of Child Neurology, 10* (Suppl. 1), S86-S91.

Zigmond, N., & Baker, J. (1990). Mainstream experiences for learning disabled students (Project MELD): Preliminary report. *Exceptional Children, 57,* 176–185.

13 Second Language Learners

SARAH HUDELSON
Arizona State University

INTRODUCTION

Between the 1980 and 1990 United States Censuses, the number of persons 5 years of age and older speaking a home language other than English increased by 38 percent. The number of U.S. residents born in other countries increased 40 percent (Waggoner, 1999). The composition of public elementary schools around the country reflects this increasing linguistic and cultural diversity, and projections suggest that the number of non–native English speaking children will continue to increase in the third millennium. Conservative estimates are that by the year 2020 there will be more than six million children in U.S. schools whose native language is other than English (Pallas, Natriello, & McDill, 1989).

Some of these children have a heritage on this continent that goes back much further than the existence of the United States as a country. Indigenous peoples, of great linguistic and cultural diversity, populated what is now North, Central, and South America long before their first encounters with Europeans. Much of the southwestern United States and California used to be part of Mexico and was populated by Spanish speakers long before the arrival of the Anglo-American settler. French speaking populations in what is now Maine and Louisiana predate the founding of the United States.

Other non-English populations have arrived more recently and are still arriving, many to escape political and social strife and/or to seek economic opportunity. In Miami, Florida, Spanish speakers from Cuba, Nicaragua, Guatemala, El Salvador, Colombia, and Puerto Rico mix with speakers of Haitian Creole and immigrants from Russia. In other parts of the country, refugees from war-torn Southeast Asia (Vietnam, Cambodia, and Laos) represent a sizable percentage of school populations; in small Ohio towns, the children of Japanese industrial employees learn alongside their native English speaking friends. Although the largest numbers of recent immigrants, especially those from Asia, are settling in California, there are fewer and fewer schools and school districts that have not been influenced by the presence of non-English speakers in the schools. Some of the children entering our schools have been in school in their native countries. Because of economic and political circumstances, some have not been able to attend school. Still others have spent time in refugee camps prior to entering the United States; some of the camps have worked with the children in educational settings.

The increase in the number of non–native English speaking children in our schools means that it is imperative that educators address the issue of how to provide learners of English as a second language (ESL) with opportunities for intellectually, socially, and emotionally enriching learning experiences that will also encourage the acquisition and development of English abilities. This chapter will focus on how to facilitate second language learners' literacy growth. The close connections between reading and writing have already been established in this book with regard to native speakers of English (see Chapter 1). These connections also hold for ESL learners; therefore, this chapter will give consideration to both of these language processes.

GRAPHIC ORGANIZER

This graphic organizer summarizes the structure of Chapter 13:

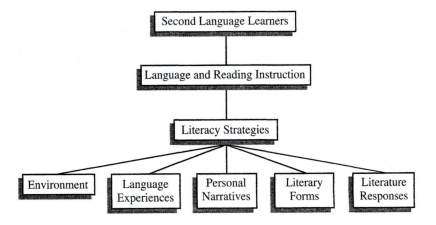

OBJECTIVES

When you finish this chapter, you should be able to understand and discuss each of these statements:

1. Native language literacy may help ESL children to become literate in English.
2. There is no one best way to facilitate ESL learners' second language literacy development.
3. Many of the literacy demands placed on ESL children are also confronted by native English speakers.
4. Work with literature in its varied forms should be an important element in a second language literacy program.
5. Work with writing across the curriculum is also crucial to second language learners' literacy development.
6. It is vital to consider the ESL reader's background of experiences and language when using commercial text material.

Language and Reading Instruction

For many schools, the first issues in providing quality instruction for second language learners are whether the children's native language will be used in school and, if so, how. One of the tenets of bilingual education in the United States, supported by both federal legislation (Title VII) and the Supreme Court (*Lau vs. Nichols* decision), is that children's native languages should be used as media of instruction, along with English, until the learners are able to function exclusively in English. Throughout its history, bilingual education has been controversial (Crawford, 1992), and it continues to be so. In California, where the largest number of non–English speaking school children reside, the passage in 1998 of Proposition 227 has caused limits to be placed on the utilization of languages other than English in classroom settings. In spite of the anti–bilingual education rhetoric, there is considerable evidence that *quality* bilingual education programs do work to facilitate overall academic achievement and the development of English language abilities. Bilingual education does not retard language or academic achievement (Ramirez, Yuen, & Ramey, 1991). Indeed, well-designed bilingual education programs enhance both academic and English language achievement (Krashen, 1999; Thomas & Collier, 1995).

Many bilingual programs have adopted the practice of first teaching non–English speaking children to read and write in their native language and then moving into English literacy. Teachers and researchers have documented that learners who become confident of their literacy abilities in a language other than English (that is, who see themselves as readers and writers) naturally begin to experiment with English (Edelsky, 1986; Hudelson, 1987, 1989; Hudelson & Serna, 1994). Learners *apply,* or *transfer,* what they have learned about reading and writing in one language to literacy in another language (Edelsky, 1982). In addition, longitudinal studies have demonstrated that children taught to read first in their native language achieve better results in the second language over time than do their peers who learn to read only in the second language (Rosier & Holm, 1979; Thomas & Collier, 1995). Given a definition of reading as a process of constructing meaning from text, it makes sense that readers will be better able to make use of all the cuing systems (graphophonic, syntactic, semantic, and pragmatic cues) needed to construct meaning in a language that they speak fluently than in a language they do not know well (Freeman & Freeman, 1998; Goodman, Goodman, & Flores, 1979; Weaver, 1994). Given a definition of writing as a process of constructing meaning through the creation of a text by utilizing a system of symbols, it makes sense that writers will be better able to create texts and use written language effectively if they are fluent speakers of the language in which they are writing (Hudelson, 1989).

Process Guide 13.1

An example of transfer, or application, may help to clarify the concept. Examine Figure 13.1, which is a page from a Navajo-language reader. What do you know about this selection? Jot down your ideas and share them with another class member.

After examining Figure 13.1, you may have decided that you know one or more of the following:

The selection is about an animal.

The name of the animal is written below the animal's picture.

The name of the animal serves as a title or part of a title to the selection.

There are many words on the page.

There are several sentences in the selection.

One sentence asks a question.

Gólízhii Yázhí

Gólízhii yázhí tizhin dóó

bikáá' dzígai. Bináá' naaki.

Bijaa' dó' naaki. Bijáád

díí'. Haash yit'é atdó'?

FIGURE 13.1   Page from a Navajo-Language Reader

You would read the selection from left to right and from top to bottom.

The writing system contains letters that represent vowels and consonants.

The diacritical marks associated with certain letters may have an effect on the pronunciation of sounds.

You may have tried to pronounce the words in the selection based on your knowledge of grapheme-phoneme relationships in another language or languages. You may have made other hypotheses about the form and content of the selection. Your hypotheses are based on what you already know about reading. But unless you are a speaker of Navajo, you are limited in the meaning you are able to construct. For example, you may know that the selection is about an animal, but what about the animal? This selection (which is titled "Little Skunk" and describes the skunk as being little, black and white, and having two eyes and ears and four legs) illustrates that (1) readers apply what they already know about reading to new reading tasks and (2) without some language ability, it is difficult to construct much meaning, even though you may be able to do a decent job of sounding out the words on the page. These points are particularly important because they are the major reasons bilingual educators believe that there is a place for native language reading in schools where the accepted medium of instruction is English.

Process Guide 13.2

Now let's look at an example of application, or transfer, in writing. Examine Figure 13.2, which is a letter written by a Spanish speaking child to an English speaking friend who has moved to another school. What does the letter say? What does this child demonstrate that he knows about English? What does this child demonstrate that he knows about written language? Jot down your ideas and share them with another class member.

The writer of the letter in Figure 13.2, a 7-year-old native Spanish speaking second grader, was enrolled in a bilingual program where his formal literacy instruction had been initiated in Spanish. At the time he wrote this letter, this child was reading and writing fluently in Spanish, but he had received no formal English literacy instruction. However, he was in a classroom where about half of his classmates were engaged daily in English literacy; he saw English around him in his classroom and in his community, and his teacher used English for a variety of activities. You may have noted that the contents of the letter make it clear that the child has been acquiring a great deal of English. He is able to ask *wh* questions. He uses a variety of verb tenses. He expresses his feelings about his missing friend. He is able to spell the English words *dear, I,* and *coming* in standard written form. You may also have discussed with your classmate that this child demonstrates that he knows how to construct a friendly letter. He has included the salutation and the closing, inserted a comma after the addressee's name, and created several sentences that form a coherent text.

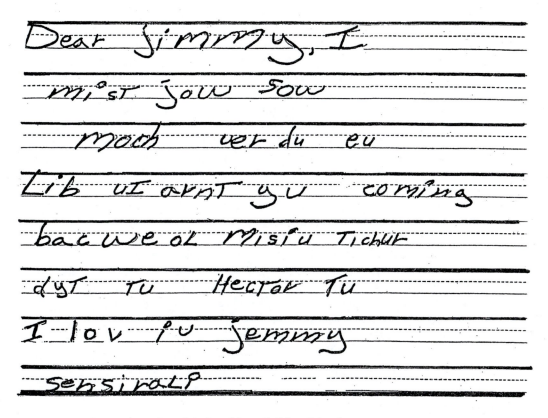

FIGURE 13.2   Letter from Spanish Speaking Child to Friend

You may have commented on the child's invented spelling and predicted that he used his knowledge of Spanish to solve his spelling problems in English. This is certainly the case. There are many examples of transfer of Spanish grapheme-phoneme correspondences to English: the words *sou* (so), *ol* (all), *tichur* (teacher), *tu* (too), and *lib* (live). The Spanish letter or combination of letters that the child believes most closely represents the English sound is used. Using Spanish orthography, the child spells "you" in several different ways (jou, eu, yu, iu), depending on its phonetic articulation in the sentence in which it occurs. These examples demonstrate that what learners learn in one setting they may apply to other settings. In this case, a child who is literate in one language (Spanish) uses that ability when he begins to develop literacy in another language (English). Literacy in a child's native language, bilingual educators argue, helps the child develop confidence as a literate person and gives the child resources to use in the second language literacy setting.

For many second language learners, however, bilingual instruction is not a viable educational alternative for one or more reasons. Children in a specific community may speak languages that the teachers do not know. Some classrooms may be populated by children from as many as a dozen different language groups, making bilingual instruction impossible. Some languages have only recently developed written systems, which means that few, if any, elementary school materials will be available. In some communities, parents and community leaders do not believe that it is appropriate to use a language other than English in school. Local or state policies may limit the use of languages other than English.

In schools where the numbers of second language learners are not large, ESL children may find themselves in regular classroom settings with a teacher who is not a bilingual/ESL specialist. In these circumstances, children will probably receive their formal education exclusively through the medium of English (although opportunities for children to pursue native language literacy in their communities and at home should be encouraged). This usually means that while children are learning to understand and speak English, they are also learning to read and write it, as well as having to cope with the English used for a variety of instructional tasks across the curriculum each school day.

For teachers who are not in bilingual programs and who do not themselves speak, read, and write the native language(s) of their students, a major concern is how best to help their children grow as English readers and writers. One way of responding to this concern is to examine recent developments in the field of second language literacy research and theory, giving special emphasis to work done with children, and to interpret these findings in terms of implications for classroom instruction. The rest of this chapter presents current information about ESL literacy and suggests that educators use this information to help second language children become effective readers and writers of English.

Making the Most of the Environment

A Literate and Collaborative Classroom Environment

Chapter 2 of this text described a print-rich classroom environment that invites learner exploration of and experimentation with literacy in a variety of forms and for a variety of purposes. For ESL learners, as well as for native speakers of the language, it is critical that classrooms demonstrate multiple functions of written language. Individual classrooms for second language learners, then, need to become print-rich environments. Special care may need to be taken by the teacher (and other children) to make sure that second language learners understand and are involved in the literacy activities taking place in such a classroom. Second language learners need to be in situations where they work with and learn both content and language from each other as well as from the teacher. A second language develops most effectively in an environment where the following conditions exist (Enright & McCloskey, 1985; Freeman & Freeman, 1998; Lindfors, 1987; TESOL, 1997):

1. The learners use the language to accomplish authentic purposes.
2. The learners use oral and written language with others, so that they are both experimenting with the new language and receiving input from other language users.

3. The learners are allowed to make mistakes, and these mistakes are acknowledged as a necessary part of language learning.
4. The learners' efforts to use the second language are encouraged by adults and peers.

The kind of classroom that second language learners need is one that fosters collaboration: children working together in small groups both independently of and in conjunction with the teacher. Second language learners benefit from a classroom in which a community has developed, so children experience a sense of belonging and well being in the class setting as well as a sense of responsibility for one another (Bridges, 1995; Townsend & Fu, 1998).

Environmental Print

For the last 20 years, research has demonstrated unequivocally that children in print-saturated or print-oriented societies are engaged, from very early on in their lives, in making sense of the printed word. One of the first contexts for many children who are grappling with the meaning and function of print is the print in the world around them—what has come to be termed *environmental print.* Work with preschoolers has demonstrated that children as young as age 3 are able to identify such familiar signs as McDonald's and STOP and such product labels as Coca-Cola and Crest (Baghban, 1984; Goodman & Altwerger, 1981; Harste, Woodward, & Burke, 1984).

Non–English speaking children in English speaking countries frequently find themselves in environments where English surrounds them (Goodman, Goodman, & Flores, 1979; Wallace, 1988). Some children are obliged to cope with English environmental print only at school, because the print in their communities is in another language. Most, however, are bombarded by English in their neighborhoods and homes, at school, and through the media, especially television. ESL learners work to make sense of the English in the environment around them by guessing about content. Many struggle with environmental print before they begin to read English texts (Goodman, Goodman, & Flores, 1979; Goodman & Altwerger, 1981; Wallace, 1988). Environmental print provides a logical area in which to plan and carry out reading activities in elementary ESL classrooms. In classrooms where native English speakers and ESL children are together, both groups of youngsters may participate.

Environmental print activities might begin with a walking field trip around the school or neighborhood so that children can examine and write down examples of the print around them. These labels can then be read and categorized (e.g., names of cars, labels on store fronts, directions for vehicles, street names). Using inexpensive instant cameras, children and/or teachers may collect environmental print samples of special interest to them, such as graffiti and signs related to child or pop culture (Orellana & Hernandez, 1999). Children may bring in examples of environmental print from their homes and neighborhoods (e.g., empty milk cartons, cereal boxes, soda cans, empty laundry detergent boxes), and these can be displayed and categorized (as names of food products, names of products you use to keep clean, etc.). Children still learning grapheme-phoneme correspondences might identify all the items that begin with a certain sound. Environmental print may form part of the "stuff" of early reading experiences in school, as children learn to read signs and other forms of print necessary for survival in school and the surrounding community. In bi- or multilingual communities, utilizing environmental print in multiple languages validates second language learners' home languages and cultures and provides opportunities for learners to experiment with reading in a language other than English (Orellana & Hernandez, 1999).

Activities that center on environmental print may be used in conjunction with content areas of the curriculum, particularly social studies. As a part of a unit on community helpers or career awareness, for example, children might role-play community persons and situations, making purchases at a grocery or convenience store, ordering and eating at a fast food restaurant, conducting business in a bank, or performing the functions of a crossing guard outside the school. A unit on communities could involve groups of children in creating their ideal community and deciding what community signs to include as part of their Utopia. Intermediate-level social studies/economics activities related to understanding the purposes of advertising could include a study of commercials, both on television and in print, and culminate in group projects in which children create their own products and advertising. If learners were studying the ways humans pollute and destroy the environment, posters and T-shirts that exhort adults and children to take particular actions could be created. These examples demonstrate the wealth of opportunities for meaningful instruction that can come out of using environmental print with second language learners.

Bringing environmental print into the classroom activates children's interest in and inquisitiveness about the print that surrounds them. It helps children see that they can construct meaning from that print. It takes advantage of their awareness of print and provides them with opportunities to demonstrate what they know and also to bring confusing print into the classroom and ask about it, facilitating vocabulary development. Using environmental print demonstrates a practical application of English reading and writing—to get along in the world. For all these reasons, the context of the physical environment as one for reading should be exploited.

Process Guide 13.3

Break into groups of three to five people. Think for a few minutes about the environmental print you see on your way to school every day. Make a list of all the examples you can generate. What different types of print have you listed? Now work together to develop a classroom activity using environmental print. You may want to consider a particular age level as you design your activity. Share your activity with other groups.

A second language develops best when learners participate in interesting experiences.

Making Use of Language Experiences

As noted earlier, second language researchers and teachers have demonstrated that a second language develops best in a language-rich environment where learners are participating in interesting experiences (Allen, 1986; Enright & McCloskey, 1985; Freeman & Freeman, 1998). Second language reading researchers have found that ESL readers' comprehension is affected by their familiarity with the content. ESL learners understand material that is experientially and/or culturally familiar to them better than they understand unfamiliar material (Barnitz, 1986; Rigg, 1986). Therefore, it seems logical to connect some of the experiences children have first to their oral expression and subsequently to text that they will read.

One way to do this is to allow the learners to create their own texts, based on their own experiences. The text of language experience stories is always comprehensible because the children themselves dictate it to the teacher. The language experience approach has long been advocated as a reading strategy for native speakers of English (see Chapter 5). Many ESL professionals also advocate its use in the second language classroom (Rigg, 1989). Rigg gives special consideration to the issue of accepting the language as the children provide it, rather than correcting it, by making the important point that language experience stories may be saved to be reread at a later date. When rereading occurs, the learners are often able to articulate grammatical and lexical changes that they would like to make in the stories, thus demonstrating to themselves and to others that they have acquired more English. Whenever possible in elementary classrooms, native speakers should be mixed heterogeneously with ESL children for the construction of language experience texts. As the native speakers participate in dictation, using their fluent English, they provide both language that will be understood by their second language counterparts and a model of fluent English. This language should have a positive impact on the ESL children's language growth.

Language experience dictation may involve the teacher in working with a single child, a small group, or the entire class. Experiences for dictations may come from a variety of sources. Stories may originate in the children's lives outside of school—for example, a movie seen, a community cultural event witnessed or participated in, a country escaped from, or a refugee camp experienced. Teachers may organize classroom activities to which first talk and then written language are attached—for example, preparing and eating a meal from a particular culture. Wordless picture books are another possible source for experiences, as children first create a story orally using the pictures from a wordless book and then dictate a version of the story. Stories from the children's own culture read or told in the classroom may inspire them to create their own versions (Rigg, 1989).

Another way language experience dictation can become a part of classroom life is through the utilization of an activity called News of the Day. Generally this activity involves children in completing such sentences as

Yesterday was _____. Today is _____. There are _____ children in class today, _____ girls and _____ boys.

In addition to these repeated sentences, children can generate unique contributions about special happenings on a particular day, such as a field trip, someone's birthday, or a regular visit to the library. Second language learners benefit especially from this kind of structured repetition of language because it provides multiple opportunities for them to understand English and to gradually participate actively in generating partial or full sentences (Peregoy & Boyle, 1993).

Finally, experiences may be connected directly to the content children are studying, so that language experience becomes a part of the content area curriculum. If, for example, children are studying light and shadow in science, the teacher may organize an activity in which groups of learners measure each other's height and chart the results. Then, the children move to a strong light source such as the sun on the playground and, after predicting the results, measure their shadows and compare the lengths of their shadows to their real heights. Next, the same learners, again after predicting what will happen, measure their shadows at other times of the day and compare the results. These predicting/measuring/charting activities may be followed by talking about what has been learned about shadows and producing a text that summarizes the learning. Thus, language experience dictations can focus directly on important content area concepts.

In working with second language learners, teachers must take special care to make content learning experiences accessible and understandable. They may do this in various ways, including (1) speaking distinctly and perhaps a little more slowly than they normally would; (2) paraphrasing comments and directions if it appears that children do not understand; (3) supporting verbal explanations with nonverbal cues such as realia, diagrams or charts, gestures or expressions, and hands-on experiences for learners; and (4) structuring group work so that more fluent users of English collaborate with less fluent English users (Peregoy & Boyle, 1993).

Using Oral and Written Personal Narratives

Over the years, many professionals in education have written about the centrality of narrative, or story, in people's lives (Bruner, 1986; Rosen, 1986; Witherell & Noddings, 1991). Their perspective is that, across cultures and individuals, narrative appears to be a fundamental process of the human mind—a basic way of making sense of the world and our own individual lives and of relating to other humans (Neumann & Peterson, 1997). All people have stories to tell, whether about something seemingly trivial that happened yesterday or about an event of more significance such as escaping one's war-torn country, living in a refugee camp, watching a drive-by shooting, or participating in a ceremony in one's own family or community. When individuals share their stories, they come to understand each other better and appreciate each other more, in terms of both how they are alike and how they are different.

The sharing of personal stories may be accomplished in different ways. One of the best documented of these is the creation of personal narratives through regular participation in what Calkins (1986) has termed *writing workshop*. Writing workshop has been practiced in classrooms around the world. With the teacher's involvement and leadership, children learn to (1) choose events from their lives about which to create stories; (2) work over time on drafts; (3) share what they are writing in small- and/or large-group conferences, in order to elicit peer and adult questions and comments; (4) make substantive changes in their pieces; (5) make editing changes to the final versions, with peer and teacher assistance; and (6) put the story into a final, published version to be shared with the class. Although writing workshop was originally carried out with native speakers of English, bilingual and second language educators have discovered that it can also be used effectively with non–native speakers of English (Edelsky, 1986; Hudelson, 1989; Peyton et al., 1994). ESL learners have proven that (1) they are able to generate their own personal stories, (2) they are capable of both giving and receiving comments on their work in progress, (3) they are able to make changes in their work, and (4) they are willing to struggle to express themselves in written English while they are still learning the language (Samway, 1987, 1992, 1993; Urzua, 1987).

While acknowledging the similarities between writing by native English speakers and writing by English language learners, teachers must also acknowledge the differences and learn to work with them in the classroom setting (Peyton et al., 1994). A major issue for many second language children writing in English is feelings of inadequacy arising from their inability to express all that they want to in English (especially in grammatically accurate English). Some learners are reluctant to share personal stories and refuse to participate in story drafting. The struggle to produce a piece of writing is often much greater for a child still developing English than for a fluent user of the language, and ESL learners may therefore be quite reluctant to make changes in what they have created (Peyton et al., 1994). The revisions ESL children do make, especially if they are early in their English language learning, may be fewer in number than those made by fluent speakers and are more likely to occur at the word level (Samway, 1987, 1993).

Sensitive teachers are able to adjust writing workshop activities to facilitate the success of ESL learners. Documented adjustments have included the following (Peyton et al., 1994):

1. Providing more time for talking and sharing stories prior to writing and modeling ways for listeners to respond to stories that have been shared
2. Slowing down the pace of drafting so that learners have more time to produce narratives
3. Providing lots of encouragement to writers and, early on, accepting and celebrating whatever is produced without concern for revising or editing
4. Allowing children to write in their native language and to use their native language to assist them with writing in English
5. Placing children's writing within the context of content study, thus providing experiences and vocabulary for them to use in their writing
6. Providing multiple experiences with reading, again to extend students' vocabulary and experiences
7. Assisting learners with vocabulary and topic development and offering visual cues such as realia, pictures, webs, diagrams, and the like
8. Offering mini-lessons that model writing processes and different kinds of writing

Some teachers of young ESL children also engage in what has been called shared writing, where children write parts of their stories themselves and then teachers (or others) write parts when the children become tired or reluctant to continue (Serna, 1991).

A question that almost always arises with regard to second language learners' draft writing is the amount of editing (particularly of syntax) that should be done, especially since ESL learners have only partial control over English and may not understand or be able to assimilate the corrections that are being made. There is no simple answer to the question of how much to edit. Some teachers of ESL children elect to encourage children's creation of personal narratives, focusing on first-draft fluency of expression and considering revision and editing later. Some choose to work on one or two syntactic irregularities or spelling inventions identified in a piece or pieces of writing. Others ask the learners themselves to identify a few words or sentences they would like to have assistance with (Hudelson, 1989). Still others choose to publish pieces only in standard written English, so they do the necessary editing to get the pieces to the standard even if the writers are not able to absorb all the changes and incorporate them into their writing (Gunkel, 1991). Acknowledging that attention needs to be paid to form as well as to content (Reyes, 1991), teachers need to be sensitive to what their ESL learners can cope with and how they will respond to instruction.

Dissatisfaction with the quality of the personal narratives that many children produced while participating in writing workshop motivated Calkins and some of her colleagues to experiment with a somewhat different approach to writing (Calkins, 1991; Fletcher, 1996). The idea for writer's notebook came from the realization that many professional authors keep notebooks in which they jot down ideas, images, lists, words, and so on, some of which they turn into complete pieces. Teachers and children who keep notebooks use them in the same way—to jot down ideas, incidents, impressions, and feelings. After several weeks, children reread their notebooks, examining them for recurring themes or musings from which they might draft a piece of some kind. When a topic has been chosen in this way, the writing process described in writing workshop begins. Calkins maintains that the use of writer's notebook contributes to a better quality of writing, particularly for young writers for whom writing workshop has become mundane and predictable. Calkins and others (e.g., Doorn, 1998) have used writer's notebook successfully with many children, both native and non–native speakers of English.

If dialogic writing can be incorporated into the sharing of personal narratives, ESL learners have the opportunity to interact with more proficient speakers of English, which is helpful in terms of both developing fluency in written communication and acquiring more English. The easiest and most direct way to do this is to use journals (see Chapter 10), so that individuals have the opportunity to carry on written conversations with each other. On a daily or regular basis, children write to their teacher about whatever they choose. The teacher reads the children's entries and writes back to them, responding to the content of the entries. Corrections of the children's written form are not made, but the teacher uses standard adult English in his or her responses. The value of this practice, which has been used in classrooms of native speakers of English for quite a few years, has also been well documented with ESL learners of various ages and English proficiency levels (Peyton, 1990; Peyton & Staton, 1993). In addition to having the child write to the teacher, it is possible to organize learner-learner pairings, matching a more fluent with a less fluent user of English (Peyton & Mackinson-Smyth, 1989) or an ESL learner with a native speaker (Bromley, 1995).

ESL learners benefit from participating in dialogue journal writing in several ways.

1. They engage in an authentic communication situation where they need to make themselves understood.
2. They receive demonstrations of standard written English.

3. They begin to see that one of the functions of written English is to establish and maintain interpersonal relationships, thus learning that English can be used for personal reasons.
4. They have an opportunity to share who they are, express their hopes and frustrations and problems, and receive personal validation from an individual who responds naturally to them.

Working with Varied Literary Forms

The kinds of student-generated texts that come out of language experiences, writing workshop, and dialogue journals are especially important to ESL learners because they give the children multiple opportunities to use their developing English and to read material that is comprehensible to them. But second language learners also need opportunities to construct meaning from texts written by authors other than themselves. When they write stories, authors take experiences and meanings from the world and re-create those experiences in print. In books and stories, authors create an experience in print, which takes the place of a direct real-life experience shared by author and reader.

Besides the shift from concrete to vicarious experience, there is also a shift in the kind of written language being read as children move from student-generated texts to published texts. In language experience stories, children often read something close to *talk talk*, or speech written down. But the language of books is not simply speech written down. Book or story talk is different from talk talk (Smith, 1982), and readers learn to deal with the more formal, conventionalized, and stylized talk of stories only as they are exposed to it over time as they listen to and read stories and books.

In addition, stories are structured and organized in highly conventionalized ways. In Western European tradition, they generally begin with an introduction of the characters and setting, move to an initiating event, present at least one if not several conflicts, and resolve the conflicts. Learners come to understand this kind of story structure, which is so critical to constructing meaning, not because someone tells them about the structure, but because they experience it in stories (Applebee, 1978; Mandler & Johnson, 1977).

Experiences with stories are especially critical for ESL learners because they will be expected, eventually, to read and comprehend them. Some ESL children, coming from different cultural as well as linguistic traditions, may have well-developed senses of story organization that differ from those used in classrooms in the United States. They need to become acquainted with typical Western story structure. Other children may come from cultures where the structure is the same but the language, of course, is different. These learners need to attach the English language to the familiar structure or organizational pattern. Stories may also help ESL learners with their overall learning of English. Research has demonstrated that a story-based ESL curriculum results in greater overall English language growth than does the regular oral sentence pattern approach (Elley & Mangubhai,

1983). For these reasons we will now take a closer look at two often underutilized forms of books—predictable books and alphabet books.

Predictable Books

This chapter takes the perspective that fluent, effective reading is a process in which readers predict their way through text, sampling the visual (graphophonic) display and using text content and the semantic and syntactic cue systems to construct meaning (Goodman, 1996; Weaver, 1994). To develop fluent, effective readers, therefore, one must use teaching strategies that help them view reading as a predicting process. Especially with beginning readers and ESL readers whose English is less than fluent, predictable books (Heald-Taylor, 1987; Seawell, 1985) may be utilized both to develop their abilities to predict their way through texts and to demonstrate the simultaneous utilization of the semantic, syntactic, and graphophonic systems of language. Additionally, the predictability of the materials should ensure readers' success in reading them, which should, in turn, make readers eager to continue reading and to stretch themselves.

Certain kinds of reading materials are more predictable than others (Heald-Taylor, 1987). Factors within the texts themselves contribute to predictability. These elements include repetition of language and incident. What some would call classic folk or fairy tales, such as *The Three Little Pigs, Little Red Riding Hood, The Three Bears, Chicken Little,* and *The Little Red Hen,* are examples of predictable reading materials. In *The Little Red Hen,* for example, the hen repeatedly carries out tasks by herself while asking over and over "Who will help me _____?" And her friends continue to respond "Not I." Thus, the reader can predict what the hen and her compatriots will both do and say.

Other stories are predictable in part because of rhythm, rhyme, and repetition. In the story *May I Bring a Friend?* (de Regniers, 1965), the main character brings a succession of wild animals to a fancy party, repeating these lines: "I told the king and the king told the queen that I had a friend I wanted to bring. The queen said to me, 'My dear, my dear. Any friend of yours is welcome here.'" In the book *Brown Bear, Brown Bear, What Do You See?* (Martin, 1983), the same two sentences occur throughout the text, with only the names and colors of the animals changing. Children's songs such as "Old MacDonald Had a Farm" and "I Know an Old Lady Who Swallowed a Fly" also fall into this category, as do poems such as "This Is the House That Jack Built." Finally some children's books such as *The Carrot Seed* (Krauss, 1945) and *The Very Hungry Caterpillar* (Carle, 1969) are predictable for readers who can take advantage of real-world knowledge, such as how plants grow and how caterpillars turn into butterflies.

Using predictable materials exposes ESL learners to one kind of literary language. Teachers should read predictable stories at story time and then make them available for children to examine on their own. Teachers who speak the native language of the ESL children may tell the story the first time in that language in order to ensure that the children have the gist of the plot. Teachers often use repeated readings of predictable books to help develop children's confidence in predicting.

Repeated readings also aid vocabulary acquisition of beginning ESL readers, as children learn new vocabulary every time they hear and participate in the reading of a predictable story (Carger, 1993). Working with teachers in New Zealand, Holdaway (1979) experimented with repeated readings of Big Books, which are highly predictable stories in enlarged text formats that enable children in a group to see the text more easily. Holdaway stressed that, with the repetitions, teachers may direct children's attention to particular features of the text, such as words and letters.

Educators in the United States (Strickland & Morrow, 1990), including those working with second language learners of varying ages (Nurss, Hough, & Enright, 1986), have also provided suggestions for repeated use of predictable books, whether in Big Book format or otherwise. For example, during a first or second reading, children might be asked to use the illustrations to predict the contents of the text. After the first or second reading, teachers may track part of the print of the story with hand or pointer and encourage children to read along as they see the words and hear them pronounced. As teachers reread a familiar story, they may stop at particularly predictable parts and ask learners to fill in the next word or phrase, urging children to think of as many words as they can that would make sense in the context of the story. This kind of oral cloze may be followed by written cloze activities in which certain words or phrases of a story are covered physically (or certain parts of a story are written on a board or on chart paper with words and/or phrases deleted) and learners are asked to predict the missing words. Teachers may also cover up a word, leaving only the initial letter or letters, so that learners use graphophonic as well as semantic and syntactic cues to predict. It is important to demonstrate to readers that, when they do not know a word, they can read ahead and use the context that follows as well as the context that precedes the missing word or phrase to aid their comprehension. Finally, teachers may focus learners' attention on certain text features such as repeated words, words that begin with a specific letter or cluster of letters, punctuation marks, and capital letters. What is crucial is that learning always begin with the experience of the whole story. Then, if the learners need specific instruction or focus on the parts, the teacher may use the text selectively to assist children in becoming independent, effective readers.

Teachers and learners may also use predictable, familiar materials for choral reading or reading in parts, for acting out stories, and for creating their own books. The incorporation of a time for independent reading (often called SSR, Sustained Silent Reading; GRAB, Go Read a Book; or DEAR, Drop Everything and Read) into daily literature experiences will give children additional opportunities to read and reread familiar, predictable stories. Predictable stories and books may also form a part of content area study. For example, when children are studying animal life cycles in science, *The Very Hungry Caterpillar* (Carle, 1969), a version of Hans Christian Anderson's *The Ugly Duckling*, and *Make Way for Ducklings* (McCloskey, 1941) could be shared. If children are learning about plant growth, *The Carrot Seed* (Krauss, 1945) is an appropriate choice. Robert Louis Stevenson's poem "I Have a Little Shadow" could be used in conjunction with a unit on light and shadow.

Teachers may be uneasy about using such seemingly "babyish" predictable stories with intermediate-school ESL learners, in spite of the fact that children can benefit from them. One solution is to create cross-age tutoring situations in which intermediate-age children share books and stories with younger children in school or at home (Cook & Urza, 1993). In order to share the books, older children must practice their own reading, which gives them added opportunities to read the predictable books for themselves. Reading to share with someone else provides an authentic reason to read and reread the same story several times, as well as an authentic reason to read orally. Reading these books may also make the older children more aware of the story structure. Projects in elementary schools with large numbers of ESL learners have demonstrated that as older children share books with younger learners, the older children become more able readers themselves and increase their own understanding of how the authors construct plots and use certain kinds of words in the books that they are sharing. The older children become more able to talk about how the stories have been put together. They are also better able to reflect on the learning of the young children, their tutees, and better able to analyze their own tutoring in terms of its effectiveness (Heath & Mangiola, 1991; Samway and Syvanen, 1999; Samway, Whang, & Pippett, 1995).

Another important factor in the utilization of predictable books with older learners is the selection of titles (Watson, 1997). There are many predictable titles that are quite sophisticated, in terms of illustrations, topic, or theme. Books such as *Guess What?* (Fox, 1988), *Yo! Yes* (Raschka, 1993), and *The Story of the Little Mole Who Went in Search of Whodunit* (Holzwarth & Erlbruch, 1993) appeal to older as well as younger listeners and readers.

Process Guide 13.4

Ask a children's librarian to help you find some predictable books. Select two or three and read them out loud several times to decide where in each story to create oral or written cloze activities (see Chapter 6). Bring these predictable books to class to share with others in a small group.

Alphabet Books

In addition to using predictable books, teachers working with second language learners who are beginning readers may want to consider the *selective* use of alphabet books. A recent review of the research on children's knowledge of the alphabet suggests that, along with reading environmental print, participating in individual and group writing projects, and reading and spelling each other's names, children in primary classrooms learn the names of the letters by sharing alphabet books (McGee & Richgels, 1989). For second language learners, the specific books chosen should be connected to something that the children are studying; for example, use animal alphabet books if the children are studying animals. Children should not use alphabet books on topics with which they have no experience, and they should not use alphabet books for drill on letters and sounds. In conjunction with reading published alphabet books, learners can create some of their own. A unit of study on animals could generate an alphabet book that reflects the animals that the children studied and what they learned about them.

Reading Aloud

If, as articulated earlier, learners become aware of narrative structure and literary language through the experience of listening to (and later reading) literature, the activity of reading to children needs to be viewed as a curriculum basic rather than as a frill. Second language learners need to be read to on a daily basis by fluent models of English reading, as do native speakers of English (Smallwood, 1991). And beyond predictable books, they need to be read to from various genres in order to (1) hear and begin to enjoy the richness and variety of the English language, (2) begin to develop knowledge of the literary and/or story heritage of varied cultures, and (3) begin to see literature as one way of coming to understand the world and the relationship of the individual to the world (Peterson & Eeds, 1990).

One source of children's literature is that written by authors, such as Natalie Babbitt and William Steig, who are known for their ability to illuminate human experience without regard to a specific cultural or ethnic group. Another source is books that reflect multicultural perspectives, particularly the perspectives of the learners but also broader human themes. Thus, with a group of Hispanic learners from the Southwest, an appropriate choice might be Soto's *Too Many Tamales* (1993), the story of a young girl who learns an important lesson when she loses her mother's diamond ring as she is making tamales. A third source for literature to share is the traditional stories of various cultural groups (Norton, 1990). If, for example, you have a significant number of children from Japan, *The Crane Maiden* (Matsustani, 1968) might be included; with Native American children from the Great Plains area of the United States, Paul Goble's renditions of Plains Indians' traditional tales could be used; with Mexican-American children, *La Llorona* is a familiar story available in many versions (Anaya, 1997; Hayes, 1987; Vigil, 1994).

When taking into account the special linguistic and cultural needs of second language learners, teachers need to be most concerned about choosing books from which learners will be able to construct some meaning, even if that meaning is not the same as the teacher's or other children's. Books that have especially clear illustrations are beneficial for second language learners early in their English literacy development. It is also important to give consideration to the level of syntactic and lexical complexity as well as the complexity of plot (Smallwood, 1991). Choosing culturally familiar stories seems to be especially helpful to ESL children because prior knowledge of characters and/or plots may make the stories more comprehensible to the learners. When read-aloud experiences are structured, grouping children heterogeneously by language proficiency and encouraging responses to shared books may assist the second language learners in developing their English.

Literature Response

It is not enough to share literature with children. Children, including second language learners, need an opportunity to respond to what they have heard (and later what they read), to construct meaning, to relate a story to their own lives, and to comment on the emotion and ideas that a piece evoked. This means that reading aloud must be followed by an opportunity to comment on the experience, ideally in a setting where children are grouped heterogeneously with respect to language ability so that less proficient speakers of English may hear more proficient speakers talk. This does *not* mean that learners should be bombarded with a variety of comprehension questions. It does mean that learners should be given time to reflect on the literary experience they have had and to respond to a general comment such as "What would you like to say about this book/chapter/poem?" (Peterson & Eeds, 1990; Samway & Whang, 1996).

Frequent opportunities for ESL children to respond to literature read aloud may facilitate these learners' subsequent literature study (Fournier & Espinosa, 1995). Although literature study was first proposed for native speakers of English (Peterson & Eeds, 1990), educators have demonstrated that second language learners can benefit from it (Fournier et al., 1993; Samway & Whang, 1996). A group of learners chooses a book that the group members want to read, usually after the teacher has introduced several books to the class. With or without adult assistance, the members of the group read the selected book and come to literature study group prepared to talk about what they have read. In the first session, the teacher opens the discussion with general questions such as "So, what did you

Reading aloud must be followed by a chance to comment on the experience.

think?" or "What do you want to say about this book?" and learners respond personally to the book. As the children talk, the teacher takes notes on their ideas and may offer some of her or his own as well. But the teacher does *not* ask a series of reading comprehension questions. Comprehension is assumed (Edelsky, 1988), so the emphasis is on the children's individual responses and how they constructed meaning when they read the piece.

After the children have shared their responses, the teacher—perhaps by reviewing some of the comments that the group members made or asking the children to think about what they would like to reexamine—guides the group in choosing a specific aspect of the book that they want to examine more closely. For example, if the children had read *Too Many Tamales* (Soto, 1993), they might have commented on the loving relationship between Maria and her mother, in this case providing the context for a further examination of this theme. The readers then return to the book to find examples of the aspect of the story that the group has decided to examine—in this case, places where the author made clear Maria's relationship with her mother. Children reexamine their constructions of meaning by going back to the author's words, using the text to justify or reconsider their interpretations. They also deal naturally with such aspects of stories as setting, characters, tension, and symbolism. The teacher may contribute ideas and opinions, but the focus is not on one right opinion or interpretation. Rather, it is on the collective construction of meaning. Together, the teacher and children decide how many sessions they will use to return to the text and investigate specific aspects of it.

Literature study recognizes that not all learners will construct the same meaning from a story or book; learners' unique prior experiences will influence their individual constructions of meaning. Thus, reading is a transaction between the reader and the text. But literature study also recognizes that learning is social and that readers can learn and grow in their interpretations of texts if they share their meaning and listen to the interpretations of others (Eeds & Peterson, 1991). Construction of meaning is enhanced when learners work together on a text. These aspects of literature study make it an especially important learning tool for second language learners.

Summary

Second language learners are entering our schools in ever increasing numbers. They are faced with an overwhelming need to become effective users of English. This chapter has made the case for native language literacy, but it has also offered English speaking educators a group of strategies that they may use to facilitate the language and literacy growth of ESL learners. These strategies are based in a perspective of language and literacy learning that emphasizes (1) experience based language and print-rich classrooms; (2) having children work together and learn from each other as well as the teacher; (3) use of natural, authentic texts for reading; (4) multiple opportunities and purposes for children to use and produce written language; (5) engagement in meaningful content study as a vehicle for language, literacy, and learning; and (6) experimentation with the new language in environments where one's efforts are appreciated and celebrated.

FOLLOW-THROUGH ACTIVITIES

Note: Level 1 activities may require limited access to children or classrooms. Level 2 activities should be completed using children and classrooms.

Level 1 Activities

1. Prepare an annotated bibliography listing at least ten predictable books and stories that you might use with ESL learners. Consult your librarian for help, if needed.

2. One kind of environmental print is the print seen on bumper stickers and tee-shirts. Choose a grade level and develop a classroom activity that utilizes these two kinds of environmental print.

3. Choose a particular ethnic group of second language learners, preferably one that is part of your local community—for example, Mexican-American, Puerto Rican, Vietnamese, Chinese speaking, or Navajo children. Create a bibliography of at least 10 books that might reflect the experiences of this specific group of learners. Bring your bibliography and at least one of the books to class to share.

Level 2 Activities

1. Choose a predictable book and read it several times to a small group of children that includes second language learners. Then ask the children to retell the story. Record the children's retelling and analyze it, paying attention both to the children's recall of the story and to their use of the language of the story.

2. Develop a language experience activity and carry it out with a group of children, including ESL learners. What was the children's response to the activity? How successful were they in dictating a language experience story? What did you learn about the children's language abilities from this activity? Did anything surprise you?

3. Choose a children's book and read all or just a chapter of it to a group of children, including second language learners. Then provide an opportunity for the learners to respond to the reading. Record the children's responses and analyze them. What kinds of responses did the children make to the story? Were there responses that surprised you?

WORKING WITH PARENTS

The scene is a parent-teacher conference in the fall in the second-grade classroom of Ms. Ramos. Most of the children in Ms. Ramos's class are speakers of English as a second language. Ms. Ramos is fluent in Spanish, so the conference is being conducted in Spanish.

MRS. ORTIZ: Good afternoon, Ms. Ramos. I have come to ask you how my daughter Teresita is doing in her reading. She doesn't bring home a reading book and workbook as her older brothers did, and she tells me that she doesn't use one at school. Is anything wrong?

MS. RAMOS: Not at all, Mrs. Ortiz. I'm glad that you came to see me so that I can explain my reading program. I am not using a reading series because I believe that the children will do better using different materials. Right now, we are doing a lot of our reading from children's books. I think that Teresita may be bringing home a book called *Caps for Sale* that she reads for homework.

MRS. ORTIZ: Yes, she has brought that book home. But I thought that it was just a fun book from the library. How does using books like that help her be a better reader?

MS. RAMOS: Well, we do a great deal of reading and rereading of stories that have a lot of repetition and rhythm and rhyme in them. The children remember these stories better than the ones in the reader. They enjoy reading them over and over, and that helps them become better readers. We also do activities, such as creating a play based on the story, and that gives the children a chance to read the story again. They actually do much more reading than they would if they were reading in the reading book. And I believe that doing a lot of reading is better for the children than doing a lot of workbook pages.

MRS. ORTIZ: Teresita certainly does seem to enjoy reading to one of us. But I was worried about how she was doing. I feel a little better now, but I do have another question. Will you ever use the reading books?

MS. RAMOS: Perhaps later in the year. The children and I will pick several stories from the book that look interesting and read them.

MRS. ORTIZ: I also have a question about Teresita's writing. She has been writing in what she calls a journal at home, and when she showed it to me, I wasn't sure that all the words were spelled correctly. When I asked her about this, she said that she was spelling the words the way she thought they should be spelled. How will she ever learn to spell if she spells with all those mistakes?

MS. RAMOS: You have raised another important question, Mrs. Ortiz. Having children write is another important part of my literacy program. What Teresita is doing is called invented spelling, which means that Teresita is using her best guesses about how some words are spelled. The reason that I encourage children to make guesses is that I want them to express their ideas in writing without being worried about how to spell words. Then, when they have their ideas expressed, we work on the accurate spellings. We will work on spelling, but after expression. And the more Teresita reads, the more accurate spellings she will see. This will also help her. I imagine that you have noticed some differences in her spelling already, from August to November. She will continue to get better, and she will also see that she is able to express her ideas in writing. That is very important for her in school and in life.

MRS. ORTIZ: Let me ask you something else, please. Some people have told me that I should try to speak English with Teresita, so that I will not interfere with her learning English. But I don't speak much English. English is very hard for me. What should I do?

MS. RAMOS: You should speak the language that you are most comfortable speaking. What you can give Teresita is a firm base in her native language, Spanish. At school, we can give her a firm base in English. It is better for you to speak to Teresita in the language that you speak fluently. That way you can share lots of experiences with her and show her how she can use language. What she knows in Spanish will help her in English.

MRS. ORTIZ: I appreciate that. I would hate not being able to talk to my own daughter. Thank you very much, Ms. Ramos. I understand better what you are doing now, and I will encourage Teresita to work hard in school.

MS. RAMOS: Thank you for your help, Mrs. Ortiz. Teresita is a hard worker, but children always need parental encouragement. Please come back any time.

RESOURCES

Cary, S. (1997). *Second language learners.* York, ME: Stenhouse.

> The specifics provided on a variety of second language teaching and assessment strategies are congruent with the framework developed in this chapter.

Edelsky, C. (1996). *With literacy and justice for all: Rethinking the social in language and education* (2nd ed.). Bristol, PA: Taylor and Francis.

> Several of the author's studies of language-minority children's literacy development are examined retrospectively, and a theoretical framework for critical literacy and whole language is set up from a critical perspective.

Freeman, Y., & Freeman, D. (1998). *ESL/EFL teaching: Principles for success.* Portsmouth, NH: Heinemann.

> This revised edition of their 1992 work, *Whole Language for Second Language Learners,* presents six principles of second language learning from a whole language perspective and then provides multiple examples of these ideas in action in bilingual, ESL, and EFL classrooms.

Genesee, F. (Ed.). (1994). *Educating second language children: The whole child, the whole curriculum, the whole community.* New York: Cambridge University Press.

> Promoting an integrated approach to the education of ESL children, the authors describe both the various contexts of the learners' experience—classroom, family, community—and the learners' learning and use of language across these contexts.

Peregoy, S., & Boyle, O. (1997). *Reading, writing and learning in ESL.* New York: Longman.

> This volume offers suggestions on how classrooms may be organized and literacy instruction carried out in ways that facilitate ESL learners' linguistic, academic, and social growth.

Peyton, J. K., & Staton, J. (1993). *Dialogue journals in the multilingual classroom: Building language fluency and writing skills through interaction.* Norwood, NJ: Ablex.

> This book presents a series of research studies on dialogue journals, carried out in a multilingual-multicultural classroom. Researcher, teacher, and learner voices are all present in the analyses of the contributions of dialogue journals to second language learners' content and language learning.

Samway, K., & Whang, G. (1996*). Literature study circles in a multicultural classroom.* York, ME: Stenhouse.

> This volume describes in detail how one teacher set up and carried out literature study in her intermediate-grade multilingual classroom. Many practical suggestions and strategies are provided.

Samway, K., Whang, G., & Pippett, M. (1995). *Buddy reading: Cross-age tutoring in a multi-cultural school*. Portsmouth, NH: Heinemann.

The authors detail how to carry out a cross-age tutoring program organized around the sharing of literature and oral and written responses to literature. Many of the child participants are ESL learners.

Spangenberg-Urbschat, K., & Pritchard, R. (Eds.). (1994*). Kids come in all languages: Reading instruction for ESL students*. Newark, DE: International Reading Association.

The articles address such topics as selecting literature for ESL learners, content area reading strategies, literacy across the curriculum, and assessing ESL learners' literacy development.

REFERENCES

Allen, R. V. (1986). Developing contexts to support second language acquisition. *Language Arts 63*, 61–66.

Anaya, R. (1997). *Maya's children: The story of La Llorona*. New York: Hyperion.

Applebee, A. (1978). *The child's concept of story*. Chicago: University of Chicago Press.

Baghban, M. (1984). *Our daughter learns to read and write*. Newark, DE: International Reading Association.

Barnitz, J. (1986). *Reading development of normative speakers of English*. Orlando, FL: Harcourt Brace Jovanovich and the Center for Applied Linguistics.

Bridges, L. (1995). *Creating your classroom community*. York, ME: Stenhouse.

Bromley, K. (1995). Buddy journals for ESL and native–English speaking students. *TESOL Journal, 4*, 7–11.

Bruner, J. (1986). *Actual minds, possible worlds*. Cambridge, MA: Harvard University Press.

Calkins, L. (1986). *The art of teaching writing*. Portsmouth, NH: Heinemann.

Calkins, L. (1991). *Living between the lines*. Portsmouth, NH: Heinemann.

Carger, C. (1993). Louie comes to life: Pretend reading with second language emergent readers. *Language Arts, 70*, 542–548.

Carle, E. (1969). *The very hungry caterpillar*. New York: World.

Cook, B., & Urzua, C. (1993). *The literacy club: A cross-aged tutoring/paired reading project*. Washington, DC: National Clearinghouse for Bilingual Education.

Crawford, J. (1992). *Language loyalties: A sourcebook on the official English controversy*. Chicago: University of Chicago Press.

de Regniers, B. (1965). *May I bring a friend?* New York: Athenaeum.

Doorn, D. (1998, November). Active roles for students in writing. Presentation at the annual convention of the National Council of Teachers of English, Nashville, TN.

Edelsky, C. (1982). Writing in a bilingual program: The relation of L1 and L2 texts. *TESOL Quarterly, 16*, 211–228.

Edelsky, C. (1986). *Writing in a bilingual program: Habia una vez*. Norwood, NJ: Ablex.

Edelsky, C. (1988). Living in the author's world: Analyzing the author's craft. *The California Reader, 21*, 14–17.

Eeds, M., & Peterson, R. (1991). Teacher as curator: Learning to talk about literature. *The Reading Teacher, 45*, 118–126.

Elley, W., & Mangubhai, F. (1983). The impact of reading on second language readers. *Reading Research Quarterly, 19*, 53–67.

Enright, D. S., & McCloskey, M. (1985). Yes talking!: Organizing the classroom to promote second language acquisition. *TESOL Quarterly, 19*, 431–453.

Fletcher, R. (1996). *A writer's notebook.* New York: Avon.

Fournier, J., & Espinosa, C. (1995). Making meaning of our lives through literature: Past, present and future. *Primary Voices, 3*, 15–21.

Fournier, J., Lansdowne, B., Pastenes, Z., Steen, P., & Hudelson, S. (1993). Learning with, about and from children: Life in a bilingual second grade. In C. Genishi (Ed.), *Ways of assessing children and curriculum,* (pp. 126–162). New York: Teachers College Press.

Fox, M. (1988). *Guess what?* San Diego, CA: Harcourt, Brace.

Freeman, Y., & Freeman, D. (1998). *ESL/EFL teaching: Principles for success.* Portsmouth, NH: Heinemann.

Goodman, K. (1996). *On reading.* Portsmouth, NH: Heinemann.

Goodman, K., Goodman, Y., & Flores, B. (1979). *Reading in the bilingual classroom: Literacy and biliteracy.* Rosslyn, VA: National Clearinghouse for Bilingual Education.

Goodman, Y., & Altwerger, B. (1981). *Print awareness in preschool children: A study of the development of literacy in preschool children. (Occasional Paper No. 4).* Tucson, AZ: Program in Language and Literacy, Arizona Center for Research and Development.

Gunkel, J. (1991). "Please teach America": Keisuke's journey into a language community. *Language Arts, 68*, 303–310.

Harste, J., Woodward, V., & Burke, C. (1984). *Language stories and literacy lessons.* Exeter, NH: Heinemann.

Hayes, J. (1987). *La llorona.* El Paso, TX: Cinco Puntos Press.

Heald-Taylor, G. (1987). Predictable literature selections and activities for language arts instruction. *The Reading Teacher, 40*, 6–12.

Heath, S. B., & Mangiola, L. (1991). *Children of promise: Literate activity in linguistically and culturally diverse classrooms.* Washington, DC: National Education Association.

Holdaway, D. (1979). *The foundations of literacy.* Exeter, NH: Heinemann.

Holzwarth, W., & Erlbruch, W. (1993). *The story of the little mole who went in search of whodunit.* New York: Stewart, Tabori & Chang.

Hudelson, S. (1987). The role of native language literacy in the education of language minority children. *Language Arts, 64*, 827–834.

Hudelson, S. (1989). *Write on: Children writing in ESL.* Englewood Cliffs, NJ: Prentice Hall.

Hudelson, S., & Serna, I. (1994). Beginning literacy in English in a whole language bilingual program. In A. Flurkey & R. Meyer (Eds.), *Many cultures, many voices* (pp. 278–294). Urbana, IL: National Council of Teachers of English.

Krashen, S. (1999). *Condemned without a trial: Bogus arguments against bilingual education.* Portsmouth, NH: Heinemann.

Krauss, R. (1945). *The carrot seed.* New York: Harper and Row.

Lindfors, J. (1987). *Children's language and learning* (2nd ed.). Englewood Cliffs, NJ: Prentice Hall.

Mandler, J. M., & Johnson, N. S. (1977). Remembrance of things parsed: Story structure and recall. *Cognitive Psychology, 9*, 111–151.

Martin, B. (1983). *Brown bear, brown bear, what do you see?* New York: Henry Holt.

Matsustani, M. (1968). *The crane maiden.* New York: Parents Magazine Press.

McCloskey, R. (1941). *Make way for ducklings.* New York: Viking.

McGee, L., & Richgels, D. (1989). "K is Kristen's": Learning the alphabet from a child's perspective. *The Reading Teacher, 43*, 216–226.

Neumann, A., & Peterson, P. (1997). *Learning from our lives: Women, research and autobiography in education.* New York: Teachers College Press.

Norton, D. (1990). Teaching multicultural literature in the reading curriculum. *The Reading Teacher, 44,* 28–40.

Nurss, J., Hough, R., & Enright, D. S. (1986). Story reading with limited English speaking children in the regular classroom. *The Reading Teacher, 39,* 510–515.

Orellana, M., & Hernandez, A. (1999). Talking the walk: Children reading urban environmental print. *The Reading Teacher, 52,* 612–620.

Pallas, A., Natriello, G., & McDill, E. (1989). The changing nature of the disadvantaged population: Current dimensions and future trends. *Educational Researcher, 18,* 16–22.

Peregoy, S., & Boyle, O. (1993). *Reading, writing and learning in ESL.* New York: Longman.

Peterson, R., & Eeds, M. (1990). *Grand conversations: Literature groups in action.* Toronto, ON: Scholastic TAB.

Peyton, J. (1990). *Students and teachers working together. Perspectives on journal writing.* Alexandria, VA: Teachers of English to Speakers of Other Languages.

Peyton, J., & Mackinson-Smyth, J. (1989). Writing and talking about writing: Computer networking with elementary students. In D. M. Johnson & D. H. Roen (Eds.), *Richness in writing: Empowering minority students* (pp. 100–119). New York: Longman.

Peyton, J. K., Jones, C., Vincent, A., & Greenblatt, L. (1994). Implementing writing workshop with ESOL students: Visions and realities. *TESOL Quarterly, 28,* 469–488.

Peyton, J. K., & Staton, J. (1993). *Dialogue journals in the multilingual classroom: Building language fluency and writing skills through interaction.* Norwood, NJ: Ablex.

Ramirez, J. D., Yuen, S., & Ramey, D. (1991). *Executive summary: Final report: Longitudinal study of structured English immersion strategy, early exit and late exit transitional bilingual education programs for language minority students.* San Mateo, CA: Aguirre International.

Raschka, C. (1993). *Yo! Yes?* New York: Scholastic.

Reyes, M. (1991). A process approach to literacy learning using dialogue journals and literature logs with second language learners. *Research in the Teaching of English, 25,* 291–313.

Rigg, P. (1986). Reading in ESL: Learning from kids. In P. Rigg & D. S. Enright (Eds.), *Children and ESL: Integrating perspectives* (pp. 55–91). Washington, DC: Teachers of English to Speakers of Other Languages.

Rigg, P. (1989). Language experience approach: Reading naturally. In P. Rigg & V. Allen (Eds.), *When they don't all speak English: Integrating the ESL student into the regular classroom* (pp. 65–76). Urbana, IL: National Council of Teachers of English.

Rosen, H. (1986). The importance of story. *Language Arts, 63,* 226–237.

Rosier, P., & Holm, W. (1979). *The Rock Point experience: An experiment in bilingual education.* Washington, DC: Center for Applied Linguistics.

Samway, K. (1987). *The writing processes of non–native English speaking children in the elementary grades.* Unpublished doctoral dissertation, University of Rochester, Rochester, NY.

Samway, K. (1992). *Writer's notebook and children acquiring English as a non-native language.* Washington, DC: National Clearinghouse for Bilingual Education.

Samway, K. (1993). "This is hard, isn't it?": Children evaluating writing. *TESOL Quarterly, 27,* 233–258.

Samway, K., & Syvanen, C. (1999). Cross-age tutoring and ESOL students. In E. Franklin (Ed.), *Reading and writing in more than one language* (pp. 49–64). Alexandria, VA: TESOL.

Samway, K., & Whang, G. (1996). *Literature study circles in a multicultural classroom.* York, ME: Stenhouse.

Samway, K., Whang, G., & Pippett, M. (1995). *Buddy reading: Cross-age tutoring in a multi-cultural school.* Portsmouth, NH: Heinemann.

Seawell, R. P. M. (1985). A micro-ethnographic study of a Spanish/English bilingual kindergarten in which literature and puppet play were used as a way of enhancing language growth. Unpublished doctoral dissertation, University of Texas, Austin.

Serna, I. (1991, March). Case studies of children developing Spanish writing in a whole language bilingual kindergarten and first grade. Paper presented at the annual TESOL Convention, New York City.

Smallwood, B. (1991). *The literature connection: A read-aloud guide for multicultural classrooms.* Reading, MA: Addison-Wesley.

Smith, F. (1982). *Writing and the writer.* New York: Holt, Rinehart and Winston.

Soto, G. (1993). *Too many tamales.* New York: G. P. Putnam's Sons.

Strickland, D., & Morrow, L. (1990). Sharing big books. *The Reading Teacher, 43,* 342–344.

TESOL. (1997). *ESL standards for pre-K–12 students.* Alexandria, VA: TESOL.

Thomas, W., & Collier, V. (1995). *Language minority student achievement and program effectiveness.* Washington, DC: National Clearinghouse for Bilingual Education.

Townsend, J., & Fu, D. (1998). A Chinese Boy's Joyful Initiation into American Literacy. *Language Arts, 75,* 193–202.

Urzua, C. (1987). "You stopped too soon": Second language children composing and revising. *TESOL Quarterly, 21,* 279–305.

Vigil, A. (1994). *The corn woman: Stories and legends of the Hispanic southwest.* Englewood, CO: Libraries Unlimited.

Waggoner, D. (1999). Who are secondary newcomer and linguistically different youth? In C. Faltis & P. Wolfe (Eds.), *So much to say: Adolescents, bilingualism, and ESL in the secondary school* (pp. 13–40). New York: Teachers College Press.

Wallace, C. (1988). *Reading in a multicultural society.* Englewood Cliffs, NJ: Prentice Hall.

Watson, C. (1997). Talking about books: Beyond decodable texts—supportive and workable literature. *Language Arts, 74,* 635–643.

Weaver, C. (1994). *Reading: Process and practice* (2nd ed.). Portsmouth, NH: Heinemann.

Witherell, C., & Noddings, N. (1991). *Stories lives tell: Narrative and dialogue in education.* New York: Teachers College Press.

PHOTO CREDITS

INDEX